No Other Book

BOOKS BY RANDALL JARRELL

POETRY

The Rage for the Lost Penny (in *Five Young American Poets*) (1940)
Blood for a Stranger (1942)
Little Friend, Little Friend (1945)
Losses (1948)
The Seven-League Crutches (1951)
Selected Poems (1955)
The Woman at the Washington Zoo (1960)
The Lost World (1965)
The Complete Poems (1969)
Selected Poems (1990)

ESSAYS

Poetry and the Age (1953)
A Sad Heart at the Supermarket (1962)
The Third Book of Criticism (1969)
Kipling, Auden & Co. (1980)
No Other Book: Selected Essays (1999)

FICTION

Pictures from an Institution (1954)

CHILDREN'S BOOKS

The Gingerbread Rabbit (1964)
The Bat-Poet (1964)
The Animal Family (1965)
Fly by Night (1976)

TRANSLATIONS

The Golden Bird and Other Fairy Tales of the Brothers Grimm (1962)
The Rabbit Catcher and Other Fairy Tales of Ludwig Bechstein (1962)
The Three Sisters (1969)
Faust, Part I (1976)

ANTHOLOGIES

The Anchor Book of Stories (1958)
The Best Short Stories of Rudyard Kipling (1961)
The English in England (Kipling stories) (1963)
In the Vernacular: The English in India (Kipling stories) (1963)
Six Russian Short Novels (1963)

Randall Jarrell

NO OTHER

BOOK

SELECTED ESSAYS

Edited and with an Introduction by

BRAD LEITHAUSER

Perennial

An Imprint of HarperCollinsPublishers

First Perennial edition published 2000.

Designed by Cynthia Krupat

Library of Congress catalog card number: 98-55353

ISBN 0-06-095638-0 (pbk.)

00 01 02 03 04 ❖/RRD 10 9 8 7 6 5 4 3 2 1

Contents

Introduction, vii

POETS AND POETRY

The Obscurity of the Poet, 3
To the Laodiceans, 19
Robert Frost's "Home Burial," 42
Paterson by William Carlos Williams, 67
An Introduction to the Selected Poems
of William Carlos Williams, 76
A Note on Poetry, 84
The Woman at the Washington Zoo, 89
Some Lines from Whitman, 98
Reflections on Wallace Stevens, 112
Her Shield, 123
Contemporary Poetry Criticism, 139
Texts from Housman, 146
Graves and the White Goddess, 156
Love and Poetry, 179
Changes of Attitude and Rhetoric
in Auden's Poetry, 186

From the Kingdom of Necessity, 208
Poets, Critics, and Readers, 216
Fifty Years of American Poetry, 230

A JARRELL GALLERY

255

THE REST OF IT

The Age of Criticism, 281
On Preparing to Read Kipling, 298
The Taste of the Age, 313
Against Abstract Expressionism, 329
An Unread Book, 334
A Sad Heart at the Supermarket, 363

Introduction

Randall Jarrell once wrote, in praise of William Carlos Williams, "When you have read *Paterson* you know for the rest of your life what it is like to be a waterfall." Yet there's another way to ascertain what it is to be a phenomenon that flows, coruscates, sings, and revitalizes: you might turn to the essays of Jarrell himself. Thirty-four years after his untimely death, at the age of fifty-one, he remains a bright, propulsive presence. A powerfully attractive personality—witty, affectionate, energetic, and positively brilliant—emerges in his letters; in his beautiful, piercing poems; in assorted memoirs and a biography; in his photographs (the camera loved his spirited brown eyes and lanky torso); in his comic novel, *Pictures from an Institution*, and his four children's books; and in the various recordings he left behind, in which the voice breaks boyishly and sounds—oddly, appealingly—just a little rubelike. But if your goal is to discover what it was like, day by day, to be a literary waterfall of a man, it is the essays to which you will most profitably turn.

Collectively, the four volumes of Jarrell's critical prose—*Poetry and the Age* (1953), *A Sad Heart at the Supermarket* (1962), and the two posthumous volumes, *The Third Book of Criticism* (1969) and *Kipling, Auden & Co.* (1980)—assemble an ample and vivid portrait. "When you know Frost's poems, you know surprisingly well what the world seemed to one man," Jarrell remarked, and much the same could be said of him and his own essays, even though these divulge precious little autobiography. A reader combs them mostly in vain for hints about Jarrell's upbringing (he was raised largely by his mother, in Nashville, to which she moved him from Long Beach, California, after divorcing a husband who ran a small photography studio); his romantic life (he was married twice); his physical health (mostly good—he was an avid tennis player); or his mental health (again mostly good, it would appear, although in the last year and a half of his life he suffered a catastrophic breakdown).

All the same, you come away from his critical prose feeling that "you know surprisingly well what the world seemed to one man," for the essays convince you that the personal background of this particular man's life is a secondary concern. What is paramount are the rewards and challenges of literature. Once you've read him on Whitman or Kafka you seem to know an intimate, key component of his personality. Which is to say, you know what he felt about Whitman or Kafka, and what could be (his essays tacitly ask) more central and revealing than that?

As a critic, Jarrell thrived during an era when American literary criticism, particularly of poetry, was itself thriving. With characteristic generosity, he extolled his competition: "I do not believe there has been another age in which so much extraordinarily good criticism of poetry has been written . . . I have been speaking of such critics as William Empson, T. S. Eliot, R. P. Blackmur, Allen Tate, Yvor Winters, John Crowe Ransom, I. A. Richards, Morton Dauwen Zabel, Cleanth Brooks, Robert Penn Warren, Delmore Schwartz, and five or six others."

It's striking, after more than half a century, how many of these remain names to reckon with. But whatever their virtues, few if any of these figures engage us as Jarrell does. Ransom is a case in point. In addition to being a bizarre and wonderful poet, he was a thoughtful and illuminating essayist; and yet the same air of dusty academic discourse which so enriched the poems (enhancing, by means of contrast, the tender sentiments at their core) nearly suffocates the essays. It's easy to esteem, and difficult to love, Ransom's critical prose.

The reader connects with Jarrell's criticism immediately, emotionally. He lures us in with his eloquent, epigrammatic aplomb ("If we judge by wealth and power, our times are the best of times; if the times have made us willing to judge by wealth and power, they are the worst of times"). With his breezy wisecracks ("The people who live in a Golden Age usually go around complaining how yellow everything looks"). With his loopy hypotheticals ("If I had to pick one writer to invent a conversation between an animal, a god, and a machine, it would be Kipling"). With his swooping range of references.

His comely humility. His psychoanalytic penetration. But what was perhaps Jarrell's most compelling trait was the passion he managed to evince, and to enkindle. He claimed that "Malraux writes a passage of ordinary exposition so that we breathe irregularly and jerk our heads from side to side, like spectators at a tennis match"—a pitch of excitement likewise quickening nearly every page of Jarrell's own criticism.

The result is that you can wind up longing to read not the actual book under examination but the ideal version located in Jarrell's head. I adore Christina Stead's *The Man Who Loved Children*, but better still, more harrowing and haunting, is that same novel as it's painstakingly dissected and reassembled in the longest essay Jarrell ever wrote (it runs to forty-eight pages in *The Third Book of Criticism*). Hence, only the purest of heart will not experience, in addition to admiration, some measure of envy and self-reproach when reading Jarrell. How can you help envying someone who can extract so much from so little, as when he focuses in upon an eight-line poem like Housman's "It nods and curtseys . . ."? Elizabeth Bishop once said of him, "He always seemed more alive than other people, as if constantly tuned up to the concert pitch that most people, including poets, can maintain only for short and fortunate stretches." He's someone who regularly prises more from a line of verse than the rest of us can smell in it and see in it and hear in it.

———

His multiple and eclectic virtues—originality, erudition, wit, probity, and an irresistible passion—combined to make him the best American poet-critic since Eliot. Or one could call him, after granting Eliot the English citizenship he so actively embraced, the best poet-critic we have ever had. Whichever side of the Atlantic one chooses to place Eliot, Jarrell was his superior in at least one significant respect. He captured a world that any contemporary poet will recognize as "the poetry scene"; his *Poetry and the Age* might even now be retitled *Poetry and Our Age.*

I have a brother-in-law who was a Vice President in the Controls Advisory Service of an investment bank—a job which kept a secure roof over his head, but what in hell is a Vice President in Controls Advisory Services? In a world of increasingly abstruse employment, we can only be grateful to any writer, of fiction or non-fiction, who opens up to us some specialized field—the world of the laser surgeon, or the ergonomist, the demographer, the talent scout for a talk-show host. In this regard—the domain of obscure professions—Jarrell takes the lay reader further into the life of the modern American poet than any other writer I know.

In essays like "Poetry and the Age" and "The Obscurity of the Poet" Jarrell captures what it is to be an artist in a squeeze—caught between the universities which, while providing a livelihood, can show condescension or even hostility to the poet, and the larger, television-centered culture which is not so much hostile as simply oblivious; this is a society (as Jarrell acerbically noted) that would grant the poet a grant if it knew of his existence. Such essays go on illuminating the lot of the contemporary poet, helping us to read not only Berryman and Roethke and Allen Tate but closer contemporaries like James Merrill and Seamus Heaney and Derek Walcott and Amy Clampitt.

By contrast, the essays of Eliot (whom Jarrell revered—the "best poetry critic of our time") are more remote from us than, chronologically speaking, we'd expect them to be. In their cool, Olympian fastidiousness, they can feel miles away from the environs of the contemporary American poet. (Eliot deliberately cultivated this remove, of course. It's characteristic of him, in a preface written in 1961, to wrap quotation marks around the word *paperback*. Having spent decades in the publishing business, he nonetheless courted the image of a man who has just now placed his first shockingly garish, pumpkin-orange Penguin on a shelf otherwise reserved for volumes bound in calfskin and gilt Moroccan leather.) One returns to Eliot for insight—much as one might turn to Coleridge. But less and less does the contemporary poet come to Eliot's essays with the expectation of hearing an inner voice exclaim, *He's talking about my daily life...*

And it is clearly Jarrell to whom we should turn if we would understand the reviews nowadays tucked away in the back of *The Hudson Review, Poetry,* or *The Threepenny Review*—or any of the other periodicals that have fought to keep the art of poetry reviewing alive. His influence on contemporary criticism has been pervasive and thoroughgoing. And to read these current reviews, intelligent and loving and well-schooled as many of them are, is to grasp how difficult to replicate is Jarrell's impulsive and insouciant style. In other hands, what might have been witty winds up looking merely whimsical; what would be irreverent, snotty; what would be biting, bilious.

———

If Jarrell addresses more tellingly than Eliot the situation of the contemporary poet, this may be partly attributable to the calendar.

Although they died in the same year—1965—Jarrell was born in 1914 (a quarter century after Eliot), into a generation most of whose leaders were absorbed into our universities. Roethke, Berryman, Kunitz, Warren, Olson: all taught for a living. And nearly all were coming of age during a period when, their sensibilities tempered by the Second World War, the juggernaut of American industry was powering the country as no country had ever been powered before. The poets saw themselves—as so many of their letters and poems attest—as small and ignored constituents of a vast and unignorable commonwealth.

The knowledge that the previous generation—Eliot's—had engineered a literary revolution that had spurred more interest and scrutiny (as well as vitriol and resistance) than anything they themselves were likely to produce only deepened the pathos of their situation. In a sketchy early essay, "The End of the Line," Jarrell took up this suspicion forthrightly. He argued (and whether he was right or wrong, his distress remains potent) that the modernism of Eliot, Stevens, Cummings, and Moore had played itself out. For the moment, there was no ground to be broken. Lovely, indeed imperishable poems were still to be written, but there wasn't to be—at least for a while—another revolution. By the mere accident of birth date, his generation might be destined for a subsidiary role, and he asked, poignantly, "Who could endure a century of *Transition*?"

Such questions bedevil succeeding generations. In the years since "The End of the Line" was published, various brilliant and magical verses have emerged—Jarrell's prominent among them—but we don't appear to be entering an age when the very mode of poetic discourse will be upended. All but the most vainglorious of contemporary poets know something of Jarrell's sensation of lying in the trough between two great waves, of belonging to a generation that posterity will classify under the heading Those Who Couldn't See What Would Come Next. It's a category into which we ourselves sometimes condescendingly place the Georgian Poets—who are seen planing and sanding and shellacking their boxlike quatrains while Eliot was putting together the firebomb of *The Waste Land*.

———

While literary history may have conspired to leave the contemporary poet feeling vulnerable and self-justifying, such feelings have been inevitably aggravated by all those social transformations that have edged the poet to the peripheries of our cultural life. If Jarrell's highly various poetry essays range around any one central theme, it would be "the obscurity of the poet," referring not to the poet's difficulty but to his social irrelevance. Time and again, implicitly and explicitly, Jarrell's essays ask, Does poetry matter to the world at large? and his answer is, Less and less.

Occasionally you'll meet contemporary poets who, vindicating some private melancholy, relish their own cultural insignificance. Or poets who, with the glazed, half-shut eyes of a swimmer doing laps in a pool, insist that poetry matters more than it ever has. And there are others who dismiss the issue as largely irrelevant, and others who close off discussion by happily hauling out that old saw about the game being murderous because the stakes are so small.

To Jarrell's credit, though, he took this crucial question—the poet's obscurity—and subjected it to probing analysis. He asked: What does it mean about the poems that will be written? How does it affect the "professionalization" of the poet? Which subjects will it unconsciously abet, and which ones unconsciously suppress?

His wit and informality can sometimes mask the essays' lunging ambition. Jarrell the critic longed to paint in broad strokes, to shoot for the horizons. He yearned to clarify the fiendishly intricate relationship between a solitary, "pure" artist and a monolithic mass culture. His essays reflect the appetites of a sociologist manqué. And in his pawky way, Jarrell got the story down: he exposed the plight of the contemporary poet as no one else has done.

———

Jarrell was fond of quoting a phrase he'd found in an essay by a psychoanalyst, "the artist and his competitor, the critic." He harbored mixed feelings about the criticism he practiced so skillfully. His essays, into which he poured hours and hours of labor, continually belittle the role of criticism. An ambitious critic, he aspired to explain, paradoxically, "why it is that critics are of so little use to writers, why it is that they are such a poor guide to the opinions of the next age."

The untangling of his ambivalence is a complicated business. By gaining a formidable reputation as a critic, he had joined a fraternity that unsettled him in all sorts of ways. In "The Age of Criticism" he lampooned the usurpations of those who would supplant the work they ostensibly served. ("Criticism *does* exist, doesn't it, for the sake of the plays and stories and poems it criticizes?" he mockingly asked—not fully foreseeing an age and a critical establishment for whom this question would be regarded not as a *reductio ad absurdum* but as a legitimate line of inquiry . . .) He was also disheartened by the obtuse reviews of early books by contemporaries (Berryman, Lowell, Bishop) whose gifts he recognized better than most everyone else. And he was, in his wholehearted, plunging way, impatient with critics who failed to respond to literature as passionately as he did; their prudent hedging exasperated him.

In addition, the renown—and fear—his criticism inspired may have psychologically undermined him. As a critic, Jarrell was a quick study; as a poet, a slow starter. It wasn't until he entered his thirties that he really began to speak with assurance in verse, and most of his best poems arrived after he'd reached forty. The celebrated critic may have threatened to overshadow the slow-germinating poet.

This uneasiness perhaps explains why he left his criticism in some disarray. Although individual reviews consumed and possessed him (he once wrote to Robert Penn Warren: "Can you recite a review from memory when you finish it? I was astonished to find I could"), he was content to be somewhat lax when treating the pieces as a collection. He made little attempt to fit them into any systematic whole, to strip them of their mutual repetitions, to track down missing citations. It's easy to understand the appeal for him of leaving a few rough edges. To be "the most powerful reviewer of poetry active in this country" (as Berryman dubbed him) was one thing. But to achieve this status casually—offhandedly—was better still.

————

For an editor of his *Selected Essays,* this issue of repetition poses a thorny problem. Although Jarrell did not repeat himself extensively, he did return to various favorite writers over the years, while writing for a range of periodicals and audiences, and a certain core of duplicated matter—both of information and of assessment—naturally resulted.

What to do about this? I suppose an editor could quietly pare and tidy the essays. (But this struck me as unthinkable: I might just as well, armed with a razor and a paintbrush and a box of oils, seek to spruce up a couple of weathered Winslow Homer seascapes.) Or an editor could leave out any essay which, by leaning heavily on a predecessor, might not be termed self-standing. (Yet this seemed, even in a book calling itself a *Selected* rather than a *Collected,* to sacrifice too much that was too good.) The compromise I've arrived at is something called "A Jarrell Gallery," which gathers favorite excerpts from essays I didn't think could be or needed to be included in entirety. The "Gallery" also allowed me—especially when rummaging around in those minor prose pieces which Jarrell himself never thought fit to reproduce in book form——to frame and hang various passages that seemed too humorous, or too trenchant, or simply too *Jarrell* to pass over.

From the outset, I had no doubt about the book's larger structure. Verse clearly was preeminent in Jarrell's artistic and intellectual life: there was Poetry, and then there was the Rest of It. This "rest" consisted of a number of passions he pursued with tenacious vigor and thoroughness (notably, anthropology, psychology, and fiction), but in the end Poetry came first, and the Rest came after——just as it does in this collection.

———

Today, Jarrell may be most widely known for his sparkling invective. He's the man who said of one of Oscar Williams's books of verse that it "gave the impression of having been written on a typewriter by a typewriter." And who noted of a contributor to *New Directions, 1941*, "Mr. Fisher is like the gold in sea water: valuable, but in impracticable concentrations." And who said of *The Shield of Achilles*, "Auden, in most of this last book, lies in himself as if he were an unmade bed, and every line in his sleepy, placid face seems to be saying: *But whoever makes beds?*"

Robert Lowell, writing a tribute to his friend after his death, offered a well-aimed corrective when he identified "eulogy" as "the glory of Randall's criticism."

Eulogies that not only impressed readers with his own enthusiasms, but which also, time and again, changed and improved opinions and values. He left many reputations permanently altered and exalted. I think particularly of his famous Frost and Whitman essays.

Jarrell's eulogies certainly can be breathtaking. Moments of an almost uncanny affinity are established, and it's as though this particular stanza of Marianne Moore's, or this little moment in Kipling's autobiography, has just now, after having lain dormant and dusty for decades, caught a blade of sun.

But later in his tribute Lowell touched on another virtue perhaps more impressive still:

One could never say of one of his admirations, "Oh, I knew *you* would like that." His progress was not the usual youthful critic's progress from callow severity to lax benevolence. With wrinkled brow and cool fresh eye, he was forever musing, discovering, and chipping away at his own misconceptions.

One thinks, by contrast, of the legion of intelligent critics (illustrious and little-known, living and dead) of whom we can say, "Oh, I knew *you* would like that," those critics whose new review we've basically read even before we pick up the magazine in which it appears. Having written of Robert Graves "he is not a good poet" and "even his best poems just miss," Jarrell subsequently declared, "Graves is the true heir of Ben Jonson, and can give to his monstrosities, occasionally, the peculiar lyric magnificence Jonson gives them in *The Alchemist*," and "Graves's poems are a marvel and a delight, the work of a fine poet who has managed, by the strangest of processes, to make himself into an extraordinary one." And Jarrell resolved this discrepancy not by recourse to some shift in the poet's development but to a shift in his own judgment; he'd learned to read Graves better. Of B. H. Haggin, the music critic, Jarrell once said, "This sort of admission of error, of change, makes us trust a critic as nothing else but omni-science could." *Trust* seems the keynote here. We have faith in the im-provisational, ever-adapting process embodied by Jarrell's essays, and it is precisely this openness to change, this awareness of fallibility, that renders so tonic and invigorating each of his return engagements with Stevens, Williams, Moore, Lowell.

This unpredictability sometimes made him an uncertain ally. Jarrell loved Marianne Moore's poetry—he composed some of the most glowing testimonials ever devoted to her verse—but when he felt she'd let her emotions run away with her in her anti-war poem "In Distrust of Merits," he chided her "lack of facts, or imagination, or *something*," and once when he thought she'd made a fatuous crit-ical judgment he referred to her as a "fool."

What is little short of astonishing, given how brutal Jarrell's dis-approval could be, is that he managed to remain friends with so many of the people he reproved. He wrote of Karl Shapiro's *Trial of a Poet* that it "has been a disappointment to everybody" and that "the first third of the book, a commonplace and derivative autobiographical series, is a sort of bobby-soxer's *Mauberley*." For good measure, he pointed out that Shapiro had "sunk and sunk until one wishes that he could go back to his best book, his first, and start over from there." Incredibly, Shapiro—though a man deeply sensitive to slights—replied that he felt as if he "had been run over but not hurt." And he later wrote this memorial:

> Jarrell tried to do the impossible: to observe and make poetry of a chaos, without being either inside or outside of it. He did it better than anyone else, better than it can be done. He did it passionately and with superb control.

For good reason, the contemporary poetry world is notorious for its thin skins and its hardy rancors, and yet Jarrell often said the seemingly unforgivable and wound up being not only forgiven but commended. How in the world did he get away with it? Surely because neither his diligence nor his integrity was ever seriously in question. He was speaking for himself, too, when he praised John Crowe Ransom as a poet "wanting the light and sorry for the dark." Jarrell paid the authors he reviewed the ultimate compliment of taking their work so deeply to heart that, when it fell short, he could sound authentically despondent, even betrayed.

Lowell made a further observation that strikes me as one of the most remarkable things any poet ever said about another:

> Randall was the only man I have ever met who could make other writers feel that their work was more important to him than his own . . . What he did was to make others feel that their realizing themselves was as close to him as his own self-realization, and that he cared as much about making the nature and goodness of someone else's work understood as he cared about making his own understood.

This unique degree of selflessness maybe explains why Jarrell, despite his harsh denunciations, was so regularly described as "generous" by those who knew him. He wrote that the writer craves a public that "reads with the calm and ease and independence that come from liking things in themselves, for themselves." And he added: "This is the kind of public that the poet would like; and if it turned out to be the kind of public that wouldn't like him, why, surely that is something he could bear. It is not his poems but poetry that he wants people to read; if they will read Rilke's and Yeats's and Hardy's poems, he can bear to have his own poems go unread forever." How plausible this sounds, and yet how far from reality it is! Jarrell's sort of generosity was rarer than he could possibly see. Think of how many poets' biographies reveal personalities who would consign Chaucer, Donne, Tennyson entirely to the flames before relinquishing even one page of their own *Selected* . . .

———

To read Jarrell is to be shown, as few critics living or dead can show us, just how strewn with posturing is the criticism daily surrounding us. We grow accustomed to various rituals of judgment, with their rote gestures and unwritten formulae. As readers we learn to accept—like citizens of a country with a collapsing monetary system—that some fair proportion of our currency will be counterfeit.

It's the usual custom, for instance, for a critic who is slamming a book to single out two or three items for praise. One does this as an earnest of one's fairness and objectivity—and, covertly, as a means of making one's indictments all the more stinging. But Jarrell went through the routine motions unroutinely. More than *any* critic I've ever read he brought sincerity to the compliments he injected into an otherwise negative review. He had an unmatched ability to find, in a book he otherwise abominated, a stanza or a paragraph that pleased him heartily. It was absolutely like Jarrell to be able to reconcile, in contiguous paragraphs, a pair of judgments as opposed as these on Yvor Winters: "His practical misvaluations, at their most extraordinary, rival the Himalayas" and "Winters's clear, independent, and serious talent has produced criticism that no cultivated person can afford to leave unread."

It's remarkable how seldom a reader of Jarrell winds up asking, *Why is he saying this?* The answer is patent: he is saying it because that's how he feels. He may be mistaken, but he isn't being devious. When he calls a book *luminous*, you sense he has personally basked in its light; when he calls it *abject*, you know he has been cast down. Placed beside him, other critics tend to look anemic and their judgments sound paltering.

———

Taking a page from Jarrell's own book, we might indulge in a fanciful hypothetical. Let's assume that someone from an alien world, a Merman, found his way into one of our university libraries and sought to understand us through our literary and scholarly journals. To such a creature, wouldn't the one unifying trait of our criticism (the one linking analyses of Homer to deconstructions of Calvin Klein ads, studies of the theme of Christian recusancy in medieval Icelandic sagas to critiques of subway performance artists) be its elaborate defensiveness? And wouldn't this tell our Merman a great deal about the larger academy where these pieces were bred? He wouldn't have to meet a single critic in order to hypothesize that this is a perilous realm, whose inhabitants perpetually expect to be preyed upon. He could deduce this merely from our penchant for qualifying our qualifications, for substantiating the inarguable, for running in place while ostentatiously huffing and puffing.

Jarrell temperamentally shrank from most such qualifications—

from the desire to protect himself. When he said "But taking the chance of making a complete fool of himself—and, sometimes, doing so—is the first demand that is made upon any real critic," he was espousing a credo he lived by. He loved sweeping utterances. In whatever he read, he was forever searching for the text's fingerprint, its unique identification, which would allow him to utter the phrase that, for him as a critic, was perhaps the richest in the language: "No other book . . ." His criticism constantly drives toward these words, or some variation on them. We are told of *The Man Who Loved Children* that it "makes you a part of one family's immediate existence as no other book quite does." Of Eleanor Ross Taylor's *A Wilderness of Ladies* that "no poems can tell you better what it is like to be a woman." Of Kipling that "the family romance, the two families of the Hero, have so predominant a place in no other writer." Of Elizabeth Bishop, "I don't know of any other poet with so high a proportion of good poems." Of Graves's *Collected Poems,* "Some are extraordinary, many are masterly, all are like nothing else ever written." Above all else, what he wanted as a critic was to be able to declare, "Not since an anonymous Akkadian scribe began to score the epic of *Gilgamesh* into a clay tablet has anyone . . ."

———

Jarrell's prescience may have worked, unfortunately, to blunt his boldness. Over time, many of his wildest pronouncements have become orthodoxy, thereby encouraging a later generation to regard him as less daring than he was. Perhaps he suffers from having been so often right.

In 1962 he delivered an extraordinary lecture, "Fifty Years of American Poetry," in which he offered a panoramic appraisal of American poetry from 1910 to 1960. It's a *tour de force* for all sorts of reasons, but primarily for the way in which its characterizations have become our own. He might be surveying a half-century of American poetry not from the perspective of the early sixties but from that of the late nineties.

The "other" Frost that Jarrell discerned behind the genial, homespun New England rustic—the "dark" Frost who was desperate, frightened, and brave—has become the Frost we've all learned to recognize, and the little-known poems Jarrell singled out as central to the Frost canon are now to be found in most anthologies. Much the same could be said about his judgments of Williams, Ransom, Stevens, Moore, Cummings, Aiken, Lowell. In recent years, Elizabeth Bishop has become an impregnable figure—a bulwark of the canon—but who except Jarrell was saying, as early as 1955, "Her *Poems* seems to me one of the best books an American poet has ever written"? And even in his quickest, most offhand judgments he prefigured much of the criticism that would follow. Jarrell never got around to an essay on Eliot, but in "Fifty Years of American Poetry" he made a few telling remarks:

> Won't the future say to us in helpless astonishment: "But did you actually believe all those things about objective correlatives, classicism, the tradition, applied to *his* poetry? Surely you must have seen that he was one of the most subjective and daemonic poets who ever lived, the victim and helpless beneficiary of his own inexorable compulsions, obsessions?"

That future is now, and our shelves are awash with Eliot studies intent on pointing up the discrepancy between Eliot the theorist and Eliot the man and poet.

I recently picked up a substantial book of essays on Frost published by a leading university press. In its contributors, topics, and methods, it seemed a representative showcase of contemporary academic criticism. I looked up Jarrell in the index . . . Now, Jarrell's two essays on Frost were milestones. As much as anything he ever did, they won him the extravagant praise that was heaped on him (by Ransom, who regarded *Poetry and the Age* as "almost epoch-making"; by Lowell, who called him "a critic of genius"; by Bishop, who deemed him "the best and most generous critic of poetry I have known"; by Tate, who rated him "a great prose-stylist"; by Berryman, who said that among living critics there was "nobody better"; by Rich, who judged him "a kind of conscience of poetry"). But Jarrell's name was hardly to be found. He was packed away in a pair of footnotes, a couple of stray and grudging quotations. On the other hand, Jarrell himself—as opposed to his name—was ubiquitous, his views having been, covertly or ignorantly, everywhere appropriated. It's a shame we have today no second Jarrell on the scene to comment on the fate of the original Jarrell. The ironies are piquant. It seems the critical establishment represented by our university English departments, for all its proud iconoclasm, is constitutionally uncomfortable with an informal, brazen, unfootnoted diamond-in-the-rough like Jarrell; his views need to be digested, and reformatted, before they can be deemed authoritative and citation-worthy.

The passing decades, having vindicated Jarrell's clairvoyance, leave us to ponder what he would have made of some of the celebrated works of our time. I've never found myself wondering what judgments Bogan or Winters or Tate or Blackmur—all critics I've read with interest—might have reached had they lived longer. But I have yearned to know what Jarrell would have made of Berryman's *Dream Songs*, Merrill's *The Changing Light at Sandover*, Walcott's *Omeros*. He is *missed* in a way those others aren't.

It's a great shame, too, he never got around to writing on Wordsworth ("one of the three or four greatest of English poets") or *Antony and Cleopatra* ("the supreme literary expression of our culture"). Had he lived to a full age, he would surely have expanded his essays, and cleaned and clarified them a bit. Various other small vices would doubtless have remained, however, woven as they were into the fiber of the man.

It seems fair to say that Jarrell devoted more time and space than was wise to poets of no lasting interest. Too often he let himself be drawn into trying to calibrate whether poet A or B was *thoroughly* bad or at times rose up and achieved mediocrity. True, he panned their verses with hilarious dexterity: he usually managed to flay rather than flog a dead horse. Still, he might better have left the corpse to decompose on its own.

One vice is simultaneously vexing and endearing: his frequent conviction that the point he's making is self-evident. He's constantly holding up a stanza or a passage and crying, in effect, "Nothing more need be said! Only an idiot could be unmoved!" Which is fine just so long as you share his enthusiasm. When you don't, you're left having to reply, "As an idiot, I wish you would further explain to me . . ."

Even so, I'd rather receive puzzlement from Jarrell's hands than elucidation from most anyone else. He once pointed out that "Art is long, and critics are the insects of the day," and added, "Unless you are one critic in a hundred thousand, the future will quote you only as an example of the normal error of the past."

Surely this one exception—the one hypothetical survivor—would need to be not only surpassingly bright but peerlessly bold. Lowell said of his friend, "Getting out on a limb was a daily occurrence for him." To my mind, Randall Jarrell was the one critic in a hundred thousand who continually climbed out on a branch that couldn't possibly support his weight and discovered that—thanks to his balance, buoyancy, nimbleness—the branch held.

BRAD LEITHAUSER

Note

After each essay, the year of first publication (usually in a literary "little magazine," occasionally in a mass-market magazine or as an introduction or a contribution to someone else's book) is given. This is followed by an abbreviation indicating in which of Jarrell's four collections the essay first appeared.

The following abbreviations are employed: *PA* for *Poetry and the Age*, *SHS* for *A Sad Heart at the Supermarket*, *TBC* for *The Third Book of Criticism*, and *KA* for *Kipling, Auden & Co.* These abbreviations are in conformity with Stuart Wright's *Randall Jarrell: A Descriptive Bibiliography, 1929–1983*, to which interested readers are referred for answers to more detailed questions about the genesis, dating, or evolution of Jarrell's essays.

B . L .

POETS AND POETRY

The Obscurity of the Poet

WHEN I WAS ASKED TO TALK about the Obscurity of the
Modern Poet I was delighted, for I have suffered from this obscurity
all my life. But then I realized that I was being asked to talk not about
the fact that people don't read poetry, but about the fact that most of
them wouldn't understand it if they did: about the difficulty, not the
neglect, of contemporary poetry. And yet it is not just modern poetry,
but poetry, that is today obscure. *Paradise Lost* is what it was; but the
ordinary reader no longer makes the mistake of trying to read it—in-
stead he glances at it, weighs it in his hand, shudders, and suddenly,
his eyes shining, puts it on his list of the ten dullest books he has ever
read, along with *Moby Dick, War and Peace, Faust,* and Boswell's *Life
of Johnson.* But I am doing this ordinary reader an injustice: it was not
the Public, nodding over its lunch-pail, but the educated reader, the
reader the universities have trained, who a few weeks ago, to the
Public's sympathetic delight, put together this list of the world's
dullest books.

Since most people know about the modern poet only that he is
obscure—i.e., that he is *difficult*, i.e., that he is *neglected*—they natu-
rally make a causal connection between the two meanings of the
word, and decide that he is unread because he is difficult. Some of the
time this is true; some of the time the reverse is true: the poet seems
difficult *because* he is not read, *because* the reader is not accustomed
to reading his or any other poetry. But most of the time neither is a
cause—both are no more than effects of that long-continued, world-

overturning cultural and social revolution (seen at its most advanced stage here in the United States) which has made the poet difficult and the public unused to any poetry exactly as it has made poet and public divorce their wives, stay away from church, dislike bull-baiting, free the slaves, get insulin shots for diabetes, or do a hundred thousand other things, some bad, some good, and some indifferent. It is superficial to extract two parts from this world-high whole, and to say of them: "This one, here, is the cause of that one, there; and that's all there is to it."

If we were in the habit of reading poets their obscurity would not matter; and, once we are out of the habit, their clarity does not help. Matthew Arnold said, with plaintive respect, that there was hardly a sentence in *Lear* that he hadn't needed to read two or three times; and three other appreciable Victorian minds, Beetle, Stalky, and McTurk, were even harder on it. They are in their study; Stalky reads:

> Never any.
> It pleased the king his master, very late,
> To strike at me, upon his misconstruction,
> When he, conjunct, and flattering in his displeasure,
> Tripped me behind: being down, insulted, railed,
> And put upon him such a deal of man
> That worthy'd him, got praises of the King
> For him attempting who was self-subdued;
> And, in the fleshment of this dread exploit,
> Drew me on here.

Stalky says: "Now, then, my impassioned bard, *construez!* That's Shakespeare"; and Beetle answers, "at the end of a blank half minute": "Give it up! He's drunk." If schoolboys were forced to read "The Phoenix and Turtle," what *would* Beetle have said of these two stanzas?

> Property was thus appalled
> That the self was not the same;
> Single nature's double name
> Neither two nor one was called,
>
> Reason, in itself confounded,
> Saw division grow together;

[4]

To themselves yet either-neither,
Simple were so well compounded . . .

You and I can afford to look at Stalky and Company, at Arnold, with dignified superiority: we know what those passages mean; we know that Shakespeare is never *obscure*, as if he were some modernist poet gleefully pasting puzzles together in his garret. Yet when we look at a variorum Shakespeare—with its line or two of text at the top of the page, its forty or fifty lines of wild surmise and quarrelsome conjecture at the bottom—we are troubled. When the Alexandrian poet Lycophron refers—and he is rarely so simple—to the *centipede, fair-faced, stork-hued daughters of Phalacra,* and they turn out to be boats, one ascribes this to Alexandrian decadence; but then one remembers that Welsh and Irish and Norse poets, the poets of a hundred barbarous cultures, loved nothing so much as referring to the very dishes on the table by elaborate descriptive epithets—periphrases, kennings—which their hearers had to be specially educated to understand. (Loved nothing so much, that is, except riddles.) And just consider the amount of classical allusions that those polite readers, our ancestors, were expected to recognize—and did recognize. If I recite to you, *The brotherless Heliades / Melt in such amber tears as these,* many of you will think, *Beautiful*; a good many will think, *Marvell*; but how many of you will know to whom Marvell is referring?

Yet the people of the past were not repelled by this obscurity (seemed, often, foolishly to treasure it); nor are those peoples of the present who are not so far removed from the past as we: who have preserved, along with the castles, the injustice, and the social discrimination of the past, a remnant of its passion for reading poetry. It is hard to be much more difficult than Mallarmé; yet when I went from bookstore to bookstore in Paris, hunting for one copy of Corbière, I began to feel a sort of mocking frustration at the poems by Mallarmé, letters by Mallarmé, letters to Mallarmé, biographies of, essays on, and homage to Mallarmé with which the shelves of those bookstores tantalized me. For how long now the French poet has been writing as if the French public did not exist—as if it were, at best, a swineherd dreaming of that faraway princess the poet; yet it looks at him with traditional awe, and reads in dozens of literary newspapers, scores of literary magazines, the details of his life, opinions, temperament, and appearance. And in the Germanic countries people still glance at one with attentive respect, as if they thought that one might at any moment be about to write a poem; I shall never forget hearing a German say, in an objective considering tone, as if I were an illustration in a book called *Silver Poets of the Americas*: "You know, he looks a little like Rilke." In several South American countries poetry has kept most of the popularity and respect it formerly enjoyed; in one country, I believe Venezuela, the president, the ambassador whom he is sending to Paris, and the waiter who serves their coffee will four out of five times be poets. "What sort of poetry do *these* poets write?" is a question of frightening moment for us poor Northern poets; if the answer is "Nice simple stuff," we shall need to question half our ways. But these poets, these truly popular poets, seem to have taken as models for their verse neither the poems of Homer, of Shakespeare, nor of Racine, but those of Pablo Picasso: they are all surrealists.

Is Clarity the handmaiden of Popularity, as everybody automatically assumes? how much does it help to be immediately plain? In England today few poets are as popular as Dylan Thomas—his magical poems have corrupted a whole generation of English poets; yet he is surely one of the most obscure poets who ever lived. Or to take an opposite example: the poems of the students of Yvor Winters are quite as easy to understand as those which Longfellow used to read during the Children's Hour; yet they are about as popular as those other poems (of their own composition) which *grave Alice, and laughing Allegra, and Edith with golden hair* used to read to Longfellow during the Poet's Hour. If Dylan Thomas is obscurely famous, such poets as these are clearly unknown.

When someone says to me something I am not accustomed to hearing, or do not wish to hear, I say to him: *I do not understand you*; and we respond in just this way to poets. When critics first read Wordsworth's poetry they felt that it was silly, but many of them *said*, with Byron, that "he who understands it would be able / To add a story to the Tower of Babel." A few years before, a great critic praising the work of that plainest of poets, John Dryden, had remarked that he "delighted to tread on the brink where sense and nonsense mingle." Dryden himself had found Shakespeare's phrases "scarcely intelligible; and of those which we understand some are ungrammatical, others coarse; and his whole style is so pestered with figurative expressions that it is as affected as it is coarse." The reviewers of "The Love Song of J. Alfred Prufrock," even those who admired it most, found it almost impossible to understand; that it was hopelessly obscure seemed to them self-evident. Today, when college girls find it exactly as easy, exactly as hard, as "The Bishop Orders His Tomb at

St. Praxed's," one is able to understand these critics' despairing or de-nunciatory misunderstanding only by remembering that the first gen-eration of critics spoke of Browning's poem in just the terms that were later applied to Eliot's. How long it takes the world to catch up! Yet it really never "catches up," but is simply replaced by another world that does not need to catch up; so that when the old say to us, "What shall I do to understand Auden (or Dylan Thomas, or whoever the latest poet is)?" we can only reply: "You must be born again." An old gentleman at a party, talking to me about a poem we both ad-mired, the *Rubaiyat*, was delighted to find that our tastes agreed so well, and asked me what modern poet I like best. Rather cutting my coat to his cloth, I answered: "Robert Frost." He looked at me with surprise, and said with gentle but undisguised finality: "I'm afraid he is a little after my time." This happened in 1950; yet surely in 1850 some old gentleman, fond of Gray and Cowper and Crabbe, must have uttered to the young Matthew Arnold the same words, but this time with reference to the poetry of William Wordsworth.

We cannot even be sure what people will find obscure; when I taught at Salzburg I found that my European students did not find *The Waste Land* half as hard as Frost's poetry, since one went with, and the other against, all their own cultural presuppositions; I had not simply to explain "Home Burial" to them, I had to persuade them that it was a poem. And another example occurs to me: that of Robert Hillyer. In a review of *The Death of Captain Nemo* that I read, the re-viewer's first complaint was that the poem is obscure. I felt as if I had seen Senator McCarthy denounced as an agent of the Kremlin; for how could Mr. Hillyer be obscure?

That the poet, the modern poet, is, understandably enough, for all sorts of good reasons, more obscure than even he has any imagin-able right to be—this is one of those great elementary (or, as people say nowadays, *elemental*) attitudes about which it is hard to write anything that is not sensible and gloomily commonplace; one might as well talk on faith and works, on heredity and environment, or on that old question: why give the poor bathtubs when they only use them to put coal in? Anyone knows enough to reply to this question: "They don't; and, even if they did, *that's* not the reason you don't want to help pay for the tubs." Similarly, when someone says, "I don't read modern poetry because it's all stuff that nobody on earth can un-derstand," I know enough to be able to answer, though not aloud: "It isn't; and, even if it were, *that's* not the reason you don't read it." Any American poet under a certain age, a fairly advanced age—the age, one is tempted to say, of Bernard Shaw—has inherited a situation in which no one looks at him and in which, consequently, everyone complains that he is invisible: for that corner into which no one looks is always dark. And people who have inherited the custom of not reading poets justify it by referring to the obscurity of the poems they have never read—since most people decide that poets are obscure very much as legislators decide that books are pornographic: by glancing at a few fragments someone has strung together to disgust them. When a person says accusingly that he can't understand Eliot, his tone implies that most of his happiest hours are spent at the fireside among worn copies of the *Agamemnon, Phèdre,* and the Symbolic Books of William Blake; and it is melancholy to find, as one commonly will, that for months at a time he can be found pushing eagerly through the pages of *Gone with the Wind* or *Forever Amber,* where *with head, hands, wings, or feet* this poor fiend *pursues his way, and swims, or sinks, or wades, or creeps, or flies*; that all his happiest memories of Shakespeare seem to come from a high school production of *As You Like It* in which he played the wrestler Charles; and that he has, by some obscure process of free association, combined James Russell, Amy, and Robert Lowell into one majestic whole: a bearded cigar-smoking ambassador to the Vatican who, after accompanying Theodore Roosevelt on his first African expedition, came home to dictate on his deathbed the "Concord Hymn." Many a man, because Ezra Pound is too obscure for him, has shut forever the pages of *Paradise Lost*; or so one would gather, from the theory and practice such people combine.

The general public [in this lecture I hardly speak of the happy few, who grow fewer and unhappier day by day] has set up a criterion of its own, one by which every form of contemporary art is condemned. This criterion is, in the case of music, melody; in the case of painting, representation; in the case of poetry, clarity. In each case one simple aspect is made the test of a complicated whole, becomes a sort of loyalty oath for the work of art. Although judging by this method is almost as irrelevant as having the artist pronounce *shibboleth,* or swear that he is not a Know-Nothing, a Locofocoist, or a Bull Moose, it is as attractive, in exactly the same way, to the public that judges: instead of having to perceive, to enter, and to interpret those new worlds which new works of art are, the public can notice at a glance whether or not these pay lip service to its own "principles," and can then praise or blame them accordingly. Most of the music of earlier centuries, of other continents, has nothing the public can consider a satisfactory melody; the tourist looking through the galleries of Europe very soon discovers that most of the Old Masters were not, representationally speaking, half so good as the painters who illustrate *Collier's Magazine*; how difficult and dull the inexperienced reader would find most of the great poetry of the past, if he could ever be induced to read it! Yet it is always in the name of the easy past that he condemns the difficult present.

Anyone who has spent much time finding out what people do when they read a poem, what poems actually mean for them, will have discovered that a surprising part of the difficulty they have comes from their almost systematic unreceptiveness, their queer unwillingness to pay attention even to the reference of pronouns, the meaning of the punctuation, which subject goes with which verb, and so on; "after all," they seem to feel, "I'm not reading *prose*." You need to read good poetry with an attitude that is a mixture of sharp intelligence and of willing emotional empathy, at once penetrating and generous: as if you were listening to *The Marriage of Figaro*, not as if you were listening to *Tristan* or to Samuel Butler's Handelian oratorios; to read poetry—as so many readers do—like Mortimer Snerd pretending to be Dr. Johnson, or like Uncle Tom recollecting Eva, is hardly to read poetry at all. When you begin to read a poem you are entering a foreign country whose laws and language and life are a kind of translation of your own; but to accept it because its stews taste exactly like your old mother's hash, or to reject it because the owl-headed goddess of wisdom in its temple is fatter than the Statue of Liberty, is an equal mark of that want of imagination, that inaccessibility to experience, of which each of us who dies a natural death will die.

That the poetry of the first half of this century often *was* too difficult—just as the poetry of the eighteenth century *was* full of antitheses, that of the metaphysicals full of conceits, that of the Elizabethan dramatists full of rant and quibbles—is a truism that it would be absurd to deny. How our poetry got this way—how romanticism was purified and exaggerated and "corrected" into modernism; how poets carried all possible tendencies to their limits, with more than scientific zeal; how the dramatic monologue, which once had depended for its effect upon being a departure from the norm of poetry, now became in one form or another the norm; how poet and public stared at each other with righteous indignation, till the poet said, "Since you won't read me, I'll make sure you can't"—is one of the most complicated and interesting of stories. But Modernism was not "that lion's den from which no tracks return," but only a sort of canvas whale from which Jonah after Jonah, throughout the late twenties and early thirties, made a penitent return, back to rhyme and meter and plain broad Statement; how many young poets today are, if nothing else, plain! Yet how little posterity—if I may speak of that imaginary point where the poet and the public intersect—will care about all the tendencies of our age, all those good or bad intentions with which ordinary books are paved; and how much it will care for those few poems which, regardless of intention, manage at once to sum up, to repudiate, and to transcend both the age they appear in and the minds they are produced by. One judges an age, just as one judges a poet, by its best poems—after all, most of the others have disappeared; when posterity hears that our poems are obscure, it will smile indifferently—just as we do when we are told that the Victorians were sentimental, the romantics extravagant, the Augustans conventional, the metaphysicals conceited, and the Elizabethans bombastic—and go back to its (and our) reading: to Hardy's "During Wind and Rain," to Wordsworth's story of the woman Margaret, to Pope's "Epistle to Dr. Arbuthnot," to Marvell's "Horatian Ode," to Shakespeare's *Antony and Cleopatra,* to Eliot's *Four Quartets,* and to all the rest of those ageless products of an age.

In this age, certainly, poetry persists under many disadvantages. Just as it has been cut off from most of the people who in another age would have read it, so it has been cut off from most of the people who in another age would have written it. Today poems, good poems, are written almost exclusively by "born poets." We have lost for good the poems that would have been written by the modern equivalents of Henry VIII or Bishop King or Samuel Johnson; born novelists, born theologians, born princes; minds with less of an innate interest in words and more of one in the world which produces words. We are accustomed to think of the poet, when we think of him at all, as someone Apart; yet was there—as so many poets and readers of poetry seem to think—*was* there in the Garden of Eden, along with Adam and Eve and the animals, a Poet, the ultimate ancestor of Robert P. Tristram Coffin? . . . When I last read poems in New York City, a lady who, except for bangs, a magenta jersey blouse, and the expression of Palamède de Charlus, was indistinguishable from any other New Yorker, exclaimed to me about a poet whom the years have fattened for the slaughter: "He read like a young god." I felt that the next poet was going to be told that I read like the young Joaquin Miller; for this lady was less interested in those wonderful things poems than in those other things, poets—not realizing that it is their subordination to the poems they write that makes them admirable. She seemed to me someone who, because he has inherited a pearl necklace, can never again look at an oyster without a shudder of awe. And this reminds one that, today, many of the readers a poet would value most have hardly learned to read any poetry; and many of those who regularly read his poems have values so different from his that he is troubled by their praise, and vexed but reassured by their blame.

Tomorrow morning some poet may, like Byron, wake up to find himself famous—for having written a novel, for having killed his wife; it will not be for having written a poem. That is still logically, but no longer socially, possible. Let me illustrate with a story. I once met on a boat, traveling to Europe with his wife and daughter, a man with whom I played ping-pong. Having learned from a friend that I wrote poetry, he asked one day with uninterested politeness, "Who are the American poets you like best?" I said, "Oh, T. S. Eliot, Robert Frost." Then this man—this father who every night danced with his daughter with the well-taught, dated, decorous attractiveness of the hero of an old *Saturday Evening Post* serial by E. Phillips Oppenheim; who had had the best professional in Los Angeles teach his wife and daughter the tennis strokes he himself talked of with wearying authority; who never in his life had gone through a doorway before anyone over the age of seven—this well-dressed, well-mannered, traveled, urbane, educated gentleman said placidly: "I don't believe I've heard of them." For so far as literature, the arts, philosophy, and science were concerned, he might better have been the policeman on the corner. But he was perfectly correct in thinking—not that he had ever thought about it—that a knowledge of these things is not an essential requirement of the society of which he is a part. We belong to a culture whose old hierarchy of values—which demanded that a girl read Pope just as it demanded that she go to church and play the pianoforte—has virtually disappeared; a culture in which the great artist or scientist, in the relatively infrequent cases in which he has become widely known, has the status of Betty Grable or of the columnist who writes that, the night before, he met both these "celebrities" at the Stork Club.

When, a hundred and fifty years ago, a man had made his fortune, he found it necessary to provide himself with lace, carriages, servants, a wife of good family, a ballerina, a fencing master, a dancing master, a chaplain, a teacher of French, a string quartet perhaps, the editions of Pope and Steele and Addison through which he worked a laborious way on unoccupied evenings: there was so much for him to learn to *do*, there in his new station in life, that he must often have thought with nostalgia of the days in which all that he had to do was make his fortune. We have changed most of that: in our day the rich are expected not to do but to be; and those ties, tenuous, ambiguous, and immemorial, which bound to the Power of a state its Wisdom and its Grace, have at last been severed.

When Mill and Marx looked at a handful of workingmen making their slow firm way through the pages of Shelley or Herbert Spencer or *The Origin of Species,* they thought with confident longing, just as Jefferson and Lincoln had, of the days when every man would be literate, when an actual democracy would make its choices with as much wisdom as any imaginary state where the philosopher is king; and no gleam of prophetic insight came to show them those workingmen, two million strong, making their easy and pleasant way through the pages of the New York *Daily News.* The very speeches in which Jefferson and Lincoln spoke of their hope for the future are incomprehensible to most of the voters of that future, since the vocabulary and syntax of the speeches are more difficult—more obscure— than anything the voters have read or heard. For when you defeat me in an election simply because you were, as I was not, born and bred in a log cabin, it is only a question of time until you are beaten by someone whom the pigs brought up out in the yard. The truth that all men are politically equal, the recognition of the injustice of fictitious differences, becomes a belief in the fictitiousness of differences, a conviction that it is reaction or snobbishness or Fascism to believe that any individual differences of real importance can exist. We dislike having to believe in what Goethe called inborn or innate merits; yet—as a later writer more or less says—many waiters are born with the taste of duchesses, and most duchesses are born (and die) with the tastes of waiters: we can escape from the level of society, but not from the level of intelligence, to which we were born.

One of our universities recently made a survey of the reading habits of the American public; it decided that forty-eight percent of all Americans read, during a year, no book at all. I picture to myself that reader—non-reader, rather; one man out of every two—and I reflect, with shame: "Our poems are too hard for him." But so, too, are *Treasure Island, Peter Rabbit,* pornographic novels—any book whatsoever. The authors of the world have been engaged in a sort of conspiracy to drive this American away from books; have, in 77 million out of 160 million cases, succeeded. A sort of dream-situation often occurs to me in which I call to this imaginary figure, "Why don't you read books?"—and he always answers, after looking at me steadily for a long time: "Huh?"

If my tone is mocking, the tone of someone accustomed to helplessness, this is natural: the poet is a condemned man for whom the State will not even buy breakfast—and as someone said, "If you're going to hang me, you mustn't expect to be able to intimidate me into sparing your feelings during the execution." The poet lives in a world whose newspapers and magazines and books and motion pictures and radio stations and television stations have destroyed, in a great many people, even the capacity for understanding real poetry, real art of any kind. The man who monthly reads, with vacant relish, the carefully predigested sentences which the *Reader's Digest* feeds to him as a mother pigeon feeds her squabs—this man *cannot* read the *Divine Comedy*, even if it should ever occur to him to try: it is too obscure. Yet one sort of clearness shows a complete contempt for the reader, just as one sort of obscurity shows a complete respect. Which patronizes and degrades the reader, the *Divine Comedy* with its four levels of meaning, or the *Reader's Digest* with its one level so low that it seems not a level but an abyss into which the reader consents to sink? The writer's real dishonesty is to give an easy paraphrase of the hard truth. Yet the average article in our magazines gives any subject whatsoever the same coat of easy, automatic, "human" interest; every year *Harper's Magazine* sounds more like *Life* and *The Saturday Evening Post*. Goethe said, "The author whom a lexicon can keep up with is worth nothing"; Somerset Maugham says that the finest compliment he ever received was a letter in which one of his readers said: "I read your novel without having to look up a single word in the dictionary." These writers, plainly, lived in different worlds.

Since the animal organism thinks, truly reasons, only when it is required to, thoughtfulness is gradually disappearing among readers; and popular writing has left nothing to the imagination for so long now that imagination too has begun to atrophy. Almost all the works of the past are beginning to seem to the ordinary reader flat and dull, because they do not supply the reader's response along with that to which he responds. Boys who have read only a few books in their lives, but a great many comic books, will tell one, so vividly that it is easy to sympathize: "I don't like books because they don't really show you things; they're too slow; you have to do all the work yourself." When, in a few years, one talks to boys who have read only a few

comic books, but have looked at a great many television programs—
what will *they* say?

On this subject of the obscurity of the poet, of the new world
that is taking the place of the old, I have written you a poem—an ob-
scure one. I once encountered, in a book, a house that had a formal
garden, an English garden, a kitchen garden, and a cutting garden;
through these gardens gentlemen walked in silk stockings, their calves
padded like those of Mephistopheles; and I made that cutting garden,
those padded calves, my symbols for the past. For the present and the
future I had so many symbols I didn't know what to do: they came into
the poem without knocking, judged it, and did not leave when they
had judged; but the one that summed them all up—that had, for me,
the sound of the Last Morning of Judgment—was a slogan from a
wine advertisement, one that I used to see every day in the New York
subways. My poem is called "The Times Worsen":

> If sixteen shadows flapping on the line
> All sleek with bluing—a Last Morning's wash—
> Whistle, "Now that was thoughty, Mrs. Bean,"
> I tell myself, I try: *A dream, a dream.*
> But my plaid spectacles are matt as gouache;
> When, Sundays, I have finished all the funnies,
> I have not finished all the funnies. Men
> Walk in all day (to try me) without knocking—
> My jurors: these just, vulgar, friendly shades.
> The cutting garden of my grandmama,
> My great-great-great-grandfather's padded calves
> (Greeted, at cockcrow, with the soft small smile
> Of Lilith, his first morganatic wife)
> Are only a tale from E. T. W. Hoffmann.
> When Art goes, what remains is Life.
> The World of the Future does not work by halves:
> Life is that "wine like Mother used to make—
> So rich you can almost cut it with a knife."

The World of the Future! That world where vegetables are ei-
ther frozen, canned, or growing in the fields; where little children, as
they gaze into the television viewplate at the Babes dead under the
heaped-up leaves of the Wood, ask pleadingly: "But where was their
electric blanket?"; where old books, hollowed out to hold fudge, grace
every coffee table; where cavemen in grammar school pageants, clad

in pelts of raw cotton, are watched by families dressed entirely—except for the Neolite of their shoe-soles—in rayon, cellulose, and spun nylon; where, among the related radiances of a kitchen's white-enameled electric stove, electric dishwasher, electric refrigerator, electric washing machine, electric dryer, electric ironer, disposal unit, air conditioner, and Waring Blendor, the homemaker sits in the trim coveralls of her profession; where, above the concrete cavern that holds a General Staff, the rockets are invisible in the sky . . . Of this world I often think.

I do not know whether, at this point, any of my hearers will feel like saying to me, "But all this is Negative. What do you want us to *do* about all this?" If I have sounded certain about "all this," let me apologize: these are conclusions which I have come to slowly and reluctantly, as the world forced them on me. Would that I were one of those happy reactionaries, born with a Greek vocabulary as other children are born with birthmarks or incomes, who at the age of four refuse indignantly to waste on that "humanitarian phantasy of a sentimental liberalism, the Kindergarten," the hours they instead devote to memorizing their catechism! But I had a scientific education and a radical youth; am old-fashioned enough to believe, like Goethe, in Progress—the progress I see and the progress I wish for and do not see. So I say what I have said about the poet, the public, and their world angrily and unwillingly. If my hearers say, "But what should we do?" what else can I answer but "Nothing"? There is nothing to do different from what we already do: if poets write poems and readers read them, each as best they can—if they try to live not as soldiers or voters or intellectuals or economic men, but as human beings—they are doing all that can be done. But to expect them (by, say, reciting one-syllable poems over the radio) to bring back that Yesterday in which people stood on chairs to look at Lord Tennyson, is to believe that General Motors can bring back "the tradition of craftsmanship" by giving, as it does, prizes to Boy Scouts for their scale-models of Napoleonic coaches; to believe that the manners of the past can be restored by encouraging country-people to say *Grüss Gott* or *Howdy, stranger* to the tourists they meet along summer lanes.

Art matters not merely because it is the most magnificent ornament and the most nearly unfailing occupation of our lives, but because it is life itself. From Christ to Freud we have believed that, if we know the truth, the truth will set us free: art is indispensable because so much of this truth can be learned through works of art and through works of art alone—for which of us could have learned for himself what Proust and Chekhov, Hardy and Yeats and Rilke, Shakespeare and Homer learned for us? and in what other way could they have made us see the truths which they themselves saw, those differing and contradictory truths which seem nevertheless, to the mind which contains them, in some sense a single truth? And all these things, by their very nature, demand to be shared; if we are satisfied to know these things ourselves, and to look with superiority or indifference at those who do not have that knowledge, we have made a refusal that corrupts us as surely as anything can. If while most of our people (the descendants of those who, ordinarily, listened to Grimm's Tales and the ballads and the Bible; who, exceptionally, listened to Aeschylus and Shakespeare) listen not to simple or naïve art, but to an elaborate and sophisticated substitute for art, an immediate and infallible synthetic as effective and terrifying as advertisements or the speeches of Hitler—if, knowing all this, we say: *Art has always been a matter of a few,* we are using a truism to hide a disaster. One of the oldest, deepest, and most nearly conclusive attractions of democracy is manifested in our feeling that through it not only material but also spiritual goods can be shared; that in a democracy bread and justice, education and art, will be accessible to everybody. If a democracy should offer its citizens a show of education, a sham art, a literacy more dangerous than their old illiteracy, then we should have to say that it is not a democracy at all, but one more variant of those "People's Democracies" which share with any true democracy little more than the name. Goethe said: The only way in which we can come to terms with the great superiority of another person is love. But we can also come to terms with superiority, with true Excellence, by denying that such a thing as Excellence can exist; and, in doing so, we help to destroy it and ourselves.

I was sorry to see this conference given its (quite traditional) name of The Defense of Poetry. Poetry does not need to be defended, any more than air or food needs to be defended; poetry—using the word in its widest sense, the only sense in which it is important—has been an indispensable part of any culture we know anything about. Human life without some form of poetry is not human life but animal existence. Our world today is not an impossible one for poets and poetry: poets can endure its disadvantages, and good poetry is still being written—Yeats, for instance, thought the first half of this century the greatest age of lyric poetry since the Elizabethan. But what will happen to the public—to that portion of it divorced from any real art even of the simplest kind—I do not know. Yet an analogy occurs to me.

One sees, in the shops of certain mountainous regions of Austria, bands of silver links, clasped like necklaces, which have at the front jeweled or enameled silver plates, sometimes quite large ones. These pieces of jewelry are called *goiter-bands*: they are ornaments which in the past were used to adorn a woman's diseased, enormously swollen neck. If the women who wore them could have been told that they had been made hideous by the lack of an infinitesimal proportion of iodine in the water of the mountain valley in which they lived, they would have laughed at the notion. They would have laughed even more heartily at the notion that their necks *were* hideous—and their lovers would have asked, as they looked greedily at the round flesh under the flaxen pigtails, how anyone could bear to caress the poor, thin, scrawny, chickenish necks of those other women they now and then saw, foreigners from that flatland which travelers call the world.

I have talked about the poet and his public; but who is his public, really? In a story by E. M. Forster called "The Machine Stops," there is a conversation between a mother and her son. They are separated by half the circumference of the earth; they sit under the surface of the earth in rooms supplied with air, with food, and with warmth as automatically as everything else is supplied to these people of the far future. "Imagine," as Forster says, "a swaddled lump of flesh—a woman, about five feet high, with a face as white as a fungus." She has just refused to go to visit her son; she has no time. Her son replies:

"'The air-ship barely takes two days to fly between me and you.'
"I dislike air-ships."
"Why?"
"I dislike seeing the horrible brown earth, and the sea, and the stars when it is dark. I get no ideas in an air-ship."
"I do not get them anywhere else."
"What kind of ideas can the air give you?"
He paused for an instant.
"Do you not know four big stars that form an oblong, and three stars close together in the middle of the oblong, and hanging from these stars, three other stars?"
"No, I do not. I dislike the stars. But did they give you an idea? How interesting; tell me."
"I had an idea that they were like a man."
"I do not understand."
"The four big stars are the man's shoulders and his knees. The three stars in the middle are like the belts that men wore once, and the three stars hanging are like a sword."

"A sword?"

"Men carried swords about with them, to kill animals and other men."

"It does not strike me as a very good idea, but it is certainly original."

As long as these stars remain in this shape; as long as there is a man left to look at them and to discover that they are the being Orion: for at least this long the poet will have his public. And when this man too is gone, and neither the poems, the poet, nor the public exist any longer—and this possibility can no longer seem to us as strange as it would once have seemed—there is surely some order of the world, some level of being, at which they still subsist: an order in which the lost plays of Aeschylus are no different from those that have been preserved, an order in which the past, the present, and the future have in some sense the same reality. Or so—whether we think so or not—so we all feel. People always ask: *For whom does the poet write?* He needs only to answer, *For whom do you do good? Are you kind to your daughter because in the end someone will pay you for being?* . . . The poet writes his poem for its own sake, for the sake of that order of things in which the poem takes the place that has awaited it.

But this has been said, better than it is ever again likely to be said, by the greatest of the writers of this century, Marcel Proust; and I should like to finish this lecture by quoting his sentences:

All that we can say is that everything is arranged in this life as though we entered it carrying the burden of obligations contracted in a former life; there is no reason inherent in the conditions of life on this earth that can make us consider ourselves obliged to do good, to be fastidious, to be polite even, nor make the talented artist consider himself obliged to begin over again a score of times a piece of work the admiration aroused by which will matter little to his body devoured by worms, like the patch of yellow wall painted with so much knowledge and skill by an artist who must for ever remain unknown and is barely identified under the name Vermeer. All these obligations which have not their sanction in our present life seem to belong to a different world, founded upon kindness, scrupulosity, self-sacrifice, a world entirely different from this, which we leave in order to be born into this world, before perhaps returning to the other to live once again beneath the sway of those unknown laws which we have obeyed because we bore their precepts in our hearts, knowing not whose hand had traced them there—those laws to which every profound work of the intellect brings us nearer and which are invisible only—and still!—to fools.

[1951/PA]

To *the* Laodiceans

BACK IN THE DAYS WHEN "serious readers of modern poetry" were most patronizing to Frost's poems, one was often moved to argument, or to article-writing, or to saying under one's breath: *What is man that Thou art mindful of him?* In these days it's better—a little, not much: the lips are pursed that ought to be parted, and they still pay lip service, or little more. But Frost's best poetry—and there is a great deal of it, at once wonderfully different and wonderfully alike— deserves the attention, submission, and astonished awe that real art always requires of us; to give it a couple of readings and a ribbon lettered First in the Old-Fashioned (or Before 1900) Class of Modern Poetry is worse, almost, than not to read it at all. Surely *we* [I don't know exactly whom this *we* includes, but perhaps I could say that it means "the friends of things in the spirit," even when the things are difficult, even when the things are in the flesh] are not going to be like the *Saturday Review* readers and writers who tell one how completely good Frost is, and in the next breath tell one how narrowly good, limitedly good, badly good Eliot is. Surely it is the excellence most unlike our own that we will be most eager to acknowledge, since it not only extends but completes us—and since only we, not the excellence, are harmed by our rejection of it.

Frost has limitations of a kind very noticeable to us, but they are no more important than those of other contemporary poets; and most of the limitations, less noticeable to us, that these poets share, Frost is free of. If it makes good sense (but a narrow and ungenerous, though essential, sense) to say about Frost, "As a poet he isn't in Rilke's class at all," it does *not* make such sense if you substitute for Rilke's name that of Eliot or Moore or Stevens or Auden, that of any living poet. We can already see, most vividly, how ridiculous posterity is going to find the people who thought Marianne Moore's poems "not poetry at all," *The Waste Land* a hoax, and so on; but is posterity going to find any less ridiculous the intellectuals who admitted Frost only as a second-class citizen of the Republic of Letters, a "bard" whom it would be absurd to compare with real modern poets like—oh, E. E. Cummings? Frost's daemonic gift of always getting on the buttered side of both God and Mammon; of doing and saying anything and everything that he pleases, and still getting the World to approve or tactfully ignore every bit of it; of not only allowing, but taking a hard pleasure in encouraging, fools and pedants to adore him as their own image magnified—all this has helped to keep us from seeing Frost for what he really is. And here one has no right to be humble and agreeable, and to concede beforehand that *what he really is* is only one's own "view" or "interpretation" of him: the regular ways of looking at Frost's poetry are grotesque simplifications, distortions, falsifications—coming to know his poetry well ought to be enough, in itself, to dispel any of them, and to make plain the necessity of finding some other way of talking about his work.

Any of us but Frost himself (and all the little Frostlings who sit round him wondering with a foolish face of praise, dealing out ten monosyllables to the homey line) can by now afford just to wonder at his qualities, not to sadden at his defects, and can gladly risk looking a little foolish in the process. The real complication, sophistication, and ambiguity of Frost's thought [what poet since Arnold has written so much about isolation, and said so much more about it than even Arnold? what other poet, long before we had begun to perfect the means of altogether doing away with humanity, had taken as an obsessive subject the wiping-out of man, his replacement by the nature out of which he arose?], the range and depth and height of his poems, have had justice done to them by neither his admirers nor his detractors—and, alas, aren't going to have justice done to them by me now. If one is talking about Frost's poetry to friends, or giving a course in it to students, one can go over thirty or forty of his best poems and feel sure about everything: one doesn't need, then, to praise or blame or generalize—the poems speak for themselves almost as well as poems can. But when one writes a little article about Frost, one feels lamentably sure of how lamentably short of his world the article is going to fall; one can never write about him without wishing that it were a whole book, a book in which one could talk about hundreds of poems and hundreds of other things, and fall short by one's essential and not accidental limitations.

I have sometimes written, and often talked, about Frost's willful, helpless, all too human mixture of virtues and vices, so I hope that this time I will be allowed simply—in the nice, old-fashioned, looked-down-on phrase—to appreciate. And I want to appreciate more than his best poems, I want to exclaim over some of the unimportantly delightful and marvelously characteristic ones, and over some of the places where all of Frost and all of what is being described are married and indistinguishable in one line. But first let me get rid, in a few sentences, of that Skeleton on the Doorstep that is the joy of his enemies and the despair of his friends. Just as a star will have, sometimes, a dark companion, so Frost has a pigheaded one, a shadowy self that grows longer and darker as the sun gets lower. I am speaking of that other self that might be called the Gray Eminence of Robert Taft, or the Peter Pan of the National Association of Manufacturers, or any such thing—this public self incarnates all the institutionalized complacency that Frost once mocked at and fled from, and later pretended to become a part of and became a part of. This Yankee Editorialist side of Frost gets in the way of *everything*—of us, of the real Frost, of the real poems and their real subject matter. And a poet so magically good at making the subtlest of points surely shouldn't evolve into one who regularly comes out and tells you the point after it's been made—and comes out and tells you, in such trudging doctrinaire lines, a point like the end of a baseball bat. Frost says in a piece of homely doggerel that he has hoped wisdom could be not only Attic but Laconic, Boeotian even—"at least not systematic"; but how systematically Frostian the worst of his later poems are! His good poems are the best refutation of, the most damning comment on, his bad: his *Complete Poems* have the air of being able to educate any faithful reader into tearing out a third of the pages, reading a third, and practically wearing out the rest.

We begin to read Frost, always, with the taste of "Birches" in our mouth—a taste a little brassy, a little sugary; and to take it out I will use not such good and familiar poems as "Mending Wall" and "After Apple-Picking," or such a wonderful and familiar (and misunderstood) poem as "An Old Man's Winter Night," but four or five of Frost's best and least familiar poems. Let me begin with a poem that, at first glance, hardly seems a Frost poem at all, but reminds us more of another kind of unfamiliar poem that Housman wrote; this poem is called "Neither Out Far Nor In Deep":

> The people along the sand
> All turn and look one way.
> They turn their back on the land.
> They look at the sea all day.
>
> As long as it takes to pass
> A ship keeps raising its hull;
> The wetter ground like glass
> Reflects a standing gull.
>
> The land may vary more;
> But wherever the truth may be—
> The water comes ashore,
> And the people look at the sea.
>
> They cannot look out far.
> They cannot look in deep.
> But when was that ever a bar
> To any watch they keep?

First of all, of course, the poem is simply there, in indifferent unchanging actuality; but our thought about it, what we are made to make of it, is there too, made to be there. When we choose between land and sea, the human and the inhuman, the finite and the infinite, the sea *has* to be the infinite that floods in over us endlessly, the hypnotic monotony of the universe that is incommensurable with us—everything into which we look neither very far nor very deep, but look, look just the same. And yet Frost doesn't say so—it is the geometry of this very geometrical poem, its inescapable structure, that says so. There is the deepest tact and restraint in the symbolism; it is like Housman's

> Stars, I have seen them fall,
> But when they drop and die
> No star is lost at all
> From all the star-sown sky.
>
> The toil of all that be
> Helps not the primal fault:

It rains into the sea
And still the sea is salt.

But Frost's poem is flatter, grayer, and at once tenderer and more ter-
rible, without even the consolations of rhetoric and exaggeration—
there is no "primal fault" in Frost's poem, but only the faint Biblical
memories of "any watch they keep." What we do know we don't care
about; what we do care about we don't know: we can't look out very
far, or in very deep; and when did that ever bother *us*? It would be hard
to find anything more unpleasant to say about people than that last
stanza; but Frost doesn't say it unpleasantly—he says it with flat ease,
takes everything with something harder than contempt, more passive
than acceptance. And isn't there something heroic about the whole
business, too—something touching about our absurdity? if the fool
persisted in his folly he would become a wise man, Blake said, and we
have persisted. The tone of the last lines—or, rather, their careful
suspension between several tones, as a piece of iron can be held in the
air between powerful enough magnets—allows for this too. This
recognition of the essential limitations of man, without denial or
protest or rhetoric or palliation, is very rare and very valuable, and
rather usual in Frost's best poetry. One is reminded of Empson's
thoughtful and truthful comment on Gray's "Elegy": "Many people,
without being communists, have been irritated by the complacence in
the massive calm of the poem . . . And yet what is said is one of the
permanent truths; it is only in degree that any improvement of soci-
ety would prevent wastage of human powers; the waste even in a for-
tunate life, the isolation even of a life rich in intimacy, cannot but be
felt deeply, and is the central feeling of tragedy."
    Another of Frost's less familiar poems is called "Provide,
Provide":

The witch that came (the withered hag)
To wash the steps with pail and rag
Was once the beauty Abishag,

The picture pride of Hollywood.
Too many fall from great and good
For you to doubt the likelihood.

Die early and avoid the fate.
Or if predestined to die late,
Make up your mind to die in state.

Make the whole stock exchange your own!
If need be occupy a throne,
Where nobody can call *you* crone.

Some have relied on what they knew;
Others on being simply true.
What worked for them might work for you.

No memory of having starred
Atones for later disregard
Or keeps the end from being hard.

Better to go down dignified
With boughten friendship at your side
Than none at all. Provide, provide!

For many readers this poem will need no comment at all, and for others it will need rather more than I could ever give. The poem is—to put it as crudely as possible—an immortal masterpiece; and if we murmur something about its crudities and provincialisms, History will smile tenderly at us and lay us in the corner beside those cultivated people from Oxford and Cambridge who thought Shakespeare a Hollywood scenario-writer. Since I can't write five or six pages about the poem, it might be better to say only that it is full of the deepest, and most touching, moral wisdom—and it is full, too, of the life we have to try to be wise about and moral in (the sixth stanza is almost unbearably actual). The Wisdom of this World and the wisdom that comes we know not whence exist together in the poem, not side by side but one inside the other; yet the whole poem exists for, lives around, the fifth stanza and its *others on being simply true*—was restraint ever more moving? One can quote about that line Rilke's *In the end the only defense is defenselessness,* and need to say no more. But the rest of the poem is the more that we need to say, if we decide to say any more: it says, in the worldliest and homeliest of terms, that expediency won't work—the poem is, even in its form, a marvelous *reductio ad absurdum* of expediency—but since you *will* try it, since you *will* provide for the morrow, then provide hard for it, be really expedient, settle yourself for life in the second-best bed around which the heirs gather, the very best second-best bed. The poem is so particularly effective because it is the Wisdom of this World which demonstrates to us that the Wisdom of this World isn't enough. The poem puts, so to speak, the minimal case for morality, and then makes the minimal recommendation of it (*What worked for them might work for you*); but this has a beauty and conclusiveness that aren't minimal.

The most awful of Frost's smaller poems is one called "Design":

I found a dimpled spider, fat and white,
On a white heal-all, holding up a moth
Like a white piece of rigid satin cloth—
Assorted characters of death and blight
Mixed ready to begin the morning right,
Like the ingredients of a witch's broth—
A snow-drop spider, a flower like froth,
And dead wings carried like a paper kite.

What had that flower to do with being white,
The wayside blue and innocent heal-all?
What brought the kindred spider to that height,
Then steered the white moth thither in the night?
What but design of darkness to appall?—
If design govern in a thing so small.

This is the Argument from Design with a vengeance; is the terrible negative from which the eighteenth century's Kodak picture (with its *Having wonderful time. Wish you were here* on the margin) had to be printed. If a watch, then a watchmaker; if a diabolical machine, then a diabolical mechanic—Frost uses exactly the logic that has always been used. And this little albino catastrophe is too whitely catastrophic to be accidental, too impossibly unlikely ever to be a coincidence: accident, chance, statistics, natural selection are helpless to account for such designed terror and heartbreak, such an awful symbolic perversion of the innocent being of the world. Frost's details are so diabolically good that it seems criminal to leave some unremarked; but notice how *dimpled, fat,* and *white* (all but one; all but one) come from our regular description of any baby; notice how the *heal-all,* because of its name, is the one flower in all the world picked to be the altar for this Devil's Mass; notice how *holding up* the moth brings something ritual and hieratic, a ghostly, ghastly formality, to this priest and its sacrificial victim; notice how terrible to the fingers, how full of the stilling rigor of death, that *white piece of rigid satin cloth* is. And *assorted characters of death and blight* is, like so many things in this poem, sharply ambiguous: *a mixed bunch of actors* or *diverse repre-*

sentative signs. The tone of the phrase *assorted characters of death and blight* is beautifully developed in the ironic Breakfast-Club-calisthenics, Radio-Kitchen heartiness of *mixed ready to begin the morning right* (which assures us, so unreassuringly, that this isn't any sort of Strindberg *Spook Sonata,* but hard fact), and concludes in the *ingredients* of the witch's broth, giving the soup a sort of cuddly shimmer that the cauldron in *Macbeth* never had; the *broth,* even, is brought to life—we realize that witch's broth *is* broth, to be supped with a long spoon. For sweet-sour, smiling awfulness *snow-drop spider* looks unsurpassable, until we come to the almost obscenely horrible (even the mouth-gestures are utilized) *a flower like froth*; this always used to seem to me the case of the absolutely inescapable effect, until a student of mine said that you could tell how beautiful the flower was because the poet compared it to froth; when I said to her, "But—but—but what does froth *remind* you of?" looking desperately into her blue eyes, she replied: "Fudge. It reminds me of making fudge."

And then, in the victim's own little line, how contradictory and awful everything is: *dead wings carried like a paper kite*! The *dead* and the *wings* work back and forth on each other heartbreakingly, and the contradictory pathos of the *carried* wings is exceeded by that of the matter-of-fact conversion into what has never lived, into a shouldered toy, of the ended life. *What had that flower to do with being white, / The wayside blue and innocent heal-all?* expresses as well as anything ever has the arbitrariness of our guilt, the fact that Original Sin is only Original Accident, so far as the creatures of this world are concerned. And *the wayside blue and innocent heal-all* is, down to the least sound, the last helpless, yearning, trailing-away sigh of too-precarious innocence, of a potentiality canceled out almost before it began to exist. The *wayside* makes it universal, commonplace, and somehow dearer to us; the *blue* brings in all the associations of the normal negated color (the poem is likely to remind the reader of Melville's chapter on the Whiteness of the Whale, just as Frost may have been reminded); and the *innocent* is given a peculiar force and life by this context, just as the name *heal-all* here comes to sad, ironic, literal life: it healed all, itself it could not heal. The *kindred* is very moving in its half-forgiving ambiguity; and the Biblical *thither in the night* and the conclusive *steered* (with its careful echoes of "To a Water-Fowl" and a thousand sermons) are very moving and very serious in their condemnation, their awful mystery. The partly ambiguous, summing-up *What but design of darkness to appall* comes as something taken for granted, a relief almost, in its mere statement and generalization, after the almost unbearable actuality and particularity of what has come before. And then this whole appalling categorical machinery of reasoning-out, of conviction, of condemnation—it reminds one of the machine in *The Penal Colony*—is suddenly made merely hypothetical, a possible contradicted shadow, by one offhand last-minute qualification: one that dismisses it, but that dismisses it only for a possibility still more terrifying, a whole new random, statistical, astronomical abyss underlying the diabolical machinery of the poem. "In large things, macroscopic phenomena of some real importance," the poem says, "the classical mechanics of design probably *does* operate—though in reverse, so far as the old Argument from Design is concerned; but these little things, things of no real importance, microscopic phenomena like a flower or moth or man or planet or solar system [we have so indissolubly identified ourselves with the moth and flower and spider that we cannot treat our own nature and importance, which theirs symbolize, as fundamentally different from theirs], are governed by the purely statistical laws of quantum mechanics, of random distribution, are they not?" I have given this statement of "what the poem says"—it says much more— an exaggeratedly physical, scientific form because both a metaphorically and literally astronomical view of things is so common, and so unremarked-on, in Frost. This poem, I think most people will admit, makes Pascal's "eternal silence of those infinite spaces" seem the hush between the movements of a cantata.

Another impressive unfamiliar poem is "The Most of It," a poem which indicates as well as any I can think of Frost's stubborn truthfulness, his willingness to admit both the falseness in the cliché and the falseness in the contradiction of the cliché; if the universe never gives us either a black or a white answer, but only a black-and-white one that is somehow not an answer at all, still its inhuman not-answer exceeds any answer that we human beings could have thought of or wished for:

He thought he kept the universe alone;
For all the voice in answer he could wake
Was but the mocking echo of his own
From some tree-hidden cliff across the lake.
Some morning from the boulder-broken beach
He would cry out on life, that what it wants
Is not its own love back in copy speech,
But counter-love, original response.
And nothing ever came of what he cried

Unless it was the embodiment that crashed
In the cliff's talus on the other side,
And then in the far distant water splashed,
But after a time allowed for it to swim,
Instead of proving human when it neared
And someone else additional to him,
As a great buck it powerfully appeared,
Pushing the crumpled water up ahead,
And landed pouring like a waterfall,
And stumbled through the rocks with horny tread,
And forced the underbrush—and that was all.

But one of the strangest and most characteristic, most dismaying and most gratifying, poems any poet has ever written is a poem called "Directive." It shows the coalescence of three of Frost's obsessive themes, those of isolation, of extinction, and of the final limitations of man—is Frost's last word about all three:

Back out of all this now too much for us,
Back in a time made simple by the loss
Of detail, burned, dissolved, and broken off
Like graveyard marble sculpture in the weather,
There is a house that is no more a house
Upon a farm that is no more a farm
And in a town that is no more a town.
The road there, if you'll let a guide direct you
Who only has at heart your getting lost,
May seem as if it should have been a quarry—
Great monolithic knees the former town
Long since gave up pretence of keeping covered.
And there's a story in a book about it:
Besides the wear of iron wagon wheels
The ledges show lines ruled southeast northwest,
The chisel work of an enormous Glacier
That braced his feet against the Arctic Pole.
You must not mind a certain coolness from him
Still said to haunt this side of Panther Mountain.
Nor need you mind the serial ordeal
Of being watched from forty cellar holes
As if by eye pairs out of forty firkins.
As for the wood's excitement over you
That sends light rustle rushes to their leaves,

Charge that to upstart inexperience.
Where were they all not twenty years ago?
They think too much of having shaded out
A few old pecker-fretted apple trees.
Make yourself up a cheering song of how
Someone's road home from work this once was,
Who may be just ahead of you on foot
Or creaking with a buggy load of grain.
The height of the adventure is the height
Of country where two village cultures faded
Into each other. Both of them are lost.
And if you're lost enough to find yourself
By now, pull in your ladder road behind you
And put a sign up CLOSED to all but me.
Then make yourself at home. The only field
Now left's no bigger than a harness gall.
First there's the children's house of make believe,
Some shattered dishes underneath a pine,
The playthings in the playhouse of the children.
Weep for what little things could make them glad.
Then for the house that is no more a house,
But only a belilaced cellar hole,
Now slowly closing like a dent in dough.
This was no playhouse but a house in earnest.
Your destination and your destiny's
A brook that was the water of the house,
Cold as a spring as yet so near its source,
Too lofty and original to rage.
(We know the valley streams that when aroused
Will leave their tatters hung on barb and thorn.)
I have kept hidden in the instep arch
Of an old cedar at the waterside
A broken drinking goblet like the Grail
Under a spell so the wrong ones can't find it,
So can't get saved, as Saint Mark says they mustn't.
(I stole the goblet from the children's playhouse.)
Here are your waters and your watering place.
Drink and be whole again beyond confusion.

There are weak places in the poem, but these are nothing be-
side so much longing, tenderness, and passive sadness, Frost's un-
derstanding that each life is pathetic because it wears away into the

death that it at last half-welcomes—that even its salvation, far back at the cold root of things, is make-believe, drunk from a child's broken and stolen goblet, a plaything hidden among the ruins of the lost cultures. Here the waters of Lethe are the waters of childhood, and in their depths, with ambiguous grace, man's end is joined to his beginning. Is the poem consoling or heartbreaking? Very much of both; and its humor and acceptance and humanity, its familiarity and elevation, give it a composed matter-of-fact magnificence. Much of the strangeness of the poem is far under the surface, or else so much on the surface, in the subtlest of details (how many readers will connect the *serial ordeal* of the eye pairs with the poem's Grail-parody?), that one slides under it unnoticing. But the first wonderful sentence; the six lines about the wood's excitement; the knowledge that produces the sentence beginning *Make yourself up a cheering song*; the *Both of them are lost*; incidental graces like the *eye pairs out of forty firkins*, the *harness gall*, the *belilaced cellar hole* closing *like a dent in dough*, the plays on the word *lost*; the whole description of the children's playhouse, with the mocking (at whom does it mock?) and beautiful *Weep for what little things could make them glad*; the grave, terrible *This was no playhouse but a house in earnest*; the four wonderful conclusive sentences—these, and the whole magical and helpless mastery of the poem, are things that many readers have noticed and will notice: the poem is hard to understand, but easy to love.

In another poem Frost worries about the bird that, waked in moonlight, "sang halfway through its little inborn tune," and then he realizes that the bird is as safe as ever, that any increase in danger must necessarily be an infinitesimal one, or else

> It could not have come down to us so far
> Through the interstices of things ajar
> On the long bead chain of repeated birth.

The thought, which would surely have made Darwin give a little gratified smile, might very well have pleased with its "interstices of things ajar" that earlier writer who said, "Absent thee from felicity awhile / And in this harsh world draw thy breath in pain." For Frost is sometimes a marvelous rhetorician, a writer so completely master of his own rhetorical effects that he can alter both their degree and kind almost as he pleases. In "The Black Cottage" he is able to write the most touchingly and hauntingly prosaic of lines about the passing away of this world:

He fell at Gettysburg or Fredericksburg.
I ought to know—it makes a difference which:
Fredericksburg wasn't Gettysburg, of course . . .

and he is also able to end the poem with the magnificence of

"As I sit here, and oftentimes, I wish
I could be monarch of a desert land
I could devote and dedicate forever
To the truths we keep coming back and back to.
So desert it would have to be, so walled
By mountain ranges half in summer snow,
No one would covet it or think it worth
The pains of conquering to force change on.
Scattered oases where men dwelt, but mostly
Sand dunes held loosely in tamarisk
Blown over and over themselves in idleness.
Sand grains should sugar in the natal dew
The babe born to the desert, the sand storm
Retard mid-waste my cowering caravans—
There are bees in this wall." He struck the clapboards,
Fierce heads looked out; small bodies pivoted.
We rose to go. Sunset blazed on the windows.

One sees this extraordinary command in the composed, thought-
ful, and traditional rhetoric of "The Gift Outright," one of the best
of Frost's smaller poems, and perhaps the best "patriotic" poem ever
written about our own country:

The land was ours before we were the land's.
She was our land more than a hundred years
Before we were her people. She was ours
In Massachusetts, in Virginia,
But we were England's, still colonials,
Possessing what we still were unpossessed by,
Possessed by what we now no more possessed.
Something we were withholding made us weak
Until we found it was ourselves
We were withholding from our land of living,
And forthwith found salvation in surrender.
Such as we were we gave ourselves outright
(The deed of gift was many gifts of war)
To the land vaguely realizing westward,

> But still unstoried, artless, unenhanced,
> Such as she was, such as she would become.

The third sentence is a little weakly and conventionally said; but the rest! And that *vaguely realizing westward*! The last three lines, both for tone and phrasing, are themselves realized with absolute finality, are good enough to survive all the repetitions that the generations of the future will give them.

We feel, here, that we understand why the lines are as good as they are; but sometimes there will be a sudden rise, an unlooked-for intensity and elevation of emotion, that have a conclusiveness and magnificence we are hardly able to explain. Frost ends a rather commonplace little poem about Time with a blaze of triumph, of calm and rapturous certainty, that is as transfiguring, almost, as the ending of "A Dialogue of Self and of Soul":

> I could give all to Time except—except
> What I myself have held. But why declare
> The things forbidden that while the Customs slept
> I have crossed to Safety with? For I am There,
> And what I would not part with I have kept.

A man finishes an axe-helve, and Frost says:

> But now he brushed the shavings from his knee
> And stood the axe there on its horse's hoof,
> Erect, but not without its waves, as when
> The snake stood up for evil in the Garden . . .

It would be hard to find words good enough for *this*. Surely anybody must feel, as he finishes reading these lines, the thrill of authentic creation, the thrill of witnessing something that goes back farther than Homer and goes forward farther than any future we are able to imagine: here the thing in itself, and man's naked wit, and Style—the elevation and composed forbearance of the Grand Style, of the truly classical—coalesce in an instant of grace.

Frost calls one poem "The Old Barn at the Bottom of the Fogs," and starts out:

> Where's this barn's house? It never had a house,
> Or joined with sheds in ring-around a dooryard.

The hunter scuffling leaves goes by at dusk,
The gun reversed that he went out with shouldered.
The harvest moon and then the hunter's moon.
Well, the moon after that came one at last
To close this outpost barn and close the season.
The fur-thing, muff-thing, rocking in and out
Across the threshold in the twilight fled him . . .

How can you resist a poet who can begin a poem like this—even if the poem later comes to nothing at all? Nor is it any easier to resist the man who says "To a Moth Seen in Winter," "with false hope seeking the love of kind," "making a labor of flight for one so airy":

Nor will you find love either nor love you.
And what I pity in you is something human,
The old incurable untimeliness,
Only begetter of all things that are . . .

What an already-prepared-for, already-familiar-seeming ring the lines have, the ring of that underlying style that great poets so often have in common beneath their own styles! I think that Dante would have read with nothing but admiration for its calm universal precision the wonderful "Acquainted with the Night," a poem in Dante's own form and with some of Dante's own qualities:

I have been one acquainted with the night.
I have walked out in rain—and back in rain.
I have outwalked the furthest city light.

I have looked down the saddest city lane.
I have passed by the watchman on his beat
And dropped my eyes, unwilling to explain.

I have stood still and stopped the sound of feet
When far away an interrupted cry
Came over houses from another street,

But not to call me back or say goodbye;
And further still at an unearthly height,
One luminary clock against the sky

Proclaimed the time was neither wrong nor right.
I have been one acquainted with the night.

Is this a "classical" poem? If *it* isn't, what is? Yet doesn't the poem itself make the question seem ignominious, a question with a fatal lack of magnanimity, of true comprehension and concern? The things in themselves, the poem itself, abide neither our questions nor our categories; they are free. And our own freedom—the freedom to look and not to disregard, the freedom to side against oneself—is treated with delicate and tender imaginativeness in "Time Out":

It took that pause to make him realize
The mountain he was climbing had the slant
As of a book held up before his eyes
(And was a text albeit done in plant).
Dwarf-cornel, gold-thread, and maianthemum,
He followingly fingered as he read,
The flowers fading on the seed to come;
But the thing was the slope it gave his head:
The same for reading as it was for thought,
So different from the hard and level stare
Of enemies defied and battles fought.
It was the obstinately gentle air
That may be clamored at by cause and sect
But it will have its moment to reflect.

There is even more delicacy and tenderness and imagination in "Meeting and Passing," a backward-looking love poem whose last two lines, by an understatement beyond statement, make tears of delight come into one's eyes—nothing else in English is so like one of those love poems that, in 1913, Hardy wrote about a woman who had just died; and nothing else in English expresses better than that last couplet—which does not rhyme, but only repeats—the transfiguring, almost inexpressible reaching-out of the self to what has become closer and more personal than the self:

As I went down the hill along the wall
There was a gate I had leaned at for the view
And had just turned from when I first saw you
As you came up the hill. We met. But all
We did that day was mingle great and small
Footprints in summer dust as if we drew

The figure of our being less than two
But more than one as yet. Your parasol

Pointed the decimal off with one deep thrust.
And all the time we talked you seemed to see
Something down there to smile at in the dust.
(Oh, it was without prejudice to me!)
Afterward I went past what you had passed
Before we met and you what I had passed.

And Frost (no poet has had even the range of his work more unforgivably underestimated by the influential critics of our time) is able once or twice to give sexual love, passion itself, as breathtakingly conclusive an embodiment. Here I am not speaking of the sinister, condemning, tender "The Subverted Flower," a flawed but extraordinary poem that at once embodies and states in almost abstract form his knowledge about part of love; I mean the wonderful conclusion of "The Pauper Witch of Grafton," where the testy, acrid mockery of the old pauper, of the "noted witch" always plagued by an adulterous generation for a sign, turns into something very different as she remembers the man who first exposed and then married her:

I guess he found he got more out of me
By having me a witch. Or something happened
To turn him round. He got to saying things
To undo what he'd done and make it right,
Like, "No, she ain't come back from kiting yet.
Last night was one of her nights out. She's kiting.
She thinks when the wind makes a night of it
She might as well herself." But he liked best
To let on he was plagued to death with me:
If anyone had seen me coming home
Over the ridgepole, 'stride of a broomstick,
As often as he had in the tail of the night,
He guessed they'd know what he had to put up with.
Well, I showed Arthur Amy signs enough
Off from the house as far as we could keep
And from barn smells you can't wash out of ploughed ground
With all the rain and snow of seven years;
And I don't mean just skulls of Roger's Rangers
On Moosilauke, but woman signs to man,
Only bewitched so I would last him longer.

Up where the trees grow short, the mosses tall,
I made him gather me wet snow berries
On slippery rocks beside a waterfall.
I made him do it for me in the dark.
And he liked everything I made him do.
I hope if he is where he sees me now
He's so far off he can't see what I've come to.
You can come down from everything to nothing.
All is, if I'd a-known when I was young
And full of it, that this would be the end,
It doesn't seem as if I'd had the courage
To make so free and kick up in folks' faces.
I might have, but it doesn't seem as if.

When I read the lines that begin *Up where the trees grow short, the mosses tall*, and that end *And he liked everything I made him do* (nobody but a good poet could have written the first line, and nobody but a great one could have forced the reader to say the last line as he is forced to say it), I sometimes murmur to myself, in a perverse voice, that there is more sexuality there than in several hothouses full of Dylan Thomas; and, of course, there is love, there. And in what poem can one find more of its distortion and frustration, its helpless derangement, than in the marvelous "A Servant to Servants"? But here I come to what makes the critic of Frost's poetry groan, and sadden, and almost despair: several of his very best poems, the poems in which he is most magnificent, most characteristic, most nearly incomparable, are far too long to quote. If I could quote "Home Burial," "The Witch of Coös," and "A Servant to Servants," Pharisee and Philistine alike would tiptoe off hand in hand, their shamed eyes starry; anyone who knows these poems well will consider the mere mention of them enough to justify any praise, any extravagance— and anybody who doesn't know them doesn't know some of the summits of our poetry, and is so much to be pitied that it would be foolish to blame him too. I don't know what to do about these poems, here: may I just make a bargain with the reader to regard them as quoted in this article?

I have used rather an odd tone about them because I feel so much frustration at not being able to quote and go over them, as I so often have done with friends and classes; they *do* crown Frost's work, are unique in the poetry of our century and perhaps in any poetry. Even such lesser poems of the sort as "The Fear" and "The Black

Cottage" would be enough to make another poet respected; and it is discouraging, while mentioning Frost's poems about love, not to be able to quote "To Earthward" and "The Lovely Shall Be Choosers," two very beautiful and very unusual poems. And this reminds me that I have not even mentioned "Desert Places," a poem almost better, at the same game, than Stevens's beautiful "The Snowman." This is the best place to say once more that such an article as this is not relatively but absolutely inadequate to a body of poetry as great as Frost's, both in quality and in quantity—can be, at best, only a kind of breathless signboard. Almost all that Frost has touched, from the greatest to the smallest things, he has transfigured.

Frost is so characteristic and delightful in slight things, often, that one feels a superstitious reluctance to dismiss them with *slight*. The little "In a Disused Graveyard" is, plainly, the slightest and least pretentious of fancies; but the justest of fancies, too—and how much there is underneath its last five lines, that changes their shape almost as the least white of a wave-top is changed by the green weight under it:

> The living come with grassy tread
> To read the gravestones on the hill;
> The graveyard draws the living still,
> But never any more the dead.
>
> The verses in it say and say:
> "The ones who living come today
> To read the stones and go away
> Tomorrow dead will come to stay."
>
> So sure of death the marbles rhyme,
> Yet can't help marking all the time
> How no one dead will seem to come.
> What is it men are shrinking from?
>
> It would be easy to be clever
> And tell the stones: Men hate to die
> And have stopped dying now forever.
> I think they would believe the lie.

Nothing could be slighter than these two lines called "The Span of Life":

> The old dog barks backward without getting up.
> I can remember when he was a pup.

Yet the sigh we give after we've read them isn't a slight one: this is age in one couplet. And another couplet, one called "An Answer," I can hardly resist using as a sort of shibboleth or Stanford-Binet Test of the imagination: if you cannot make out the sea-change this strange little joke, this associational matrix, has undergone somewhere down in Frost's head, so that it has become worthy of Prospero himself, all nacreous with lyric, tender, amused acceptance and understanding and regret—if you can't feel any of this, you *are* a Convention of Sociologists. Here it is, "An Answer":

> But Islands of the Blessèd, bless you son,
> I never came upon a blessèd one.

Frost's account of a battle, in "Range-Finding," is an unprecedentedly slight one. This battle, before it killed any of the soldiers—and Frost does not go on to them—cut a flower beside a ground bird's nest, yet the bird kept flying in and out with food; and a butterfly, dispossessed of the flower, came back and flutteringly clung to it. Besides them there was

>   a wheel of thread
> And straining cables wet with silver dew.
> A sudden passing bullet shook it dry.
> The indwelling spider ran to greet the fly,
> But finding nothing, sullenly withdrew.

That is all. An occasional lameness or tameness of statement mars the poem, gives it a queer rather attractive old-fashionedness, but does not destroy it. This is the minimal case, the final crystalline essence of Stendhal's treatment of Waterloo: a few fathoms down the sea is always calm, and a battle, among other things, at bottom is always this; the spider can ask with Fabrizio, "Was that it? Was I really at Waterloo?"

I mustn't go on quoting slight things forever, yet there are many more that I would like to quote—or that the reader might like to reread, or read: "An Empty Threat," "The Telephone," "Moon Compasses," "The Hill Wife," "Dust of Snow," "The Oven Bird," "Gathering Leaves" (that saddest, most-carefully-unspecified symbol for our memories), "For Once, Then, Something," "The Runaway," "In Hardwood Groves," "Beech," "The Ingenuities of Debt," "The Investment," the "Books" part of "A Fountain, a Bottle, a Donkey's Ear and Some Books"—these, and poems like "The Pasture" and "Stopping by Woods on a Snowy Evening," that many readers will not need to reread, but will simply repeat. (Frost is, often, as automatically memorable as any savage chronicle rhymed and metered for remembrance: I was floating in a quarry with my chin on a log when I first discovered that I knew "Provide, Provide" by heart, and there are six or eight more that I know without ever having memorized them.) Here is a poem titled "Atmosphere," and subtitled "Inscription for a Garden Wall":

> Winds blow the open grassy places bleak;
> But where this old wall burns a sunny cheek,
> They eddy over it too toppling weak
> To blow the earth or anything self-clear;
> Moisture and color and odor thicken here,
> The hours of daylight gather atmosphere.

Now this is more than slight, it's nothing; I admit it; yet, admit it, isn't it a nothing that Marvell himself could have been proud of? And after reading it, can you understand how *any* critic could have patronizingly pigeonholed the man who wrote it? Frost writes a poem about a barn that is left over after its farmhouse has burnt down (of the house only the chimney is left, to stand "like a pistil after the petals go"); the poem is called "The Need of Being Versed in Country Things," and it ends:

> The birds that came to it through the air
> At broken windows flew out and in,
> Their murmur more like the sigh we sigh
> From too much dwelling on what has been.
>
> Yet for them the lilac renewed its leaf,
> And the aged elm, though touched with fire;
> And the dry pump flung up an awkward arm;
> And the fence post carried a strand of wire.
>
> For them there was really nothing sad.
> But though they rejoiced in the nest they kept,

> One had to be versed in country things
> Not to believe the phoebes wept.

But here I am not only left helpless to say whether this is slight or not, I don't even want to know: I am too sure of what I have even to want to say what it is, so that I will say if you ask me, as St. Augustine did about Time: "I know if you don't ask me."

I don't want to finish without saying how much *use* Frost's poems are to one, almost in the way that Hardy's are, when one has read them for many years—without saying how little they seem performances, no matter how brilliant or magical, how little things made primarily of words (or of ink and paper, either), and how much things made out of lives and the world that the lives inhabit. For how much this poetry *is* like the world, "the world wherein we find our happiness or not at all," "the world which was ere I was born, the world which lasts when I am dead," the world with its animals and plants and, most of all, its people: people working, thinking about things, falling in love, taking naps; in these poems men are not only the glory and jest and riddle of the world, but also the habit of the world, its strange ordinariness, its ordinary strangeness, and they too trudge down the ruts along which the planets move in their courses. Frost is that rare thing, a complete or representative poet, and not one of the brilliant partial poets who do justice, far more than justice, to a portion of reality, and leave the rest of things forlorn. When you know Frost's poems you know surprisingly well how the world seemed to one man, and what it was to seem that way: the great *Gestalt* that each of us makes from himself and all that isn't himself is very clear, very complicated, very contradictory in the poetry. The grimness and awfulness and untouchable sadness of things, both in the world and in the self, have justice done to them in the poems, but no more justice than is done to the tenderness and love and delight; and everything in between is represented somewhere too, some things willingly and often and other things only as much—in Marianne Moore's delicate phrase—"as one's natural reticence will allow." If some of the poems come out of a cynical common sense that is only wisdom's backward shadow, others come out of wisdom itself—for it is, still, just possible for that most old-fashioned of old-fashioned things, wisdom, to maintain a marginal existence in our world. If we compare this wisdom with, say, that of the last of the Old Ones, Goethe, we are saddened and frightened at how much the poet's scope has narrowed, at how difficult and partial and idiosyncratic the application of his intelligence has become, at what terrible sacrifices he has had to make in order to avoid making others still more terrible. Yet how many poems, how many more lines, are immediately and supplely responsive with the unseparated unspecialized intelligence that is by now almost as natural to man—that being men have so laboriously created—as dreams and hunger and desire. To have the distance from the most awful and most nearly unbearable parts of the poems, to the most tender, subtle, and loving parts, a distance so great; to have this whole range of being treated with so much humor and sadness and composure, with such plain truth; to see that a man can still include, connect, and make humanly understandable or humanly ununderstandable so *much*—this is one of the freshest and oldest of joys, a joy strong enough to make us forget the limitations and excesses and baseness that these days seem unforgettable, a joy strong enough to make us say, with the Greek poet, that many things in this world are wonderful, but of all these the most wonderful is man.

[1952/PA]

Robert Frost's
"Home Burial"

"HOME BURIAL" and "The Witch of Coös" seem to me the best of all Frost's dramatic poems—though "A Servant to Servants" is nearly as good. All three are poems about women in extreme situations: neurotic or (in "A Servant to Servants") psychotic women. The circumstances of the first half of his life made Frost feel for such women a sympathy or empathy that amounted almost to identification. He said that, "creature of literature that I am," he had learned to "make a virtue of my suffering / From nearly everything that goes on round me," and that "Kit Marlowe taught me how to say my prayers: / 'Why, this is Hell, nor am I out of it.' " It is with such women that he says this—this and more than this: the Pauper Witch of Grafton's

> Up where the trees grow short, the mosses tall,
> I made him gather me wet snow berries
> On slippery rocks beside a waterfall.
> I made him do it for me in the dark.
> And he liked everything I made him do . . .

shows us, as few passages can, that for a while the world was heaven too.

"Home Burial" is a fairly long but extraordinarily concentrated poem; after you have known it long enough you feel almost as the Evangelist did, that if all the things that could be said about it were written down, "I suppose that even the world itself could not contain the books that should be written." I have written down a few of these things; but, first of all, here is "Home Burial" itself:

He saw her from the bottom of the stairs
Before she saw him. She was starting down,
Looking back over her shoulder at some fear.
She took a doubtful step and then undid it
To raise herself and look again. He spoke
Advancing toward her: "What is it you see
From up there always—for I want to know."
She turned and sank upon her skirts at that,
And her face changed from terrified to dull.
He said to gain time: "What is it you see,"
Mounting until she cowered under him.
"I will find out now—you must tell me, dear."
She, in her place, refused him any help
With the least stiffening of her neck and silence.
She let him look, sure that he wouldn't see,
Blind creature; and awhile he didn't see.
But at last he murmured, "Oh," and again, "Oh."

"What is it—what?" she said.

                    "Just that I see."

"You don't," she challenged. "Tell me what it is."

"The wonder is I didn't see at once.
I never noticed it from here before.
I must be wonted to it—that's the reason.
The little graveyard where my people are!
So small the window frames the whole of it.
Not so much larger than a bedroom, is it?
There are three stones of slate and one of marble,
Broad-shouldered little slabs there in the sunlight
On the sidehill. We haven't to mind *those*.
But I understand: it is not the stones,
But the child's mound—"

                    "Don't, don't, don't, don't," she cried.

She withdrew shrinking from beneath his arm
That rested on the banister, and slid downstairs;

[*43*]

And turned on him with such a daunting look,
He said twice over before he knew himself:
"Can't a man speak of his own child he's lost?"

"Not you! Oh, where's my hat? Oh, I don't need it!
I must get out of here. I must get air.
I don't know rightly whether any man can."

"Amy! Don't go to someone else this time.
Listen to me. I won't come down the stairs."
He sat and fixed his chin between his fists.
"There's something I should like to ask you, dear."

"You don't know how to ask it."

                              "Help me, then."

Her fingers moved the latch for all reply.

"My words are nearly always an offence.
I don't know how to speak of anything
So as to please you. But I might be taught,
I should suppose. I can't say I see how.
A man must partly give up being a man
With women-folk. We could have some arrangement
By which I'd bind myself to keep hands off
Anything special you're a-mind to name.
Though I don't like such things 'twixt those that love.
Two that don't love can't live together without them.
But two that do can't live together with them."
She moved the latch a little. "Don't—don't go.
Don't carry it to someone else this time.
Tell me about it if it's something human.
Let me into your grief. I'm not so much
Unlike other folks as your standing there
Apart would make me out. Give me my chance.
I do think, though, you overdo it a little.
What was it brought you up to think it the thing
To take your mother-loss of a first child
So inconsolably—in the face of love.
You'd think his memory might be satisfied—"

"There you go sneering now!"

                            "I'm not, I'm not!
You make me angry. I'll come down to you.
God, what a woman! And it's come to this,
A man can't speak of his own child that's dead."

"You can't because you don't know how to speak.
If you had any feelings, you that dug
With your own hand—how could you?—his little grave;
I saw you from that very window there,
Making the gravel leap and leap in air,
Leap up, like that, like that, and land so lightly
And roll back down the mound beside the hole.
I thought, Who is that man? I didn't know you.
And I crept down the stairs and up the stairs
To look again, and still your spade kept lifting.
Then you came in. I heard your rumbling voice
Out in the kitchen, and I don't know why,
But I went near to see with my own eyes.
You could sit there with the stains on your shoes
Of the fresh earth from your own baby's grave
And talk about your everyday concerns.
You had stood the spade up against the wall
Outside there in the entry, for I saw it."

"I shall laugh the worst laugh I ever laughed.
I'm cursed. God, if I don't believe I'm cursed."

"I can repeat the very words you were saying.
'Three foggy mornings and one rainy day
Will rot the best birch fence a man can build.'
Think of it, talk like that at such a time!
What had how long it takes a birch to rot
To do with what was in the darkened parlor.
You *couldn't* care! The nearest friends can go
With anyone to death, comes so far short
They might as well not try to go at all.
No, from the time when one is sick to death,
One is alone, and he dies more alone.
Friends make pretense of following to the grave,

But before one is in it, their minds are turned
And making the best of their way back to life
And living people, and things they understand.
But the world's evil. I won't have grief so
If I can change it. Oh, I won't, I won't!"

"There, you have said it all and you feel better.
You won't go now. You're crying. Close the door.
The heart's gone out of it: why keep it up.
Amy! There's someone coming down the road!"

"*You*—oh, you think the talk is all. I must go—
Somewhere out of this house. How can I make you—"

"If—you—do!" She was opening the door wider.
"Where do you mean to go? First tell me that.
I'll follow and bring you back by force. I *will!*— "

The poem's first sentence, "He saw her from the bottom of the stairs / Before she saw him," implies what the poem very soon states: that, knowing herself seen, she would have acted differently—she has two sorts of behavior, behavior for him to observe and spontaneous immediate behavior. "She was starting down, / Looking back over her shoulder at some fear" says that it is *some fear*, and not a specific feared object, that she is looking back at; and, normally, we do not look back over our shoulder at what we leave, unless we feel for it something more than fear. "She took a doubtful step" emphasizes the queer attraction or fascination that the fear has for her; her departing step is not sure it should depart. "She took a doubtful step and then *undid* it": the surprising use of *undid* gives her withdrawal of the tentative step a surprising reality. The poem goes on: "To raise herself and look again." It is a little vertical ballet of indecision toward and away from a fearful but mesmerically attractive object, something hard to decide to leave and easy to decide to return to. "He spoke / Advancing toward her": having the old line end with "spoke," the new line begin with "advancing," makes the very structure of the lines express the way in which he looms up, gets bigger. (Five lines later Frost repeats the effect even more forcibly with: "He said to gain time: 'What is it you see,' / Mounting until she cowered under him.") Now when the man asks: "What is it you see / From up there always—for I want to know," the word "always" tells us that all this has gone on many times before, and that he has seen it—without speaking of it—a number of times before. The phrase "for I want to know" is a characteristic example of the heavy, willed demands that the man makes, and an even more characteristic example of the tautological, rhetorical announcements of his actions that he so often makes, as if he felt that the announcement somehow justified or excused the action.

The poem goes on: "She turned and sank upon her skirts at that . . ." The stairs permit her to subside into a modest, compact, feminine bundle; there is a kind of smooth deftness about the phrase, as if it were some feminine saying: "When in straits, sink upon your skirts." The next line, "And her face changed from terrified to dull," is an economically elegant way of showing how the terror of surprise (perhaps with another fear underneath it) changes into the dull lack of response that is her regular mask for him. The poem continues: "He said to gain time"—to gain time in which to think of the next thing to say, to gain time in which to get close to her and gain the advantage of his physical nearness, his physical bulk. His next "What is it you see" is the first of his many repetitions; if one knew only this man one would say, "Man is the animal that repeats." In the poem's next phrase, "mounting until she cowered under him," the identity of the vowels in "mounting" and "cowered" physically connects the two, makes his mounting the plain immediate cause of her cowering. "I will find out now" is another of his rhetorical announcements of what he is going to do: "this time you're going to tell me, I'm going to make you." But this heavy-willed compulsion changes into sheer appeal, into reasonable beseeching, in his next phrase: "you must tell me, dear." The "dear" is affectionate intimacy, the "must" is the "must" of rational necessity; yet the underlying form of the sentence is that of compulsion. The poem goes on: "She, in her place, refused him any help . . ." The separated phrase "in her place" describes and embodies, with economical brilliance, both her physical and spiritual lack of outgoingness, forthcomingness; she brims over none of her contours, remains sitting upon her skirts upon her stairstep, in feminine exclusion. "Refused him any help / With the least stiffening of her neck and silence": she doesn't say Yes, doesn't say No, doesn't say; her refusal of any answer is worse than almost any answer. "The least stiffening of her neck," in its concise reserve, its slight precision, is more nearly conclusive than any larger gesture of rejection. He, in extremities, usually repeats some proverbial or rhetorical generalization; at such moments she usually responds either with a particular, specific sentence or else with something more particular than any sentence: with some motion or gesture.

The next line, "She let him look, sure that he wouldn't see," reminds one of some mother bird so certain that her nest is hidden that she doesn't even flutter off, but sits there on it, risking what is no risk, in complacent superiority. "Sure that he wouldn't see, / Blind creature": the last phrase is quoted from her mind, is her contemptuous summing up. "And awhile he didn't see"; but at last when he sees, he doesn't tell her what it is, doesn't silently understand, but with heavy slow comprehension murmurs, "Oh," and then repeats, "Oh." It is another announcement of what he is doing, a kind of dramatic rendition of his understanding. (Sometimes when we are waiting for someone, and have made some sound or motion we are afraid will seem ridiculous to the observer we didn't know was there, we rather ostentatiously look at our watch, move our face and lips into a "What on earth could have happened to make him so late?" as a way of justifying our earlier action. The principle behind our action is the principle behind many of this man's actions.) With the undignified alacrity of someone hurrying to reestablish a superiority that has been questioned, the woman cries out like a child: "What is it—what?" Her sentence is, so to speak, a rhetorical question rather than a real one, since it takes it for granted that a correct answer can't be made. His reply, "Just that I see," shows that his unaccustomed insight has given him an unaccustomed composure; she has had the advantage, for so long, of being the only one who knows, that he for a moment prolongs the advantage of being the only one who knows that he knows. The immediately following " 'You don't,' she challenged. 'Tell me what it is' " is the instant, childishly assertive exclamation of someone whose human position depends entirely upon her knowing what some inferior being can never know; she cannot let another second go by without hearing the incorrect answer that will confirm her in her rightness and superiority.

The man goes on explaining, to himself, and to mankind, and to her too, in slow rumination about it and about it. In his "The wonder is I didn't see at once. / I never noticed it from here before. / I must be wonted to it—that's the reason," one notices how "wonder" and "once" prepare for "wonted," that provincial-, archaic-sounding word that sums up—as "used" never could—his reliance on a habit or accustomedness which at last sees nothing but itself, and hardly sees that; and when it does see something through itself, beyond itself, slowly marvels. In the next line, "The little graveyard where my people are!" we feel not only the triumph of the slow person at last comprehending, but also the tender, easy accustomedness of habit, of long use, of a kind of cozy social continuance—for him the graves are not the healed scars of old agonies, but are something as comfortable and accustomed as the photographs in the family album. "So small the window frames the whole of it," like the later "Broad-shouldered little slabs there in the sunlight / On the sidehill," not only has this easy comfortable acceptance, but also has the regular feel of a certain sort of Frost nature description: this is almost the only place in the poem where for a moment we feel that it is Frost talking first and the man talking second. But the man's "Not so much larger than a bedroom, is it?"—an observation that appeals to her for agreement—carries this comfortable acceptance to a point at which it becomes intolerable: the only link between the bedroom and the graveyard is the child conceived in their bedroom and buried in that graveyard. The sentence comfortably establishes a connection which she cannot bear to admit the existence of—she tries to keep the two things permanently separated in her mind. (What he says amounts to his saying about their bedroom: "Not so much smaller than the graveyard, is it?") "There are three stones of slate and one of marble, / Broad-shouldered little slabs there in the sunlight / On the sidehill" has a heavy tenderness and accustomedness about it, almost as if he were running his hand over the grain of the stone. The "little" graveyard and "little" slabs are examples of our regular way of making something acceptable or dear by means of a diminutive.

Next, to show her how well he understands, the man shows her how ill he understands. He says about his family's graves: "We haven't to mind *those*"; that is, we don't have to worry about, grieve over, my people: it is not your obligation to grieve for them at all, nor mine to give them more than their proper share of grief, the amount I long ago measured out and used up. But with the feeling, akin to a sad, modest, relieved, surprised pride, with which he regularly responds to his own understanding, he tells her that he does understand: what matters is not the old stones but the new mound, the displaced earth piled up above the grave which he had dug and in which their child is buried.

When he says this, it is as if he had touched, with a crude desecrating hand, the sacred, forbidden secret upon which her existence depends. With shuddering hysterical revulsion she cries: "Don't, don't, don't, don't." (If the reader will compare the effect of Frost's four *don't*'s with the effect of three or five, he will see once more how exactly accurate, perfectly effective, almost everything in the poem is.) The poem continues: "She withdrew shrinking from beneath his arm / That rested on the banister, and slid downstairs"; the word "slid" says, with vivid indecorousness, that anything goes in extremities, that you can't be bothered, then, by mere appearance or propriety; "slid" has the ludicrous force of actual fact, is the way things are instead of the way we agree they are. In the line "And turned on him with such a daunting look," the phrase "turned on him" makes her resemble a cornered animal turning on its pursuer; and "with such a daunting look" is the way he phrases it to himself, is quoted from his mind as "blind creature" was quoted from hers. The beautifully provincial, old-fashioned, folk-sounding "daunting" reminds one of the similar, slightly earlier "wonted," and seems to make immediate, as no other word could, the look that cows him. The next line, "He said twice over before he knew himself," tells us that repetition, saying something twice over, is something he regresses to under stress; unless he can consciously prevent himself from repeating, he repeats. What he says twice over (this is the third time already that he has repeated something) is a rhetorical question, a querulous, plaintive appeal to public opinion: "Can't a man speak of his own child he's lost?" He does not say specifically, particularly, with confidence in himself: "I've the right to speak of our dead child"; instead he cites the acknowledged fact that any member of the class *man* has the acknowledged right to mention, just to mention, that member of the class of his belongings, *his own child*—and he has been unjustly deprived of this right. "His own child he's lost" is a way of saying: "You act as if he were just yours, but he's just as much just mine; that's an established fact." "Can't a man speak of his own child he's lost" has a magnificently dissonant, abject, aggrieved querulousness about it, in all its sounds and all its rhythms; "Can't a man" prepares us for the even more triumphantly ugly dissonance (or should I say consonance?) of the last two words in her "I don't know rightly whether any man can."

Any rhetorical question demands, expects, the hearer's automatic agreement; there is nothing it expects less than a particular, specific denial. The man's "Can't a man speak . . ." means "Isn't any man allowed to speak . . . ," but her fatally specific answer, "Not you!" makes it mean, "A man cannot—is not able to—speak, if the man is you." Her "Oh, where's my hat?" is a speech accompanied by action, means: "I'm leaving. Where's the hat which social convention demands that a respectable woman put on, to go out into the world?" The immediately following "Oh, I don't need it!" means: in extremities, in cases when we come down to what really matters, what does social convention or respectability really matter? Her "I must get out of here. I must get air" says that you breathe understanding and suffocate without it, and that in this house, for her, there is none. Then, most extraordinarily, she gives a second specific answer to his rhetorical question, that had expected none: "I don't know rightly whether any man can." The line says: "Perhaps it is not the individual *you* that's to blame, but man in general; perhaps a woman is wrong to expect that any man can speak—really *speak*—of his dead child."

His "Amy! Don't go to someone else this time" of course tells us that another time she *has* gone to someone else; and it tells us the particular name of this most particular woman, something that she and the poem never tell us about the man. The man's "Listen to me. I won't come down the stairs" tells us that earlier he *has* come down the stairs, hasn't kept his distance. It (along with "shrinking," "cowered," and many later things in the poem) tells us that he has given her reason to be physically afraid of him; his "I won't come down the stairs" is a kind of euphemism for "I won't hurt you, won't even get near you."

The poem's next sentence, "He sat and fixed his chin between his fists"—period, end of line—with its four short *i*'s, its "fixed" and "fists," fixes him in baffled separateness; the sentence fits into the line as he fits into the isolated perplexity of his existence. Once more he makes a rhetorical announcement of what he is about to do, before he does it: "There's something I should like to ask you, dear." The sentence tiptoes in, gentle, almost abjectly mollifying, and ends with a reminding "dear"; it is an indirect rhetorical appeal that expects for an answer at least a grudging: "Well, go ahead and ask it, then." His sentence presupposes the hearer's agreement with what it implies: "Anyone is at least allowed to *ask*, even if afterwards you refuse him what he asks." The woman once more gives a direct, crushing, *particular* answer: "You don't know how to ask it." "Anyone may be allowed to ask, but *you* are not because you are not able to ask"; we don't even need to refuse an animal the right to ask and be refused, since if we gave him the right he couldn't exercise it. The man's "Help me, then," has an absolute, almost abject helplessness, a controlled childlike simplicity, that we pity and sympathize with; yet we can't help remembering the other side of the coin, the heavy, brutal, equally simple and helpless anger of his later *I'll come down to you.*

The next line, "Her fingers moved the latch for all reply" (like the earlier "She . . . refused him any help / With the least stiffening of her neck and silence"; like "And turned on him with such a daunting look"; like the later "She moved the latch a little"; like the last

"She was opening the door wider"), reminds us that the woman has a motion language more immediate, direct, and particular than words—a language she resorts to in extremities, just as he, in extremities, resorts to a language of repeated proverbial generalizations. "Home Burial" starts on the stairs but continues in the doorway, on the threshold between the old life inside and the new life outside.

The man now begins his long appeal with the slow, heavy, hopeless admission that "My words are nearly always an offence." This can mean, "Something is nearly always wrong with me and my words," but it also can mean—does mean, underneath—that she is to be blamed for nearly always finding offensive things that certainly are not meant to offend. "I don't know how to speak of anything / So as to please you" admits, sadly blames himself for, his baffled ignorance, but it also suggests that she is unreasonably, fantastically hard to please—if the phrase came a little later in his long speech he might pronounce it "so as to please *you*." (Whatever the speaker intends, there are no long peacemaking speeches in a quarrel; after a few sentences the speaker always has begun to blame the other again.) The man's aggrieved, blaming "But I might be taught, / I should suppose" is followed by the helpless, very endearing admission: "I can't say I see how"; for the moment this removes the blame from her, and his honesty of concession makes us unwilling to blame him. He tries to summarize his dearly bought understanding in a generalization, almost a proverb: "A man must partly give up being a man / With women-folk." The sentence begins in the dignified regretful sunlight of the main floor, in "A man must partly give up being a man," and ends huddled in the basement below, in "With women-folk." He doesn't use the parallel, coordinate "with a woman," but the entirely different "with women-folk"; the sentence tries to be fair and objective, but it is as completely weighted a sentence as "A man must partly give up being a man with the kiddies," or "A man must partly give up being a man with Bandar-log." The sentence presupposes that the real right norm is a man being a man with men, and that some of this rightness and normality always must be sacrificed with that special case, that inferior anomalous category, "women-folk."

He goes on: "We could have some arrangement [it has a hopeful, indefinite, slightly helter-skelter sound] / By which I'd bind myself to keep hands off"—the phrases "bind myself" and "keep hands off" have the primitive, awkward materiality of someone taking an oath in a bad saga; we expect the sentence to end in some awkwardly impressive climax, but get the almost ludicrous anticlimax of

"Anything special you're a-mind to name." And, too, the phrase makes whatever she names quite willful on her part, quite unpredictable by reasonable man. His sensitivity usually shows itself to be a willing, hopeful form of insensitivity, and he himself realizes this here, saying, "Though I don't like such things 'twixt those that love." Frost then makes him express his own feeling in a partially truthful but elephantine aphorism that lumbers through a queerly stressed line a foot too long ("Two that don't love can't live together without them") into a conclusion ("But two that do can't live together with them") that has some of the slow, heavy relish just in being proverbial that the man so often shows. (How hard it is to get through the monosyllables of the two lines!) His words don't convince her, and she replies to them without words: "She moved the latch a little." He repeats in grieved appeal: "Don't—don't go. / Don't carry it to someone else this time." (He is repeating an earlier sentence, with "Don't go" changed to "Don't carry it.") The next line, "Tell me about it if it's something human," is particularly interesting when it comes from him. When is something inside a human being not human, so that it can't be told? Isn't it when it is outside man's understanding, outside all man's categories and pigeonholes—when there is no proverb to say for it? It is, then, a waste or abyss impossible to understand or manage or share with another. His next appeal to her, "Let me into your grief," combines an underlying sexual metaphor with a child's "Let me in! let me in!" This man who is so much a member of the human community feels a helpless bewilderment at being shut out of the little group of two of which he was once an anomalous half; the woman has put in the place of this group a group of herself-and-the-dead-child, and he begs or threatens—reasons with her as best he can—in his attempt to get her to restore the first group, so that there will be a man-and-wife grieving over their dead child.

He goes on: "I'm not so much / Unlike other folks as your standing there / Apart would make me out." The "standing there / Apart" is an imitative, expressive form that makes her apart, shows her apart. Really her apartness makes him out *like* other folks, all those others who make pretense of following to the grave, but who before one's back is turned have made their way back to life; but he necessarily misunderstands her, since for him being like others is necessarily good, being unlike them necessarily bad. His "Give me my chance"— he doesn't say *a* chance—reminds one of those masculine things fairness and sportsmanship, and makes one think of the child's demand for justice, equal shares, which follows his original demand for exclusive possession, the lion's share. "Give me my chance" means: "You, like everybody else, must admit that anybody deserves a chance—so give me mine"; he deserves his chance not by any particular qualities, personal merit, but just by virtue of being a human being. His "I do think, though, you overdo it a little" says that he is forced against his will to criticize her for so much exceeding (the phrase "a little" is understatement, politeness, and caution) the norm of grief, for mourning more than is usual or reasonable; the phrase "overdo it a little" manages to reduce her grief to the level of a petty social blunder. His next words, "What was it brought you up to think it the thing / To take your mother-loss of a first child / So inconsolably—in the face of love," manage to crowd four or five kinds of condemnation into a single sentence. "What was it brought you up" says that it is not your essential being but your accidental upbringing that has made you do this—it reduces the woman to a helpless social effect. "To think it the thing" is particularly insulting because it makes her grief a mere matter of fashion; it is as though he were saying, "What was it brought you up to think it the thing to wear your skirt that far above your knees?" The phrase "To take your mother-loss of a first child" pigeonholes her loss, makes it a regular, predictable category that demands a regular, predictable amount of grief, and no more. The phrase "So inconsolably—in the face of love" condemns her for being so unreasonable as not to be consoled by, for paying no attention to, that unarguably good, absolutely general thing, love; the generalized *love* makes demands upon her that are inescapable, compared to those which would be made by a more specific phrase like "in the face of my love for you." The man's "You'd think his memory might be satisfied" again condemns her for exceeding the reasonable social norm of grief; condemns her, jealously, for mourning as if the dead child's demands for grief were insatiable.

Her interruption, "There you go sneering now!" implies that he has often before done what she calls "sneering" at her and her excessive sensitivity; and, conscious of how hard he has been trying to make peace, and unconscious of how much his words have gone over into attack, he contradicts her like a child, in righteous anger: "I'm not, I'm not!" His "You make me angry" is another of his rhetorical, tautological announcements about himself, one that is intended somehow to justify the breaking of his promise not to come down to her; he immediately makes the simple childish threat, "I'll come down to you"—he is repeating his promise, "I won't come down to you," with the "not" removed. "God, what a woman!" righteously and despairingly calls on God and public opinion (that voice of the people which is the voice of God) to witness and marvel at what he is being forced to put up with: the fantastic, the almost unbelievable wrongness and unreasonableness of this woman. "And it's come to this," that regular piece of rhetorical recrimination in quarrels, introduces his *third* use of the sentence "Can't a man speak of his own child he's lost"; but this time the rhetorical question is changed into the factual condemnation of "A man can't speak of his own child that's dead." This time he doesn't end the sentence with the more sentimental, decorous, sympathy-demanding "that's lost," but ends with the categorical "that's dead."

Earlier the woman has given two entirely different, entirely specific and unexpected answers to this rhetorical question of his; this time she has a third specific answer, which she makes with monosyllabic precision and finality: "You can't because you don't know how to speak." He has said that it is an awful thing not to be permitted to speak of his own dead child; she replies that it is not a question of permission but of ability, that he is too ignorant and insensitive to be *able* to speak of his child. Her sentence is one line long, and it is only the second sentence of hers that has been that long. He has talked at length during the first two-thirds of the poem, she in three- or four-word phrases or in motions without words; for the rest of the poem she talks at length, as everything that has been shut up inside her begins to pour out. She opens herself up, now—is far closer to him, striking at him with her words, than she has been sitting apart, in her place. His open attack has finally elicited from her, by contagion, her open anger, so that now he is something real and unbearable to attack, instead of being something less than human to be disregarded.

This first sentence has indicted him; now she brings in the specific evidence for the indictment. She says: "If you had any feelings, you that dug / With your own hand"—but after the three stabbing, indicting stresses of

<pre>
      /   /   /
    your own hand
</pre>

she breaks off the sentence, as if she found the end unbearable to go on to; interjects, her throat tightening, the incredulous rhetorical question, "how could you?"—and finishes with the fact that she tries to make more nearly endurable, more euphemistic, with the tender word "little": "his little grave." The syntax of the sentence doesn't continue, but the fact of things continues; she says, "I saw you from that very window there."

<pre>
    /   /   /   /
  That very window there
</pre>

has the same stabbing stresses, the same emphasis on a specific, damning actuality, that

> / / /
> your own hand

had—and that, soon,

> / / /
> my own eyes

and

> / / / /
> your own baby's grave

and other such phrases will have. She goes on: "Making the gravel leap and leap in air, / Leap up, like that, like that, and land so lightly / And roll back down the mound beside the hole." As the sentence imitates with such terrible life and accuracy the motion of the gravel, her throat tightens and aches in her hysterical repetition of "like that, like that": the sounds of "leap and leap in air, / Leap up, like that, like that, and land so lightly" are "le! le! le! li! li! la! li!" and re-create the sustained hysteria she felt as she first watched; inanimate things, the very stones, leap and leap in air, or when their motion subsides land "so lightly," while the animate being, her dead child, does not move, will never move. (The foxes have holes, and the birds of the air have nests; but the Son of man hath not where to lay his head.) Her words "leap and leap in air, / Leap up, like that, like that" keep the stones alive! alive! alive!—in the words "and land" they start to die away, but the following words "so lightly" make them alive again, for a last moment of unbearable contradiction, before they "*roll* back *down* the *mound* beside the *hole.*" The repeated *o*'s (the line says "oh! ow! ow! oh!") make almost crudely actual the abyss of death into which the pieces of gravel and her child fall, not to rise again. The word "hole" (insisted on even more by the rhyme with "roll") gives to the grave the obscene actuality that watching the digging forced it to have for her.

She says: "I thought, Who is that man? I didn't know you." She sees the strange new meaning in his face (what, underneath, the face has meant all along) so powerfully that the face itself seems a stranger's. If her own husband can do something so impossibly alien to all her expectations, he has never really been anything but alien; all her repressed antagonistic knowledge about his insensitivity comes to the surface and masks what before had masked it. In the next sentence, "And I crept down the stairs and up the stairs / To look again," the word "crept" makes her a little mouselike thing crushed under the weight of her new knowledge. But the truly extraordinary word is the "and" that joins "down the stairs" to "up the stairs." What is so extraordinary is that she sees nothing extraordinary about it: the "and" joining the two coordinates hides from her, shows that she has repressed, the thoroughly illogical, contradictory nature of her action; it is like saying: "And I ran out of the fire and back into the fire," and seeing nothing strange about the sentence.

Her next words, "and still your spade kept lifting," give the man's tool a dead, mechanical life of its own; it keeps on and on, crudely, remorselessly, neither guided nor halted by spirit. She continues: "Then you came in. I heard your rumbling voice / Out in the kitchen"; the word "rumbling" gives this great blind creature an insensate weight and strength that are, somehow, hollow. Then she says that she did something as extraordinary as going back up the stairs, but she masks it, this time, with the phrase "and I don't know why." She doesn't know why, it's unaccountable, "But I went near to see with my own eyes." Her "I don't know why" shows her regular refusal to admit things like these; she manages by a confession of ignorance not to have to make the connections, consciously, that she has already made unconsciously.

She now says a sentence that is an extraordinarily conclusive condemnation of him: "You could sit there with the stains on your shoes / Of the fresh earth from your own baby's grave / And talk about your everyday concerns." The five hissing or spitting s's in the strongly accented "sit," "stains," "shoes"; the whole turning upside down of the first line, with four trochaic feet followed by one poor iamb; the concentration of intense, damning stresses in

fresh earth from your own baby's grave

—all these things give an awful finality to the judge's summing up, so that in the last line, "And talk about your everyday concerns," the criminal's matter-of-fact obliviousness has the perversity of absolute insensitivity: Judas sits under the cross matching pennies with the soldiers. The poem has brought to life an unthought-of literal meaning of its title: this is home burial with a vengeance, burial *in* the home; the fresh dirt of the grave stains her husband's shoes and her kitchen floor, and the dirty spade with which he dug the grave stands there in the entry. As a final unnecessary piece of evidence, a last straw that comes long after the camel's back is broken, she states:

"You had stood the spade up against the wall / Outside there in the entry, for I saw it." All her pieces of evidence have written underneath them, like Goya's drawing, that triumphant, traumatic, unarguable I SAW IT.

The man's next sentence is a kind of summing-up-in-little of his regular behavior, the ways in which (we have come to see) he *has* to respond. He has begged her to let him into her grief, to tell him about it if it's something human; now she lets him into not her grief but her revolted, hating condemnation of him; she does tell him about it and it isn't human, but a nightmare into which he is about to fall. He says: "I shall laugh the worst laugh I ever laughed. / I'm cursed. God, if I don't believe I'm cursed." The sounds have the gasping hollowness of somebody hit in the stomach and trying over and over to get his breath—of someone nauseated and beginning to vomit: the first stressed vowel sounds are "agh! uh! agh! uh! agh! uh!" He doesn't reply to her, argue with her, address her at all, but makes a kind of dramatic speech that will exhibit him in a role public opinion will surely sympathize with, just as he sympathizes with himself. As always, he repeats: "laugh," "laugh," and "laughed," "I'm cursed" and "I'm cursed" (the rhyme with "worst" gives almost the effect of another repetition): as always, he announces beforehand what he is going to do, rhetorically appealing to mankind for justification and sympathy. His "I shall laugh the worst laugh I ever laughed" has the queer effect of seeming almost to be quoting some folk proverb. His "I'm cursed" manages to find a category of understanding in which to pigeonhole this nightmare, makes him a reasonable human being helpless against the inhuman powers of evil—the cursed one is not to blame. His "God, if I don't believe I'm cursed" is akin to his earlier "God, what a woman!"—both have something of the male's outraged, incredulous, despairing response to the unreasonableness and immorality of the female. He responds hardly at all to the exact situation; instead he demands sympathy for, sympathizes with himself for, the impossibly unlucky pigeonhole into which Fate has dropped him.

His wife then repeats the sentence that, for her, sums up everything: "I can repeat the very words you were saying. / 'Three foggy mornings and one rainy day / Will rot the best birch fence a man can build.' " We feel with a rueful smile that he has lived by proverbs and—now, for her—dies by them. He has handled his fresh grief by making it a part of man's regular routine, man's regular work; and by quoting man's regular wisdom, that explains, explains away, pigeonholes, anything. Nature tramples down man's work, the new fence rots, but man still is victorious, in the secure summing up of the proverb.

  The best birch fence

is, so far as its stresses are concerned, a firm, comfortable parody of all those stabbing stress systems of hers. In his statement, as usual, it is not *I* but *a man*. There is a resigned but complacent, almost relishing wit about this summing up of the transitoriness of human effort: to understand your defeat so firmly, so proverbially, is in a sense to triumph. He has seen his ordinary human ambition about that ordinary human thing, a child, frustrated by death; so there is a certain resignation and pathos about his saying what he says. The word "rot" makes the connection between the fence and the child, and it is the word "rot" that is unendurable to the woman, since it implies with obscene directness: how many foggy mornings and rainy days will it take to rot the best flesh-and-blood child a man can have? Just as, long ago at the beginning of the poem, the man brought the bedroom and the grave together, he brings the rotting child and the rotting fence together now. She says in incredulous, breathless outrage: "Think of it, talk like that at such a time!" (The repeated sounds, *th, t, t, th, t, t*, are thoroughly expressive.) But once more she has repressed the connection between the two things: she objects to the sentence not as what she knows it is, as rawly and tactlessly relevant, but as something absolutely irrelevant, saying: "What had how long it takes a birch to rot / To do with"—and then she puts in a euphemistic circumlocution, lowers her eyes and lowers the shades so as not to see—"what was in the darkened parlor."

But it is time to go back and think of just what it was the woman saw, just how she saw it, to make her keep on repeating that first occasion of its sight. She saw it on a holy and awful day. The child's death and burial were a great and almost unendurable occasion, something that needed to be accompanied with prayer and abstention, with real grief and the ritual expression of grief. It was a holy or holi-day that could only be desecrated by "everyday concerns"; the husband's digging seemed to the wife a kind of brutally unfeeling, secular profanation of that holy day, her holy grief. Her description makes it plain that her husband dug strongly and well. And why should he not do so? Grief and grave digging, for him, are in separate compartments; the right amount of grief will never flow over into the next compartment. To him it is the workaday, matter-of-fact thing that necessarily comes first; grieving for the corpse is no excuse for not having plenty of food at the wake. If someone had said to him: "You dig mighty well for a man that's just lost his child," wouldn't he have replied: "Grief's no reason for doing a bad job"? (And yet, the muscles tell the truth; a sad enough man shovels badly.) When, the grave dug and the spade stood up in the entry, he went into the kitchen, he may very well have felt: "A good job," just as Yakov, in *Rothschild's Fiddle,* taps the coffin he has made for his wife and thinks: "A good job."

But unconsciously, his wife has far more compelling reasons to be appalled at this job her husband is doing. Let me make this plain. If we are told how a woman dreams of climbing the stairs, and of looking out through a window at a man digging a hole with a spade— digging powerfully, so that the gravel leaps and leaps into the air, only to roll back down into the hole; and still the man's spade keeps lifting and plunging down, lifting and plunging down, as she watches in fascinated horror, creeps down the stairs, creeps back up against her will, to keep on watching; and then, she doesn't know why, she has to go to see with her own eyes the fresh earth staining the man's shoes, has to see with her own eyes the man's tool stood up against the wall, in the entrance to the house—if we are told such a dream, is there any doubt what *sort* of dream it will seem to us? Such things have a sexual force, a sexual meaning, as much in our waking hours as in our dreams—as we know from how many turns of speech, religious rites, myths, tales, works of art. When the plowman digs his plow into the earth, Mother Earth, to make her bear, this does not have a sexual appropriateness only in the dreams of neurotic patients—it is something that we all understand, whether or not we admit that we understand. So the woman understood her husband's digging. If the spade, the tool that he stands up in the entry, stands for man's workaday world, his matter-of-fact objectivity and disregard of emotion, it also stands for his masculinity, his sexual power; on this holy day he brings back into the house of grief the soiling stains of fresh earth, of this digging that, to her, is more than digging.

That day of the funeral the grieving woman felt only misery and anguish, passive suffering; there was nobody to blame for it all except herself. And how often women do blame themselves for the abnormality or death of a baby! An old doctor says they keep blaming themselves; they should have done this, that, something; they forget all about their husbands; often they blame some doctor who, by not coming immediately, by doing or not doing something, was responsible for it all: the woman's feeling of guilt about other things is displaced

onto the child's death. Now when this woman sees her husband dig-
ging the grave (doing what seems to her, consciously, an intolerably in-
sensitive thing; unconsciously, an indecent thing) she *does* have some-
one to blame, someone upon whom to shift her own guilt: she is able
to substitute for passive suffering and guilt an active loathing and
condemnation—as she blames the man's greater guilt and wrongness
her own lesser guilt can seem in comparison innocence and rightness.
(The whole matrix of attitudes available to her, about woman as
Madonna-and-child and man as brute beast, about sexuality as a de-
filing thing forced upon woman, helps her to make this shift.) The
poem has made it easy for us to suspect a partial antagonism or un-
congeniality, sexually, between the weak oversensitive woman and
the strong insensitive man, with his sexual force so easily transformed
into menace. (The poem always treats it in that form.) The woman's
negative attitudes have been overwhelmingly strengthened, now; it is
plain that since the child's death there has been no sort of sexual or
emotional union between them.

To her, underneath, the child's death must have seemed a pun-
ishment. Of whom for what? Of them for what they have done—sex-
ual things are always tinged with guilt; but now her complete grief,
her separateness and sexual and emotional abstention, help to cancel
out her own guilt—the man's matter-of-fact physical obliviousness,
his desire to have everything what it was before, reinforce his own
guilt and help to make it seem absolute. Yet, underneath, the woman's
emotional and physiological needs remain unchanged, and are satis-
fied by this compulsory symptomatic action of hers—this creeping up
the stairs, looking, looking, creeping down and then back up again,
looking, looking; she stares with repudiating horror, with accepting
fascination, at this obscenely symbolic sight. It is not the child's
mound she stares at, but the scene of the crime, the site of this terri-
ble symbolic act that links sexuality and death, the marriage bed and
the grave. (Afterwards she had gone down into the kitchen to see the
man flushed and healthy, breathing a little harder after physical ex-
ertion; her words "I heard your *rumbling* voice / Out in the kitchen"
remind us of that first telling description of him on the stairs,
"*Mounting* until she *cowered* under him." Her first response to the
sight, "I thought: Who *is* that man? I didn't know you," makes him
not her husband but a stranger, a guilty one, whom she is right to re-
main estranged from, must remain estranged from.) Her repeated
symptomatic act has the consciousness of obsessional-compulsive
symptoms, not the unconsciousness of hysterical blindness or paraly-

sis: she is conscious of what she is doing, knows how it all began; and yet she cannot keep from doing it, does not really know why she does it, and is conscious only of a part of the meaning it has for her. She has isolated it, and refuses to see its connections, consciously, because the connections are so powerful unconsciously: so that she says, "And I crept down the stairs *and* up the stairs"; says, *"And I don't know why,* / But I went near to see with my own eyes"; says, "What had how long it takes a birch to rot / To do with what was in the darkened parlor."

This repeated symptomatic action of hers satisfies several needs. It keeps reassuring her that she is right to keep herself fixed in separation and rejection. By continually revisiting this scene, by looking again and again at—so to speak—this indecent photograph of her husband's crime, she is making certain that she will never come to terms with the criminal who, in the photograph, is committing the crime. Yet, underneath, there is a part of her that takes guilty pleasure in the crime, that is in identifying complicity with the criminal. A symptom or symptomatic action is an expression not only of the defense against the forbidden wish, but also of the forbidden wish.

If the reader doubts that this symptomatic action of hers has a sexual root, he can demonstrate it to himself by imagining the situation different in one way. Suppose the wife had looked out of the window and seen her husband animatedly and matter-of-factly bargaining to buy a cemetery lot from one of the next day's funeral guests. She would have been angered and revolted. But would she have crept back to look again? have gone into the kitchen so as to see the bargainer with her own eyes? have stared in fascination at the wallet from which he had taken the money? Could she as easily have made a symptom of it?

After she has finished telling the story of what she had seen, of what he had done, she cries: "You *couldn't* care!" The words say: "If you could behave as you behaved, it proves that you didn't care and, therefore, that you couldn't care; if you, my own husband, the child's own father, were unable to care, it proves that it must be impossible for anyone to care." So she goes on, not about him but about everyone: "The nearest friends can go / With anyone to death, comes so far short / They might as well not try to go at all." The sentence has some of the rueful, excessive wit of Luther's "In every good act the just man sins"; man can do so little he might as well do nothing. Her next sentence, "No, from the time when one is sick to death, / One is alone, and he dies more alone," tolls like a lonely bell for the human being who grieves for death and, infected by what she grieves for, dies alone in the pesthouse, deserted by the humanity that takes good care not to be infected. When you truly feel what death is, you must die: all her phrases about the child's death and burial make them her own death and burial.

She goes on: "Friends make pretense of following to the grave, / But before one is in it, their minds are turned"—her "make pretense" blames their, his, well-meant hypocrisy; her "before one is in it" speaks of the indecent haste with which he hurried to dig the grave into which the baby was put, depriving her of it—of the indecent haste with which he forgot death and wanted to resume life. The phrases "their minds are turned" and "making the best of their way back" are (as so often with Frost) queerly effective adaptations of ordinary idioms, of "their backs are turned" and "making the best of things"; these are the plain roots, in the woman's mind, of her less direct and more elaborate phrases. But when we have heard her whole sentence: "Friends make pretense of following to the grave, / But before one is in it, their minds are turned / And making the best of their way back to life / And living people, and things they understand," we reply: "As they must." She states as an evil what we think at worst a necessary evil; she is condemning people for not committing suicide, for not going down into the grave with the corpse and dying there. She condemns the way of the world, but it is the way of any world that continues to be a world: the world that does otherwise perishes. Her "But the world's evil. I won't have grief so / If I can change it. Oh, I won't, I won't!" admits what grief is to everybody else; is generally; and says that she will change the universal into her own contradictory particular if she can: the sentence has its own defeat inside it. What this grieving woman says about grief is analogous to a dying woman's saying about death: "I won't have death so if I can change it. Oh, I won't, I won't!" Even the man responds to the despairing helplessness in her "Oh, I won't, I won't!" She is still trying to be faithful and unchanging in her grief, but already she has begun to be faithless, has begun to change. Saying "I never have colds any more," an hour or two before one has a cold, is one's first unconscious recognition that one has caught cold; similarly, she says that other people forget and change but that she never will, just when she has begun to change—just when, by telling her husband the cause of her complete separation, she has begun to destroy the completeness of the separation. Her "Oh, I won't, I won't!" sounds helplessly dissolving, running down; already contains within it the admission of what it denies. Her "I won't have grief so" reminds us that grief *is* so, is by its very nature a transition to something that isn't grief. She knows it too, so that she says that everybody else is that way, the world is that way, but they're wrong, they're evil; *someone* must be different; *someone* honorably and quixotically, at no matter what cost, must contradict the nature of grief, the nature of the world.

All this is inconceivable to the man: if everybody is that way, it must be right to be that way; it would be insanity to think of any other possibility. She has put grief, the dead child, apart on an altar, to be kept separate and essential as long as possible—forever, if possible. He has immediately filed away the child, grief, in the pigeonhole of man's wont, man's proverbial understanding: the weight is off his own separate shoulders, and the shoulders of all mankind bear the burden. In this disaster of her child's death, her husband's crime, her one consolation is that she is inconsolable, has (good sensitive woman) grieved for months as her husband (bad insensitive man) was not able to grieve even for hours. Ceasing to grieve would destroy this consolation, would destroy the only way of life she has managed to find.

And yet she has begun to destroy them. When she says at the end of the poem: "How can I make you—" understand, see, she shows in her baffled, longing despair that she *has* tried to make him understand; has tried to help him as he asked her to help him. Her "You *couldn't* care," all her lines about what friends and the world necessarily are, excuse him in a way, by making him a necessarily insensitive part of a necessarily insensitive world that she alone is sensitive in: she is the one person desperately and forlornly trying to be different from everyone else, as she tries to keep death and grief alive in the middle of a world intent on its own forgetful life. At these last moments she does not, as he thinks, "set him apart" as "so much / Unlike other folks"; if he could hear and respond to what she actually has said, there would be some hope for them. But he doesn't; instead of understanding her special situation, he dumps her into the pigeonhole of the crying woman—any crying woman—and then tries to *manage* her as one manages a child. She does try to let him into her grief, but he won't go; instead he tells her that now she's had her cry, that now he feels better, that the heart's gone out of it, that there's really no grief left for him to be let into.

The helpless tears into which her hard self-righteous separateness has dissolved show, underneath, a willingness to accept understanding; she has denounced him, made a clean breast of things, and now is accessible to the understanding or empathy that he is unable to give her. Women are oversensitive, exaggerate everything, tell all, weep, and then are all right: this is the pigeonhole into which he drops her. So rapid an understanding can almost be called a form of stupidity, of not even trying really to understand. The bewitched, uncanny, almost nauseated helplessness of what he has said a few lines before: "I shall laugh the worst laugh I ever laughed. / I'm cursed. God, if I don't believe I'm cursed," has already changed into a feeling of mastery, of the strong man understanding and managing the weak hysterical woman. He is the powerful one now. His "There, you have said it all and you feel better. / You won't go now" has all the grown-up's condescension toward the child, the grown-up's ability to make the child do something simply by stating that the child is about to do it. The man's "You're crying. Close the door. / The heart's gone out of it: why keep it up" shows this quite as strikingly; he feels that he can manipulate her back into the house and into his life, back out of the grief that—he thinks or hopes—no longer has any heart in it, so that she must pettily and exhaustingly "keep it up."

But at this moment when the depths have been opened for him; at this moment when the proper management might get her back into the house, the proper understanding get her back into his life; at this moment that it is fair to call the most important moment of his life, someone happens to come down the road. Someone who will see her crying and hatless in the doorway; someone who will go back to the village and tell everything; someone who will shame them in the eyes of the world. Public opinion, what people will say, is more important to him than anything she will do; he forgets everything else, and expostulates: "Amy! There's someone coming down the road!" His exclamation is full of the tense, hurried fear of social impropriety, of public disgrace; nothing could show more forcibly what he *is* able to understand, what he *does* think of primary importance. Her earlier "Oh, where's my hat? Oh, I don't need it!" prepares for, is the exact opposite of, his "Amy! There's someone coming down the road!"

She says with incredulous, absolute intensity and particularity, *"You—"*

That italicized *you* is the worst, the most nearly final thing that she can say about him, since it merely points to what he is. She doesn't go on; goes back and replies to his earlier sentences: "oh, you think the talk is all." Her words have a despairing limpness and sadness: there is no possibility of his being made to think anything different, to see the truth under the talk. She says: "I must go—" and her words merely recognize a reality— "Somewhere out of this house." Her final words are full of a longing, despairing, regretful realization of a kind of final impossibility: "How can I make you—" The word that isn't said, that she stops short of saying, is as much there as anything in the poem. All her insistent anxious pride in her own separateness and sensitiveness and superiority is gone; she knows, now, that she is separate from him no matter what she wants. Her "How can I make you—" amounts almost to "If only I could make you—if only there were some way to make you—but there is no way."

He responds not to what she says but to what she does, to "She was opening the door wider." He threatens, as a child would threaten: "If—you—do!" He sounds like a giant child, or a child being a giant or an ogre. The "If—you—do!" uses as its principle of being the exaggerated slowness and heaviness, the *willedness* of his nature. (Much about him reminds me of Yeats's famous definition: "Rhetoric is the will trying to do the work of the imagination"; "Home Burial" might be called the story of a marriage between the will and the imagination.) The dashes Frost inserts between the words slow down the words to the point where the slowedness or heaviness itself, as pure force and menace, is what is communicated. Then the man says, trying desperately—feebly—to keep her within reach of that force or menace: "Where do you mean to go? First tell me that. / I'll follow and bring you back by force. I *will!*—" The last sentences of each of her previous speeches (her despairing emotional "Oh, I won't, I won't!" and her despairing spiritual "How can I make you—") are almost the exact opposite of the "I *will!*" with which he ends the poem. It is appropriate that "force," "I," and *"will"* are his last three words: his proverbial, town-meeting understanding has failed, just as his blankly imploring humility has failed; so that he has to resort to the only thing he has left, the will or force that seems almost like the mass or inertia of a physical body. We say that someone "throws his weight around," and in the end there is nothing left for him to do but throw his weight around. Appropriately, his last line is one more rhetorical announcement of what he is going to do: he will follow and bring her back by force; and, appropriately, he ends the poem with one more repetition—he repeats: "I *will!*"

[1962/TBC]

Paterson

by William Carlos Williams

PATERSON (BOOK I) seems to me the best thing William Carlos Williams has ever written; I read it seven or eight times, and ended lost in delight. It is a shame to write a little review of it, instead of going over it page by page, explaining and admiring. And one hates to quote much, since the beauty, delicacy, and intelligence of the best parts depend so much upon their organization in the whole; quoting from it is like humming a theme and expecting a hearer to guess from that its effect upon its third repetition in a movement. I have used this simile deliberately, because—over and above the organization of argument or exposition—the organization of *Paterson* is musical to an almost unprecedented degree: Dr. Williams introduces a theme that stands for an idea, repeats it over and over in varied forms, develops it side by side with two or three more themes that are being developed, recurs to it time and time again throughout the poem, and echoes it for ironic or grotesque effects in thoroughly incongruous contexts. Sometimes this is done with the greatest complication and delicacy; he wants to introduce a bird whose call will stand for the clear speech of nature, in the midst of all the confusion and ugliness in which men could not exist except for "imagined beauty where there is none": so he says in disgust, "Stale as a whale's breath: breath! / Breath!" and ten lines later (during which three themes have been repeated and two of them joined at last in a "silent, uncommunicative," and satisfying resolution) he says that he has

Only of late, late! begun to know, to
know clearly (as through clear ice) whence
I draw my breath or how to employ it
clearly—if not well:

        Clearly!
speaks the red-breast his behest. Clearly!
   clearly!

These double exclamations have so prepared for the bird's call
that it strikes you, when you are reading the poem itself, like the blow
which dissolves an enchantment. And really the preparation has been
even more complicated: two pages before there was the line "divorce!
divorce!" and, half a page before, the birds and weeds by the river
were introduced with

. . . white, in
the shadows among the blue-flowered
Pickerel-weed, in summer, summer! if it should
ever come . . .

If you want to write a long poem which doesn't stick to one subject,
but which unifies a dozen, you can learn a good deal from *Paterson.*
    The subject of *Paterson* is: How can you tell the truth about
things?—that is, how can you find a language so close to the world
that the world can be represented and understood in it?

Paterson lies in the valley under the Passaic Falls
its spent waters forming the outline of his back. He
lies on his right side, head near the thunder
of the water filling his dreams! Eternally asleep,
his dreams walk about the city where he persists
incognito. Butterflies settle on his stone ear.

How can he—this city that is man—find the language for what he
sees and is, the language without which true knowledge is impossible?
He starts with the particulars ("Say it, no ideas but in things") which
stream to him like the river, "rolling up out of chaos, / a nine months'
wonder"; with the interpenetration of everything with everything,
"the drunk the sober; the illustrious / the gross; one":

It is the ignorant sun
rising in the slot of
hollow suns risen, so that never in this
world will a man live well in his body
save dying—and not know himself
dying . . .

The water falls and then rises in "floating mists, to be rained down and / regathered into a river that flows / and encircles"; the water, in its time, is "combed into straight lines / from that rafter of a rock's / lip," and attains clarity; but the people are like flowers that the bee misses, they fail and die and "Life is sweet, they say"—but their speech has failed them, "they do not know the words / or have not / the courage to use them," and they hear only "a false language pouring—a / language (misunderstood) pouring (misinterpreted) without / dignity, without minister, crashing upon a stone ear." And the language available to them, the language of scholarship and science and the universities, is

a bud forever green
tight-curled, upon the pavement, perfect
in justice and substance but divorced, divorced
from its fellows, fallen low—
                    Divorce is
the sign of knowledge in our time,
divorce! divorce!

Girls walk by the river at Easter and one, bearing a willow twig in her hand as Artemis bore the moon's crescent bow,

holds it, the gathered spray,
upright in the air, the pouring air,
strokes the soft fur—
                    Ain't they beautiful!

(How could words show better than these last three the touching half-success, half-failure of their language?) And Sam Patch, the professional daredevil who jumped over the Falls with his pet bear, could *say* only: "Some things can be done as well as others"; and Mrs. Cumming, the minister's wife, shrieked unheard and fell unseen from the brink; and the two were only

a body found next spring
frozen in an ice-cake; or a body
fished next day from the muddy swirl—

both silent, uncommunicative.

The speech of sexual understanding, of natural love, is represented by three beautifully developed themes: a photograph of the nine wives of a Negro chief; a tree standing on the brink of a waterfall; and two lovers talking by the river:

We sit and talk and the
silence speaks of the giants
who have died in the past and have
returned to those scenes unsatisfied
and who is not unsatisfied, the
silent, Singac the rock-shoulder
emerging from the rocks—and the giants
live again in your silence and
unacknowledged desire . . .

But now the air by the river "brings in the rumors of separate worlds," and the poem is dragged from its highest point in the natural world, from the early, fresh, and green years of the city, into the slums of Paterson, into the collapse of this natural language, into a "delirium of solutions," into the back streets of that "great belly / that no longer laughs but mourns / with its expressionless black navel love's / deceit." Here is the whole failure of Paterson's ideas and speech, and he is forced to begin all over; Part II of the poem ends with the ominous, "No ideas but / in the facts."

Part III opens with this beautiful and unexpected passage:

How strange you are, you idiot!
So you think because the rose
is red that you shall have the mastery?
The rose is green and will bloom,
overtopping you, green, livid
green when you shall no more speak, or
taste, or even be. My whole life
has hung too long upon a partial victory.

The underlying green of the facts always cancels out the red in which we had found our partial, temporary, aesthetic victory; and the poem now introduces the livid green of the obstinate and contorted lives, the lifeless perversions of the industrial city. Here are the slums; here is the estate with its acre hothouse, weedlike orchids, and French maid whose only duty is to "groom / the pet Pomeranians—who sleep"; here is the university with its clerks

> spitted on fixed concepts like
> roasting hogs, sputtering, their drip sizzling
> in the fire

> Something else, something else the same.

Then (in one of the fine prose quotations—much altered by the poet, surely—which interrupt the verse) people drain the lake there, all day and all night long kill the fish and eels with clubs, carry them away in baskets; there is nothing left but the mud. The sleeping Paterson, "moveless," envies the men who could run off "toward the peripheries—to other centers, direct," for some "loveliness and / authority in the world," who could leap like Sam Patch and be found " 'the following spring, frozen in / an ice cake'." But he goes on thinking to a very bitter end, and reproduces the brutal ignorance of his city as something both horrible and pathetic:

> And silk spins from the hot drums to a music
> of pathetic souvenirs, a comb and nail-file
> in an imitation leather case—to
> remind him, to remind him! and
> a photograph-holder with pictures of himself
> between the two children, all returned
> weeping, weeping—in the back room
> of the widow who married again, a vile tongue
> but laborious ways, driving a drunken
> husband . . .

But he contrasts his own mystery, the mystery of people's actual lives, with the mystery that "the convent of the Little Sisters of / St. Ann pretends"; and he understands the people "wiping the nose on sleeves, come here / to dream"; he understands that

Things, things unmentionable
the sink with the waste farina in it and
lumps of rancid meat, milk-bottle-tops: have
here a still tranquillity and loveliness . . .

Then Paterson "shifts his change," and an earthquake and a "remarkable rumbling noise" frighten the city but leave it undamaged—this in the prose of an old newspaper account; and at the end of the poem he stands in the flickering green of the cavern under the waterfall (the dark, skulled world of consciousness), hedged in by the pouring torrent whose thunder drowns out any language: "The myth / that holds up the rock, / that holds up the water thrives there— / in that cavern, that profound cleft"; and the readers of the poem have shown to them, in the last words of the poem,

standing, shrouded there, in that din,
Earth, the chatterer, father of all
speech . . .

It takes several readings to work out the poem's argument (it is a poem that *must* be read over and over), and it seemed to me that I could do most for its readers by roughly summarizing that argument. There are hundreds of things in the poem that deserve specific mention. The poem is weakest in the middle of the third section—I'd give page numbers if New Directions had remembered to put any in—but this seems understandable and almost inevitable. Everything in the poem is interwoven with everything else, just as the strands of the Falls interlace: how wonderful and unlikely that this extraordinary mixture of the most delicate lyricism of perception and feeling with the hardest and homeliest actuality should ever have come into being! There has never been a poem more American (though the only influence one sees in it is that of the river scene from *Finnegans Wake*); if the next three books are as good as this one, which introduces "the elemental character of the place," the whole poem will be the best very long poem that any American has written.

[*1946/PA*]

PATERSON (BOOK I) seemed to me a wonderful poem; I should not have supposed beforehand that William Carlos Williams could do the organizing and criticizing and selecting that a work of this length requires. Of course, Book I is not organized quite so well as a long poem *ought* to be, but this is almost a defining characteristic of long poems—and I do not see how anyone could do better using only those rather mosaic organizational techniques that Dr. Williams employs, and neglecting as much as he does narrative, drama, logic, and sustained movement, the primary organizers of long poems. I waited for the next three books of *Paterson* more or less as you wait for someone who has gone to break the bank at Monte Carlo for the second, third, and fourth times; I was afraid that I knew what was going to happen, but I kept wishing as hard as I could that it wouldn't.

Now that Book IV has been printed, one can come to some conclusions about *Paterson* as a whole. My first conclusion is this: it doesn't seem to *be* a whole; my second: *Paterson* has been getting rather steadily worse. Most of Book IV is much worse than II and III, and neither of them even begins to compare with Book I. Book IV is so disappointing that I do not want to write about it at any length: it would not satisfactorily conclude even a quite mediocre poem. Both form and content often seem a parody of those of the "real" *Paterson*; many sections have a scrappy inconsequence, an arbitrary irrelevance, that is extraordinary; poetry of the quality of that in Book I is almost completely lacking—though the forty lines about a new Odysseus coming in from the sea are particularly good, and there are other fits and starts of excellence. There are in Part III long sections of a measure that sounds exactly like the stuff you produce when you are demonstrating to a class that any prose whatsoever can be converted into four-stress accentual verse simply by inserting line-endings every four stresses. These sections *look* like blank verse, but are flatter than the flattest blank verse I have ever read—for instance: "Branching trees and ample gardens gave / the village streets a delightful charm and / the narrow old-fashioned brick walls added / a dignity to the shading trees. It was a fair / resort for summer sojourners on their way / to the Falls, the main object of interest." This passage suggests that the guidebook of today is the epic of tomorrow; and a worse possibility, the telephone book put into accentual verse, weighs upon one's spirit.

Books II and III are much better than this, of course: Book II is decidedly what people call "a solid piece of work," but most of the magic is gone. And one begins to be very doubtful about the organization: should there be so much of the evangelist and his sermon? Should so much of this book consist of what are—the reader is forced to conclude—real letters from a real woman? One reads these letters with involved, embarrassed pity, quite as if she had walked into the room and handed them to one. What has been done to them to make it possible for us to respond to them as art, not as raw reality? to make them part of the poem *Paterson*? I can think of no answer except: "They have been copied out on the typewriter." Anyone can object, "But the context makes them part of the poem"; and anyone can reply to this objection, "It takes a lot of context to make somebody else's eight-page letter the conclusion to a book of a poem."

Book II introduces—how one's heart sinks!—Credit and Usury, those enemies of man, God, and contemporary long poems. Dr. Williams has always put up a sturdy resistance to Pound when Pound has recommended to him Santa Sophia or the Parthenon, rhyme or meter, European things like that; yet he takes Credit and Usury over from Pound and gives them a good home and maintains them in practically the style to which they have been accustomed—his motto seems to be, *I'll adopt your child if only he's ugly enough*. It is interesting to see how much some later parts of *Paterson* resemble in their structure some middle and later parts of the *Cantos*: the Organization of Irrelevance (or, perhaps, the Irrelevance of Organization) suggests itself as a name for this category of structure. Such organization is *ex post facto* organization: if something is somewhere, one can always find Some Good Reason for its being there, but if it had not been there would one reader have missed it? if it had been put somewhere else, would one reader have guessed where it should have "really" gone? Sometimes these anecdotes, political remarks, random comments seem to be where they are for one reason: because Dr. Williams chose—happened to choose—for them to be there. One is reminded of that other world in which Milton found Chance "sole arbiter."

Book III is helped very much by the inclusion of "Beautiful Thing," that long, extremely effective lyric that was always intended for *Paterson*; and Book III, though neither so homogeneous nor so close to Book I, is in some respects superior to Book II. But all three later books are worse organized, more eccentric and idiosyncratic, more self-indulgent, than the first. And yet that is not the point, the real point: the *poetry*, the lyric rightness, the queer wit, the improbable and dazzling perfection of so much of Book I have disappeared—or at least, reappear only fitfully. Early in Book IV, while talking to his son, Dr. Williams quotes this to him: "What I miss, said your mother, is the poetry, the pure poem of the first parts." She is right.

I have written a good deal about Dr. Williams's unusual virtues, so I will take it for granted that I don't need to try to demonstrate, all over again, that he is one of the best poets alive. He was the last of the good poets of his generation to become properly appreciated; and some of his appreciators, in the blush of conversion, rather overvalue him now. When one reads that no "living American poet has written anything better and more ambitious" than *Paterson*, and that Dr. Williams is a poet who gives us "just about everything," one feels that the writer has in some sense missed the whole point of William Carlos Williams. He is a *very* good but *very* limited poet, particularly in vertical range. He is a notably unreasoning, intuitive writer—is not, of course, an intellectual in any sense of the word; and he has further limited himself by volunteering for and organizing a long dreary imaginary war in which America and the Present are fighting against Europe and the Past. But go a few hundred years back inside the most American American and it is Europe: Dr. Williams is just as much Darkest Europe as any of us, down there in the middle of his past.

In his long one-sided war with Eliot Dr. Williams seems to me to come off badly—particularly so when we compare the whole of *Paterson* with the *Four Quartets*. When we read the *Four Quartets* we are reading the long poem of a poet so temperamentally isolated that he does not even put another character, another human being treated at length, into the whole poem; and yet the poem (probably the best long poem since the *Duino Elegies*) impresses us not with its limitations but with its range and elevation, with how much it knows not simply about men but about Man—not simply about one city or one country but about the West, that West of which America is no more than the last part.

[*1951/PA*]

An Introduction to the Selected Poems of William Carlos Williams

AN INTRODUCTION TO THESE POEMS can be useful to the reader in the way that an introduction to Peirce or William James can be: the reader is entering a realm that has some of the confusion and richness of the world, and any sort of summary is useful that keeps him reassured for a while—after that the place is its own justification. But most readers will automatically make any adjustments they need to make for writers so outspoken, warmhearted, and largely generous as Peirce and James and Williams. Their voices are introduction enough.

Anyone would apply to Williams—besides *outspoken, warmhearted,* and *generous*—such words as *fresh, sympathetic, enthusiastic, spontaneous, open, impulsive, emotional, observant, curious, rash, courageous, undignified, unaffected, humanitarian, experimental, empirical, liberal, secular, democratic.* Both what he keeps and what he rejects are unusual: how many of these words would fit the other good poets of the time? He was born younger than they, with more of the frontier about him, of the this-worldly optimism of the eighteenth century; one can imagine his reading *Rameau's Nephew* with delighted enthusiasm, but wading along in Karl Barth with a dour blank frown. (I don't mean altogether to dissociate myself from these responses.) And he is as Pelagian as an obstetrician should be: as he points to the poor red thing mewling behind plate-glass, he says with professional, observant disbelief: "You mean you think *that's* full of

Original Sin?" He has the honesty that consists in writing down the way things seem to you yourself, not the way that they really must be, that they *are*, that everybody but a misguided idealist or shallow optimist or bourgeois sentimentalist *knows* they are. One has about him the amused, admiring, and affectionate certainty that one has about Whitman: *Why, he'd say anything*—creditable or discreditable, sayable or unsayable, so long as he believes it. There is a delightful generosity and extravagance about the man in and behind the poems: one is attracted to him so automatically that one is "reminded of a story" of how S——was defined (quite unjustly) as the only man in the universe who didn't like William James.

A *Selected Poems* does far less than justice to Williams. Any fair selection would have to include his wonderful *Paterson (Part I),* which is itself a book; and Williams is one of those poets, like Hardy, whose bad or mediocre poems do repay reading and do add to your respect for the poet. Williams's bad poems are usually rather winning machine parts minus their machine, irrepressible exclamations about the weather of the world, interesting but more or less autonomous and irrelevant entries in a Lifetime Diary. But this is attractive; the usual bad poem in somebody's *Collected Works* is a learned, mannered, valued habit, a habit a little more careful than, and a little emptier than, brushing one's teeth.

The first thing one notices about Williams's poetry is how radically sensational and perceptual it is: "Say it! No ideas but in things." Williams shares with Marianne Moore and Wallace Stevens a feeling that almost nothing is more important, more of a true delight, than the way things look. Reading their poems is one long shudder of recognition; their reproduction of things, in its empirical gaiety, its clear abstract refinement of presentation, has something peculiarly and paradoxically American about it—English readers usually talk about their work as if it had been produced by three triangles fresh from Flatland. All three of these poets might have used, as an epigraph for their poetry, that beautiful saying that it is nicer to think than to do, to feel than to think, but nicest of all merely to look. Williams's poems, so far as their spirit is concerned, remind one of Marianne Moore's "It is not the plunder, / but 'accessibility to experience' "; so far as their letter is concerned, they carry scrawled all over them Stevens's "The greatest poverty is not to live / In a physical world"—and Stevens continues, quite as if he were Williams looking with wondering love at all the unlikely beauties of the poor:

One might have thought of sight, but who could think
Of what it sees, for all the ill it sees.

All three poets did their first good work in an odd climate of po-
etic opinion. Its expectations of behavior were imagist (the poet was
supposed to see everything, to feel a great deal, and to think and to do
and to make hardly anything), its metrical demands were minimal,
and its ideals of organization were mosaic. The subject of poetry had
changed from the actions of men to the reactions of poets—*reactions*
being defined in a way that left the poet almost without motor system
or cerebral cortex. This easily led to a strange kind of abstraction: for
what is more abstract than a fortuitous collocation of sensations?
Stevens, with his passion for philosophy, order, and blank verse, was
naturally least affected by the atmosphere of the time, in which he
was at most a tourist; and Marianne Moore synthesized her own novel
organization out of syllabic verse, extravagantly elaborated, half-
visual patterns, and an extension of moral judgment, feeling, and
generalization to the whole world of imagist perception. Williams
found his own sort of imagism considerably harder to modify. He had
a boyish delight and trust in Things: there is always on his lips the fa-
miliar, pragmatic, American *These are the facts*—for he is the most
pragmatic of writers, and so American that the adjective itself seems
inadequate . . . one exclaims in despair and delight: He is the America
of poets. Few of his poems had that pure crystalline inconsequence
that the imagist poem ideally has—the world and Williams himself
kept breaking into them; and this was certainly their salvation.

Williams's poetry is more remarkable for its empathy, sympathy,
its muscular and emotional identification with its subjects, than any
modern poetry except Rilke's. When you have read *Paterson* you know
for the rest of your life what it is like to be a waterfall; and what other
poet has turned so many of his readers into trees? Occasionally one re-
alizes that this latest tree of Williams's is considerably more active
than anybody else's grizzly bear; but usually the identification is so
natural, the feel or rhythm of the poem so hypnotic, that the problem
of belief never arises. Williams's knowledge of plants and animals,
our brothers and sisters in the world, is surprising for its range and in-
tensity; and he sets them down in the midst of the real weather of the
world, so that the reader is full of an innocent lyric pleasure just in
being out in the open, in feeling the wind tickling his skin. The poems
are full of "Nature": Williams has reproduced with exact and loving
fidelity both the illumination of the letter and the movement of the

spirit. In these poems emotions, ideals, whole attitudes are implicit in a tone of voice, in the feel of his own overheard speech; or are expressed in terms of plants, animals, the landscape, the weather. You see from his instructions "To a Solitary Disciple" that it is what the landscape does—its analogical, anthropomorphized life—that matters to Williams; and it is only as the colors and surfaces reveal this that they are important.

At first people were introduced into the poems mainly as overheard or overlooked landscape; they spread. Williams has the knowledge of people one expects, and often does not get, from doctors; a knowledge one does not expect, and almost never gets, from contemporary poets. (For instance, what is probably the best poem by a living poet, *Four Quartets,* has only one real character, the poet, and a recurrent state of that character which we are assured is God; even the ghostly mentor encountered after the air-raid is half Eliot himself, a sort of Dostoevsky double.) One believes in and remembers the people in Williams's poems, though they usually remain behavioristic, sharply observed, sympathetic and empathetic sketches, and one cannot get from these sketches the knowledge of a character that one gets from some of Frost's early dramatic monologues and narratives, from a number of Hardy's poems, or from Williams's detailed and conclusive treatment of the most interesting character in the poems, himself. Some of the narrative and dramatic elements of his poetry seem to have drained off into his fiction. Williams's attitude toward his people is particularly admirable: he has neither that condescending, impatient, Pharisaical dismissal of the illiterate mass of mankind, nor that manufactured, mooing awe for an equally manufactured Little or Common Man, that disfigures so much contemporary writing. Williams loves, blames, and yells despairingly at the Little Men just as naturally and legitimately as Saint-Loup got angry at the servants: because he *feels,* not just says, that the differences between men are less important than their similarities—that he and you and I, together, are the Little Men.

Williams has a real and unusual dislike of, distrust in, Authority; and the Father-surrogate of the average work of art has been banished from his Eden. His ability to rest (or at least to thrash happily about) in contradictions, doubts, and general guesswork, without ever climbing aboard any of the monumental certainties that go perpetually by, perpetually on time—this ability may seem the opposite of Whitman's gift for boarding every certainty and riding off into every infinite, but the spirit behind them is the same. Williams's range (it is roughly Paterson, that microcosm which he has half-discovered, half-invented) is narrower than Whitman's, and yet there too one is reminded of Whitman: Williams has much of the freeness of an earlier America, though it is a freedom haunted about by desperation and sorrow. The little motto one could invent for him—*In the suburbs, there one feels free*—is particularly ambiguous when one considers that those suburbs of his are overshadowed by, are a part of, the terrible industrial landscape of northeastern New Jersey. But the ambiguity is one that Williams himself not only understands but insists upon: if his poems are full of what is clear, delicate, and beautiful, they are also full of what is coarse, ugly, and horrible. There is no optimistic blindness in Williams, though there is a fresh gaiety, a stubborn or invincible joyousness. But when one thinks of the poems, of Williams himself, in the midst of these factories, dumps, subdivisions, express highways, patients, children, weeds, and wildflowers of theirs—with the city of New York rising before them on the horizon, a pillar of smoke by day, a pillar of fire by night; when one thinks of this, one sees in an ironic light, the flat matter-of-fact light of the American landscape, James's remark that America "has no ruins." America is full of ruins, the ruins of hopes.

There are continually apparent in Williams that delicacy and subtlety which are sometimes so extraordinarily present, and sometimes so extraordinarily absent, in Whitman; and the hair-raising originality of some of Whitman's language is another bond between the two—no other poet of Whitman's time could have written

> The orchestra whirls me wider than Uranus flies,
> It wrenches such ardors from me I did not know I possessed them,
> It sails me, I dab with bare feet, they are lick'd by the indolent waves,
> I am cut by bitter and angry hail, I lose my breath,
> Steep'd amid honey'd morphine, my windpipe throttled in fakes of
>   death,
> At length let up again to feel the puzzle of puzzles . . .

I suppose that the third line and the *fakes of death* are the most extraordinary things in the passage; yet the whole seems more overwhelming than they. In spite of their faults—some of them obvious to, and some of them seductive to, the most foolish reader—poets like Whitman and Williams have about them something more valuable than any faultlessness: a wonderful largeness, a quantitative and qualitative generosity.

Williams's imagist-objectivist background and bias have helped his poems by their emphasis on truthfulness, exactness, concrete "presentation"; but they have harmed the poems by their underemphasis on organization, logic, narrative, generalization—and the poems are so short, often, that there isn't time for much. Some of the poems seem to say, "Truth is enough"—*truth* meaning *data brought back alive.* But truth isn't enough. Our crudest demand for excitement, for the "actions of men," for the "real story" of something "important," something strange—this demand is legitimate because it is the nature of the animal, man, to make it; and the demand can hardly be neglected so much as a great deal of the poetry of our time—of the good poetry of our time—has neglected it. The materials of Williams's unsuccessful poems have as much reality as the brick one stumbles over on the sidewalk; but how little has been done to them!—the poem is pieces or, worse still, a piece. But sometimes just enough, exactly as little as is necessary, has been done; and in these poems the Nature of the edge of the American city—the weeds, clouds, and children of vacant lots—and its reflection in the minds of its inhabitants, exist for good.

One accepts as a perfect criticism of his own insufficiently organized (i.e., insufficiently living) poems Williams's own lines: "And we thought to escape rime / by imitation of the senseless / unarrangement of wild things—the stupidest rime of all"; and one realizes at the same time, with a sense of reassurance, that few people know better than Williams how sensible the arrangement of wild things often is. Williams's good poems are in perfect agreement with his own explanation of what a poem is:

A poem is a small (or large) machine made of words. When I say there's nothing sentimental about a poem I mean that there can be no part, as in any other machine, that is redundant . . . Its movement is intrinsic, undulant, a physical more than a literary character. Therefore each speech having its own character, the poetry it engenders will be peculiar to that speech also in its own intrinsic form. The effect is beauty, what in a single object resolves our complex feelings of propriety . . . When a man makes a poem, makes it, mind you, he takes words as he finds them interrelated about him and composes them—without distortion which would mar their exact significances—into an intense expression of his perceptions and ardors that they may constitute a revelation in the speech that he uses. It isn't what he *says* that counts as a work of art, it's what he makes, with such intensity of perception that it lives with an intrinsic movement of its own to verify its authenticity.

It is the opposition between the *without distortion* and the repeated *makes* of this passage that gives Williams's poetry the type of organization that it has.

One is rather embarrassed at the necessity of calling Williams original; it is like saying that a Cheshire Cat smiles. Originality is one of his major virtues and minor vices. One thinks about some of his best poems, *I've never read or imagined anything like this*; and one thinks about some of his worst, *I wish to God this were a little more like ordinary poetry.* He is even less logical than the average good poet—he is an intellectual in neither the good nor the bad sense of the word—but loves abstractions for their own sake, and makes accomplished, characteristic, inveterate use of them, exactly as if they were sensations or emotions; there is no "dissociation of sensibility" in Williams. Both generalizations and particulars are handled with freshness and humor and imagination, with a delicacy and fantasy that are especially charming in so vigorous, realistic, and colloquial a writer.

The mosaic organization characteristic of imagism or "objectivism" develops naturally into the musical, thematic organization of poems like *Paterson (Part I)*; many of its structural devices are interestingly, if quite independently, close to those of *Four Quartets* and "Coriolan," though Eliot at the same time utilizes a good many of the traditional devices that Williams dislikes. A large-scale organization which is neither logical, dramatic, nor narrative is something that contemporary poetry has particularly desired; such an organization seems possible but improbable, does not exist at present, and is most nearly approached in *Four Quartets* and *Paterson (Part I)*.

Williams's poems are full of imperatives, exclamations, trochees—the rhythms and dynamics of their speech are being insisted upon as they could not be in any prose. It is this insistence upon dynamics that is fundamental in Williams's reading of his own poems: the listener realizes with astonished joy that he is hearing a method of reading poetry that is both excellent—for these particular poems—and completely unlike anything he has ever heard before. About Williams's meters one remark might be enough, here: that no one has written more accomplished and successful free verse. It seems to me that ordinary accentual-syllabic verse, in general, has tremendous advantages over "free," accentual, or syllabic verse—in English, of course. But that these other kinds of verse, in some particular situations or with some particular materials, can work out better for some poets, is so plain that any assertion to the contrary seems obstinate dogmatism. We want to explain *why* Williams's free verse or Marianne Moore's syllabic verse is successful, not to make fools of ourselves by arguing that it isn't. The verse-form of one of their poems, as anyone can see, is essential to its success; and it is impossible to produce the same effect by treating their material in accentual-syllabic verse. Anyone can invent the genius who might have done the same thing even better in ordinary English verse, but he is the most fruitless of inventions.

Contemporary criticism has not done very well by Williams; most of the good critics of poetry have not written about him, and one or two of the best, when they did write, just twitched as if flies were crawling over them. Yvor Winters has been Williams's most valuable advocate, and has written extremely well about one side of Williams's poetry; but his praise has never had enough effect on the average reader, who felt that Williams came as part of the big economy-sized package that included Elizabeth Daryush, Jones Very, and Winters's six best students. The most important thing that criticism can do for a poet, while he is alive, is to establish that atmosphere of interested respect which gets his poems a reasonably careful reading; it is only in the last couple of years that any such atmosphere has been established for Williams.

Williams's most impressive single piece is certainly *Paterson (Part I)*: a reader has to be determinedly insensitive to modern poetry not to see that it has an extraordinary range and reality, a clear rightness that sometimes approaches perfection. I imagine that almost any list of Williams's best poems would include the extremely moving, completely realized "The Widow's Lament in Springtime"; that terrible poem (XVIII in "Spring and All") that begins, *The pure products of America / go crazy*; "The Yachts," a poem that is a paradigm of all the unjust beauty, the necessary and unnecessary injustice of the world; "These," a poem that is pure deprivation; "Burning the Christmas Greens"; the long poem (called "Paterson: Episode 17" in Williams's *Collected Poems*) that uses for a refrain the phrase *Beautiful Thing*; the unimaginably delicate "To Waken an Old Lady"; the poem that begins, *By the road to the contagious hospital*; the beautiful "A Unison," in which Nature is once again both ritual and myth; and, perhaps, "The Sea-Elephant," "The Semblables," and "The Injury." And how many other poems there are that one never comes on without pleasure!

That Williams's poems are honest, exact, and original, that some of them are really *good* poems, seems to me obvious. But in concluding I had rather mention something even more obvious: their generosity and sympathy, their moral and human attractiveness.

[*1949/PA*]

A Note on Poetry

I MAY AS WELL SAY what the reader will soon enough see, that I don't want to write a preface. I am not even sure what sort I am expected to write: one telling what I meant these poems to be or do, I suppose, along with sections about the function of poetry and its state at present. Now, the reader may be interested in what the poems are; but why should he care what I meant them to be? And the thought of saying anything about the function of poetry or its present condition, in a couple of pages, makes me uncomfortable. Worse, suppose I say "modern" poetry is A; then the reader will probably think I meant my poems to be A, if I consider myself a "modern" poet, not-A if I don't. I could give plenty of other reasons; but the best reason is simply that I don't want the poems mixed up with my life or opinions or picture or any other regrettable concomitants. I look like a bear and live in a cave; but you should worry.

If, after all this, I go on and write my preface, surely the reader will pay no attention to it?

If you consider "modern" poetry—Pound, Eliot, Crane, Tate, Stevens, Cummings, Marianne Moore, and so on—in isolation, it will seem both more original (this is the favorable side of the mistake) and more disquieting (or *crazy* or *inexplicable* or any other disapproving adjective) than it really is; if you consider it as an end product, a limit, in most cases a *reductio ad absurdum*, of a long historical process, what will puzzle you is why it didn't happen sooner. (That is, as early as it did in France: Rimbaud wrote "modern" poetry. The causes are mostly economic, I think: France didn't have the Victorian prosperity which slowed up the whole series of changes in England; also, the rate of change could be greater because romanticism was more of a surface phenomenon there.) When I say *historical process* I use it in the full sense of the word, I don't mean literary-historical; without the economic and scientific and political changes that accompany—and, mostly, cause—the changes in the poetry itself, the history of English poetry is nothing but a magician's catalogue. I don't mean that I believe in the sort of psycho-physical parallelism between literature and economics in which literary phenomena are merely shadows of economic ones, with no causal efficacy of their own; once a literary process is really started, it works itself out on its own momentum. But the great changes in literature are non-literary in origin; and the same causes that produce the new work produce, in time, its audience. Wordsworth's poems did not produce the Wordsworthians—the things that made Wordsworth write a certain type of poetry at the beginning of the nineteenth century, by the middle of the century had prepared its readers. If poetry were produced by large groups and consumed by a few responsive individuals, the order would be reversed, and the consumers would have to hunger vaguely for something not even ready to exist for thirty or forty years.

"Modern" poetry is, essentially, an extension of romanticism; it is what romantic poetry wishes or finds it necessary to become. It is the end product of romanticism, all past and no future; it is impossible to go further by any extrapolation of the process by which we have arrived, and certainly it is impossible to remain where we are— who could endure a century of *Transition?* Modernism, like Spinoza's *substance*, is the den from which no tracks return: at least, none whose makers have not come to an understanding with the lion. One is reminded of some species which carried evolutionary tendencies so far past the point of maximum utility that they actually became destructive to them: Titanotherium, whose size and horns increased until the species became extinct; or certain shellfish whose coils became so complicated they could at last barely be opened. Romanticism is necessarily a process of extension, a vector; this is striking even when the observer looks at it as a purely literary process, and leaves out of account the changes in society that are forcing it to its extremes. (Neoclassicism, *in theory,* is a static system.) Most of the tendencies which differentiate romantic from neoclassical poetry exist in an hypertrophied state in modernist poetry, but there are a great many factors that help conceal this: a big quantitative change looks like a qualitative one; the best modern criticism of poetry is extremely anti-romantic, and the change in theory covers up the lack of any essential change in practice—because of Eliot's critical opinions, many people think his poetry a sort of classicism; modern poetry often so noticeably lacks some romantic qualities that the reader disregards all the others it possesses, especially since many of them are too common to be noticed as specifically romantic; the reader tends to be confused by the continual surface novelty romanticism demands; and, finally, there are some genuinely non-romantic tendencies—premonitions, perhaps—in modern poetry. I have no space for the enormous amount of evidence all these generalizations require; but consider some of the qualities of typical modernistic poetry: very interesting language, a great emphasis on connotation, "texture"; extreme intensity, forced emotion—violence; a good deal of obscurity; emphasis on sensation, perceptual nuances; emphasis on details, on the part rather than on the whole; experimental or novel qualities of some sort; a tendency toward external formlessness and internal disorganization—these are justified, generally, as the disorganization required to express a disorganized age, or, alternatively, as newly discovered and more complex types of organization; an extremely personal style—*refine your singularities*; lack of restraint—all tendencies are forced to their limits; there is a good deal of emphasis on the unconscious, dream structure, the thoroughly subjective; the poet's attitudes are usually anti-scientific, anti-common-sense, anti-public—he is, essentially, removed; poetry is primarily lyric, intensive—the few long poems are aggregations of lyric details; poems usually have, not a logical, but the more or less associational structure of dramatic monologue; and so on and so on. This complex of qualities is essentially romantic; and the poetry that exhibits it represents the culminating point of romanticism.

I obviously do not mean that the poets and their public have arrived at this point en masse; the poetry of the age is extremely heterogeneous, and the indifferent mass of poets and readers are distributed haphazardly through the various earlier stages of romanticism, unwilling or unable to go any further—cultural liberals, so to speak; or, to put it more prettily, vestiges, anachronisms, reptiles surviving into an age of mammals. For modernistic poetry has certainly been the most successful and influential body of poetry of this century; most good poets outside it have been influenced by it, the most successful poet of the time, Yeats, had his poetry so changed by it that his later work is neglected or disliked as "modern" by most of the admirers of his earlier poems. What has begun to weaken so much the enormous attraction (in the physical sense) that modernist poetry exerted? What has become of the animal certainty with which the young poet of the twenties began to write experimental poetry? Why have not the successful modernist poets continued confidently their original lines of development?

Modernist poetry exerted its attraction because it was carrying the tendencies of romanticism to their necessary conclusions; now most of those conclusions have been arrived at; and how can the poet go any further? How can poems be written that are more violent? more disorganized? more obscure? more—the adjectives throng to me—than those that have already been written? And the poets, at the ends of their processes of specialization, are more or less conscious of what has happened. Some of them have tried to make their poetry conform to their critical principles, spoiling their poetry in the process: Winters is my *locus classicus*, but I can spare Eliot a glance. (Here I am certainly not recommending any divergence of practice and theory, I am simply noticing that it is difficult for a poet in an advanced state of romanticism to write good non-romantic poetry because he thinks he ought to.) Imagism was a *reductio ad absurdum* of one or two tendencies of romanticism, such a beautifully and finally absurd one that it is hard to believe it existed as anything but a logical construction; and what imagist found it possible to go on writing imagist poetry? A number of poets have stopped writing entirely; others, like recurring decimals, repeat the novelties they commenced with, each time less valuably than before. And there are surrealist poetry, and political poetry, and all the other refuges of the indigent. Auden is the only poet who has been influential very recently; and this is because, very partially and uncertainly, and often very mechanically, he represents new tendencies, a departure from modernist romanticism.

We have reached one of those points in the historical process at which the poet has the uncomfortable illusion of choice; when he too says, "But what was it? What am I?" The *it* he asks about is the dying tradition (which dies because the world it represented is dying)—the determinants which once were axiomatic, permitting neither disagreement nor understanding; today, for him, they are no longer determining: the marionette looks reluctantly for another hand. So the poets repeat the old heartlessly, or make their guesses at the new; meanwhile, quantity is being transformed into quality, the water goes over into steam—today, for most of Europe, even the illusion of choice is impossible, and we see or shall see literature being determined, in the strictest and most immediate sense, by economics.

I have not been saying that modernist poetry is romantic, hence bad; *romantic,* as I used it, is a neutral descriptive term. I wished to stress the fundamental kinship of modern and romantic poetry because it is their differences that are insisted on by the two common critical positions: the essentially Victorian view that regards metaphysical, eighteenth-century, and modern poetry as regrettable divergences from the real tradition of English poetry, which skips from the Elizabethans (i.e., Spenser and Shakespeare) and Milton on to the romantics and Victorians; and the other view, which approves of the Elizabethans, metaphysicals, and moderns, tolerates the eighteenth century, and condemns the Victorians and romantics.

I have had no space for evidence, qualification, or detail—and there needs to be a great deal of each; I hope the reader will be indulgent toward a tentative sketch. During the course of the article, the reader may have thought curiously, "Does he really suppose he writes the sort of poetry that replaces modernism?" Let me answer, like the man in the story, "I must decline the soft impeachment." But I am sorry I need to.

[*1940/KA*]

The Woman at
the Washington Zoo

Critics fairly often write essays about how some poem was written; the
poet who wrote it seldom does. When Robert Penn Warren and Cleanth
Brooks were making a new edition of Understanding Poetry, they asked
several poets to write such essays. I no longer remembered much about
writing "The Woman at the Washington Zoo"—a poem is, so to speak,
a way of making you forget how you wrote it—but I had almost all the
sheets of paper on which it was written, starting with a paper napkin
from the Methodist Cafeteria. If you had asked me where I had begun
the poem I'd have said: "Why, sir, at the beginning"; it was a surprise
to me to see that I hadn't.

As I read, arranged, and remembered the pages it all came
back to me. I went over them for several days, copying down most
of the lines and phrases and mentioning some of the sights and cir-
cumstances they came out of; I tried to give a fairly good idea of
the objective process of writing the poem. You may say, "But isn't a
poem a kind of subjective process, like a dream? Doesn't it come out
of unconscious wishes of yours, childhood memories, parts of your
own private emotional life?" It certainly does: part of them I don't
know about and the rest I didn't write about. Nor did I write about or
copy down something that begins to appear on the last two or three
pages: lines and phrases from a kind of counter-poem, named
"Jerome," in which St. Jerome is a psychoanalyst and his lion is at the
zoo.

If after reading this essay the reader should say: "You did all that *you could to the things, but the things just came," he would feel about it as I do.*

LATE IN THE SUMMER OF 1956 my wife and I moved to Washington. We lived with two daughters, a cat, and a dog, in Chevy Chase; every day I would drive to work through Rock Creek Park, past the zoo. I worked across the street from the Capitol, at the Library of Congress. I knew Washington fairly well, but had never lived there; I had been in the army, but except for that had never worked for the government.

Some of the new and some of the old things there—I was often reminded of the army—had a good deal of effect on me: after a few weeks I began to write a poem. I have most of what I wrote, though the first page is gone; the earliest lines are:

>   any color
> My print, that has clung to its old colors
> Through many washings; this dull null
> Navy I wear to work, and wear from work, and so
> ~~And so to bed~~   To bed
> With no complaint, no comment—neither from my chief,
>   nor
> The Deputy Chief Assistant, ~~from~~ his chief,
> Nor   nor
> ~~From~~ Congressmen, ~~from~~ their constituents—
>   ~~thin~~
> Only I complain; this ~~poor~~ worn serviceable . . .

The woman talking is a near relation of women I was seeing there in Washington—some at close range, at the Library—and a distant relation of women I had written about before, in "The End of the Rainbow" and "Cinderella" and "Seele im Raum." She is a kind of aging machine part. I wrote, as they say in suits, "acting as next friend"; I had for her the sympathy of an aging machine part. (If I was also something else, that was just personal; and she also was something else.) I felt that one of these hundreds of thousands of government clerks might feel all her dresses one dress, a faded navy blue print, and that dress her body. This work- or life-uniform of hers excites neither complaint, nor comment, nor the mechanically protective *No comment* of the civil servant; excites them neither from her "chief," the Deputy Chief Assistant, nor from his, nor from any being on any level of that many-leveled machine: all the system is silent, except for her own cry, which goes unnoticed just as she herself goes unnoticed. (I had met a Deputy Chief Assistant, who saw nothing remarkable in the title.) The woman's days seem to her the going-up-to-work and coming-down-from-work of a worker; each ends in *And so to bed,* the diarist's conclusive unvarying entry in the daybook of his life.

These abruptly opening lines are full of duplications and echoes, like what they describe. And they are wrong in the way in which beginnings are wrong: either there is too much of something or it is not yet there. The lines break off with *this worn serviceable*—the words can apply either to her dress or to her body, but anything so obviously suitable to the dress must be intended for the body. *Body that no sunlight dyes, no hand suffuses,* the page written the next day goes on; then after a space there is *Dome-shadowed, withering among columns, / Wavy upon the pools of fountains, small beside statues . . .* No sun colors, no hand suffuses with its touch, this used, still-useful body. It is subdued to the element it works in: is shadowed by the domes, grows old and small and dry among the columns, of the buildings of the capital; becomes a reflection, its material identity lost, upon the pools of the fountains of the capital; is dwarfed beside the statues of the capital—as year by year it passes among the public places of this city of space and trees and light, city sinking beneath the weight of its marble, city of graded voteless workers.

The word *small,* as it joins the reflections in the pools, the trips to the public places, brings the poem to its real place and subject—to its title, even: next there is *small and shining,* then (with the star beside it that means *use, don't lose*) *small, far-off, shining in the eyes of animals*; the woman ends at the zoo, looking so intently into its cages that she sees her own reflection in *the eyes of animals, these wild ones trapped / As I am trapped but not, themselves, the trap . . .* The lines have written above them "The Woman at the Washington Zoo."

The next page has the title and twelve lines:

This print, that has kept the memory of color
Alive through many cleanings; this dull null
Navy I wear to work, and wear from work, and so
To bed (with no complaints, no comment: neither from my chief,
The Deputy Chief Assistant, nor her chief,
Nor his, nor Congressmen, nor their constituents
                    ~~wan~~
—Only I complain); this ~~plain~~, worn, serviceable

<pre>   sunlight
Body that no ~~sunset~~ dyes, no hand suffuses
But, dome-shadowed, withering among columns,
Wavy beneath fountains—small, far-off, shining
                              ~~wild~~
In the eyes of animals, these beings trapped
As I am trapped but not, themselves, the trap . . .</pre>

Written underneath this, in the rapid, ugly, disorganized handwriting of most of the pages, is *bars of my body burst blood breath breathing— lives aging but without knowledge of age / Waiting in their safe prisons for death, knowing not of death*; immediately this is changed into two lines, *Aging, but without knowledge of their age, / Kept safe here, knowing not of death, for death*—and out at the side, scrawled heavily, is: *O bars of my own body, open, open!* She recognizes herself in the animals—and recognizes herself, also, in the cages.

Written across the top of this page is *2nd and 3rd alphabet.* Streets in Washington run through a one-syllable, a two-syllable, and a three-syllable (Albemarle, Brandywine, Chesapeake . . .) alphabet, so that people say about an address: "Let's see, that's in the second alphabet, isn't it?" It made me think of Kronecker's "God made the integers, all else is the work of man"; but it seemed right for Washington to have alphabets of its own—I made up the title of a detective story, *Murder in the Second Alphabet.* The alphabets were a piece of Washington that should have fitted into the poem, but didn't; but the zoo was a whole group of pieces, a little Washington, into which the poem itself fitted.

Rock Creek Park, with its miles of heavily wooded hills and valleys, its rocky stream, is like some National Forest dropped into Washington by mistake. Many of the animals of the zoo are in unroofed cages back in its ravines. My wife and I had often visited the zoo, and now that we were living in Washington we went to it a great deal. We had made friends with a lynx that was very like our cat that had died the spring before, at the age of sixteen. We would feed the lynx pieces of liver or scraps of chicken and turkey; we fed liver, sometimes, to two enormous white timber wolves that lived at the end of one ravine. Eager for the meat, they would stand up against the bars on their hind legs, taller than a man, and stare into our eyes; they reminded me of Akela, white with age, in the *Jungle Books,* and of the wolves who fawn at the man Mowgli's brown feet in *In the Rukh.* In one of the buildings of the zoo there was a lioness with two big cubs; when the keeper came she would come over, purring her bass purr, to rub her head against the bars almost as our lynx would rub his head against the turkey skin, in rapture, before he finally gulped it down. In the lions' building there were two black leopards; when you got close to them you saw they had not lost the spots of the ordinary leopards—were the ordinary leopards, but spotted black on black, dingy somehow.

On the way to the wolves one went by a big unroofed cage of foxes curled up asleep; on the concrete floor of the enclosure there would be scattered two or three white rats—stiff, quite untouched—that the foxes had left. (The wolves left their meat, too—big slabs of horse-meat, glazing, covered with flies.) Twice when I came to the foxes' cage there was a turkey buzzard that had come down for the rats; startled at me, he flapped up heavily, with a rat dangling underneath. (There are usually vultures circling over the zoo; nearby, at the tennis courts of the Sheraton-Park, I used to see vultures perched on the tower of WTTG, above the court on which Defense Secretary McElroy was playing doubles—so that I would say to myself, like Peer Gynt: "Nature is witty.") As a child, coming around the bend of a country road, I had often seen a turkey buzzard, with its black wings and naked red head, flap heavily up from the mashed body of a skunk or possum or rabbit.

A good deal of this writes itself on the next page, almost too rapidly for line endings or punctuation: *to be and never know I am   when the vulture buzzard comes for the white rat that the foxes left   May he take off his black wings, the red flesh of his head, and step to me as man—a man at whose brown feet the white wolves fawn—to whose hand of power / The lioness stalks, leaving her cubs playing / and rubs her head along the bars as he strokes it.* Along the side of the page, between these lines, two or three words to a line, is written *the animals who are trapped but are not themselves the trap black leopards spots, light and darkened, hidden except to the close eyes of love, in their life-long darkness, so I in decent black, navy blue.*

As soon as the zoo came into the poem, everything else settled into it and was at home there; on this page it is plain even to the writer that all the things in the poem come out of, and are divided between, color and colorlessness. Colored women and colored animals and colored cloth—all that the woman sees as her own opposite—come into the poem to begin it. Beside the typed lines are many hurried phrases, most of them crossed out: *red and yellow as October maples   rosy, blood seen through flesh in summer   colors wild and easy natural   leaf-yellow cloud-rose leopard-yellow, cloth from another planet the leopards look back at their wearers, hue for hue   the women look back at the leopard.* And on the back of the vulture's page there is a flight of ideas, almost a daydream, coming out of these last phrases: *we have never mistaken you for the others   among the legations one of a different architecture women, saris of a different color envoy impassive   clear bullet-proof glass   lips, through the clear glass of a rose sedan   color of blood   you too are represented on this earth* . . .

One often sees on the streets of Washington—fairly often sees at the zoo—what seem beings of a different species: women from the embassies of India and Pakistan, their sallow skin and black hair leopard-like, their yellow or rose or green saris exactly as one imagines the robes of Greek statues before the statues had lost their colors. It was easy for me to see the saris as cloth from another planet or satellite; I have written about a sick child who wants "a ship from some near star / To land in the yard and beings to come out / And think to me: 'So this is where you are!' " and about an old man who says that it is his ambition to be the pet of visitors from another planet; as an old reader of science fiction, I am used to looking at the sun red over the hills, the moon white over the ocean, and saying to my wife in a sober voice: "It's like another planet." After I had worked a little longer, the poem began as it begins now:

The saris go by me from the embassies.

Cloth from the moon. Cloth from another planet.
They look back at the leopard like the leopard.

And I . . . This print of mine, that has kept its color
Alive through so many cleanings; this dull null
Navy I wear to work, and wear from work, and so
To my bed, so to my grave, with no
Complaints, no comment: neither from my chief,
The Deputy Chief Assistant, nor his chief—
Only I complain; this serviceable
Body that no sunlight dyes, no hand suffuses
But, dome-shadowed, withering among columns,
Wavy beneath fountains—small, far-off, shining
In the eyes of animals, these beings trapped
As I am trapped but not, themselves, the trap,
Aging, but without knowledge of their age,
Kept safe here, knowing not of death, for death
—Oh, bars of my own body, open, open!

It is almost as if, once all the materials of the poem were there, the middle and end of the poem made themselves, as the beginning seemed to make itself. After the imperative *open, open!* there is a space, and the middle of the poem begins evenly—since her despair is beyond expression—in a statement of accomplished fact: *The world goes by my cage and never sees me.* Inside the mechanical official cage of her life, her body, she lives invisibly; no one feeds this animal, reads out its name, pokes a stick through the bars at it—the cage is empty. She feels that she is even worse off than the other animals of the zoo: they are still wild animals—since they do not know how to change into domesticated animals, beings that are their own cages— and they are surrounded by a world that does not know how to surrender them, still thinks them part of itself. This natural world comes through or over the bars of the cages, on its continual visits to those within: to those who are not machine parts, convicts behind the bars of their penitentiary, but wild animals—the free beasts come to their imprisoned brothers and never know that they are not also free. Written on the back of one page, crossed out, is *Come still, you free*; on the next page this becomes

> The world goes by my cage and never sees me.
> And there come not to me, as come to these,
> The wild ~~ones~~ beasts, sparrows pecking the llamas' grain,
> Pigeons ~~fluttering to~~ settling on the bears' bread, turkey buzzards
> ~~Coming with grace first, then with horror~~ ~~Vulture seizing~~
> Tearing the meat the flies have clouded . . .

In saying mournfully that the wild animals do not come to her as they come to the animals of the zoo, she is wishing for their human equivalent to come to her. But she is right in believing that she has become her own cage—she has changed so much, in her manless, childless, fleshless existence, that her longing wish has inside it an increasing repugnance and horror: the innocent sparrows *pecking* the llamas' grain become larger in the pigeons *settling on* (not *fluttering to*) the bears' bread; and these grow larger and larger, come (with grace first, far off in the sky, but at last with horror) as turkey buzzards seizing, no, *tearing* the meat the flies have clouded. She herself is that stale leftover flesh, nauseating just as what comes to it is horrible and nauseating. The series *pecking, settling on,* and *tearing* has inside it a sexual metaphor: the stale flesh that no one would have is taken at last by the turkey buzzard with his naked red neck and head.

Her own life is so terrible to her that, to change, she is willing to accept even this, changing it as best she can. She says: *Vulture* [it is a euphemism that gives him distance and solemnity], *when you come for the white rat that the foxes left* [to her the rat is so plainly herself that she does not need to say so; the small, white, untouched thing is more accurately what she is than was the clouded meat—but, also, it is euphemistic, more nearly bearable], *take off the red helmet of your head* [the bestiality, the obscene sexuality of the flesh-eating death-bird is really—she hopes or pretends or desperately is sure—merely external, *clothes,* an intentionally frightening war garment like a Greek or Roman helmet], *the black wings that have shadowed me* [she feels that their inhuman colorless darkness has always, like the domes of the inhuman city, shadowed her; the wings are like a black parody of the wings the Swan Brothers wear in the fairy tale, just as the whole costume is like that of the Frog Prince or the other beast-princes of the stories] *and step* [as a human being, not fly as an animal] *to me as* [what you really are under the disguising clothing of red flesh and black feathers] *man*—not the machine part, the domesticated animal that is its own cage, but man as he was first, still must be, is: the animals' natural lord,

> The wild brother at whose feet the white wolves fawn,
> To whose hand of power the great lioness
> Stalks, purring . . .

And she ends the poem when she says to him:

> You know what I was,
> You see what I am: change me, change me!

Here is the whole poem:

THE WOMAN AT THE WASHINGTON ZOO

> The saris go by me from the embassies.
>
> Cloth from the moon. Cloth from another planet.
> They look back at the leopard like the leopard.
>
> And I . . .
>   This print of mine, that has kept its color

Alive through so many cleanings; this dull null
Navy I wear to work, and wear from work, and so
To my bed, so to my grave, with no
Complaints, no comment: neither from my chief,
The Deputy Chief Assistant, nor his chief—
Only I complain; this serviceable
Body that no sunlight dyes, no hand suffuses
But, dome-shadowed, withering among columns,
Wavy beneath fountains—small, far-off, shining
In the eyes of animals, these beings trapped
As I am trapped but not, themselves, the trap,
Aging, but without knowledge of their age,
Kept safe here, knowing not of death, for death
—Oh, bars of my own body, open, open!

The world goes by my cage and never sees me.
And there come not to me, as come to these,
The wild beasts, sparrows pecking the llamas' grain,
Pigeons settling on the bears' bread, buzzards
Tearing the meat the flies have clouded . . .
                                        Vulture,
When you come for the white rat that the foxes left,
Take off the red helmet of your head, the black
Wings that have shadowed me, and step to me as man,
The wild brother at whose feet the white wolves fawn,
To whose hand of power the great lioness
Stalks, purring . . .
                You know what I was,
You see what I am: change me, change me!

[*1960/SHS*]

Some Lines from Whitman

WHITMAN, DICKINSON, AND MELVILLE seem to me the best poets of the nineteenth century here in America. Melville's poetry has been grotesquely underestimated, but of course it is only in the last four or five years that it has been much read; in the long run, in spite of the awkwardness and amateurishness of so much of it, it will surely be thought well of. (In the short run it will probably be thought entirely too well of. Melville is a great poet only in the prose of *Moby Dick.*) Dickinson's poetry has been thoroughly read, and well though undifferentiatingly loved—after a few decades or centuries almost everybody will be able to see through Dickinson to her poems. But something odd has happened to the living changing part of Whitman's reputation: nowadays it is people who are not particularly interested in poetry, people who say that they read a poem for what it says, not for how it says it, who admire Whitman most. Whitman is often written about, either approvingly or disapprovingly, as if he were the Thomas Wolfe of nineteenth-century democracy, the hero of a De Mille movie about Walt Whitman. (People even talk about a war in which Walt Whitman and Henry James chose up sides, to begin with, and in which you and I will go on fighting till the day we die.) All this sort of thing, and all the bad poetry that there of course is in Whitman—for any poet has written enough bad poetry to scare away anybody—has helped to scare away from Whitman most "serious readers of modern poetry." They do not talk of his poems, as a rule, with any real liking or knowledge. Serious readers, people who are ashamed of not knowing all Hopkins by heart, are not at all ashamed to say, "I don't really know Whitman very well." This may harm Whitman in your eyes, they know, but that is a chance that poets have to take. Yet "their" Hopkins, that good critic and great poet, wrote about Whitman, after seeing five or six of his poems in a newspaper review: "I may as well say what I should not otherwise have said, that I always knew in my heart Walt Whitman's mind to be more like my own than any other man's living. As he is a very great scoundrel this is not a very pleasant confession." And Henry James, the leader of "their" side in that awful imaginary war of which I spoke, once read Whitman to Edith Wharton (much as Mozart used to imitate, on the piano, the organ) with such power and solemnity that both sat shaken and silent; it was after this reading that James expressed his regret at Whitman's "too extensive acquaintance with the foreign languages." Almost all the most "original and advanced" poets and critics and readers of the last part of the nineteenth century thought Whitman as original and advanced as themselves, in manner as well as in matter. Can Whitman really be a sort of Thomas Wolfe or Carl Sandburg or Robinson Jeffers or Henry Miller—or a sort of Balzac of poetry, whose every part is crude but whose whole is somehow great? He is not, nor could he be; a poem, like Pope's spider, "lives along the line," and all the dead lines in the world will not make one live poem. As Blake says, "all sublimity is founded on minute discrimination," and it is in these "minute particulars" of Blake's that any poem has its primary existence.

To show Whitman for what he is one does not need to praise or explain or argue, one needs simply to quote. He himself said, "I and mine do not convince by arguments, similes, rhymes, / We convince by our presence." Even a few of his phrases are enough to show us that Whitman was no sweeping rhetorician, but a poet of the greatest and oddest delicacy and originality and sensitivity, so far as words are concerned. This is, after all, the poet who said, "Blind loving wrestling touch, sheath'd hooded sharp-tooth'd touch"; who said, "Smartly attired, countenance smiling, form upright, death under the breast-bones, hell under the skull-bones"; who said, "Agonies are one of my changes of garments"; who saw grass as the "flag of my disposition," saw "the sharp-peak'd farmhouse, with its scallop'd scum and slender shoots from the gutters," heard a plane's "wild ascending lisp," and saw and heard how at the amputation "what is removed drops horribly in a pail." This is the poet for whom the sea was "howler and scooper of storms," reaching out to us with "crooked inviting fingers"; who went "leaping chasms with a pike-pointed staff, clinging to topples of brittle and blue"; who, a runaway slave, saw how "my gore dribs, thinn'd with the ooze of my skin"; who went "lithographing Kronos . . . buying drafts of Osiris"; who stared out at the "little plentiful mannikins skipping around in collars and tail'd coats, / I am aware who they are, (they are positively not worms or fleas)." For he is, at his best, beautifully witty: he says gravely, "I find I incorporate gneiss, coals, long-threaded moss, fruits, grain, esculent roots, / And am stucco'd with quadrupeds and birds all over"; and of these quadrupeds and birds "not one is respectable or unhappy over the whole earth." He calls advice: "Unscrew the locks from the doors! Unscrew the doors from their jambs!" He publishes the results of research: "Having pried through the strata, analyz'd to a hair, counsel'd with doctors and calculated close, / I find no sweeter fat than sticks to my own bones." Everybody remembers how he told the Muse to "cross out please those immensely overpaid accounts, / That matter of Troy and Achilles' wrath, and Aeneas', Odysseus' wanderings," but his account of the arrival of the "illustrious emigré" here in the New World is even better: "Bluff'd not a bit by drainpipe, gasometer, artificial fertilizers, / Smiling and pleas'd with palpable intent to stay, / She's here, install'd amid the kitchenware." Or he sees, like another Bruegel, "the mechanic's wife with the babe at her nipple interceding for every person born, / Three scythes at harvest whizzing in a row from three lusty angels with shirts bagg'd out at their waists, / The snag-toothed hostler with red hair redeeming sins past and to come"—the passage has enough wit not only (in Johnson's phrase) to keep it sweet, but enough to make it believable. He says:

> I project my hat, sit shame-faced, and beg.
>
> Enough! Enough! Enough!
> Somehow I have been stunn'd. Stand back!
> Give me a little time beyond my cuff'd head, slumbers,
>   dreams, gaping,
> I discover myself on the verge of a usual mistake.

There is in such changes of tone as these the essence of wit. And Whitman is even more farfetched than he is witty; he can say about Doubters, in the most improbable and explosive of juxtapositions: "I know every one of you, I know the sea of torment, doubt, despair and unbelief. / How the flukes splash! How they contort rapid as lightning, with splashes and spouts of blood!" Who else would have said about God: "As the hugging and loving bed-fellow sleeps at my side through the night, and withdraws at the break of day with stealthy tread, / Leaving me baskets cover'd with white towels, swelling the house with their plenty"?—the Psalmist himself, his cup running over, would have looked at Whitman with dazzled eyes. (Whitman was persuaded by friends to hide the fact that it was God he was talking about.) He says, "Flaunt of the sunshine I need not your bask— lie over!" This unusual employment of verbs is usual enough in participle-loving Whitman, who also asks you to "look in my face while I snuff the sidle of evening," or tells you, "I effuse my flesh in eddies, and drift it in lacy jags." Here are some typical beginnings of poems: "City of orgies, walks, and joys . . . Not heaving from my ribb'd breast only . . . O take my hand Walt Whitman! Such gliding wonders! Such sights and sounds! Such join'd unended links . . ." He says to the objects of the world, "You have waited, you always wait, you dumb, beautiful ministers"; sees "the sun and stars that float in the open air, / The apple-shaped earth"; says, "O suns— O grass of graves— O perpetual transfers and promotions, / If you do not say anything how can I say anything?" Not many poets have written better, in queerer and more convincing and more individual language, about the world's *gliding wonders*: the phrase seems particularly right for Whitman. He speaks of those "circling rivers the breath," of the "savage old mother incessantly crying, / To the boy's soul's questions sullenly timing, some drown'd secret hissing"—ends a poem, once, "We have voided all but freedom and our own joy." How can one quote enough? If the reader thinks that all this is like Thomas Wolfe he *is* Thomas Wolfe; nothing else could explain it. Poetry like this is as far as possible from the work of any ordinary rhetorician, whose phrases cascade over us like suds of the oldest and most-advertised detergent.

The interesting thing about Whitman's worst language (for, just as few poets have ever written better, few poets have ever written worse) is how unusually absurd, how really ingeniously bad, such language is. I will quote none of the most famous examples; but even a line like *O culpable! I acknowledge. I exposé!* is not anything that you and I could do—only a man with the most extraordinary feel for language, or none whatsoever, could have cooked up Whitman's worst messes. For instance: what other man in all the history of this planet would have said, "I am a habitan of Vienna"? (One has an immediate vision of him as a sort of French-Canadian halfbreed to whom the Viennese are offering, with trepidation, through the bars of a zoological garden, little mounds of whipped cream.) And *enclaircise*—why, it's as bad as *explicate*! We are right to resent his having made up his own horrors, instead of sticking to the ones that we ourselves employ. But when Whitman says, "I dote on myself, there is that lot of me and all so luscious," we should realize that we are not the only ones who are amused. And the queerly bad and merely queer and queerly good will often change into one another without warning: "Hefts of the moving world, at innocent gambols silently rising, freshly exuding, / Scooting obliquely high and low"—not good, but *queer*!—suddenly becomes, "Something I cannot see puts up libidinous prongs, / Seas of bright juice suffuse heaven," and it is sunrise.

But it is not in individual lines and phrases, but in passages of some length, that Whitman is at his best. In the following quotation Whitman has something difficult to express, something that there are many formulas, all bad, for expressing; he expresses it with complete success, in language of the most dazzling originality:

> The orchestra whirls me wider than Uranus flies,
> It wrenches such ardors from me I did not know I possess'd them,
> It sails me, I dab with bare feet, they are lick'd by the indolent waves,
> I am cut by bitter and angry hail, I lose my breath,
> Steep'd amid honey'd morphine, my windpipe throttled in fakes of
>   death,
> At length let up again to feel the puzzle of puzzles,
> And that we call Being.

One hardly knows what to point at—everything works. But *wrenches* and *did not know I possess'd them*; the incredible *it sails me, I dab with bare feet*; *lick'd by the indolent*; *steep'd amid honey'd morphine*; *my windpipe throttled in fakes of death*—no wonder Crane admired Whitman! This originality, as absolute in its way as that of Berlioz's orchestration, is often at Whitman's command:

> I am a dance—play up there! the fit is whirling me fast!
> I am the ever-laughing—it is new moon and twilight,
> I see the hiding of douceurs, I see nimble ghosts whichever way I look,
> Cache and cache again deep in the ground and sea, and where it is
>   neither ground nor sea.
> Well do they do their jobs those journeymen divine,
> Only from me can they hide nothing, and would not if they could,
> I reckon I am their boss and they make me a pet besides,
> And surround me and lead me and run ahead when I walk,

To lift their sunning covers to signify me with stretch'd arms, and
    resume the way;
Onward we move, a gay gang of blackguards! with mirth-shouting
    music and wild-flapping pennants of joy!

If you did not believe Hopkins's remark about Whitman, that *gay gang of blackguards* ought to shake you. Whitman shares Hopkins's passion for "dappled" effects, but he slides in and out of them with ambiguous swiftness. And he has at his command a language of the calmest and most prosaic reality, one that seems to do no more than present:

The little one sleeps in its cradle.
I lift the gauze and look a long time, and silently brush away flies with
    my hand.
The youngster and the red-faced girl turn aside up the bushy hill,
I peeringly view them from the top.

The suicide sprawls on the bloody floor of the bedroom.
I witness the corpse with its dabbled hair, I note where the pistol has
    fallen.

It is like magic: that is, something has been done to us without our knowing how it was done; but if we look at the lines again we see the *gauze, silently, youngster, red-faced, bushy, peeringly, dabbled*—not that this is all we see. "Present! present!" said James; these are presented, put down side by side to form a little "view of life," from the cradle to the last bloody floor of the bedroom. Very often the things presented form nothing but a list:

The pure contralto sings in the organ loft,
The carpenter dresses his plank, the tongue of his foreplane whistles
    its wild ascending lisp,
The married and unmarried children ride home to their Thanksgiving
    dinner,
The pilot seizes the king-pin, he heaves down with a strong arm,
The mate stands braced in the whale-boat, lance and harpoon are
    ready,
The duck-shooter walks by silent and cautious stretches,
The deacons are ordain'd with cross'd hands at the altar,
The spinning-girl retreats and advances to the hum of the big wheel,

The farmer stops by the bars as he walks on a First-day loafe and looks
    at the oats and rye,
The lunatic is carried at last to the asylum a confirm'd case,
(He will never sleep any more as he did in the cot in his mother's bed-
    room;)
The jour printer with gray head and gaunt jaws works at his case,
He turns his quid of tobacco while his eyes blur with the manuscript,
The malform'd limbs are tied to the surgeon's table,
What is removed drops horribly in a pail . . .

It is only a list—but what a list! And how delicately, in what differ-
ent ways—likeness and opposition and continuation and climax and
anticlimax—the transitions are managed, whenever Whitman wants
to manage them. Notice them in the next quotation, another "mere
list":

The bride unrumples her white dress, the minute-hand of the clock
    moves slowly,
The opium-eater reclines with rigid head and just-open'd lips,
The prostitute draggles her shawl, her bonnet bobs on her tipsy and
    pimpled neck . . .

The first line is joined to the third by *unrumples* and *draggles, white
dress* and *shawl*; the second to the third by *rigid head, bobs, tipsy,
neck*; the first to the second by *slowly, just-open'd,* and the slowing-
down of time in both states. And occasionally one of these lists is
metamorphosed into something we have no name for; the man who
would call the next quotation a mere list—anybody will feel this—
would boil his babies up for soap:

Ever the hard unsunk ground,
Ever the eaters and drinkers, ever the upward and downward sun,
Ever myself and my neighbors, refreshing, wicked, real,
Ever the old inexplicable query, ever that thorned thumb, that breath
    of itches and thirsts,
Ever the vexer's hoot! hoot! till we find where the sly one hides and
    bring him forth,
Ever the sobbing liquid of life,
Ever the bandage under the chin, ever the trestles of death.

Sometimes Whitman will take what would generally be consid-
ered an unpromising subject (in this case, a woman peeping at men

in bathing naked) and treat it with such tenderness and subtlety and
understanding that we are ashamed of ourselves for having thought
it unpromising, and murmur that Chekhov himself couldn't have
treated it better:

> Twenty-eight young men bathe by the shore,
> Twenty-eight young men and all so friendly,
> Twenty-eight years of womanly life and all so lonesome.
>
> She owns the fine house by the rise of the bank,
> She hides handsome and richly drest aft the blinds of the window.
>
> Which of the young men does she like the best?
> Ah the homeliest of them is beautiful to her.
>
> Where are you off to, lady? for I see you,
> You splash in the water there, yet stay stock still in your room.
> Dancing and laughing along the beach came the twenty-ninth
>   bather,
> The rest did not see her, but she saw them and loved them.
>
> The beards of the young men glistened with wet, it ran from their
>   long hair,
> Little streams pass'd all over their bodies.
>
> An unseen hand also pass'd over their bodies,
> It descended tremblingly from their temples and ribs.
>
> The young men float on their backs, their white bellies bulge to the
>   sun, they do not ask who seizes fast to them,
> They do not know who puffs and declines with pendant and bending
>   arch,
> They do not know whom they souse with spray.

And in the same poem (that "Song of Myself" in which one
finds half his best work) the writer can say of a sea-fight:

> Stretched and still lies the midnight,
> Two great hulls motionless on the breast of the darkness,
> Our vessel riddled and slowly sinking, preparations to pass to the one
>   we have conquer'd,

The captain on the quarter-deck coldly giving his orders through a
    countenance white as a sheet,
Near by the corpse of the child that serv'd in the cabin,
The dead face of an old salt with long white hair and carefully curl'd
    whiskers,
The flames spite of all that can be done flickering aloft and below,
The husky voices of the two or three officers yet fit for duty,
Formless stacks of bodies and bodies by themselves, dabs of flesh upon
    the masts and spars,
Cut of cordage, dangle of rigging, slight shock of the soothe of waves,
Black and impassive guns, litter of powder-parcels, strong scent,
A few large stars overhead, silent and mournful shining,
Delicate snuffs of sea-breeze, smells of sedgy grass and fields by the
    shore, death-messages given in charge to survivors,
The hiss of the surgeon's knife, the gnawing teeth of his saw,
Wheeze, cluck, swash of falling blood, short wild scream, and long,
    dull, tapering groan,
These so, these irretrievable.

There are faults in this passage, and they *do not matter*: the serious truth, the complete realization of these last lines make us remember that few poets have shown more of the tears of things, and the joy of things, and of the reality beneath either tears or joy. Even Whitman's most general or political statements sometimes are good: everybody knows his "When liberty goes out of a place it is not the first to go, nor the second or third to go, / It waits for all the rest to go, it is the last"; these sentences about the United States just before the Civil War may be less familiar:

Are those really Congressmen? are those the great Judges? is that the
    President?
Then I will sleep awhile yet, for I see that these States sleep, for
    reasons;
(With gathering murk, with muttering thunder and lambent shoots we
    all duly awake,
South, North, East, West, inland and seaboard, we will surely awake.)

How well, with what firmness and dignity and command, Whitman does such passages! And Whitman's doubts that he has done them or anything else well—ah, there is nothing he does better:

The best I had done seemed to me blank and suspicious,
My great thoughts as I supposed them, were they not in reality
     meagre?
I am he who knew what it was to be evil,
I too knitted the old knot of contrariety . . .
Saw many I loved in the street or ferry-boat or public assembly, yet
     never told them a word,
Lived the same life with the rest, the same old laughing, gnawing,
     sleeping,
Played the part that still looks back on the actor and actress,
The same old role, the role that is what we make it . . .

Whitman says once that the "look of the bay mare shames silliness out of me." This is true — sometimes it is true; but more often the silliness and affection and cant and exaggeration are there shamelessly, the Old Adam that was in Whitman from the beginning and the awful new one that he created to keep it company. But as he says, "I know perfectly well my own egotism, / Know my omnivorous lines and must not write any less." He says over and over that there are in him good and bad, wise and foolish, anything at all and its antonym, and he is telling the truth; there is in him almost everything in the world, so that one responds to him, willingly or unwillingly, almost as one does to the world, that world which makes the hairs of one's flesh stand up, which seems both evil beyond any rejection and wonderful beyond any acceptance. We cannot help seeing that there is something absurd about any judgment we make of its whole — for there is no "point of view" at which we can stand to make the judgment, and the moral categories that mean most to us seem no more to apply to its whole than our spatial or temporal or causal categories seem to apply to its beginning or its end. (But we need no arguments to make our judgments seem absurd — we feel their absurdity without argument.) In some like sense Whitman is a world, a waste with, here and there, systems blazing at random out of the darkness. Only an innocent and rigidly methodical mind will reject it for this disorganization, particularly since there are in it, here and there, little systems as beautifully and astonishingly organized as the rings and satellites of Saturn:

I understand the large hearts of heroes,
The courage of present times and all times,
How the skipper saw the crowded and rudderless wreck of the steam-
     ship, and Death chasing it up and down the storm,

How he knuckled tight and gave not back an inch, and was faithful of
    days and faithful of nights,
And chalked in large letters on a board, Be of good cheer, we will not
    desert you;
How he follow'd with them and tack'd with them three days and
    would not give it up,
How he saved the drifting company at last,
How the lank loose-gown'd women looked when boated from the side
    of their prepared graves,
How the silent old-faced infants and the lifted sick, and the sharp-
    lipp'd unshaved men;
All this I swallow, it tastes good, I like it well, it becomes mine,
I am the man, I suffered, I was there.

In the last lines of this quotation Whitman has reached—as great writers always reach—a point at which criticism seems not only unnecessary but absurd: these lines are so good that even admiration feels like insolence, and one is ashamed of anything that one can find to say about them. How anyone can dismiss or accept patronizingly the man who wrote them, I do not understand.

The enormous and apparent advantages of form, of omission and selection, of the highest degree of organization, are accompanied by important disadvantages—and there are far greater works than *Leaves of Grass* to make us realize this. But if we compare Whitman with that very beautiful poet Alfred Tennyson, the most skillful of all Whitman's contemporaries, we are at once aware of how limiting Tennyson's forms have been, of how much Tennyson has had to leave out, even in those discursive poems where he is trying to put everything in. Whitman's poems *represent* his world and himself much more satisfactorily than Tennyson's do his. In the past a few poets have both formed and represented, each in the highest degree; but in modern times what controlling, organizing, selecting poet has created a world with as much in it as Whitman's, a world that so plainly *is* the world? Of all modern poets he has, quantitatively speaking, "the most comprehensive soul"—and, qualitatively, a most comprehensive and comprehending one, with charities and concessions and qualifications that are rare in any time.

"Do I contradict myself? Very well then I contradict myself," wrote Whitman, as everybody remembers, and this is not naïve, or something he got from Emerson, or a complacent pose. When you organize one of the contradictory elements out of your work of art, you are getting rid not just of it, but of the contradiction of which it was a part; and it is the contradictions in works of art which make them able to represent to us—as logical and methodical generalizations cannot—our world and our selves, which are also full of contradictions. In Whitman we do not get the controlled, compressed, seemingly concordant contradictions of the great lyric poets, of a poem like, say, Hardy's "During Wind and Rain"; Whitman's contradictions are sometimes announced openly, but are more often scattered at random throughout the poems. For instance: Whitman specializes in ways of saying that there is in some sense (a very Hegelian one, generally) no evil—he says a hundred times that evil is not Real; but he also specializes in making lists of the evil of the world, lists of an unarguable reality. After his minister has recounted "the rounded catalogue divine complete," Whitman comes home and puts down what has been left out: "the countless (nineteen-twentieths) low and evil, crude and savage . . . the barren soil, the evil men, the slag and hideous rot." He ends another such catalogue with the plain unexcusing "All these—all meanness and agony without end I sitting look out upon, / See, hear, and am silent." Whitman offered himself to everybody, and said brilliantly and at length what a good thing he was offering:

> Sure as the most certain sure, plumb in the uprights, well entretied,
>> braced in the beams,
> Stout as a horse, affectionate, haughty, electrical,
> I and this mystery here we stand.

Just for oddness, characteristicalness, differentness, what more could you ask in a letter of recommendation? (Whitman sounds as if he were recommending a house—haunted, but what foundations!) But after a few pages he is oddly different:

> Apart from the pulling and hauling stands what I am,
> Stands amused, complacent, compassionating, idle, unitary,
> Looks down, is erect, or bends an arm on an impalpable certain rest
> Looking with side curved head curious what will come next,
> Both in and out of the game and watching and wondering at it.

Tamburlaine is already beginning to sound like Hamlet: the employer feels uneasily, "Why, I might as well hire myself . . ." And, a few pages later, Whitman puts down in ordinary-sized type, in the middle of the page, this warning to any *new person drawn toward me*:

Do you think I am trusty and faithful?
Do you see no further than this façade, this smooth and tolerant
    manner of me?
Do you suppose yourself advancing on real ground toward a real heroic
    man?
Have you no thought O dreamer that it may be all maya, illusion?

Having wonderful dreams, telling wonderful lies, was a temptation Whitman could never resist; but telling the truth was a temptation he could never resist, either. When you buy him you know what you are buying. And only an innocent and solemn and systematic mind will condemn him for his contradictions: Whitman's catalogues of evils represent realities, and his denials of their reality represent other realities, of feeling and intuition and desire. If he is faithless to logic, to Reality As It Is—whatever that is—he is faithful to the feel of things, to reality as it seems; this is all that a poet has to be faithful to, and philosophers have been known to leave logic and Reality for it.

Whitman is more coordinate and parallel than anybody, is *the* poet of parallel present participles, of twenty verbs joined by a single subject: all this helps to give his work its feeling of raw hypnotic reality, of being that world which also streams over us joined only by *ands*, until we supply the subordinating conjunctions; and since as children we see the *ands* and not the *becauses*, this method helps to give Whitman some of the freshness of childhood. How inexhaustibly interesting the world is in Whitman! Arnold all his life kept wishing that he could see the world "with a plainness as near, as flashing" as that with which Moses and Rebekah and the Argonauts saw it. He asked with elegiac nostalgia, "Who can see the green earth any more / As she was by the sources of Time?"—and all the time there was somebody alive who saw it so, as plain and near and flashing, and with a kind of calm, pastoral, Biblical dignity and elegance as well, sometimes. The *thereness* and *suchness* of the world are incarnate in Whitman as they are in few other writers.

They might have put on his tombstone WALT WHITMAN: HE HAD HIS NERVE. He is the rashest, the most inexplicable and unlikely—the most impossible, one wants to say—of poets. He somehow *is* in a class by himself, so that one compares him with other poets about as readily as one compares *Alice* with other books. (Even his free verse has a completely different effect from anybody else's.) Who would think of comparing him with Tennyson or Browning or Arnold or Baudelaire?—it is Homer, or the sagas, or something far away and long ago, that comes to one's mind only to be dismissed; for sometimes Whitman *is* epic, just as *Moby Dick* is, and it surprises us to be able to use truthfully this word that we have misused so many times. Whitman *is* grand, and elevated, and comprehensive, and real with an astonishing reality, and many other things—the critic points at his qualities in despair and wonder, all method failing, and simply calls them by their names. And the range of these qualities is the most extraordinary thing of all. We can surely say about him, "He was a man, take him for all in all. I shall not look upon his like again"— and wish that people had seen this and not tried to be his like: one Whitman is miracle enough, and when he comes again it will be the end of the world.

I have said so little about Whitman's faults because they are so plain: baby critics who have barely learned to complain of the lack of ambiguity in *Peter Rabbit* can tell you all that is wrong with *Leaves of Grass.* But a good many of my readers must have felt that it is ridiculous to write an essay about the obvious fact that Whitman is a great poet. It is ridiculous—just as, in 1851, it would have been ridiculous for anyone to write an essay about the obvious fact that Pope was no "classic of our prose" but a great poet. Critics have to spend half their time reiterating whatever ridiculously obvious things their age or the critics of their age have found it necessary to forget: they say despairingly, at parties, that Wordsworth is a great poet, and *won't* bore you, and tell Mr. Leavis that Milton is a great poet whose deposition *hasn't* been accomplished with astonishing ease by a few words from Eliot . . . There is something essentially ridiculous about critics, anyway: what is good is good without our saying so, and beneath all our majesty we know this.

Let me finish by mentioning another quality of Whitman's—a quality, delightful to me, that I have said nothing of. If someday a tourist notices, among the ruins of New York City, a copy of *Leaves of Grass,* and stops and picks it up and reads some lines in it, she will be able to say to herself: "How very American! If he and his country had not existed, it would have been impossible to imagine them."

[*1952/PA*]

Reflections
on Wallace Stevens

LET ME BEGIN WITH a quotation from Stendhal: " 'What I find completely lacking in all these people,' thought Lucien, 'is the unexpected . . .' He was reduced to philosophizing." In my quotation Lucien stands for Stevens, "these people" for America and Business, "the unexpected" for Culture, the exotic, the past, the Earth-minus-America; "philosophizing" stands for, alas! philosophizing . . . But before Stevens was reduced to it, he drew the unexpected from a hundred springs. There has never been a travel poster like *Harmonium*: how many of its readers must have sold what they had, given the money to steamship agents, and gone to spend the rest of their lives in Lhasa. Yet there was nothing really unusual in what Stevens felt. To have reached, in 1900, in the United States, the age of twenty-one, or fifteen, or twelve—as Stevens and Pound and Eliot did—this was so hard a thing for poets, went so thoroughly against the grain, that they emigrated as soon as they could, or stayed home and wrote poems in which foreignness, pastness, is itself a final good. "But how absurd!" a part of anyone protests. "Didn't they realize that, to a poet, New York City means just as much as Troy and Jerusalem and all the rest of those *immensely overpaid accounts* that Whitman begged the Muse, *install'd amid the kitchenware*, to cross out?" They didn't realize it; if one realizes it, one is not a poet. The accounts have been overpaid too many years for people ever to stop paying; to keep on paying them is to be human. To be willing to give up Life for the last local slice of it, for all those Sears, Roebuck catalogues which, as businessmen and generals say, would be the most effective propaganda we could possibly drop on the Russians—this is a blinded chauvinism, a provincialism in space and time, which is even worse than that vulgar exoticism which disregards both what we have kept and what we are unique in possessing, which gives up *Moby Dick* for the Journals of André Gide. Our most disastrous lacks—delicacy, awe, order, natural magnificence and piety, "the exquisite errors of time," and the rest; everything that is neither bought, sold, nor imagined on Sunset Boulevard or in Times Square; everything the absence of which made Lorca think Hell a city very like New York—these things were the necessities of Stevens's spirit. Some of his poems set about supplying these lacks—from other times and places, from the underlying order of things, from the imagination; other poems look with mockery and despair at the time and place that cannot supply them, that do not even desire to supply them; other poems reason or seem to reason about their loss, about their nature, about their improbable restoration. His poetry is obsessed with lack, a lack at last almost taken for granted, that he himself automatically supplies; if sometimes he has restored by imagination or abstraction or re-creation, at other times he has restored by collection, almost as J. P. Morgan did—Stevens likes something, buys it (at the expense of a little spirit), and ships it home in a poem. The feeling of being a leisured, cultivated, and sympathetic tourist (in a time-machine, sometimes) is essential to much of his work; most of his contact with values is at the distance of knowledge and regret—an aesthetician's or an archaeologist's contact with a painting, not a painter's.

Many of Stevens's readers have resented his—so to speak—spending his time collecting old porcelain: "If old things are what you want," they felt, "why don't you collect old Fords or Locomobiles or Stutz Bearcats, or old Mother Bloors, right here at home?" But, for an odd reason, people have never resented the cruel truths or half-truths he told them about the United States. Once upon a time Richard Dehmel's poems, accused of obscenity, were acquitted on the grounds that they were incomprehensible—and almost exactly this happened to Stevens's home-truths. Yet they were plain, sometimes. Looking at General Jackson confronting the "mockers, the mickey mockers," Stevens decided what the "American Sublime" is: the sublime "comes down / To the spirit itself, / The spirit and space, / The empty spirit / In vacant space." Something like this is true, perhaps, always and everywhere; yet it is a hard truth for your world to have reduced you to: it is no wonder the poem ends, "What wine does one drink? / What bread does one eat?" And in "The Common Life" the church steeple is a "black line beside a white line," not different in any way from "the stack of the electric plant"; in the "flat air," the "morbid light," a man is "a result, a demonstration"; the men "have no shadows / And the women only one side." We live "no longer on the ancient cake of seed, / The almond and deep fruit . . . We feast on human heads"; the table is a mirror and the diners eat reflections of themselves. "The steeples are empty and so are the people," he says in "Loneliness in Jersey City"; the poem is full of a despairing frivol- ity, as Stevens looks from Room 2903 out over that particular coun- tryside which, I think, God once sent angels to destroy, but which the angels thought worse than anything they could do to it. And "In Oklahoma, / Bonnie and Josie, / Dressed in calico, / Danced around a stump. / They cried, / 'Ohoyaho, / Ohoo' . . . / Celebrating the marriage / Of flesh and air." Without what's superfluous, the excess of the spirit, man is a poor, bare, forked animal. In "Country Words" the poet sits under the willows of exile, and sings "like a cuckoo clock" to Belshazzar, that "putrid rock, / putrid pillar of a putrid people"; he sings "an old rebellious song, / An edge of song that never clears." But if it should clear, if the cloud that hangs over his heart and mind should lift, it would be because Belshazzar heard and understood:

> What is it that my feeling seeks?
> I know from all the things it touched
> And left beside and left behind.
> It wants the diamond pivot bright.
> It wants Belshazzar reading right
> The luminous pages on his knee,
> Of being, more than birth and death.
> It wants words virile with his breath.

If this intellectual is "isolated," it is not because he wants to be . . . But Stevens's most despairing, amusing, and exactly realized complaint is "Disillusionment of Ten O'Clock":

> The houses are haunted
> By white nightgowns.
> None are green,
> Or purple with green rings,
> Or green with yellow rings,
> Or yellow with blue rings.
> None of them are strange,
> With socks of lace

And beaded ceintures.
People are not going
To dream of baboons and periwinkles.
Only, here and there, an old sailor,
Drunk and asleep in his boots,
Catches tigers
In red weather.

Any schoolboy (of the superior Macaulayish breed) more or less feels what this poem means, but it is interesting to look at one or two details. Why *ten o'clock*? They have all gone to bed early, like good sensible machines; and the houses' ghosts, now, are only nightgowns, the plain white nightgowns of the Common Man, Economic Man, Rational Man—pure commonplace, no longer either individual or strange or traditional; and the dreams are as ordinary as the nightgowns. Here and there a drunken and disreputable *old sailor* still lives in the original reality (he doesn't dream of catching, he *catches*): *sailor* to bring in old-fashioned Europe, old-fashioned Asia, the old-fashioned ocean; *old* to bring in the past, to make him a dying survival. What indictment of the Present has ever compared, for flat finality, with "People are not going / To dream of baboons and periwinkles"? Yet isn't this poem ordinarily considered a rather nonsensical and Learish poem?

It is not until later that Stevens writes much about what America has in common with the rest of the world; then he splits everything differently, and contrasts with the past of America and of the world their present. In *Harmonium* he still loves America best when he can think of it as wilderness, naturalness, pure potentiality (he treats with especial sympathy Negroes, Mexican Indians, and anybody else he can consider wild); and it is this feeling that is behind the conclusion of "Sunday Morning":

She hears, upon that water without sound,
A voice that cries, "The tomb in Palestine
Is not the porch of spirits lingering.
It is the grave of Jesus, where he lay."
We live in an old chaos of the sun,
Or old dependency of day and night,
Or island solitude, unsponsored, free,
Of that wide water, inescapable.
Deer walk upon our mountains, and the quail
Whistle about us their spontaneous cries;

Sweet berries ripen in the wilderness;
And, in the isolation of the sky,
At evening, casual flocks of pigeons make
Ambiguous undulations as they sink
Downward to darkness, on extended wings.

Here—in the last purity and refinement of the grand style, as perfect, in its calm transparency, as the best of Wordsworth—is the last wilderness, come upon so late in the history of mankind that it is no longer seen as the creation of God, but as the Nature out of which we evolve; man without myth, without God, without anything but the universe which has produced him, is given an extraordinarily pure and touching grandeur in these lines—lines as beautiful, perhaps, as any in American poetry. Yet Stevens himself nearly equals them in two or three parts of *Esthétique du Mal*, the best of his later poems; there are in *Harmonium* six or eight of the most beautiful poems an American has written; and a book like *Parts of a World* is delightful as a whole, even though it contains no single poem that can compare with the best in *Harmonium*. But *Auroras of Autumn*, Stevens's last book, is a rather different affair. One sees in it the distinction, intelligence, and easy virtuosity of a master—but it would take more than these to bring to life so abstract, so monotonous, so overwhelmingly *characteristic* a book. Poems like these are, always, the product of a long process of evolution; in Stevens's case the process has been particularly interesting.

———

The habit of philosophizing in poetry—or of seeming to philosophize, of using a philosophical tone, images, constructions, of having quasi-philosophical daydreams—has been unfortunate for Stevens. Poetry is a bad medium for philosophy. Everything in the philosophical poem has to satisfy irreconcilable requirements: for instance, the last demand that we should make of philosophy (that it be interesting) is the first we make of a poem; the philosophical poet has an elevated and methodical, but forlorn and absurd air as he works away at his flying tank, his sewing machine that also plays the piano. (One thinks of Richard Wilbur's graceful "Tom Swift has vanished too, / Who worked at none but wit's expense, / Putting dirigibles together, / Out in the yard, in the quiet weather, / Whistling behind Tom Sawyer's fence.") When the first thing that Stevens can find to say of the Supreme Fiction is that "it must be *abstract*," the reader protests, "Why, even Hegel called it a *concrete* universal"; the poet's medium, words, is abstract to begin with, and it is only his unique organization of the words that forces the poem, generalizations and all, over into the concreteness and singularity that it exists for. But Stevens has the weakness—a terrible one for a poet, a steadily increasing one in Stevens—of thinking of particulars as primarily illustrations of general truths, or else as aesthetic, abstracted objects, simply there to be contemplated; he often treats things or lives so that they seem no more than generalizations of an unprecedentedly low order. But surely a poet *has* to treat the concrete as primary, as something far more than an instance, a hue to be sensed, a member of a laudable category—for him it is always the generalization whose life is derived, whose authority is delegated. Goethe said, quite as if he were talking about Stevens: "It makes a great difference whether the poet seeks the particular in relation to the universal or contemplates the universal in the particular . . . [In the first case] the particular functions as an example, as an instance of the universal; but the second indeed represents the very nature of poetry. He who grasps this particular as living essence also encompasses the universal."

As a poet Stevens has every gift but the dramatic. It is the lack of immediate contact with lives that hurts his poetry more than anything else, that has made it easier and easier for him to abstract, to philosophize, to treat the living dog that wags its tail and bites you as the "canoid patch" of the epistemologist analyzing that great problem, the world; as the "cylindrical arrangement of brown and white" of the aesthetician analyzing that great painting, the world. Stevens knows better, often for poems at a time:

> At dawn,
> The paratroopers fall and as they fall
> They mow the lawn. A vessel sinks in waves
> Of people, as big bell-billows from its bell
> Bell-bellow in the village steeple. Violets,
> Great tufts, spring up from buried houses
> Of poor, dishonest people, for whom the steeple,
> Long since, rang out farewell, farewell, farewell.

This is a map with people living on it. Yet it is fatally easy for the scale to become too small, the distance too great, and us poor, dishonest people no more than data to be manipulated.

As one reads Stevens's later poetry one keeps thinking that he needs to be possessed by subjects, to be shaken out of himself, to have his subject individualize his poem; one remembers longingly how much more individuation there was in *Harmonium*—when you're young you try to be methodical and philosophical, but reality keeps breaking in. The best of *Harmonium* exists at a level that it is hard to rise above; and Stevens has had only faintly and intermittently the dramatic insight, the capacity to be obsessed by lives, actions, subject matter, the chameleon's shameless interest in everything but itself, that could have broken up the habit and order and general sobering matter-of-factness of age. Often, nowadays, he seems disastrously set in his own ways, a fossil imprisoned in the rock of himself—the best marble but, still, marble.

All his *tunk-a-tunks*, his *hoo-goo-boos*—those mannered, manu-factured, individual, uninteresting little sound-inventions—how typ-ical they are of the lecture-style of the English philosopher, who makes grunts or odd noises, uses homely illustrations, and quotes day in and day out from *Alice,* in order to give what he says some appear-ance of that raw reality it so plainly and essentially lacks. These "toot-ings at the wedding of the soul" are fun for the tooter, but get as dreary for the reader as do all the foreign words—a few of these are brilliant, a few more pleasant, and the rest a disaster: "one cannot help deploring his too extensive acquaintance with the foreign languages," as Henry James said, of Walt Whitman, to Edith Wharton.

Stevens is never more philosophical, abstract, rational, than when telling us to put our faith in nothing but immediate sensations, perceptions, aesthetic particulars; for this is only a generalization of-fered for assent, and where in the ordinary late poem are the real particulars of the world—the people, the acts, the lives—for us to put our faith in? And when Stevens makes a myth to hold together aesthetic particulars and generalizations, it is as if one were revisited by the younger Saint-Simon, Comte, and that actress who played Reason to Robespierre's approving glare; Stevens's myths spring not from the soil but from the clouds, the arranged, scrubbed, reasoning clouds in someone's head. He is too rational and composedly fanciful a being to make up a myth—one could as easily imagine his starting a cult in Los Angeles. When one reads most eighteenth-century writ-ing one is aware of some man of good sense and good taste and good will at the bottom of everything and everybody; but in Stevens—who is always swinging between baroque and rococo, and reminds one of the eighteenth century in dozens of ways—this being at the bottom of everything is cultivated and appreciative and rational out of all reason: the Old Adam in everybody turns out to be not Robinson Crusoe but Bernard Berenson.

Metastasio began as an improviser and ended as a poet; as one reads the average poem in *Auroras of Autumn* one feels that the opposite has been happening to Stevens. A poem begins, revealingly: "An exercise in viewing the world. / On the motive! But one looks at the sea / As one improvises, on the piano." And not the sea only. One reads a book like this with odd mixed pleasure, not as if one were reading poems but as if one were reading some *Travel-Diary of an Aesthetician*, who works more for pleasure than for truth, puts in entries regularly, and gives one continual pleasure in incidentals, in good phrases, interesting ideas, delicate perceptions, but who hardly tries to subordinate his Method to the requirements of any particular situation or material. The individual poems are less and less differentiated; the process is always more evident than what is being processed; everything is so familiarly contrived by will and habit and rule of thumb (for improvisation, as Virgil Thomson says, "among all the compositional techniques is the one most servile to rules of thumb") that it does not seem to matter exactly which being is undergoing these immemorial metamorphoses. Stevens's passagework, often, is so usual that we can't believe past the form to the matter: what truth could survive these pastry-cook's, spun-sugar, parallel qualifications?

> It was like sudden time in a world without time,
> This world, this place, the street in which I was,
> Without time: as that which is not has not time,
> Is not, or is of what there was, is full . . .

And on the shelf below:

> It was nowhere else, it was there and because
> It was nowhere else, its place had to be supposed,
> Itself had to be supposed, a thing supposed
> In a place supposed, a thing that reached
> In a place that he reached . . .

It is G. E. Moore at the spinet. And it looks worst of all when one compares it with a passage from that classic of our prose, that generalizer from an Age of Reason, that hapless victim of Poetic Diction, that— but let me quote:

> As Hags hold Sabbaths, less for joy than spite,
> So these their merry, miserable Night;
> Still round and round the Ghosts of Beauty glide,
> And haunt the places where their Honor died.

> See how the World its Veterans rewards!
> A Youth of Frolics, an old Age of Cards;
> Fair to no purpose, artful to no end,
> Young without Lovers, old without a Friend;
> A Fop their Passion, but their Prize a Sot;
> Alive, ridiculous, and dead, forgot!

The immediacy and precision and particularity, the live touch of things, the beauty that exists in precarious perfection in so many poems in *Harmonium*—

> the beauty
> Of the moonlight
> Falling there,
> Falling
> As sleep falls
> In the innocent air—

this, at last, is lost in rhetoric, in elaboration and artifice and contrivance, in an absolutely ecumenical Method of seeing and thinking and expressing, in *craftsmanship*: why has no loving soul ever given Stevens a copy of that *Principles of Art* in which Collingwood argues at length—many people might say *proves*—that art is not a craft at all? (I hardly dare to quote one great poet's even more sweeping "But I deny that poetry is an art.") In *Auroras of Autumn* one sees almost everything through a shining fog, a habitualness not just of style but of machinery, perception, anything: the green spectacles show us a world of green spectacles; and the reader, staring out into this Eden, thinks timidly: "But it's all so *monotonous*." When Marx said that he wasn't a Marxist he meant, I suppose, that he himself was not one of his own followers, could not be taken in by the prolongation and simplification of his own beliefs that a disciple would make and believe; and there is nothing a successful artist needs to pray so much as: "Lord, don't let me keep on believing *only this*; let me have the courage of something besides my own convictions; let me escape at last from the maze of myself, from the hardening quicksilver womb of my own characteristicalness."

———

I have felt as free as posterity to talk in this way of Stevens's weaknesses, of this later mold in which he has cast himself, since he seems to me—and seems to my readers, I am sure—one of the true poets of our century, someone whom the world will keep on reading just as it keeps on listening to Vivaldi or Scarlatti, looking at Tiepolo or Poussin. His best poems are the poetry of a man fully human—of someone sympathetic, magnanimous, both brightly and deeply intelligent; the poems see, feel, and think with equal success; they treat with mastery that part of existence which allows of mastery, and experience the rest of it with awe or sadness or delight. Minds of this quality of genius, of this breadth and delicacy of understanding, are a link between us and the past, since they are, for us, the past made living; and they are our surest link with the future, since they are the part of us which the future will know. As one feels the elevation and sweep and disinterestedness, the thoughtful truthfulness of the best sections of a poem like *Esthétique du Mal,* one is grateful for, over-awed by, this poetry that knows so well the size and age of the world; that reminds us, as we sit in chairs produced from the furniture exhibitions of the Museum of Modern Art, of that immemorial order or disorder upon which our present scheme of things is a monomolecular film; that counsels us—as Santayana wrote of Spinoza—"to say to those little gnostics, to those circumnavigators of being: *I do not believe you; God is great.*" Many of the poems look grayly out at "the immense detritus of a world / That is completely waste, that moves from waste / To waste, out of the hopeless waste of the past / Into a hopeful waste to come"; but more of the poems see the unspoilable delights, the inexhaustible interests of existence—when you have finished reading Stevens's best poems you remember once more that man is not only the jest and riddle of the world, but the glory.

Some of my readers may feel about all this, "But how can you reconcile what you say with the fact that *Auroras of Autumn* is not a good book? Shouldn't the Mature poet be producing late masterpieces even better than the early ones?" (They might ask the same thing about *The Cocktail Party.*) All such questions show how necessary it is to think of the poet as somebody who has prepared himself to be visited by a daemon, as a sort of accident-prone worker to whom poems happen—for otherwise we *expect* him to go on writing good poems, better poems, and this is the one thing you cannot expect even of good poets, much less of anybody else. Good painters in their sixties may produce good pictures as regularly as an orchard produces apples; but Planck is a great scientist because he made one discovery as a young man—and I can remember reading in a mathematician's memoirs a sentence composedly recognizing the fact that, since the writer was now past forty, he was unlikely ever again to do any important creative work in mathematics. A man who is a good poet at forty *may* turn out to be a good poet at sixty; but he is more likely to have stopped writing poems, to be doing exercises in his own manner, or to have reverted to whatever commonplaces were popular when he was young. A good poet is someone who manages, in a lifetime of standing out in thunderstorms, to be struck by lightning five or six times; a dozen or two dozen times and he is great.

[1951/PA]

Her Shield

MARIANNE MOORE'S POEMS judge what is said about them almost as much as poems can, so that even one's praise is hesitant, uncertain of its welcome. As her readers know, her father used to say, "The deepest feeling always shows itself in silence; / not in silence, but restraint"; and she herself has said, "If tributes cannot / be implicit, give me diatribes and the fragrance of iodine." Quotation is a tribute as near implicit as I can get; so I will quote where I can, and criticize where I can't. (My father used to say, "The deepest feeling always shows itself in scratches; / not in scratches, but in iodine.") And I have found one little hole through which to creep to criticism, Miss Moore's "If he must give an opinion it is permissible that the / critic should know what he likes." I know; and to have to give an opinion is to be human. Besides, I have never believed her father about feeling; "entire affection hateth nicer hands," as Spenser says, and I should hate to trust to "armor's undermining modesty / instead of innocent depravity." And that last quotation isn't Spenser.

It felt queer to see all over again this year, in English reviews of Miss Moore's *Collected Poems*, those sentences—sentences once so familiarly American—saying that she isn't a poet at all. I can understand how anyone looking into her book for the first time, and coming on an early passage like "Disbelief and conscious fastidiousness were the staple / ingredients in its / disinclination to move. Finally its hardihood was / not proof against its / proclivity to more fully appraise such bits / of food as the stream / bore counter to it," might make this mistake; but what goes on in the mind that experiences

And Bluebeard's Tower above the coral-reefs,
the magic mouse-trap closing on all points of the compass,
capping like petrified surf the furious azure of the bay,
where there is no dust, and life is like a lemon-leaf,
a green piece of tough translucent parchment,

and, dissatisfied, decides that it is prose? Aren't these lines (ordinary enough lines for her) the work of someone even at first glance a poet, with the poet's immemorial power to make the things of this world seen and felt and living in words? And even if the rhythms were those of prose—these are not—wouldn't we rather have poetry in prose than prose in verse? I wouldn't trade *Prudence is a rich, ugly old maid courted by Incapacity* for some epics.

Nowadays, over here, Miss Moore wins all the awards there are; but it took several decades for what public there is to get used to her—she was, until very recently, read unreasonably little and praised reasonably much. Even the circumstances hindered. The dust jacket of her *Collected Poems* says: "Since the former volumes are out of print many readers will now, for the first time, have the opportunity to own the treasure of her poetry." This *is* a felicitous way for a publishing firm to say that it has allowed to remain out of print, for many years, most of the poetry of one of the great living poets. Miss Moore's prose-seeming, matter-of-factly rhythmed syllabic verse, the odd look most of her poems have on the page (their unusual stanzaic patterns, their words divided at the ends of lines, give many of them a consciously, sometimes misleadingly experimental or modernist look), their almost ostentatious lack of transitions and explanations, the absence of romance and rhetoric, of acceptedly Poetic airs and properties, did most to keep conservative readers from liking her poetry. Her restraint, her lack—her wonderful lack—of arbitrary intensity or violence, of sweep and overwhelmingness and size, of cant, of sociological significance, and so on, made her unattractive both to some of the conservative readers of our age and to some of the advanced ones. Miss Moore was for a long time (in her own phrase about something else) "like Henry James 'damned by the public for decorum,' / not decorum but restraint." She demands, "When I Buy Pictures," that the pictures "not wish to disarm anything." (Here I feel like begging for the pictures, in a wee voice: "Can't they be just a *little* disarming?" My tastes are less firmly classical.) The poems she made for herself were so careful never to wish to disarm anyone, to appeal to anyone's habitual responses and grosser instincts, to sweep anyone resistlessly away, that they seemed to most readers eccentrically but forbiddingly austere, so that the readers averted their faces from her calm, elegant, matter-of-fact face, so exactly moved and conscientiously unappealing as itself to seem averted. It was not the defects of her qualities but the qualities that made most of the public reluctant to accept her as more than a special case: her extraordinary discrimination, precision, and restraint, the odd propriety of her imagination, her gifts of "natural promptness" (I use the phrase she found, but her own promptness is preternatural)—all these stood in her way and will go on standing in her way.

These people who *can't read modern poetry because it's so*—this or that or the other—why can't they read "Propriety" or "The Mind Is an Enchanting Thing" or "What Are Years" or "The Steeple-Jack"? Aren't these plain-spoken, highly formed, thoughtful, sincere, magnificently expressive—the worthy continuation of a great tradition of English poetry? Wouldn't the poet who wrote the *Horatian Ode* have been delighted with them? Why should a grown-up, moderately intelligent reader have any trouble with an early poem like, say, "New York"? The words that follow the title, the first words of the poem, are *the savage's romance*—here one stops and laughs shortly, as anybody but a good New Yorker will. (Her remark about Brooklyn, "this city of freckled / integrity," has a more ambiguous face.) She goes on, by way of the fact that New York is the center of the wholesale fur trade, to the eighteenth century when furs were the link between the Five Nations and Bath, between Natty Bumppo and the Trianon:

> It is a far cry from the "queen full of jewels"
> and the beau with the muff,
> from the gilt coach shaped like a perfume-bottle,
> to the conjunction of the Monongahela and the Allegheny,
> and the scholastic philosophy of the wilderness
> to combat which one must stand outside and laugh
> since to go in is to be lost.

And she finishes by saying about America—truthfully, one thinks and hopes—that "it is not the dime-novel exterior, / Niagara Falls, the calico horses and the war-canoe" that matter, it is not the resources and the know-how, "it is not the plunder, / but 'accessibility to experience.' "

The only way to combat a poem like this is to stand outside and laugh—to go in is to be lost, and in delight; how can you say better, more concretely and intelligently and imaginatively, what that long central sentence says? Isn't the word *scholastic* worth some books? Of course, if the eighteenth century and the frontier don't interest you, if you've never read or thought anything about them, the poem will seem to you uninteresting or incommunicative; but it is unreasonable to blame the poet for that. In grammar school, bent over the geography book, all of us lingered over the unexpected geometrical magnificence of "the conjunction of the Monongahela and the Allegheny," but none of the rest of us saw that it was part of a poem—our America was here around us, then, and we didn't know. And isn't the conclusion of Miss Moore's poem the best and truest case that can be made out for Americans?

It is most barbarously unjust to treat her (as some admiring critics do) as what she is only when she parodies herself: a sort of museum poet, an eccentric shut-in dealing in the collection, renovation, and exhibition of precise exotic properties. For she is a lot more American a writer (if to be an American is to be the heir, or heiress, of all the ages) than Thomas Wolfe or Erskine Caldwell or—but space fails me; she looks lovingly and knowingly at this "grassless / linksless [no longer], languageless country in which letters are written / not in Spanish, not in Greek, not in Latin, not in shorthand, / but in plain American which cats and dogs can read!" Doesn't one's heart reverberate to that last phrase "as to a trumpet"?

Miss Moore is one of the most perceptive of writers, sees extraordinarily—the words fit her particularly well because of the ambiguity that makes them refer both to sensation and intelligence. One reads, at random among lines one likes: *But we prove, we do not explain our birth*; reads about the pangolin *returning before sunrise; stepping in the moonlight, / on the moonlight peculiarly*; reads, *An aspect may deceive; as the / elephant's columbine-tubed trunk / held waveringly out— / an at will heavy thing—is / delicate. / Art is unfortunate. / One may be a blameless / bachelor, and it is but a / step to Congreve.* One relishes a fineness and strangeness and firmness of discrimination that one is not accustomed to, set forth with a lack of fuss that one is not accustomed to either; it is the exact opposite of all those novels which present, in the most verbose and elaborate of vocabularies, with the greatest and most obvious of pains, some complacently and irrelevantly Sensitive perceptions. How much has been left out, here! (One remembers Kipling's *A cut story is like a poked fire.*) What intelligence vibrates in the sounds, the rhythms, the pauses, in all the minute particulars that make up the body of the poem! The tone of Miss Moore's poems, often, is enough to give the reader great pleasure, since it is a tone of much wit and precision

and intelligence, of irony and forbearance, of unusual moral pene-
tration—is plainly the voice of a person of good taste and good sense
and good will, of a genuinely human being. Because of the curious
juxtaposition of curious particulars, most of the things that inhabit
her poetry seem extraordinarily bright, exact, and there—just as un-
familiar colors, in unfamiliar combinations, seem impossibly vivid.
She is *the* poet of the particular—or, when she fails, of the peculiar;
and is also, in our time, *the* poet of general moral statement. Often, be-
cause of their exact seriousness of utterance, their complete individ-
uality of embodiment, these generalizations of hers seem almost
more particular than the particulars.

———

In some of her poems Miss Moore has discovered both a new
sort of subject (a queer many-headed one) and a new sort of connec-
tion and structure for it, so that she has widened the scope of poetry;
if poetry, like other organisms, wants to convert into itself everything
there is, she has helped it to. She has shown us that the world is more
poetic than we thought. She has a discriminating love of what others
have seen and made and said, and has learned (like a burglar who
marks everything that he has stolen with the owner's name, and then
exhibits it in his stall in the marketplace) to make novel and beauti-
ful use of such things in her own work, where they are sometimes set
off by their surroundings, sometimes metamorphosed. But for Miss
Moore I'd never have got to read about "the emerald's 'grass-lamp
glow,' " or about the Abbé Berlèse, who said, "In the camellia-house
there must be / no smoke from the stove, or dew on / the windows,
lest the plants ail . . . / mistakes are irreparable and nothing will
avail," or about "our clasped hands that swear, 'By Peace / Plenty;
as / by Wisdom, Peace,' " or about any of a thousand such things—
so I feel as grateful to her memory as to a novelist's. Novelists are the
most remembering of animals, but Miss Moore comes next.

Her poems have the excellences not of some specialized, pri-
marily or exclusively Poetic expression, but of expression in general;
she says so many good things that, call it prose or poetry or what you
will, her work is wonderful. She says, for instance:

> . . . The polished wedge
>   that might have split the firmament
>   was dumb. At last it threw itself away
> and falling down, conferred on some poor fool, a privilege.

Is this an aphorism in the form of a fable, or a fable in the form of an aphorism? It doesn't matter. But how sadly and firmly and mockingly *so* it is, whatever it is; we don't need to search for an application.

Miss Moore speaks well, memorably well, unforgettably well, in many different ways. She is, sometimes, as tersely conclusive as Grimm:

> Jacob when a-dying, asked
> Joseph: Who are these? and blessed
> both sons, the younger most, vexing Joseph. And
> Joseph was vexing to some . . .

or as wise as Goethe:

> Though white is
> the colour of worship and of mourning, he
> is not here to worship and he is too wise
> to mourn,—a life prisoner but reconciled.
> With trunk tucked up compactly—the elephant's
> sign of defeat—he resisted, but is the child
>
> of reason now. His straight trunk seems to say: when
> what we hoped for came to nothing, we revived . . .

or as beguiling, as full of becoming propriety, as Beatrix Potter:

> The fish-spine
> on firs, on
>   sombre trees
>   by the sea's
> walls of wave-worn rock—have it; and
> a moonbow and Bach's cheerful firmness
>   in a minor key.
>   It's an owl-and-a-pussy-
>
> both-content
> agreement.
>   Come, come. It's
>   mixed with wits;
> it's not a graceful sadness. It's
>   resistance with bent head, like foxtail
>   millet's . . .

or as purely magical as Alban Berg:

Plagued by the nightingale
in the new leaves,
with its silence—
not its silence but its silences,
he says of it:
"It clothes me with a shirt of fire . . ."

or as elevated as the Old Testament:

Sun and moon and day and night and man and beast
    each with a splendour
        which man in all his vileness cannot
        set aside; each with an excellence! . . .

or as morally and rhetorically magnificent as St. Paul, when she says
about man, at the end of the best of all her poems, "The Pangolin":

        Unignorant,
      modest and unemotional, and all emotion,
    he has everlasting vigor,
      power to grow,
        though there are few creatures who can make one
        breathe faster and make one erecter.

Not afraid of anything is he,
    and then goes cowering forth, tread paced to meet an obstacle
at every step. Consistent with the
    formula—warm blood, no gills, two pairs of hands and a few
                                hairs—that
    is a mammal; there he sits in his own habitat,
      serge-clad, strong-shod. The prey of fear, he, always
      curtailed, extinguished, thwarted by the dusk, work partly done,
    says to the alternating blaze,
      "Again the sun!
        anew each day; and new and new and new,
      that comes into and steadies my soul."

The reader may feel, "You're certainly quoting a lot." But I have
only begun to quote—or wish that I had; these are just a few of the
things I can't bear not to quote, I haven't yet come to the things I want
to quote—I may never get to them. But how can I resist telling you
"that one must not borrow a long white beard and tie it on / and

threaten with the scythe of time the casually curious"? Or say noth-
ing about the "swan, with swart blind look askance / and gondolier-
ing legs" (the "swart blind look askance" makes us not only see, but
also feel ourselves into, the swan); or about the jerboa that "stops its
gleaning / on little wheel castors, and makes fern-seed / footprints
with kangaroo speed"; or about "this graft-grown briar-black
bloom"?—a phrase that would have made Hopkins say with a com-
placent smile, "Now, *that's* the way you use words." But there are
hundreds of phrases as good or better: one goes through "The Steeple-
Jack" and "The Hero" hating to leave anything unquoted. There
"the / whirlwind fife-and-drum of the storm bends the salt / marsh
grass, disturbs stars in the sky and the / star in the steeple; it is a
privilege to see so / much confusion"; there one finds "presidents
who have repaid / sin-driven / senators by not thinking about them";
there one hears "the 'scare-babe voice' / from the neglected yew set
with / the semi-precious cat's eyes of the owl"; there

> the decorous frock-coated Negro
> by the grotto
>
> answers the fearless sightseeing hobo
>   who asks the man she's with, what's this,
>   what's that, where's Martha
>   buried, "Gen-ral Washington
>   there; his lady, here"; speaking
>   as if in a play, not seeing her . . .

Even admiration seems superfluous. But expostulation doesn't:
where is Ambrose the student, with his not-native hat? and the pitch,
not true, of the church steeple? and that "elegance the source of
which is not bravado" that we and the student like? I think that Miss
Moore was right to cut "The Steeple-Jack"—the poem seems plainer
and clearer in its shortened state—but she has cut too much: when the
reader comes, at the end, to "the hero, the student, the steeple-jack,
each in his way, is at home," he must go to the next poem for the hero,
has lost the student entirely, and has to make out as best he can with
the steeple-jack. I wish that the poet had cut only as far as "but here
they've cats not cobras to keep out the rats"; this would keep the best
things, the things necessary for the sense of the poem, and still get rid
of the tropical digression. The reader may feel like saying, "Let her
do as she pleases with the poem; it's hers, isn't it?" No; it's much too

good a poem for that, it long ago became everybody's, and we can protest just as we could if Donatello cut off David's left leg.

———

The change in Miss Moore's work, between her earliest and latest poems, is an attractive and favorable change. How much more modernist, special-case, dryly elevated and abstract, she was to begin with! "As for butterflies, I can hardly conceive / of one's attending upon you, but to question / the congruence of the complement is vain, if it exists." Butter not only wouldn't melt in this mouth, it wouldn't go in; one runs away, an urchin in the gutter and glad to be, murmuring: "The Queen of Spain *has* no legs." Or Miss Moore begins a poem, with melting grace: "If yellow betokens infidelity, / I am an infidel. / I could not bear a yellow rose ill will / Because books said that yellow boded ill, / White promised well." One's eyes widen; one sits the poet down in the porch swing, starts to go off to get her a glass of lemonade, and sees her metamorphosed before one's eyes into a new *Critique of Practical Reason*, feminine gender: for her next words are, "However, your particular possession, / The sense of privacy, / Indeed might deprecate / Offended ears, and need not tolerate / Effrontery." And that is all; the poem is over. Sometimes, in her early poems, she has not a tone but a manner, and a rather mannered manner at that—two or three such poems together seem a dry glittering expanse, i.e., a desert. But in her later work she often escapes entirely the vice most natural to her, this abstract, mannered, descriptive, consciously prosaic commentary (accompanied, usually, by a manneredness of leaving out all introductions and transitions and explanations, as if one could represent a stream by reproducing only the stepping-stones one crossed it on). As she says, compression is the first grace of style—is almost a defining characteristic of the poetry our age most admires; but such passages as those I am speaking of are not compressed—the time wasted on Being Abstract more than makes up for the time saved by leaving out. Looking at a poem like "What Are Years," we see how much her style has changed. And the changes in style represent a real change in the poet: when one is struck by the poet's seriousness and directness and lack of manner—by both her own individual excellence and by that anonymous excellence the best poets sometimes share—it is usually in one of the poems written during the thirties and forties. I am emphasizing this difference too much, since even its existence is ignored, usually; but it is interesting what a different general impression the *Collected*

Poems gives, compared to the old *Selected Poems*. (Not that it wasn't wonderful too.)

How often Miss Moore has written about Things (hers are aesthetic-moral, not commercial-utilitarian—they persist and reassure); or Plants (how can anything bad happen to a plant?); or Animals with holes, a heavy defensive armament, or a massive and herbivorous placidity superior to either the dangers or temptations of aggression. The way of the little jerboa on the sands—at once true, beautiful, and good—she understands; but the little shrew or weasel, that kills, if it can, two or three dozen animals in a night? the little larvae feeding on the still-living caterpillar their mother has paralyzed for them? Nature, in Miss Moore's poll of it, is overwhelmingly in favor of morality; but the results were implicit in the sampling—like the *Literary Digest*, she sent postcards to only the nicer animals. In these poems the lion never eats Androcles—or anything else except a paste of seeded rotten apples, the national diet of Erewhon; so that her truthful and surprising phrase, *the lion's ferocious chrysanthemum head*, may seem less surprising than it would for a wilder lion. Because so much of our own world is evil, she has transformed the Animal Kingdom, that amoral realm, into a realm of good; her consolatory, fabulous bestiary is more accurate than, but is almost as arranged as, any medieval one. We need it as much as she does, but how can we help feeling that she relies, some of the time, too surely upon this last version of pastoral? "You reassure me and people don't, except when they are like you—but really they are always like you," the poems say sometimes, to the beasts; and it is wonderful to have it said so, and for a moment to forget, behind the animals of a darkening landscape, their dark companions.

Some of the changes in Miss Moore's work can be considered in terms of Armor. Queer terms, you say? They are hers, not mine: a good deal of her poetry is specifically (and changingly) about armor, weapons, protection, places to hide; and she is not only conscious that this is so, but after a while writes poems about the fact that it is so. As she says, "armor seems extra," but it isn't; and when she writes about "another armored animal," about another "thing made graceful by adversities, conversities," she does so with the sigh of someone who has come home. She asks whether a woman's looks are weapons or scalpels; comments, looking out on a quiet town: "It could scarcely be dangerous to be living / in a town like this"; says about a man's nonchalance: "his by- / play was more terrible in its effectiveness / than the fiercest frontal attack. / The staff, the bag, the feigned inconsequence / of manner, best bespeak that weapon, self-protectiveness."

That weapon, self-protectiveness! The poet knows that morals are not "the memory of success that no longer succeeds," but a part of survival.

She writes: "As impassioned Handel / . . . never was known to have fallen in love, / the unconfiding frigate-bird hides / in the height and in the majestic / display of his art." If Handel (or the frigate-bird) had been less impassioned he wouldn't have hidden, and if his feelings had been less deep they'd have been expressed with less restraint, we are meant to feel; it was because he was so impassioned that he "never was known to have fallen in love," the poem almost says. And how much sisterly approval there is in that *unconfiding!* When a frigate-bird buys pictures, you can bet that the pictures "must not wish to disarm anything." (By being disarming we sometimes disarm others, but always disarm ourselves, lay ourselves open to rejection. But if we do not make ourselves disarming or appealing, everything can be a clear, creditable, take-it-or-leave-it affair, rejection is no longer rejection. Who would be such a fool as to make advances to his reader, advances which might end in rejection or, worse still, in acceptance?) Miss Moore spoke as she pleased, and did not care whether or not it pleased; mostly this made her firm and good and different, but sometimes it had its drawbacks.

She says of some armored animals that they are "models of exactness." The association was natural: she thought of the animals as models and of the exactness as armor—and for such a writer, there was no armor like exactness, concision, irony. She wished to trust, as absolutely as she could, in flat laconic matter-of-factness, in the minimal statement, understatement: these earlier poems of hers approach as a limit a kind of ideal minimal statement, a truth thought of as underlying, prior to, all exaggeration and error; the poet has tried to strip or boil everything down to this point of hard, objective, absolute precision. But the most extreme precision leads inevitably to quotation; and quotation is armor and ambiguity and irony all at once—turtles are great quoters. Miss Moore leaves the stones she picks up carefully uncut, but places them in an unimaginably complicated and difficult setting, to sparkle under the Northern Lights of her continual irony. Nobody has ever been better at throwing away a line than this Miss Facing-Both-Ways, this La Rochefoucauld who has at last rid himself of La Rochefoucauld, and can disabusedly say about man:

> he loves himself so much,
> he can permit himself
> no rival in that love . . .

and about woman:

> one is not rich but poor
> when one can always seem so right . . .

and about both:

> What can one do for them—
> these savages
> condemned to disaffect
> all those who are not visionaries
> alert to undertake the silly task
> of making people noble?

All this is from "Marriage," the most ironic poem, surely, written by man or woman; and one reads it with additional pleasure because it was written by the woman who was later to say, so tenderly and magically: "What is more precise than precision? Illusion."

Along with precision she loved difficulty. She said about James and others: "It is the love of doing hard things / that rebuffed and wore them out—a public out of sympathy with neatness. / Neatness of finish! Neatness of finish!" Miss Moore almost despairs of us in one poem, until she comes across some evidence which shows that, in spite of everything, "we are precisionists"; and Santa Claus's reindeer, in spite of cutwork ornaments and fur like edelweiss, are still "rigorists," so she names the poem that for them. How much she cares for useless pains, difficulties undertaken for their own sake! Difficulty is the chief technical principle of her poetry, almost. (For sureness of execution, for originality of technical accomplishment, her poetry is unsurpassed in our time; Auden says almost that, and the author of "Under Sirius" ought to know. Some of her rhymes and rhythms and phrases look quite undiscoverable.) Such unnecessary pains, such fantastic difficulties! Yet with manners, arts, sports, hobbies, they are always there—so perhaps they are necessary after all.

———

But some of her earlier poems do seem "averted into perfection." You can't put the sea into a bottle unless you leave it open at the end, and sometimes hers is closed at both ends, closed into one of those crystal spheres inside which snowflakes are falling onto a tiny house, the house where the poet lives—or says that she lives. Sometimes Miss Moore writes about armor and wears it, the most

delicately chased, live-seeming scale-armor anybody ever put to-
gether: armor hammered out of fern seed, woven from the silk of in-
visible cloaks—for it is almost, though not quite, as invisible as it
pretends to be, and is when most nearly invisible most nearly pro-
tecting. One is often conscious while reading the poetry, the earlier
poetry especially, of a contained removed tone; of the cool precise un-
touchedness, untouchableness, of fastidious rectitude; of innate mer-
its and their obligations, the obligations of ability and intelligence
and aristocracy—for if aristocracy has always worn armor, it has also
always lived dangerously: the association of aristocracy and danger
and obligation is as congenial to Miss Moore as is the rest of the
"flower and fruit of all that noted superiority." Some of her poems
have the manners or manner of ladies who learned a little before
birth not to mention money, who neither point nor touch, and who
scrupulously abstain from the mixed, live vulgarity of life. "You sit
still if, whenever you move, something jingles," Pound quotes an of-
ficer of the old school as saying. There is the same aristocratic ab-
stention behind the restraint, the sitting still as long as it can, of this
poetry. "The passion for setting people right is in itself an afflictive
disease. / Distaste which takes no credit to itself is best," she says in
an early poem; and says, broadly and fretfully for her, "We are sick of
the earth, / sick of the pig-sty, wild geese and wild men." At such
moments she is a little disquieting (she speaks for everybody, in the
best of the later poems, in a way in which she once could not); one
feels like quoting against her her own, "As if a death-mask could re-
place / Life's faulty excellence," and blurting that life-masks have
their disadvantages too. We are uncomfortable—or else too comfort-
able—in a world in which feeling, affection, charity, are so entirely
divorced from sexuality and power, the bonds of the flesh. In this
world of the poems there are many thoughts, things, animals, senti-
ments, moral insights; but money and passion and power, the brute
fact that *works*, whether or not correctly, whether or not precisely—
the whole Medusa-face of the world: these are gone. In the poem
called "Marriage" marriage, with sex, children, and elementary eco-
nomic existence missing, is an absurd unlikely affair, one that
wouldn't fool a child; and, of course, children don't get married. But
this reminds me how un-childish, un-young, Miss Moore's poems al-
ways are; she is like one of those earlier ages that dressed children as
adults, and sent them off to college at the age of eleven—though the
poems dress their children in animal skins, and send them out into
the wilderness to live happily ever after. Few poets have as much
moral insight as Miss Moore; yet in her poems morality usually *is*

simplified into self-abnegation, and Gauguin always seems to stay home with his family—which is right, but wrong in a way, too. Poems which celebrate morality choose more between good and evil, and less between lesser evils and greater goods, than life does, so that in them morality is simpler and more beautiful than it is in life, and we feel our attachment to it strengthened.

"Spine-swine (the edgehog misnamed hedgehog)," echidna, echinoderm, rhino, the spine pig or porcupine—"everything is battle-dressed"; so the late poem named "His Shield" begins. But by then Miss Moore has learned to put no trust in armor, says, "Pig-fur won't do, I'll wrap / myself in salamander-skin like Presbyter John," the "inextinguishable salamander" who "revealed / a formula safer than / an armorer's: the power of relinquishing / what one would keep," and whose "shield was his humility." And "What Are Years" begins "All are naked, none are safe," and speaks of overcoming our circumstances by accepting them; just as "Nevertheless" talks not about armor, not about weapons, but about what is behind or above them both: "The weak overcomes its / menace, the strong over- / comes itself. What is there / like fortitude? What sap / went through that little thread / to make the cherry red!" All this is a wonderfully appealing, a disarming triumph; yet not so appealing, so disarming, so amused and imaginative and doubtful and tender, as her last look at armor, the last poem of her *Collected Poems*. It is called "Armor's Undermining Modesty"; I don't entirely understand it, but what I understand I love, and what I don't understand I love almost better. I will quote most of the last part of it:

> No wonder we hate poetry,
> and stars and harps and the new moon. If tributes cannot
> be implicit,
>
>   give me diatribes and the fragrance of iodine,
>   the cork oak acorn grown in Spain;
>   the pale-ale-eyed impersonal look
>   which the sales-placard gives the bock beer buck.
> What is more precise than precision? Illusion.
> Knights we've known,
>
>   like those familiar
>   now unfamiliar knights who sought the Grail . . .

. . . did not let self bar
their usefulness to others who were
different. Though Mars is excessive
in being preventive,
heroes need not write an ordinall of attributes to enumerate
what they hate.

I should, I confess,
like to have a talk with one of them about excess,
and armor's undermining modesty
instead of innocent depravity.
A mirror-of-steel uninsistence should countenance
continence,

objectified and not by chance,
there in its frame of circumstance
of innocence and altitude
in an unhackneyed solitude.
There is the tarnish; and there, the imperishable wish.

One doesn't need to say that this is one of Miss Moore's best
poems. Some of the others are, I think, "The Pangolin"; "Propriety"
(if ever a poem was perfect "Propriety" is; how *could* a poem end
better?); "The Mind Is an Enchanting Thing"; "Melancthon";
"Elephants"; the first half of "The Jerboa," that poem called "Too
Much"; "Spenser's Ireland"; "Bird-Witted"; "Smooth Gnarled Crape
Myrtle"; "In Distrust of Merits"; "What Are Years"; "The Steeple-
Jack"; "The Hero"; "Those Various Scalpels"; "Marriage"; "His
Shield"; and "New York." "Virginia Britannia" is a beautiful poem
that some of the time gets lost in the maze of itself; "Nevertheless"
and "No Swan So Fine" are two of the most beautiful of the slighter
poems; "Camellia Sabina" is—but I must stop.

Miss Moore's *Collected Poems* is a neat little book, with all its
verse tucked into a hundred and thirty-eight pages; a reader could,
with a reference to size, rather easily put her into her minor place, and
say—as I heard a good or even great critic say—that it is easy to see
the difference between a poet like this and a major poet. It is; is so easy
that Miss Moore's real readers, who share with her some of her "love
of doing hard things," won't want to do it—not for a century or two,
at least, and then only with an indifferent, "I suppose so." There is so
much of a life concentrated into, objectified on, these hard, tender, se-

rious pages, there is such wit and truth and moral imagination inhabiting this small space, that we are surprised at possibility, and marvel all over again at the conditions of human making and being. What Miss Moore's best poetry does, I can say best in her words: it "comes into and steadies the soul," so that the reader feels himself "a life prisoner, but reconciled."

[*1952/PA*]

Contemporary
Poetry Criticism

A POEM, TODAY, IS BOTH an aesthetic object and a commodity. It is an unimportant commodity for which there is a weak and limited demand; it is produced, distributed, and consumed like any other commodity. Poems are produced by a peculiar submarginal class, only a dozen or so of whom live by the sale of their products. They are distributed, as a relatively negligible sideline, by publishers. The consumers are a heterogeneous group; their demand is, for the most part, characterized by a somewhat apathetic and pious conventionality. A cynical observer might say that many of them have inherited from another age both their respect for and their taste in poetry, and are afraid that if one is questioned the other will disappear. What this public likes (and buys) the publisher publishes. Some people—regular publishers, occasionally—are shocked at what the public does like, and publish unprofitably what it won't buy.

A commercial magazine or newspaper is a rather elaborate device for inducing people to read advertisements. Most present-day poetry criticism consists of reviews in such magazines and newspapers; if we disregard its function and the conditions of its production—both commercial—we must misunderstand it. Reviews are demanded by both publishers and public; publishers buy advertisements, the public buys magazines (and advertising rates vary with circulation): so an editor necessarily demands reviews that will satisfy publishers and public. (Here, let me emphasize, I am disregarding subsidized noncommercial magazines and magazines only secondarily supported by advertising; however, the criticism of these to some extent influences and is influenced by that of the commercial magazines and newspapers.)

From the publisher's point of view criticism is a quite important subspecies of advertising; reviews are free publicity, free testimonials. Good criticism is criticism that sells books. A good critic is a man who likes as much as possible as persuasively as possible. (Woollcott's pall-bearers will all be publishers; and those tears will be real.) The publisher naturally advertises in magazines that print *good* criticism— naturally; so, naturally, an editor farms out his reviews to reliable producers of just such criticism; there is a process of natural selection going on all the time among reviewers. In heaven all reviews will be favorable; here on earth, the publisher realizes, plausibility demands an occasional bad one, some convincing lump in all that leaven, and he accepts it somewhat as a theologian accepts Evil. Newspapers sometimes print free news stories about their advertisers; reporters call such a story a Business Office Must. To the publisher reviews are a kind of Business Office Must.

The public—let me put it bluntly—the public wants a review to tell it what it is going to think of a book. The critic usually avoids the ambiguity of "You'll like this, you won't like that," and tactfully or ingenuously phrases his prediction: "This is a good book; that is a bad." The public likes the good, dislikes the bad, and is pleased with both its taste and the reviewer's. The reviewer preferably is someone who can be considered an expert: there is more prestige in agreeing with him, and he can speak with a knowledge and finality that will reassure the reader (that what he likes *is* art)—and since modern poetry is to the average reader, if not terra incognita, at least No Man's Land, he welcomes reassurance. But often the reviewer is not expert on any subject except Reviews: he derives his authority from his position, rather than the reverse. The reviewer, from the public's point of view, should be the Collective Me, a sort of hypostatized, apotheosized common denominator of public taste. (Many people—booksellers and librarians, for instance—have an actual commercial interest in the coincidence of the reviewer's taste and the public's.) The reviewer is like the juror, drawn by lot, who nevertheless takes on the authority and prestige of the People he represents. But all the reviewer's powers are delegated powers; if he tries to elevate the public taste, writes real criticism and consistently disagrees with the public, these powers are withdrawn, and he will be revealingly condemned for arbitrary dogmatism, the assumption of powers that are not his.

Reviews are codified in critical articles and anthologies; it is the nature of both to be approving, or to manifest their disapproval only negatively. Editors seldom print unfavorable articles on poets, so critics rarely write them. The anthologist has a vital financial interest in there being a large body of current poetry that can be called—that he can call—good. Poetry is always reviving today from yesterday's revival.

This is the system; but there is a good deal of play in it, precisely because the publishing of poetry is commercially such a negligible affair. Publishers are hardly vitally concerned; no one, so far as I know, makes a living by reviewing poetry. Another thing that makes the system more disapproving than it otherwise would be is that so much of the poetry of the last twenty years has been modernist poetry (often printed by non-commercial publishers), which the public dislikes, misunderstands, and enjoys seeing condemned.

I have given a rather abstract analysis of the situation. Now I could go in for details, and tell you about the prominent reviewer Mr. B., who said, when Auden was first published here, that his six-year-old boy could write better poetry than Auden; or about the most prominent Mr. U., who says that Marianne Moore's poetry isn't poetry at all, but criticism; or about that inveterate reviewer Miss W., who has just published a textbook full of explanations of modern poetry—explanations that show she is quite incapable of understanding any modern poem of even the slightest difficulty. But it is like trying to define a haystack by drawing straws from it. And I am not interested in the individual depravity of reviewers; they are standardized, eminently replaceable parts of the machine: I suppose even for Louis Untermeyer a substitute could be found. I am afraid I have not exaggerated the situation; if for a few months the reader will look at the poetry reviews in the *Times* and the *Herald Tribune*, the *Saturday Review*, and other such places, he can see for himself. Such reviews are extraordinarily similar—that is because they are a technique not for pointing out but for obscuring differences; from the hands of most reviewers best and worse emerge with the same winning and vacant smile. In the dark all cats are gray.

Most of the criticism of any age is bad—for instance, who were the popular reviewers and critics of the year 1841? But today the only commercially practicable body of criticism is a bad one. Good criticism, which points out badness or mediocrity, and actually scares away buyers from most books, is something the publishers necessarily cannot tolerate. Good criticism, which is often involved or difficult, and which always tells the public not what it wants but what is good for it, is something the commercial public doesn't care for either. I am not condemning the body of criticism for being as bad as it is, I am giving it a certificate of necessity: for it to be anything else is a commercial impossibility.

The poetry of the present is mostly written about by reviewers; that of the past is mostly written about by scholars: i.e., English professors. Scholars produce scholarly articles, for which there is a great demand; the steady publication of quantities of scholarly articles will obtain for a person with the proper academic qualifications steadily increasing salaries. Consequently, scholarly criticism is being produced in immense amounts. Unfortunately, most scholarly criticism is negligible as scholarship and worthless as criticism. Much of the performance is bad, of course, because the performers are incompetent or mediocre; but the real trouble is the nature of the performance.

During the last part of the nineteenth century the prestige that had formerly attended the methods and practitioners of literary, philosophical, and theological wisdom was largely transferred to those of scientific knowledge. Professors of English tried to "cash in on" (Burke's phrase) this prestige by the naïve application of scientific quantitative methods to literature. They tried to make "English" a science, and they succeeded in making it a pseudo-science of the most forbidding variety, in amassing a gigantic rubbish heap of facts about literature. (Of scholars, as of bees, the criterion is industry.) Criticism is necessarily based on very fine qualitative distinctions, the critic's responses to and judgments about works of art; the discipline that neglects and condemns these as subjective, unreliable, impressionistic, that is satisfied only with the "objective reliability" of "facts"—such a discipline is absurd in theory and disastrous in practice, and can produce criticism of any value only in spite of itself. Some scholars have attained their ideal of perfect objectivity, and seem unwilling or even unable to make the slightest distinction between good, bad, and mediocre—all are data for scholarship. Robert Graves was examined by such a professor, who gave him the considered reproof: "Mr. Graves, I believe you *prefer* some authors to others." Carl Becker has defined a professor as a man who thinks otherwise; a scholar is a man who otherwise thinks.

But, do what he will, feeling, taste, the subjectivity of judgment constantly do creep into the scholar's articles and teachings; not the trained and scrupulous taste, the reasoned critical judgment of the expert, but the unexamined conventions, prejudices, and idiosyncrasies that the scholar has acquired at random in the course of his career of facts. His taste in poetry is, very slightly modified, the academic late-Victorian taste of his high-school and college teachers. The last twenty-five years have seen part of a great change in taste, a revaluation of most English poetry—I do not believe there is a good critic living who shares the taste of the scholars. So the scholar, who already looks down on the critic in theory, is able in practice to condemn him, even more severely and sincerely, for the immense disparity in all their judgments. Today there is not merely a division between scholars and critics, but open war; and since scholars are a thousand to one, and occupy every important position in the colleges, there is not much hope for the critic.

I hope the summary quality of this account has not antagonized the reader; I do not question the value of scholarship. But most scholarship is a means, and when it is exalted into an end—as it is today—the real end of scholarship is defeated. Our universities should produce good criticism; they do not—or, at best, they do so only as federal prisons produce counterfeit money: a few hardened prisoners are more or less surreptitiously continuing their real vocations.

I might have taken as a motto for this essay, "If a way there be to the Better, it exacts a full look at the Worse." Now I have come to the Better—the Best, even: I do not believe there has been another age in which so much extraordinarily good criticism of poetry has been written. (Incidentally, it is usually printed in non-commercial magazines and often published by non-commercial publishers.) Too much of the criticism of the past seems to us morals or biography or information—anything but criticism. Modern criticism of poetry, at its best, is relatively pure; it is really concerned, as it should be, with understanding (in the most active and comprehensive sense) and evaluating poetry. This criticism has been extremely catholic and extremely acute; there has been no analysis too complicated, delicate, or surprising for these critics to undertake. Modern criticism has accomplished a change in taste, a critical revolution, even greater than the change in poetic performance which modernist poets have effected. I myself believe that modernist poetry is essentially an extension of romanticism (with a few neoclassic elements à la Stravinsky), and that along with great virtues it exhibits many of the vices of romanticism in their most exaggerated form. This certainly could not be said of modern criticism, which has repudiated romanticism so wholeheartedly that many critics condemn in their criticism the vices that they exploit in their poetry. This criticism has helped us understand and value modernist poetry—which academic criticism simply rejected—but its work with the poetry of the past has been even more important: it has resurrected or defended dozens of poets whom academic criticism had discarded or disgracefully undervalued. One immediately thinks of Donne, Webster, Raleigh, Jonson, Wyatt, Fulke Greville, Herbert, Marvell, Hopkins, and those poets who Matthew Arnold said were not poets at all: Dryden and Pope. And modern criticism has reexamined, carefully and often damningly, many of the Victorians and romantics whom academic criticism so uncritically received and exalted. It is only by connecting the past with the present, by examining the past in the light of the present, that we can really either understand or value the past; academic and scholarly criticism have failed because they have not done this. After knowing the best modern criticism, one reads more poetry and reads it better: English poetry is, one sees, more varied, complicated, and astonishing than anybody had thought.

I have been speaking of such critics as William Empson, T. S. Eliot, R. P. Blackmur, Allen Tate, Yvor Winters, John Crowe Ransom, I. A. Richards, Morton Dauwen Zabel, Cleanth Brooks, Robert Penn Warren, Delmore Schwartz, and five or six others. They have written a good many books, almost any of which is worth reading; their criticism is often printed in such magazines as *The Southern Review,* the *Kenyon Review,* and *Partisan Review.* I do not mean to be saying, "Here they are—all perfect!" They are highly imperfect; the reader and I will probably agree that we would not be caught dead saying some of the things they say; but, all in all, they are about as good as we can find—and better than we deserve.

This criticism is not better known for several reasons. Much of it has been published recently and rather obscurely. It is *hard* criticism, of unusual depth and complication, written—one might almost say—by critics for critics. It makes great demands of its readers in more than one way: its characteristic complication of surface, its self-conscious employment of so much knowledge, sensitivity, and superiority may dishearten or antagonize the reader. Another deterrent is the political and social position of the majority of these writers. It is an odd fact that most good criticism of poetry today is being written by critics who can only be called—who call themselves—reactionary. (The best leftist critics of poetry, men like Edmund Wilson and Kenneth Burke, have gone over almost entirely into general criticism.) But neglecting criticism because we are annoyed at the critic's politics (or tone or style or anything else) is a fool's game; if we can learn nothing at all from his political views—that is unlikely, but possible—we can simply disregard them, and have that much more time for the criticism. As readers of criticism, we must allow ourselves to be disheartened or antagonized by nothing but bad criticism.

Personally, I believe that it would be profitable for critics to show less concern with poets, periods, society (big-scale extensive criticism), and more concern with the poems themselves (intensive criticism). In extensive criticism the data on which the critic bases his judgments are necessarily not given. The critic says that A.'s poetry is such-and-such because of the influence of So-and-So on the age; you summon your memories, clear or vague, of a few dozen of A.'s poems—the right ones, you hope—and after comparing these with your memories of So-and-So and the age, you make up your mind about the critic's remark. Your need and understanding of the remark vary inversely. In intensive criticism, the analysis of specific poems, what the critic says and exactly what he is saying it about are both there: the criticism is ideally accessible. Nothing would have more value for criticism than the existence of a few hundred or thousand detailed critical analyses, done by first-rate critics, of important English poems—*important* includes both good and bad. Good criticism is based on very good reading: unless we can do the same sort of reading the critic does we cannot even understand his judgments, much less accept or reject them. These intensive critical analyses at once convict and improve our own reading—there is no way in which we can learn so much about poetry so quickly and surely. I know plenty of critics who agree with me about such analyses; why aren't they being written? Because there are one or two magazines in the world that occasionally print such analyses; because no publisher has ever published a book of them. The critic not only can't make his living by them; he can't even get them printed.

We have a good many critics who are perfectly capable, under favorable conditions, of producing a large amount of extremely valuable criticism of poetry; they are, instead, producing a small amount under quite unfavorable conditions. All through this article, with shy persistence, I have kept recurring to the topic of money. This is an incongruous subject for a critic—what does he know about money? Only what everybody else knows: that he must get some somehow; by writing criticism if that is possible, by doing something else if that is not. People who are interested in criticism can do something for it in two ways: by being good critics or by encouraging good critics. *Encouraging* means buying or publishing their books, running magazines for them, giving them fellowships, hiring them in universities: it is a mercenary word.

[*1941/KA*]

Texts from Housman

THE LOGIC poetry has or pretends to have generally resembles in-
duction more than deduction. Of four possible procedures (dealing en-
tirely with particulars, dealing entirely with generalizations, inferring
the relatively general from the relatively particular, and deducing the
particular from the more general), the third is very much the most
common, and the first and second are limits which "pure" and di-
dactic poetry timidly approach. The fourth is seldom seen. In this
essay I am interested in that variety of the third procedure in which
the generalizations are implicit. When such generalizations are sim-
ple ones, very plainly implied by the particulars of the poem, there
will be little tendency to confuse this variety of the third procedure
with the first procedure; when they are neither simple nor very
plainly implied, the poem will be thought of as "pure" (frequently,
"nature") poetry. This is all the more likely to occur since most "pure"
poetry is merely that in which the impurity, like the illegitimate child
of the story, is "such a little one" that we feel it ought to be disre-
garded. Of these poems of implicit generalization there is a wide
range, extending from the simplest, in which the generalizations are
made obvious enough to vex the average reader (some of the "Satires
of Circumstance," for instance), to the most complicated, in which
they entirely escape his observation ("To the Moon"). The two poems
of Housman's which I am about to analyze are more nearly of the
type of "To the Moon."

II

Crossing alone the nighted ferry
With the one coin for fee,
Whom, on the wharf of Lethe waiting,
Count you to find? Not me.

The brisk fond lackey to fetch and carry,
The true, sick-hearted slave,
Expect him not in the just city
And free land of the grave.

The first stanza is oddly constructed; it manages to carry over several more or less unexpressed statements, while the statement it makes on the surface, grammatically, is arranged so as to make the reader disregard it completely. Literally, the stanza says: *Whom do you expect to find waiting for you? Not me.* But the denying and elliptical *not me* is not an answer to the surface question; that question is almost rhetorical, and obviously gets a *me*; the *not me* denies *And I'll satisfy your expectations and be there?*—the implied corollary of the surface question; and the flippant and brutal finality of the *not me* implies that the expectations are foolish. (A belief that can be contradicted so carelessly and completely—by a person in a position to know—is a foolish one.) The stanza says: *You do expect to find me and ought not to* and *You're actually such a fool as to count on my being there?* and *So I'll be there, eh? Not me.*

Some paraphrases of the two stanzas will show how extraordinarily much they do mean; they illustrate the quality of poetry that is almost its most characteristic, compression. These paraphrases are not very imaginative—the reader can find justification for any statement in the actual words of the poem. (Though not in any part considered in isolation. The part as part has a misleading look of independence and reality, just as does the word as word; but it has only that relationship to the larger contexts of the poem that the words which compose it have to it, and its significance is similarly controlled and extended by those larger units of which it is a part. A poem is a sort of onion of contexts, and you can no more locate any of the important meanings exclusively in a part than you can locate a relation in one of its terms. The significance of a part may be greatly modified or even in extreme cases completely reversed by later and larger parts and by the whole. This will be illustrated in the following discussion: most of the important meanings attached to the first stanza do not exist when the stanza is considered in isolation.) And the paraphrases are not hypertrophied, they do not even begin to be exhaustive.

Stanza I: Do you expect me to wait patiently for you there, just as I have done on earth? expect that, in hell, after death, things will go on for you just as they do here on earth? that there, after crossing and drinking Lethe and oblivion, I'll still be thinking of human you, still be waiting faithfully there on the wharf for you to arrive, with you still my only interest, with me still your absolutely devoted slave—just as we are here? Do you really? Do you actually suppose that you yourself, then, will be able to expect it? Even when dead, all alone, on that grim ferry, in the middle of the dark forgetful river, all that's left of your human life one coin, you'll be stupid or inflexible or faithful enough to *count* on (you're sure, are you, so sure that not even a doubt enters your mind?) finding me waiting there? How are we to understand an inflexibility that seems almost incredible? Is it because you're pathetically deluded about love's constancy, my great lasting love for you? (This version makes the *you* sympathetic; but it is unlikely, an unstressed possibility, and the others do not.) Or is it that you're so sure of my complete enslavement that you know death itself can't change it? Or are you so peculiarly stupid that you can't even conceive of any essential change away from your past life and knowledge, even after the death that has destroyed them both? Or is it the general inescapable stupidity of mankind, who can conceive of death only in human and vital terms? (Housman's not giving the reasons, when the reasons must be thought about if the poem is to be understood, forces the reader to make them for himself, and to see that there is a wide range that must be considered. This is one of the most important principles of compression in poetry; these implied foundations or justifications for a statement might be called *bases*.) Are you actually such a fool as to believe that? So I'll be there? Not me. You're wrong. There things are really different.

One of the most important elements in the poem is the tone of the *not me*. Its casualness, finality, and matter-of-fact bluntness give it almost the effect of slang. It is the crudest of denials. There is in it a laconic brutality, an imperturbable and almost complacent vigor; it has certainly a sort of contempt. Contempt for what? Contempt at himself for his faithlessness? contempt at himself for his obsessing weakness—for not being faithless now instead of then? Or contempt at her, for being bad enough to keep things as they are, for being stupid enough to imagine that they will be so always? The tone is both threatening and disgusted. It shivers between all these qualities like a just-thrown knife. And to what particular denial does this tone attach? how specific, how general a one? These are changes a reader can easily ring for himself; but I hope he will realize their importance. Variations of this formula of alternative possibilities make up one of the most valuable resources of the poet.

The second stanza is most thoroughly ambiguous; there are two entirely different levels of meaning for the whole, and most of the parts exhibit a comparable stratification. I give a word-for-word analysis:

Do not expect me to be after death what I was alive and human: the *fond* (1. *foolish*; 2. *loving*—you get the same two meanings in the synonym *doting*) *brisk* (the normal meanings are favorable: *full of life, keenly alive or alert, energetic*; but here the context forces it over into *officious, undignified, solicitous, leaping at your every word*—there is a pathetic ignoble sense to it here) *lackey* (the most contemptuous and degrading form of the word *servant*: a servile follower, a toady) *to fetch and carry* (you thought so poorly of me that you let me perform nothing but silly menial physical tasks; thus, our love was nothing but the degrading relationship of obsequious servant and contemptuous master), *the true* (1. *constant, loyal, devoted, faithful*; 2. *properly so-called, ideally or typically such*—the perfectly slavish slave), *sick-hearted* (1. cowardly, disheartened in a weak discouraged ignoble way, as a Spartan would have said of helots, "These sick-hearted slaves"; 2. sick at heart at the whole mess, his own helpless subjection. There was a man in one of the sagas who had a bad boil on his foot; when he was asked why he didn't limp and favor it, he replied: "One walks straight while the leg is whole." If the reader imagines this man as a slave he will see sharply the more elevated sense of the phrase *sick-hearted slave*) *slave* (1. the conventional hardly meant sense in which we use it of lovers, as an almost completely dead metaphor; this sense has very little force here; or 2. the literal *slave*: the relation of slave to master is not pleasant, not honorable, is between lovers indecent and horrible, but immensely comprehensive—their love is made even more compulsive and even less favorable). But here I leave the word-by-word analysis for more general comment. I think I hardly need remark on the shock in this treatment, which forces over the conventional unfelt terms into their literal degrading senses; and this shock is amplified by the paradoxical fall through *just city* and *free land* into *the grave*. (Also, the effect of the *lackey / carry* and versification of the first line of the stanza should be noted.)

Let me give first the favorable literal surface sense of *the just city and free land of the grave*, its sense on the level at which you take Housman's Greek underworld convention seriously. The house of Hades is the *just city* for a number of reasons: in it are the three just judges; in it are all the exemplary convicts, from Ixion to the Danaïdes, simply dripping with justice; here justice is meted equally to the anonymous and rankless dead; there is no corruption here. It is the *free land* because here the king and the slave are equal (though even on the level of death as the Greek underworld, the horrid irony has begun to intrude—Achilles knew, and Housman knows, that it is better to be the slave of a poor farmer than king among the hosts of the dead); because here we are free at last from life; and so on and so on.

But at the deeper level, the *just* fastened to *city*, the *city* fastened to *grave*, have an irony that is thorough. How are we to apply *just* to a place where corruption and nothingness are forced on good and bad, innocent and guilty alike? (From Housman's point of view it might be called mercy, but never justice.) And the *city* is as bad; the cemetery looks like a city of the graves, of the stone rectangular houses—but a city without occupations, citizens, without life: a shell, a blank check that can never be filled out. And can we call a land *free* whose inhabitants cannot move a finger, are compelled as completely as stones? And can we call the little cave, the patch of darkness and pressing earth, the *land* of the grave?

And why are we told to expect him not, the slave, the lackey, in the just city and free land of the grave? Because he is changed now, a citizen of the Greek underworld, engrossed in its games and occupations, the new interests that he has acquired? Oh no, the change is complete, not from the old interests to new ones, but from any interests to none; do not expect him because he has ceased to exist, he is really, finally different now. It is foolish to expect *anything* of the world after death. But we can expect nothingness; and that is better than this world, the poem is supposed to make us feel; there, even though we are overwhelmed impartially and completely, we shall be free of the evil of this world—a world whose best thing, love, is nothing but injustice and stupidity and slavery. This is why the poet resorts to the ambiguity that permits him to employ the adjectives *just* and *free*: they seem to apply truly on the surface level, and ironically at the other; but in a way they, and certainly the air of reward and luck and approbation that goes with them, apply truly at the second level as well. This is the accusation and condemnation of life that we read so often in Housman: that the grave seems better, we are glad to be in it.

We ought not to forget that this poem is a love poem by the living "me" of the poem to its equally living "you": *when we are dead, things will be different—and I'm glad of it.* It is, considerably sublimated, the formula familiar to such connections: *I wish I were dead;* and it has more than a suspicion of the child's *when I'm dead, then they'll be sorry.* It is an accusation that embodies a very strong statement of the underlying antagonism, the real ambivalence of most such relationships. The condemnation applied to the world for being bad is extended to the *you* for not being better. And these plaints are always pleas; so the poem has an additional force. Certainly this particular-seeming little poem turns out to be general enough: it carries implicit in it attitudes (aggregates of related generalizations) toward love, life, and death.

III

It nods and curtseys and recovers
    When the wind blows above,
The nettle on the graves of lovers
    That hanged themselves for love.

The nettle nods, the wind blows over,
    The man, he does not move,
The lover of the grave, the lover
    That hanged himself for love.

This innocent-looking little nature poem is actually, I think, a general quasi-philosophical piece meant to infect the reader with Housman's own belief about the cause of any action. (I am afraid it is a judgment the reader is likely neither to resist nor recognize.) The nettle and the wind are Housman's specific and usual symbols. Housman's poetry itself is a sort of homemade nettle wine ("Out of a stem that scored the hand / I wrung it in a weary land"); the nettle has one poem entirely to itself, XXXII in *More Poems.* No matter what you sow, only the nettle grows; no matter what happens, it flourishes and remains—"the numberless, the lonely, the thronger of the land." It peoples cities, it waves above the courts of kings; "and touch it and it stings." Stating what symbols "mean" is a job the poet has properly avoided; but, roughly, the nettle stands for the hurting and inescapable conditions of life, the prosperous (but sympathetically presented and almost admiringly accepted) evil of the universe—

"great Necessity," if you are not altogether charmed by it. What the wind is Housman states himself (in "On Wenlock Edge the wood's in trouble"; but it is given the same value in several other poems, notably "The weeping Pleiads wester"): the "tree of man" is never quiet because the wind, "the gale of life," blows through it always.

What I said just before the analysis of the first stanza of "Crossing alone the nighted ferry" is true here too; many of one's remarks about the first stanza of this poem will be plausible or intelligible only in the light of one's consideration of the whole poem. In the first line, *It nods and curtseys and recovers,* there is a shock which grows out of the contrast between this demure performance and its performer, the Housman nettle. The nettle is merely repeating above the grave, compelled by the wind, what the man in the grave did once, when the wind blew through him. So living is (we must take it as being) just a repetition of little meaningless nodding actions, actions that haven't even the virtue of being our own—since the wind forces them out of us; life as the wind makes man as the tree or nettle helpless and determined. This illustrates the general principle that in poetry you make judgments by your own preliminary choice of symbols, and force the reader who accepts the symbols to accept the judgments implicit in them. A symbol, like Bowne's "concept," is a nest of judgments; the reader may accept the symbols, and then be cautious about accepting judgments or generalizations, but the damage is done.

The images in the poem are quite general: "the nettle on the graves of lovers that hanged themselves for love" is not any one nettle, not really any particular at all, but a moderately extensive class. (If Housman were writing a pure poem, a nature poem, he would go about it differently; here the generality is insisted on—any lover, any nettle will do well enough: if you prove something for *any* you prove it for *all,* and Housman is arranging all this as a plausible *any.*) There is of course irony, at several levels, in a nettle's dancing obliviously (*nod* and *curtsey* and *recover* add up to *dance*) on the grave of the dead lover. All flesh is grass; but worse here, because the grass which is the symbol for transitoriness outlasts us. (The reader may say, remembering *The stinging nettle only will still be found to stand*: "But the nettle is a symbol of lasting things to Housman, not of transitory ones." Actually it manages for both here, for the first when considered as a common symbol, for the second when considered as Housman's particular one. But this ambiguity in symbols is frequent; without it they would be much less useful. Take a similar case, *grass*: this year's grass springs up and withers, and is shorter than man; but *grass*, all grass, lasts forever. With people we have different words for the two aspects, *men* and *man*. The whole business of thinking of the transitory grass as just the same more lasting than man—in one form or another, one of the stock poetic subjects—is a beautiful fallacy that goes like this: *Grass*—the year-after-year process—is more lasting than *men*; substituting *man* for *men* and this year's blade for the endless grass, you end by getting a proposition that everybody from Job on down or up has felt, at one time or another, thoroughly satisfactory.) Why a nettle to dance on the grave? Because in English poetry flowers grow on the graves of these lovers who have died for love, to show remembrance; Housman puts the nettle there, for forgetfulness. In the other poems the flower "meant" their love—here the nettle means it. All the nettle's actions emphasize its indifference and removedness. The roses in the ballads were intimately related to the lovers, and entwined themselves above the graves—the nature that surrounded the lovers was thoroughly interested in their game, almost as human as they; the nettle above this grave is alone, inhuman and casual, the representative of a nature indifferent to man.

The fifth and sixth lines of the poem are there mainly to establish this shocking paradox: here is a sessile thing, a plant, that curtseys and nods, while the man, the most thoroughly animate of all beings, cannot even move. Looked at in the usual way this is gloomy and mortifying, and that is the surface force it has here; but looked at in another way, Housman's way, there is a sort of triumph in it: the most absolute that man can know. That is what it is for Housman. Once man was tossed about helplessly and incessantly by the wind that blew through him—now the toughest of all plants is more sensitive, more easily moved than he. In other words, death is better than life, nothing is better than anything. Nor is this a silly adolescent pessimism peculiar to Housman, as so many critics assure you. It is better to be dead than alive, best of all never to have been born—said a poet approvingly advertised as seeing life steadily and seeing it whole; and if I began an anthology of such quotations there it would take me a long time to finish. The attitude is obviously inadequate and just as obviously important.

The triumph here leads beautifully into the poem's final statement: the triumph at being in the grave, one with the grave, prepares us for the fact that it was the grave, not any living thing, that the lover loved, and hanged himself for love of. The statement has some plausibility: hanging yourself for love of someone is entirely silly, so far as any possession or any furthering of your love is concerned, but if you are in love with death, killing yourself is the logical and obvious and only way to consummate your love. For the lover to have killed himself for love of a living thing would have been senseless; but his love for her was only ostensible, concealing—from himself too—the "common wish for death," his real passion for the grave.

But if this holds for this one case; if in committing this most sincere and passionate, most living of all acts (that is, killing yourself for love; nothing else shows so complete a contempt for death and consequences, so absolute a value placed on another living creature), the lover was deceiving himself about his motives, and did it, not for love of anything living, but because of his real love for death; then everybody must do everything for the same reason. (This is a judgment too exaggerated for anyone to expect to get away with, the reader may think; but judgments of life tend to this form—"Vanity, vanity, all is vanity.") For the lover is the perfectly simplified, extreme case. This is what is called a crucial experiment. (It is one of Mill's regular types of induction.) The logic runs: If you can prove that in committing this act—an act about the motives of which the actor is so little likely to be deceived, an act so little likely to have the love of death as its motive—the actor was deceived, and had the love of death as his motive, then you can prove it for any other act the motive of which is more likely to be the love of death, and about the motives of which it is more likely that the actor might be deceived.

But for the conclusion to be true the initial premise must be true, the lover's one motive must have been the wish for death; and Housman has of course not put in even a word of argument for the truth of that premise, he has merely stated it, with the most engaging audacity and dogmatism—has stated it innocently, as a fact obvious as any other of these little natural facts about the wind and the nettle and the cemetery. He has produced it not as a judgment but as a datum, and the sympathetic reader has accepted it as such. He is really treating it as a percept, and percepts have no need for proof, they are neither true nor false, they are just there. If he had tried to prove the truth of the premise he would have convinced only those who already believed in the truth of the conclusion, and those people (i.e., himself) didn't need to be convinced. With the poem as it is, the reader is convinced; or if he objects, the poet can object disingenuously in return, "But you've made the absurd error of taking hypothetical reasoning as categorical. My form is: *If* A, *then* B; I'm not interested in *proving* A. Though, of course, if you decide to remove the *if,* and assert A, then B is asserted also; and A is awfully plausible, isn't it?—just part of the data of the poem; you could hardly reject it, could you?"

Two of the generalizations carried over by this poem—that our actions are motivated by the wish for death, that our ostensible reasons for acts are merely rationalizations, veneers of apparent motive overlying the real levels of motivation—are, in a less sweeping form, psychological or psychoanalytical commonplaces today. But I am not going to hold up Housman's poem as a masterly anticipation of our own discoveries; so far as I can see, Housman was not only uninterested but incapable in such things, and pulled these truths out of his pie, not because of wit, but because of the perverse and ingenious obstinacy that pulled just such gloomy judgments out of any pie at all. Here the shock and unlikeliness of what he said were what recommended it to him; and the discovery that these have been mitigated would merely have added to his gloom.

[1939/KA]

Graves and

the White Goddess

AT THE BEGINNING OF ROBERT GRAVES'S *Collected Poems* (1955) there is a list of thirty-three books and three translations. The list makes it seem foolish to talk only of the poems, and if you think of *Goodbye to All That* and *The White Goddess*, it seems foolish to talk only of the writing: there is a great deal of Graves's life in what he has written, and a great deal of his writing seems plausible—explicable, even—only in terms of his life. I want to write, in the first half of this essay, about what his poetry seems to me; and later, about how his life (all I know of it comes from him) has made his poetry and his understanding of the world into the inimitable, eccentric marvels that they are.

Looking along his list, I see that I have read two of the translations and twenty-nine and a half of the books—three haven't got to me yet, and I quit in the middle of *Homer's Daughter*—but I have read three or four of the books Graves doesn't list. And I have read *I, Claudius* (a good book singular enough to be immortal) and its slightly inferior continuation three or four times; *King Jesus*, a wonderfully imagined, adequately written novel, three times; *The White Goddess*, that erudite, magical (or, as Eliot calls it, "prodigious, monstrous, stupefying, indescribable") masterwork of fantastic exposition, twice; the poems scores or hundreds of times. In two months I have had time to read *The Greek Myths* only once, but it is, both in matter and in manner, an odd rare classic that people will be rereading for many years. And they will be reading, I think, the book with which, in 1929, I began: the thirty-three-year-old Robert Graves's autobiography, *Goodbye to All That*. If you are interested in Graves—and how can anyone help being interested in so good and so queer a writer?—there is no better place to begin. No better, except for the *Collected Poems*: that, with Graves, is where one begins and ends.

For Graves is, first and last, a poet: in between he is a Graves. "There is a coldness in the Graveses which is anti-sentimental to the point of insolence," he writes. The Graveses have good minds "for examinations . . . and solving puzzles"; are loquacious, eccentric individualists "inclined to petulance"; are subject to "most disconcerting spells of complete amnesia . . . and rely on their intuition and bluff to get them through"; and, no matter how disreputable their clothes and friends, are always taken for gentlemen. This is a fine partial summary of one side of Robert von Ranke Graves: of that professional, matter-of-fact-to-the-point-of-insolence, complacent, prosaic competence of style and imagination that weighs down most of his fiction, gives a terse, crusty, Defoe-esque plausibility to even his most imaginative nonfiction, and is present in most of his poetry only as a shell or skeleton, a hard lifeless something supporting or enclosing the poem's different life. Graves has spoken of the "conflict of rival sub-personalities," of warring halves or thirds or quarters, as what makes a man a poet. He differentiates the two sides of his own nature so sharply that he speaks of the first poem "I" wrote and the first poem "I wrote as a Graves"; he calls his prose "potboiling"—much of it is—and puts into his autobiography a number of his mother's sayings primarily to show how much more, as a poet, he owes to the von Rankes than to the Graveses. (One of these sayings was, "There was a man once, a Frenchman, who died of grief because he could never become a mother." I find it delightful to think of the mother bending to the child who was to become the excavator or resurrector of the White Goddess, and repeating to him this Delphic sentence.)

The sincere and generous von Rankes, with their castles, venison, blind trout, and black honey; their women who "were noble and patient, and always kept their eyes on the ground when out walking"; their great historian of whom Graves says, "To him I owe my historical method"—a tribute that must have made Leopold von Ranke's very bones grow pale—the von Rankes are certainly, as Graves considers them, the more attractive side of himself. He speaks of his "once aquiline, now crooked nose" as being "a vertical line of demarcation between the left and right sides of my face, which are naturally unassorted—my eyes, eyebrows, and ears all being notably crooked and my cheek-bones, which are rather high, being on different levels." I do not propose to tell you which is the Graves, and which the von Ranke, eye, eyebrow, ear, and cheekbone, but I am prepared to do as much for almost any sentence in Robert Graves—to tell you whether it was written by the cold, puzzle-solving, stamp-collecting, logic-chopping Regimental Explainer; or by the Babe, Lover, and Victim howling, in dreadful longing, for the Mother who bears, possesses, and destroys; or, as happens sometimes, by both. But I am being drawn, not much against my will, into the second part of this essay; let me get back to the poetry.

Graves's poems seem to divide naturally into six or seven types. These are: mythical-archaic poems, poems of the White Goddess; poems about extreme situations; expressive or magical landscapes; grotesques; observations—matter-of-fact, tightly organized, tersely penetrating observations of types of behavior, attitude, situation, of the processes and categories of existence; love poems; ballads or nursery rhymes.

These last are early poems, and disappear as soon as Graves can afford to leave "what I may call the folk-song period of my life," the time when "country sentiment," childlike romance, were a refuge from "my shellshocked condition." The best of these poems is his grotesquely and ambiguously moving, faintly Ransomesque ballad of the Blatant Beast, "Saint." Some others are "Frosty Night," "Apples and Water," "Richard Roe and John Doe," "Allie," "Henry and Mary," "Vain and Careless," "The Bedpost," and the beautiful "Love without Hope":

> Love without hope, as when the young bird-catcher
> Swept off his tall hat to the Squire's own daughter,
> So let the imprisoned larks escape and fly
> Singing about her head, as she rode by.

The young birdcatcher might have stepped from "Under the Greenwood Tree" or "Winter Night in Woodland (Old Time)"— and in all Italy where is there a halo like his, made from such live and longing gold?

Graves has never forgotten the child's incommensurable joys; nor has he forgotten the child's and the man's incommensurable, irreducible agonies. He writes naturally and well—cannot keep himself from writing—about bad, and worse, and worst, the last extremities of existence:

Walls, mounds, enclosing corrugations
Of darkness, moonlight on dry grass.
Walking this courtyard, sleepless, in fever;
Planning to use—but by definition
There's no way out, no way out—
Rope-ladders, baulks of timber, pulleys,
A rocket whizzing over the walls and moat—
Machines easy to improvise.

                  No escape,
No such thing; to dream of new dimensions,
Cheating checkmate by painting the king's robe
So that he slides like a queen;
Or to cry, "Nightmare, nightmare!"
Like a corpse in the cholera-pit
Under a load of corpses;
Or to run the head against these blind walls,
Enter the dungeon, torment the eyes
With apparitions chained two and two,
And go frantic with fear—
To die and wake up sweating in moonlight
In the same courtyard, sleepless as before.

This poem, "The Castle," and such poems as "Haunted House," "The Pier-Glass," "Down," "Sick Love," "Mermaid, Dragon, and Fiend," "The Suicide in the Copse," "The Survivor," "The Devil at Berry Pomeroy," "The Death Room," and "The Jealous Man" are enough to make any reader decide that Graves is a man to whom terrible things have happened.

At the end of the First World War, Graves says, "I could not use a telephone, I was sick every time I travelled in a train, and if I saw more than two new people in a single day it prevented me from sleeping . . . Shells used to come bursting on my bed at midnight even when Nancy was sharing it with me; strangers in daytime would assume the faces of friends who had been killed." Graves has removed from his *Collected Poems* any poem directly about the war; only the generalized, decade-removed "Recalling War" remains. When he had said *Goodbye to All That* he had meant it—meant it more than he had known, perhaps. The worst became for him, from then on, a civilian worst, and his thoughts about war dried and hardened into the routine, grotesque professionalism that is the best way of taking for granted, canceling out, the unbearable actualities of war. Who would have believed that the author who wrote about these, in *Goodbye to All That,* with plain truth, would in a few years be writing such a G. A. Henty book as *Count Belisarius?*

To Graves, often, the most extreme situation is truth, the mere seeing of reality; we can explain away or destroy the fabulous, traditional mermaids or dragons or devils of existence, but the real "mermaids will not be denied / The last bubbles of our shame, / The dragon flaunts an unpierced hide, / The true fiend governs in God's name." In "A Jealous Man" Graves writes with this truth about another war in which he has fought—writes about it in nightmarishly immediate, traditional, universal terms. The objectively summarizing, held-in, held-back lines seem, in Hopkins's phrase, to "wince and sing" under the hammering of this grotesque, obscene, intolerable anguish—an anguish that ends in untouched, indifferent air:

> To be homeless is a pride
> To the jealous man prowling
> Hungry down the night lanes,
>
> Who has no steel at his side,
> No drink hot in his mouth,
> But a mind dream-enlarged,
>
> Who witnesses warfare,
> Man with woman, hugely
> Raging from hedge to hedge:
>
> The raw knotted oak-club
> Clenched in the raw fist,
> The ivy-noose well flung,
>
> The thronged din of battle,
> Gaspings of the throat-snared,
> Snores of the battered dying,
>
> Tall corpses, braced together,
> Fallen in clammy furrows,
> Male and female,
>
> Or, among haulms of nettle
> Humped, in noisome heaps,
> Male and female.

He glowers in the choked roadway
Between twin churchyards,
Like a turnip ghost.

(Here, the rain-worn headstone,
There, the Celtic cross
In rank white marble.)

This jealous man is smitten,
His fear-jerked forehead
Sweats a fine musk;

A score of bats bewitched
By the ruttish odor
Swoop singing at his head;

Nuns bricked up alive
Within the neighbouring wall
Wail in cat-like longing.

Crow, cocks, crow loud!
Reprieve the doomed devil,
Has he not died enough?

Now, out of careless sleep,
She wakes and greets him coldly,
The woman at home,

She, with a private wonder
At shoes bemired and bloody—
His war was not hers.

Often these poems of extreme situation, like those of observa-
tion, are grotesques—this neither by chance nor by choice, but by ne-
cessity. Much of life comes to Graves already sharpened into carica-
ture: "another caricature scene" and "plenty of caricature scenes"
are ordinary remarks in his autobiography. ("Another caricature
scene to look back on," he writes of his wedding.) The best of his
grotesques have a peculiar mesmeric power, shock when touched,
since they are the charged caricatures of children, of dreams, of the
unconscious:

All horses on the racecourse of Tralee
  Have four more legs in gallop than in trot—
  Two pairs fully extended, two pairs not;
And yet no thoroughbred with either three
  Or five legs but is mercilessly shot.
I watched a filly gnaw her fifth leg free,
Warned by a speaking mare since turned silentiary.

Somewhere in Kafka there is a man who is haunted by two bouncing balls; living with this poem is like being haunted by a Gestalt diagram changing from figure to ground, ground to figure, there in the silent darkness, until we get up and turn on the light and look at it, and go back to sleep with it ringing—high, hollow, sinister, yet somehow lyric and living—in our dream-enlarged ears. One can say about this poem of Graves's, as about others: "If I weren't looking at it I wouldn't believe it." According to Stalky and Company, the impassioned Diderot burst forth, "O Richardson, thou singular genius!" When one reads "It Was All Very Tidy," "The Worms of History," "Ogres and Pygmies," "Lollocks," "The Laureate," "The Death Room," one feels just like Diderot; nor is one willing to dismiss grotesques like "Song: Lift-Boy," "The Suicide in the Copse," "Grotesques" II, "The Villagers and Death," "Welsh Incident," "Wm. Brazier," "General Bloodstock's Lament for England," "Vision in the Repair Shop," and "Front Door Soliloquy" with a mere "Singular, singular!"

Sometimes these grotesques are inspired hostile observations, highly organized outbursts of dislike, revulsion, or rejection: where these observations (and much else) are concerned, Graves is the true heir of Ben Jonson, and can give to his monstrosities, occasionally, the peculiar lyric magnificence Jonson gives them in *The Alchemist*. It is easy for him to see God or Death as grotesque monsters; and the White Goddess, with all her calm, grave, archaic magnificence, is monstrous. But sometimes Graves writes grotesques of local color, traditional properties, comfortable-enough types, and these can be good-humored—are even, once, wistful:

Even in hotel beds the hair tousles.
But this is observation, not complaint—
"Complaints should please be dropped in the complaint-box"—
"Which courteously we beg you to vacate
In that clean state as you should wish to find it."

And the day after Carnival, today,
I found, in the square, a crimson cardboard heart:
"Anna Maria," it read. Otherwise, friends,
No foreign news—unless that here they drink
Red wine from china bowls; here anis-roots
Are stewed like turnips; here funiculars
Light up at dusk, two crooked constellations . . .

"It is not yet the season," pleads the Porter,
"That comes in April, when the rain most rains."
Trilingual Switzer fish in Switzer lakes
Pining for rain and bread-crumbs of the season,
In thin reed-beds you pine!

           In bed drowsing,
(While the hair slowly tousles) uncomplaining . . .
Anna Maria's heart under my pillow
Evokes no furious dream. Who is this Anna?
A Switzer maiden among Switzer maidens,
Child of the children of that fox who never
Ate the sour grapes: her teeth not set on edge.

The reader can murmur: "Why—why, this is life." But Graves—as mercilessly good a critic of his own poetry as he is a mercilessly bad critic of everybody else's—has here had a most disconcerting spell of complete amnesia: "Hotel Bed" isn't included in his new *Collected Poems.* "My poetry-writing has always been a painful process of continual corrections and corrections on top of corrections and persistent dissatisfaction," he writes. He is the only one who can afford to be dissatisfied with the process or the poems it has produced: he is the best rewriter and corrector of his own poetry that I know. Lately I have gone over the new, and old, and very old versions of all the poems in *Collected Poems,* and I am still dazzled by the magical skill, the inspiration apparently just there for use when needed, with which Graves has saved a ruined poem or perfected a good one. Usually the changes are so exactly right, so thoroughly called for, that you're puzzled at his ever having written the original; it grieves me that I have no space in which to quote them.

About sixty of Graves's collected poems are what one might call Observations—observations of types, functions, states; of characteristic strategies and attitudes, people's "life-styles"; of families, genetic development in general; of the self; of well-known stories or characters; of good reasons and real reasons; of dilemmas; of many of the processes and categories of existence. Ordinarily these observations are witty, detailed, penetrating, disabused, tightly organized, logical-sounding, matter-of-fact, terse: Graves sounds, often, as if he were Defoe attempting to get his Collected Works into the "Sayings of Spartans." Frequently an observation is put in terms of landscape or grotesque, organized as an approach to a limit or a *reductio ad absurdum*; sometimes a set of observations (for instance, "To Bring the Dead to Life" and "To Evoke Posterity") reminds one of a set of non-Euclidean geometries, differing assumptions rigorously worked out. Such a poem seems an organized, individual little world, this and no other. Finishing one we may feel, as in Graves's dry masterpiece, that It Was All Very Tidy—tidier, certainly, than life and our necessities; we feel about it a gnawing lack, the lack of anything lacking, of a way out—between the inside of the poem and the great outside there is no communication, and we long for an explosion or an implosion, we are not sure which. But these local actions, limited engagements, punitive expeditions; these poems which do, with elegance and dispatch, all that they set out to do; these bagatelles—on occasion Beethoven bagatelles; these complete, small-scale successes, are poems in which Graves excels. Few poets have written more pretty-good poems: "Midway," "The Devil's Advice to Story Tellers," "The Fallen Tower of Siloam," "The Reader over My Shoulder," "To Bring the Dead to Life," "To Walk on Hills," "The Persian Version," "The Furious Voyage," "The Climate of Thought," and "The Shot" are some examples of notably successful "observations," but there are many more; and the grotesques and landscapes and love poems are full of such small successes.

Landscapes have always been of particular importance to Graves; shell-shocked, he spent an entire leave walking through some favorite country, and went back to France half cured. When he writes about landscapes he puts into them or gets out of them meanings, attitudes, and emotions that Poets rarely get from Poetic landscapes; like Wordsworth, he is not interested in landscape as landscape. Some of the best of these poems describe magical landscapes—inside-out, box-inside-a-box, infinite regress—that seem to express, or correspond to, emotional or physiological states in Graves that I am not sure of, and that Graves may not be sure of: "Warning to Children," "Interruption," and, especially, "The Terraced Valley" are better than I can explain, and I listen to

... Neat outside-inside, neat below-above,
Hermaphrodizing love.
Neat this-way-that-way and without mistake:
On the right hand could slide the left glove.
Neat over-under: the young snake
Through an unyielding shell his path could break.
Singing of kettles, like a singing brook,
Made out-of-doors a fireside nook.

... I knew you near me in that strange region,
So searched for you, in hope to see you stand
On some near olive-terrace, in the heat,
The left-hand glove drawn on your right hand,
The empty snake's egg perfect at your feet—

with, at the climax, a kind of rapt uneasy satisfaction.

But Graves's richest, most moving, and most consistently beautiful poems—poems that almost deserve the literal *magical*—are his mythical-archaic pieces, all those the reader thinks of as "White Goddess poems": "To Juan at the Winter Solstice," "Theseus and Ariadne," "Lament for Pasiphaë," "The Sirens' Welcome to Cronos," "A Love Story," "The Return of the Goddess," "Darien," and eight or ten others. The best of these are different from anything else in English; their whole meaning and texture and motion are different from anything we could have expected from Graves or from anybody else. "The Sirens' Welcome to Cronos," for instance, has a color or taste that is new because it has been lost for thousands of years. In the second part of this essay I mean to discuss exactly what these poems are, and how they got to be that, along with the more ordinary love poems which form so large a part of Graves's work; but here I should like simply to quote the poem that represents them best, "To Juan at the Winter Solstice":

There is one story and one story only
That will prove worth your telling,
Whether as learned bard or gifted child;
To it all lines or lesser gauds belong
That startle with their shining
Such common stories as they stray into.

Is it of trees you tell, their months and virtues,
Or strange beasts that beset you,

Of birds that croak at you the Triple will?
Or of the Zodiac and how slow it turns
Below the Boreal Crown,
Prison of all true kings that ever reigned?

Water to water, ark again to ark,
From woman back to woman:
So each new victim treads unfalteringly
The never altered circuit of his fate,
Bringing twelve peers as witness
Both to his starry rise and starry fall.

Or is it of the Virgin's silver beauty,
All fish below the thighs?
She in her left hand bears a leafy quince;
When, with her right she crooks a finger smiling,
How may the King hold back?
Royally then he barters life for love.

Or of the undying snake from chaos hatched,
Whose coils contain the ocean,
Into whose chops with naked sword he springs,
Then in black water, tangled by the reeds,
Battles three days and nights,
To be spewed up beside her scalloped shore?

Much snow is falling, winds roar hollowly,
The owl hoots from the elder,
Fear in your heart cries to the loving-cup:
Sorrow to sorrow as the sparks fly upward.
The log groans and confesses
There is one story and one story only.

Dwell on her graciousness, dwell on her smiling,
Do not forget what flowers
The great boar trampled down in ivy time.
Her brow was creamy as the crested wave,
Her sea-blue eyes were wild
But nothing promised that is not performed.

Graves's best poems, I think, are "To Juan at the Winter Solstice,"
"A Jealous Man," "Theseus and Ariadne," "Lament for Pasiphaë,"

"The Sirens' Welcome to Cronos," "Ogres and Pygmies," "The Worms of History," "It Was All Very Tidy," "Saint," "The Terraced Valley," "The Devil at Berry Pomeroy," "Lollocks"; poems like "The Laureate," "The Castle," "Hotel Bed," "A Love Story," and "The Death Room" might end this list and begin a list of what seem to me Graves's next-best poems: "Interruption," "Warning to Children," "The Young Cordwainer," "Down," "Reproach," "Recalling War," "Song: Lift-Boy" (with the old coda), "The Bards," and "The Survivor." Quite as good as some of these are the best of Graves's slighter poems, delicate or witty or beautiful pieces without much weight or extent of subject and movement: "Love without Hope," "She Tells Her Love While Half Asleep," "Advocates," "Dawn Bombardment," "Sick Love," "Grotesques" II and VI, "The Suicide in the Copse," "Like Snow," "An English Wood," "The Shot," "On Dwelling," "The Portrait"; and I have already listed what seem to me some of his best grotesques and observations.

Graves is a poet of varied and consistent excellence. He has written scores, almost hundreds, of poems that are completely realized, different either from one another or from the poems of any other poet. His poems have to an extraordinary degree the feeling of one man's world, one man's life: what he loves and loathes; what he thinks and feels and doesn't know that he feels; the rhythms of his voice, his walk, his gestures. To meet Robert Graves is unnecessary: all his life has transformed itself into his poetry. The limitations of his poetic world come more from limitations of temperament than from limitations of gift or ability—anything Graves is really interested in he can do. He writes, always, with economical strength, with efficient distinction. Both the wording and the rhythm of his verse are full of personal force and impersonal skill: the poems have been made by a craftsman, but a craftsman whose heart was in his fingers. His wit; terseness; matter-of-factness; overmastering organizational and logical skill; penetrating observation; radical two-sidedness; gifts of skewness, wryness, cater-corneredness, sweet-sourness, of "English eccentricity," of grotesque humor, of brotherly acceptance of the perverse random contingency of the world; feeling for landscapes and for Things; gifts of ecstasy, misery, and confident command; idiosyncratic encyclopedic knowledge of our world and the worlds that came before it; the fact that love—everyday, specific, good-and-bad, miraculous-and-disastrous love, not the Love most writers write about—is the element he is a native of; his—to put it in almost childish terms—invariable *interestingness*, are a few of the many qualities that make Graves extraordinary.

Later on I should like to discuss Graves's limitations, which are as interesting as any of his qualities—which are, so to speak, the grotesque shadow of his qualities. His poems seem to me in no sense the work of a great poet; when you compare Graves with Wordsworth or Rilke, you are comparing a rearrangement of the room with a subsidence of continents. But Graves's poems are a marvel and a delight, the work of a fine poet who has managed, by the strangest of processes, to make himself into an extraordinary one. In the "Fiend, Dragon, Mermaid" that is not included in this last *Collected Poems*, Graves tells how he escaped from the monstrous fiend, dragon, mermaid, each dying—and how, quit of them, "I turned my gaze to the encounter of / The later genius, who of my pride and fear / And love / No monster made but me." This is true: he is, now, somewhat of a monster, a marvelous and troubling one, and it is by means of this "later genius," the White Goddess, the monstrous Muse, that he has made himself into what he is. In the second half of this essay I shall try to show how it was done.

II

"There is one story and one story only," Graves writes; all poems have the same theme. "The theme," he says in *The White Goddess*, "is the antique story . . . of the birth, life, death, and resurrection of the God of the Waxing Year; the central chapters concern the God's long battle with the God of the Waning Year for love of the capricious and all-powerful Threefold Goddess, their mother, bride, and layer-out. The poet identifies himself with the God of the Waxing Year and his muse with the Goddess; the rival is his blood-brother, his other self, his weird. All true poetry—true by Housman's practical test—celebrates some incident or scene in this very ancient story, and the main characters are so much a part of our racial inheritance that they not only assert themselves in poetry but recur on occasions of emotional stress in the form of dreams, paranoiac visions and delusions . . . The Goddess is a lovely, slender woman with a hooked nose, deathly pale face, lips red as rowanberries, startlingly blue eyes and long fair hair; she will suddenly transform herself into sow, mare, bitch, vixen, she-ass, weasel, serpent, owl, she-wolf, tigress, mermaid or loathsome hag . . . I cannot think of any true poet from Homer on who has not independently recorded his experience of her . . . The reason why the hairs stand on end, the skin crawls and a shiver runs down the spine when one writes or reads a true poem is that a true poem is necessarily an Invocation of the White Goddess, or Muse, the Mother of All Living, the ancient power of fright and lust—the female spider or the queen-bee whose embrace is death.

"... The true poet must always be original, but in a simpler sense: he must address only the Muse—not the King or Chief Bard or the people in general—and tell her the truth about himself and her in his own passionate and peculiar words ... Not that the Muse is ever completely satisfied. Laura Riding has summed her up in three memorable lines:

> Forgive me, giver, if I destroy the gift:
> It is so nearly what would please me
> I cannot but perfect it."

The Muse or Triple Goddess "was a personification of primitive woman—woman the creatress and destructress. As the New Moon or Spring she was girl; as the Full Moon or Summer she was woman; as the Old Moon or Winter she was hag ... The revolutionary institution of fatherhood, imported into Europe from the East, brought with it the institution of individual marriage ... Once this revolution had occurred, the social status of women altered: man took over many of the sacred practices from which his sex had debarred him, and finally declared himself head of the household." Graves describes with disgust the progressive degradation of this patriarchal world, as it moved farther and farther from its matriarchal beginnings, and as the "female sense of orderliness" was replaced by "the restless and arbitrary male will." This "female sense of orderliness" seems a rationalization or secondary elaboration: usually Graves speaks, without any disguise, of "the cruel, capricious, incontinent White Goddess," and values above all things the prospect of being destroyed by her. *Though she slay me, yet will I trust in her* is his motto, almost; if one substitutes *if* and *then* for *though* and *yet*, the sentence exactly fits his attitude.

One sees both from *The White Goddess* and the lectures recently published in England that almost no poets seem "true poets" to Graves; most of the poets of the past belonged to the Apollonian or "Classical homosexual" tradition, and most modern poets have ceased "to make poetic, prosaic, or even pathological sense." Woman "is not a poet: she is either a Muse or she is nothing." (One of his poems to Laura Riding is dedicated "To the Sovereign Muse": of all the poets who erstwhile bore the name, he says, "none bore it clear, not one";

she is the first to do so.) A woman should "either be a silent Muse" or "she should be the Muse in a complete sense; she should be in turn Arianrhod, Blodenwedd and the Old Sow of Maenawr Penarrd who eats her farrow." For the poet "there is no other woman but Cerridwen and he desires one thing above all else in the world: her love. As Blodenwedd, she will gladly give him her love, but at only one price: his life . . . Poetry began in the matriarchal age . . . No poet can hope to understand the nature of poetry unless he has had a vision of the Naked King crucified to the lopped oak, and watched the dancers, red-eyed from the acrid smoke of the sacrificial fires, stamping out the measure of the dance, their bodies bent uncouthly forward; with a monotonous chant of 'Kill! kill! kill!' and 'Blood! blood! blood!' "

But the reader before now will have interrupted this summary of Graves's world picture with an impatient "Why repeat all this to me? It's an ordinary wish fantasy reinforced with extraordinary erudition—a kind of family romance projected upon the universe. Having the loved one the mother is the usual thing. Of course, some of the details of this Mother-Muse, female spider, are unusual: she always *has* to kill, so that she is called cruel, capricious, incontinent, and yet is worshipped for being so; she—but case histories always are unusual. Let's admit that it's an unusual, an extraordinary fantasy; still, why quote it to me?"

I quote it for two reasons:

(1) It is the fantastic theory that has accompanied a marvelous practice: some of the best poems of our time have been written as a result of this (I think it fair to say) objectively grotesque account of reality. If the Principle of Indeterminacy had been discovered as a result of Schrödinger or Heisenberg's theory that the universe is a capricious, intuitive Great Mother whose behavior must always rightfully disappoint the predictions of her prying son—*a fingering slave, / One that would peep and botanize / Upon his mother's grave*—the theory would have an extrinsic interest that it now lacks. Because of the poems it enabled Yeats to write, many of us read *A Vision*. That Graves's astonishing theories should be so necessary to him, so right and proper for him, that by means of them he could write "To Juan at the Winter Solstice," "Theseus and Ariadne," "The Sirens' Welcome to Cronos," is a thing worthy of our admiration and observation.

(2) Graves's theories, so astonishing in themselves, are—when we compare them with Graves's life and with psychoanalytical observation of lives in general, of the Unconscious, of children, neu-

rotics, savages, myths, fairy tales—not astonishing at all, but logical and predictable; are so *natural* that we say with a tender smile, "Of course!" We see, or fancy that we see, why Graves believes them and why he is helped by believing them. Few poets have made better "pathological sense." I wish to try to explain these theories in terms of Graves's life; I shall try as far as possible to use Graves's own words.

In *Goodbye to All That* Graves cannot speak with enough emphasis of the difference between the side of him that is Graves and the side that is von Ranke. He writes with rather patronizing exactness of the Graveses, who are made to seem dry English eccentrics, excellent at puzzle solving, but writes with real warmth of the "goodness of heart" of his mother and the von Rankes; he seems to associate her idealism and *Gemütlichkeit*, her *Children, as your mother I command you* . . . with all that is spontaneous and emotional in his own nature—he has a heartfelt sentence telling "how much more I owe, as a writer, to my mother than to my father." His father was a poet. Graves writes: "I am glad in a way that my father was a poet. This at least saved me from any false reverence for poets . . . Some of his songs I sing without prejudice; when washing up after meals or shelling peas or on similar occasions. He never once tried to teach me how to write, or showed any understanding of my serious work; he was always more ready to ask advice about his own work than to offer it for mine." Graves also says that "we children saw practically nothing of him except during the holidays." It is not difficult to see why, in Graves's myth of the world, it is a shadowy left-handed "blood-brother" or "other self," and not the father in his own form, against whom the hero struggles for the possession of the mother.

Graves's mother was forty, his father forty-nine, when he was born; she "was so busy running the household and conscientiously carrying out her obligations as my father's wife that we did not see her continuously"; he writes about his nurse: "In a practical way she came to be more to us than our mother. I began to despise her at the age of twelve—she was then nurse to my younger brothers—when I found that my education was now in advance of hers, and that if I struggled with her I was able to trip her up and bruise her quite easily." Graves says that his religious training developed in him, as a child, "a great capacity for fear (I was perpetually tortured by the fear of hell), a superstitious conscience and a sexual embarrassment." Graves's reading was "carefully censored"; after two years of trench service he had still been to the theater only twice, to children's plays; his mother "allowed us no hint of its [humanity's] dirtiness and intrigue and lustfulness, believing that innocence was the surest protection against them." Two of his earlier memories seem particularly important to him:

"And the headmaster had a little daughter with a little girl friend, and I was in a sweat of terror whenever I met them; because, having no brothers, they once tried to find out about male anatomy from me by exploring down my shirt-neck when we were digging up pig-nuts in the garden.

"Another frightening experience of this part of my life was when I once had to wait in the school cloakroom for my sisters . . . I waited about a quarter of an hour in the corner of the cloakroom. I suppose I was about ten years old, and hundreds and hundreds of girls went to and fro, and they all looked at me and giggled and whispered things to each other. I knew they hated me, because I was a boy sitting in the cloakroom of a girls' school, and when my sisters arrived they looked ashamed of me and quite different from the sisters I knew at home. I realized that I had blundered into a secret world, and for months and even years afterwards my worst nightmares were of this girls' school, which was filled with coloured toy balloons. 'Very Freudian,' as one says now.

"My normal impulses were set back for years by these two experiences. When I was about seventeen we spent our Christmas holidays in Brussels. An Irish girl stopping at the same *pension* made love to me in a way that I see now was really very sweet. I was so frightened I could have killed her.

"In English preparatory and public schools romance is necessarily homosexual. The opposite sex is despised and hated, treated as something obscene. Many boys never recover from this perversion. I only recovered by a shock at the age of twenty-one. For every born homosexual there are at least ten permanent pseudo-homosexuals made by the public school system. And nine of these ten are as honorably chaste and sentimental as I was."

His strained affection for Dick, a boy at his school, ended disastrously only after two years of military service. Graves went directly from what seemed to him the organized masculine nightmare of the public schools into the organized masculine nightmare of the First World War. He was an excellent soldier. His sense of professional tradition, of regimental loyalty, was extreme ("We all agreed that regimental pride was the greatest force that kept a battalion going as an effective fighting unit, contrasting it particularly with patriotism and religion"), but it led him only into prolonged service at the front,

murderous and routine violence, wounds so serious that he was re-
ported dead, shell shock, neurosis, and an intense hatred for govern-
ments, civilians, the whole established order of the world. Jung says,
in a sentence that might have been written to apply specifically to
Graves: "It is no light matter to stand between a day-world of ex-
ploded ideals and discredited values, and a night-world of apparently
senseless fantasy. The weirdness of this standpoint is in fact so great
that there is nobody who does not reach out for security, even though
it be a reaching back to the mother who shielded his childhood from
the terrors of night."

When, on sick leave, he met a young artist, Nancy Nicholson,
Graves reached back. "Of course I also accepted the whole patriarchal
system of things," he writes. "It is difficult now to recall how com-
pletely I believed in the natural supremacy of male over female. I
never heard it even questioned until I met Nancy, when I was about
twenty-two, towards the end of the war. *The surprising sense of ease*
that I got from her frank statement of equality between the sexes
was among my chief reasons for liking her . . . Nancy's crude sum-
mary: 'God is a man, so it must be all rot,' *took a load off my shoul-
ders.*" [My italics.]

Champagne was scarce at their wedding; "Nancy said: 'Well,
I'm going to get something out of this wedding, at any rate,' and
grabbed a bottle. After three or four glasses she went off and
changed into her land-girl's costume of breeches and smock . . . The
embarrassments of our wedding night were somewhat eased by an
air-raid . . . Nancy's mother was a far more important person to her
than I was . . . The most important thing to her was judicial equal-
ity of the sexes; she held that all the wrong in the world was caused
by male domination and narrowness. She refused to see my experi-
ences in the war as in any way comparable with the sufferings that
millions of married women of the working-class went through . . .
Male stupidity and callousness became an obsession with her and she
found it difficult not to include me in her universal condemnation of
men."

In country cottages; living from hand to mouth; ashamed of
himself "as a drag on Nancy"; a friend, rather than a father, to
Nancy's children; helping with the housework, taking care of the ba-
bies; so hauntedly neurotic that he saw ghosts at noon, couldn't use a
telephone, couldn't see more than two new faces without lying awake
all that night; writing child-poems or "country sentiment" poems to
escape from his everyday reality, or else haunted nightmarish poems

to express that everyday reality—so Graves spent the next six or eight years. (The keenest sense of the pathetic strangeness of that household comes to me when I read Graves's "I realized too that I had a new loyalty, to Nancy and the baby, tending to overshadow regimental loyalty now that the war was over.") "I had bad nights," Graves writes. "I thought that perhaps I owed it to Nancy to go to a psychiatrist to be cured; yet I was not sure. Somehow I thought that the power of writing poetry, which was more important than anything else I did, would disappear if I allowed myself to get cured; my *Pier-Glass* haunting would end and I would become a dull easy writer. It seemed to me less important to be well than to be a good poet. I also had a strong repugnance against allowing anyone to have the power over me that psychiatrists always seem to win over their patients." *Anyone,* here, means *any man,* I think; in the end Graves decided that he "would read the modern psychological books and apply them to my case," and "cure myself."

Their marriage, regretted by both husband and wife, ended after the two read an American poem and invited its author to come and live with them. Its author was a violent feminist, an original poet, a more than original thinker, and a personality of seductive and overmastering force. Judging from what Graves has written about her (in many poems, in some novels, and in his ecstatic epilogue to *Goodbye to All That,* in which he tells how he and she "went together to the land where the dead parade the streets and there met with demons and returned with the demons still treading behind us," speaks of the "salvation" that, through her, he has neared, and calls her a being essentially different from all others, a mystic savior "living invisibly, against kind, as dead, beyond event"), I believe that it is simplest to think of her as, so to speak, the White Goddess incarnate, the Mother-Muse in contemporary flesh. She seems to have had a radical influence on Graves's life, poetry, and opinions until 1939; and it was only after Graves was no longer in a position to be dominated by her in specific practice that he worked out his general theory of the necessary dominance of the White Goddess, the Mother-Muse, over all men, all poets.

Graves's theoretical picture of what life necessarily must be is so clearly related to what his life actually has been that it is possible to make summaries or outlines of the two, to put these outlines side by side, and to see that they match in every detail: this is what I have tried to do. (If the reader feels that he understands no better than before how and why Graves's world picture came into existence, either

I have made very bad summaries or else I have deluded myself with an imaginary resemblance.) One does not need much of a psychoanalytical or anthropological background to see that Graves's world picture is a projection upon the universe of his own unconscious, of the compulsively repeated situation in which, alone, it is able to find satisfaction; or to see that this world picture is one familiar, in structure and in much detail, in the fantasies of children and neurotics, in dreams, in fairy tales, and, of course, in the myths and symbols of savages and of earlier cultures. Many details of case histories, much of Freud's theoretical analysis, are so specifically illuminating about Graves's myth that I would have quoted or summarized them here, if it had been possible to do so without extending this essay into a third issue of the *Review.* That all affect, libido, mana should be concentrated in this one figure of the Mother-Muse; that love and sexuality should be inseparably intermingled with fear, violence, destruction in this "female spider"—that the loved one should be, necessarily, the Bad Mother who, necessarily, deserts and destroys the child; that the child should permit against her no conscious aggression of any kind, and intend his *cruel, capricious, incontinent,* his *bitch, vixen, hag,* to be neither condemnation nor invective, but only fascinated description of the loved and worshipped Mother and Goddess, She-Who-Must-Be-Obeyed—all this is very interesting and very unoriginal. One encounters a rigorous, profound, and quite unparalleled understanding of such cases as Graves's in the many volumes of Freud; but one can read an excellent empirical, schematic description of them in Volume VII of Jung's *Collected Works,* in the second part of the essay entitled "The Relations between the Ego and the Unconscious." Anyone familiar with what Jung has written about the *persona* and *anima,* and what happens when a man projects this *anima* upon the world and identifies himself with it, will more than once give a laugh of astonished recognition as he goes through *The White Goddess.*

The double-natured Graves has continually written about this split in himself—thought of it, once, as the poet's necessary condition: "I regarded poetry as, first, a personal cathartic for the poet suffering from some inner conflict, and then as a cathartic for readers in a similar conflict." One side of Robert Graves was—and is—the Graves or Father-of-the-Regiment side: the dry, matter-of-fact, potboiling, puzzle-solving, stamp-collecting, "anti-sentimental to the point of insolence" side, which notes, counts, orders, explains, explains away, which removes all affect from the world and replaces it by professional technique, pigeonholing, logic chopping. When this side is haunted or possessed by the childish, womanly, disorderly, emotional nightside of things, by the irresistible or inconsequential Unconscious—when the *dusty-featured Lollocks, by sloth on sorrow fathered, play hide and seek* among the *unanswered letters, empty medicine bottles* of *disordered drawers; plague little children* who cannot sleep; *are nasty together in the bed's shadow,* when *the imbecile aged are overlong in dying;* are invisible to, denied by, the men they torment; are visible to women, *naughty wives* who *slyly allow them* to lick their *honey-sticky fingers*—when all this happens, the dry masculine Ego can protect itself from them only by *hard broom and soft broom, / To well comb the hair, / To well brush the shoe, / And to pay every debt / So soon as it's due.* These measures—so Graves says—are *sovereign against Lollocks.*

And so they are, much of the day, a little of the night; that they are ever sovereign against "the Mother of All Living, the ancient power of fright and lust—the female spider or the queen-bee whose embrace is death," I doubt. The whole Tory, saddle-soap, regimental-song-singing side of Graves can only drug, quiet temporarily, disregard as long as routine and common sense have power, the demands, manifestations, and existence of Graves's other side, the side that says: "Oh, *him*! He's just something I fool people with in the daytime."

Yet we should be foolish to believe its remark—to insist, with Graves's unconscious, that the male principle is without all affect, libido, mana. (We can see from Graves's early life, from his public-school experiences, why it is necessary for *him* to insist that this is so.) It would be equally foolish to believe that the White Goddess does not exist: she is as real as the Unconscious which she inhabits and from which she has been projected, first upon actual women and later upon the universe. (A car's headlights can rest upon a deer until the deer moves away, but then the beam of light goes out to the sky beyond.) The usefulness of this projection, the therapeutic value of Graves's myth, is obvious: it has been able to bring into efficient and fairly amiable symbiosis the antagonistic halves of his nature.

Graves understands men far better than he understands women; has taken as his own *persona* or mask or life style the terse, professional, matter-of-fact, learned Head of the Regiment—Colonel Ben Jonson of the Royal Welch Fusiliers, so to speak. Men are as dry and as known to him as his own Ego; women are as unknown, and therefore as all-powerful and as all-attractive, as his own Id. Salvation, Graves has to believe, comes through Woman alone; regimented masculinity can work only for, by means of, everyday routine, unless it is *put into the service of Woman.* Graves is willing to have the Ego do anything for the Id except notice that it *is* the Id, analyze it, explain it as subjective necessity; instead the Ego completely accepts the Id and then, most ingeniously and logically and disingenuously, works out an endless explanation of, justification for, every aspect of what it insists is objective necessity. (All of Graves's readers must have felt: "Here is a man who can explain anything.") Graves's Ego can dismiss any rebellion against the reign of Woman with a hearty matter-of-fact—next to the White Goddess, matter-of-factness is the most important thing in the world to Graves—"Nonsense! nonsense!"; can dryly, grotesquely, and cruelly satirize those who rebel; can pigeonhole them, explain them, explain them away—and all in the service of the Mother! No wonder that the once-torn-in-two Graves becomes sure, calm, unquestioning; lives in the satisfied certainty that he is right, and the world wrong, about anything, anything! He has become, so to speak, his own Laura Riding. *There is only one Goddess, and Graves is her prophet*—and isn't the prophet of the White Goddess the nearest thing to the White Goddess?

If you break your neck every time you climb over a stile, soon you will be saying that the necessary condition of all men is to break, not rib, not thigh, not arm, not shin, but always, without fail, T H E N E C K when climbing over stiles; by making the accidental circumstances of your life the necessary conditions of all lives, you have transformed yourself from an accident-prone analysand into an emblematic Oedipus. Instead of going on thinking of himself, with shaky hope, as an abnormal eccentric, a "spiritual Quixote" better than the world, perhaps, in his own queer way, Graves now can think of himself as representing the norm, as being the one surviving citizen of that original matriarchal, normal state from which the abnormal, eccentric world has departed. The Mother whom he once clung to in personal shame ("childishly / I dart to Mother-skirts of love and peace / To play with toys until those horrors leave me")—what will the Fathers of the Regiment say?—turns out to be, as he can show with impersonal historical objectivity, the "real" Father of the Regiment: the Father-Principle, if you trace it back far enough, is really the Mother-Principle, and has inherited from the Primal Mother what legitimacy it has. Graves wants all ends to be Woman, and Man no more than the means to them. Everything has an original matriarchal core; all Life (and all "good" Death) comes from Woman. Authority is extremely important to Graves: by means of his myth he is able to get rid of the dry, lifeless, external authority of the father, the public school, the regiment, and to replace it with the wet, live, internal authority of the mother. All that is finally important to Graves is condensed in the one figure of the Mother-Mistress-Muse, she who creates, nourishes, seduces, destroys; she who saves us—or, as good as saving, destroys us—as long as we love her, write poems to her, submit to her without question, use all our professional, Regimental, masculine qualities in her service. Death is swallowed up in victory, said St. Paul; for Graves Life, Death, everything that exists is swallowed up in the White Goddess.

Graves's poems will certainly seem to the reader, as they seem to me, a great deal more interesting than any explanation of their origin. This account is no more than a sketch: the psychoanalytically or anthropologically minded reader will find in the poems, in *Goodbye to All That*, in *The White Goddess*, many things that I should have liked to discuss, many that I should have liked to understand. Because of the White Goddess, some of the most beautiful poems of our time have come into existence. But our gratitude to her need not stop there: as we read Graves's account of her we can say to ourselves, "We *are* the ancients," for it furnishes an almost incomparably beautiful illustration of the truth of Freud's "The power of creating myths is not extinct, but still produces in the neuroses the same psychical products as in the most ancient times."

[*1956/TBC*]

Love and Poetry

———————

Children of the future Age
Reading this indignant page,
Know that in a former time
Love! sweet Love! was thought a crime.

SO BLAKE WROTE, LONG AGO; and long ago, back in what my daughter calls the Gay Twenties; back when a girl's waist was at her knees and her hat brim at her eyes and she wasn't a girl at all but a flapper; back when, day after day, I stared speechlessly at the head one desk up and one desk over, with its pilot's helmet of shining red hair—back then, long ago, I read what Blake had written.

I had just finished H. G. Wells's *Men Like Gods*, a magazine serial of beings who never were and, I guess, never will be: the good and naked people of the future. As I read Blake's stanza, I saw those shining children of the future Age gazing in perplexed wonder at this page from the criminal, miserable past. It seemed to me that I, like Blake, was one of them; under the Keds and khaki riding trousers and ribbed brown cotton stockings in which the past had clothed me, I was naked and I shone. I didn't think it queer that, 150 years after Blake, the future still hadn't come, so that Blake and it and I were still stuck miserably in the dark, perpetually present past; I didn't ask myself: What past or present or future ever made a little boy wear tennis shoes, riding trousers, and brown cotton stockings? When, at a hotel, I was allowed to order anything I pleased for breakfast and got a chocolate éclair and a strawberry milk shake, I didn't think that queer either.

It seemed to me that I did only two things: the things people made me do, and reasonable things. And how many of the reasonable things were Thought A Crime! The future in which, naked, shining,

I was to sit eating my éclair, drinking my milk shake, and staring across the aisle at Joyce Meek for all eternity, with nobody minding, not even Joyce Meek—the future in which we would all live so, in liberty, in the reasonable working out of our desires—that was the world to which I belonged; if I had had a watch it would have ticked: Come quick, O world, come quick, come quick!

That world never came, of course; tomorrow never comes; the children of the future are only you. And it is tempting to someone on the side of poetry to tell you that it is always the arbitrary, contingent Past in which we live; that the bright, rational Future is only the illusion of youth, of that hopeful, romantic potentiality that existence always thwarts; that it is the poet, and not the social worker or marriage counselor, who is our true guide to love and marriage, since he writes about the real, cater-cornered past in which Achilles and Swann and you and I live and love, and not about that projected, upright future in which the mean marries the median and they have four siblings and live happily ever after.

But to say so would be false. The dark past and the bright future and the lightless and timeless Unconscious lie side by side, in unchanging contradiction, within the poet's stories and pictures and songs and poems, just as they do in our lives—the poems repeat in their own structure the structure of existence, and have, consequently, a representative truth. A poet was the first psychoanalyst, the poet who wrote, "Sooner murder an infant in its cradle than nurse unacted desires"; wrote, "Energy is the only life . . . and Reason is the bound or outward circumference of Energy. Energy is Eternal Delight"; wrote, "What is it men in women do require? / The lineaments of Gratified Desire. / What is it women do in men require? / The lineaments of Gratified Desire"; wrote,

"Love seeketh not Itself to please,
Nor for itself hath any care,
But for another gives its ease,
And builds a Heaven in Hell's despair."

So sung a little Clod of Clay
Trodden with the cattle's feet,
But a Pebble of the brook
Warbled out these metres meet:

"Love seeketh only Self to please,
To bind another to Its delight,

Joys in another's loss of ease
And builds a Hell in Heaven's despite."

And if the first psychoanalyst was the poet William Blake, the sec-
ond—he who said that he had only rediscovered, systematized, what
the poets had found out before him—was surely a poet of a strange
and penetrating kind, the poet Sigmund Freud; any essay on love and
marriage and poetry might well ask for itself the blessing of one of the
most loving and most married of mortals, a husband and father who
could describe with lyric humor the very tables and chairs, keys and
sewing baskets of a household, and finish by calling it "a little world
of happiness, of silent friends and emblems of honorable humanity."

So much of the poetry of the past is poetry about love—once
readers expected love poems from poets almost as they expected ser-
mons from preachers—that our eyes are still dazzled, our ears still
ringing, with the bright blur of "O thou weed, / Who art so lovely fair
and smell'st so sweet / That the sense aches at thee"; of "With thee
conversing I forget all time"; of "Make the violent wheels / Of Time
and Fortune stand; and great Existence, / The Maker's Treasury, now
seem not to be / To all but my approaching friend and me"; of "They
flee from me that sometime did me seek / With naked foot stalking
within my chamber"; of "Then tell, O tell, how thou didst murder
me!"; of "Stay for me there! I will not fail / To meet thee in that
hollow vale"; of

> Ay me! ay me! with what another heart
> In days far-off, and with what other eyes
> I used to watch—if I be he that watched—
> The lucid outline forming round thee; saw
> The dim curls kindle into sunny rings;
> Changed with thy mystic change, and felt my blood
> Glow with the glow that slowly crimson'd all
> Thy presence and thy portals, while I lay,
> Mouth, forehead, eyelids, growing dewy-warm
> With kisses balmier than half-opening buds
> Of April, and could hear the lips that kiss'd
> Whispering I knew not what of wild and sweet,
> Like that strange song I heard Apollo sing
> While Ilion like a mist rose into towers.

Today it is a private preoccupation, and not a public expecta-
tion, that love poems are written to satisfy; and if these are hardly

more common than poems about lovelessness, the distortions and frustrations of love—"Portrait of a Lady," "Prufrock," "Gerontion," and *The Waste Land* are, in one sense, a long personal poem on the subject—still, such poets as Hardy, Rilke, Yeats, Frost, Lawrence, and Graves have written in our century love poems that can compare with almost any of the love poems of the past. And, too, the last hundred or so years have produced all those unprecedentedly magnificent extensive treatments of that extensive process, love, by such poets (in the larger sense of the word) as Proust, Tolstoy, Chekhov, Emily Brontë, a hundred more. Even in the free, the rational, the impossible future, won't Shakespeare and Proust and Goethe tell us more than any *Textbook of Modern Marriage*, no matter how colorful its graphs, anatomical its diagrams, inclusive its tables? When the mean marries the median and they go home and sit down beside the firepl—beside the radiant heating unit in the wallboard, won't it still be Elizabeth Barrett Browning's *Sonnets from the Portuguese* that he puts on the tape recorder for her?

And even if the tomorrow of our dreams and predictions never comes, our todays already are changing so fast that the people of a photograph are old-fashioned before its paper can yellow, and the middle-aged live in an unpredicted future. You who read are the children of an age in which Love is a third the Crime it was, and a third an Industry, and a third a Right, the right of youth. (And youth too has become the right, the almost obligatory right, of anybody younger than Marlene Dietrich: the sexy grandma has replaced the foxy grandpa, and stores sell or will soon sell matching grandmother-and-granddaughter sets, so that the milkman can murmur, "I took you for her sister.") The good and two-thirds naked children of the future blaze out at one, in panties and girdles or all ungirdled, from every other advertisement—for Sex Sells, sells anything; and as one looks at what is sold, and the associated flesh that sells it, one sees that the greatest power, and the sweetest—Eros, builder and destroyer of cities—is for these not joy, not necessity, but only the policy of the firm. O Future, here around me now, in which junior-high-school girls go steady with junior-high-school boys, marry in high school and repent at college! Or rather, do not repent but begin with assured hope the life in which, without father, mother, aunt, or servant, alone with their little boys and little girls and an electric dishwasher, they await the day when these steady-going children of theirs marry, set out for college, and leave the still-young parents alone forever with the washer . . . You cannot have your cake and eat it too? We have changed all that. Romeo's and Juliet's parents sit with a social worker and a marriage broker—ah no, marriage counselor—until the well-counseled Montagues, the well-worked-over Capulets ship the children off to the University of Padua, where, with part-time jobs, allowances from both families, and a freezer full of TV Dinners, they live in bliss with their babies. And the moral is: *The course of true love ever did run smooth; Why should I make it at home when the store makes it better?; Love is the piece that finishes every puzzle.*

If England is a nation of shopkeepers, surely our own country is a nation of homemakers—of homemakers and their consorts. Blake wrote:

> I went to the Garden of Love,
> And saw what I never had seen:
> A Chapel was built in the midst,
> Where I used to play on the green.
>
> And the gates of this Chapel were shut,
> And "Thou shalt not" writ over the door;
> So I turn'd to the Garden of Love
> That so many sweet flowers bore;
>
> And I saw it was filled with graves,
> And tomb-stones where flowers should be:
> And Priests in black gowns were walking their rounds,
> And binding with briars my joys and desires.

The anguish that vibrates in the rhymes of those last two lines is not an obsolescent anguish: under the surface, the first green Garden and the last black one are what they were. But instead of *Thou shalt not*, now, there is *Nobody else does, and surely my little girl wouldn't want to be different from everybody else*; the angel with the flaming sword has put down his sword and taken up his card index and whispers: *Adjust, adjust—when there is not one left that I can tell from another, Paradise will have come again.*

And love, which is nourished on difficulties and prohibitions—which grows as rankly in caves in the dark, or under fig leaves, as in sunlight—how does love thrive on this bland, salt-free, even-caloried diet, the diet of a good invalid? For love *is* a crime, if something that is stronger than society itself, something in which the deluded, absolute desire of the individual triumphs over, forgets the existence of all public considerations, is a crime; and our American attempt to base society itself upon the crime, to have or pretend to have all marriages, marriages of love and none the loveless works of expedience— this attempt is as audacious as our attempt to have or pretend to have no one poor and everyone equal. Our audacity, like love itself, is partly an ideal and partly a delusion; and, I have to confess, I sympathize with each part. It is only human to be deluded so; without such delusions is humanity possible? Eighteenth-century warfare, historians say, was one of the greatest triumphs of Western civilization; and how much greater a triumph or discovery or invention is the Love! sweet Love! of Blake's stanza, the romantic love that so many cultures know nothing of . . . If *Antony and Cleopatra* is actually, as it seems to me, the supreme literary expression of our culture, this is the most fitting and appropriate of actualities.

Samuel Johnson could speak, with marvelous contempt, of "wretched unidea'd girls"; but he could also call love "that passion which he who never felt never was happy," and could declare, with superb conclusiveness: "Marriage has many pains but celibacy has no pleasures." My heart—my poor representative Western heart—goes out to him, just as it goes out to Darwin when, deciding between a married and a single life, the great scientist writes in his diary: "What is the use of working without sympathy from near and dear friends? Who are near and dear friends to the old, except relatives? My God, it is intolerable to think of spending one's whole life like a neuter bee working, working, and nothing after all. —No, no won't do. —Imagine living all one's days solitarily in smoky, dirty London house— Only picture to yourself a nice soft wife on a sofa, with good fire and books and music perhaps— Marry, marry, marry. Q.E.D."

A nice soft wife on a sofa, with good fire and books and music perhaps: this is the poetry of marriage; what bachelor can hear it without a pang, what husband hear it without wanting to leave his nasty hard typewriter, light the fire, put *Verklärte Nacht* on the phonograph and sit with his wife—his nice soft wife—on the sofa? Love makes poets of us all. When Richard Garnett writes: "Eros is the wisest of the gods, because the oldest, and because there is nothing from which he does not learn," he is as truly a poet as is Rilke when he writes: "Love consists in this, that two solitudes protect and touch and greet one another." The solitude that another solitude greets, protects, and touches—learns, by love—is no longer able to believe in its own solitariness, and hears with perplexed wonder the voices that tell it that each of us is, now and forever, alone.

"Do what you will, this life's a fiction / And is made up of Contradiction," Blake wrote. I can't believe the first line, can't help believing the second. Love, and the marriages and poems which grow out of love, contain these vital contradictions in concentrated form. Love makes less than sense and much more than sense—says to us, like the universe: "Do I contradict myself? Well then I contradict myself."

Love removes none of the contradictions of our lives but, by adding one more, induces us to accept them all; transfigured by it, we had rather be loved than right—are willing, even, to be happy. Whether it moves the sun and the other stars we cannot tell, but that it moves the men and women and children and cats and dogs among whom we live we can hardly doubt. The house not built upon it, blessed by it, is founded upon the sand. We can call Eros the best and the worst of the gods, and the strangest, and the strongest. And yet often it is not bad at all, but sweet and dear and shining; and when it *is* bad, dark, nameless, turns upon us its

> . . . soft unchristened smile
> That shadows neither love nor guile,
> But shameless will and power intense
> In secret sensuous innocence—

is it so bad, always, even then? Our lives question and explain what they need only accept.

[1956/KA]

Changes of Attitude and Rhetoric in Auden's Poetry

We never step twice into the same Auden.
—HERACLITUS

IN THE FIRST PART of this article I want to analyze the general position Auden makes for himself in his early poems, and to show how the very different attitude of the later poems developed from it; in the second part I shall describe the language of the early poems and the rhetoric of the late, and try to show why one developed from the other. I have borrowed several terms from an extremely good book—Kenneth Burke's *Attitudes toward History*—and I should like to make acknowledgments for them.

I

The date is *c.* 1930, the place England. Auden (and the group of friends with whom he identifies himself) is unable or unwilling to accept the values and authority, the general world picture of the late-capitalist society in which he finds himself. He is conscious of a profound alienation, intellectual, moral, and aesthetic—financial and sexual, even. Since he rejects the established order, it is necessary for him to find or make a new order, a myth by which he and his can possess the world. Auden synthesizes (more or less as the digestive organs synthesize enzymes) his own order from a number of sources: (1) Marx—Communism in general. (2) Freud and Groddeck: in gen-

eral, the risky and nonscientific, but fertile and imaginative, side of
modern psychology. (3) A cluster of related sources: the folk, the
blood, intuition, religion and mysticism, fairy tales, parables, and so
forth—this group includes a number of semi-Fascist elements.
(4) The sciences, biology particularly: these seem to be available to
him because they have been only partially assimilated by capitalist
culture, and because, like mathematics, they are practically incapable
of being corrupted by it. (5) All sorts of boyish sources of value: fly-
ing, polar exploration, mountain climbing, fighting, the thrilling side
of science, public-school life, sports, big-scale practical jokes, "the
spies' career," etc. (6) Homosexuality: if the ordinary sexual values are
taken as negative and rejected, this can be accepted as a source of pos-
itive revolutionary values.

Auden is able to set up a We (whom he identifies himself with—
rejection loves company) in opposition to the enemy They; neither We
nor They are the relatively distinct or simple entities one finds in po-
litical or economic analyses, but are tremendous clusters of elements
derived from almost every source: Auden is interested in establishing
a dichotomy in which one side, naturally, gets all the worst of it, and
he wants this *all the worst* to be as complete as possible, to cover every-
thing from imperialism to underlining too many words in letters. A
reader may be indifferent to some or most of Their bad points, but
They are given so many that even the most confirmed ostrich will at
some point break down and consent to Auden's rejection. Auden wants
a total war, a total victory; he does not make the political mistake of
taking over a clear limited position and leaving to the enemy every-
thing else. Sometimes his aptitude for giving all he likes to Us, all he
doesn't like to Them, passes over from ingenuity into positive ge-
nius—or disingenuousness. I am going to treat this We–They oppo-
sition at the greatest length—a treatment of it is practically a treat-
ment of Auden's early position; and I shall mix in some discussion of
the sources of value I have listed.

Auden begins: The death of the old order is inevitable; it is al-
ready economically unsound, morally corrupt, intellectually bank-
rupt, and so forth. We = the Future, They = the Past. (So any reader
tends to string along with Us and that perpetual winner, the Future.)
Auden gets this from Marxism, of course; but never at any time was
he a thorough Marxist: it would have meant giving up too much to the
enemy. He keeps all sorts of things a Marxist rejects, and some of his
most cherished doctrines—as the reader will see—are in direct con-
tradiction to his Marxism. At the ultimate compulsive level of belief

most of his Marxism drops away (and, in the last few years, *has* dropped away); his psychoanalytical, vaguely medical beliefs are so much more essential to Auden—"son of a nurse and doctor, loaned a dream"—that the fables he may have wanted to make Marxist always turn out to be psychoanalytical. But Marxism as a source of energy, of active and tragic insight, was invaluable; it was badly needed to counteract the passivity, the trust in Understanding and Love and God, that are endemic in Auden. Marxism has always supplied most of the terror in his poetry; in his latest poems all that remains is the pity—an invalid's diet, like milk toast.

Obviously They represent Business, Industrialism, Exploitation—and, worse than that, a failing business, an industrialism whose machines are already rusting. Auden had seen what happened to England during a long depression, and he made a romantic and beautifully effective extension of this, not merely into decadence, but into an actual breakdown of the whole machinery, a Wellsish state where commerce and transportation have gone to pieces, where the ships lie "long high and dry," where no one goes "further than railhead or the end of pier," where the professional traveler "asked at fireside . . . is dumb." The finest of these poems is XXV in *Poems*: history before the event, one's susceptible and extravagant heart tells one. (Incidentally, this vision is entirely non-Marxist.) Here Auden finds a symbol whose variants are obsessive for him, reasonably so for the reader, another machine's child: *grass-grown pitbank, abandoned seam, the silted harbors, derelict works*—these, and the wires that carry nothing, the rails over which no one comes, are completely moving to Auden, a boy who wanted to be a mining engineer, who "Loved a pumping-engine, / Thought it every bit as / Beautiful as you." The thought of those "beautiful machines that never talked / But let the small boy worship them," abandoned and rusting in the wet countryside—the early Auden sees even his machines in rural surroundings—was perhaps, unconsciously, quite as influential as some political or humanitarian considerations.

Auden relates science to Marxism in an unexpected but perfectly orthodox way: Lenin says somewhere that in the most general sense Marxism is a theory of evolution. Auden quite consciously makes this connection; evolution, as a source both of insight and image, is always just at the back of his earliest poems. (This, along with his countryishness—Auden began by writing poetry like Hardy and Thomas—explains his endless procession of birds and beasts, symbols hardly an early poem is without.) IV in *Poems* is nothing

but an account of evolution—by some neo-Hardyish *I* behind it—
and a rather Marxist extension of it into man's history and everyday
life. The critical points where quantity changes into quality, the
Hegelian dialectic, what Burke calls neo-Malthusian limits—all these
are plain in the poem. There are many examples of this coalition of
Marxism and biology; probably the prettiest is IX, a poem with the re-
frain, "Here am I, here are you: / But what does it mean? What are
we going to do?" The *I* of the poem is supposed to be anonymous and
typical, a lay figure of late capitalism; he has not retained even the
dignity of rhetoric, but speaks in a style that is an odd blank parody
of popular songs. He has finally arrived at the end of his blind alley:
he has a wife, a car, a mother complex, a vacation, and no use or de-
sire for any. All he can make himself ask for is some fresh tea, some
rugs—this to remind you of Auden's favorite view of capitalism: a so-
ciety where everyone is sick. Even his instincts have broken down: he
doesn't want to go to bed with Honey, all the wires to the base in his
spine are severed. The poem develops in this way up to the next to the
last stanza: "In my veins there is a wish, / And a memory of
fish: / When I lie crying on the floor, / It says, 'You've often done
this before.' " The "wish" in the blood is the evolutionary will, the
blind urge of the species to assimilate the universe. He remembers the
fish, that at a similar impasse, a similar critical point, changed over to
land, a new form of being. Here for the millionth time (the racial
memory tells the weeping individual) is the place where the contra-
diction has to be resolved; where the old answer, useless now, has to
be transcended; where all the quantitative changes are over, where the
qualitative leap has to occur. The individual remembers all these crit-
ical points because he is the product of them. And the individual, in
the last stanza, is given a complete doom ("I've come a very long way
to prove / No land, no water, and no love"). But his bankruptcy and
liquidation are taken as inevitable for the species, a necessary mode of
progression: the destructive interregnum between the old form and
the new is inescapable, as old as life. The strategic value in Auden's
joining of Marxism and evolution, his constant shifting of terms from
one sphere to the other, is this: the reader will tend to accept the de-
sired political and economic changes (and the form of these) as them-
selves inevitable, something it is as ludicrous or pathetic to resist as
evolution.

When compared with the folkish Us, They are complicated, sub-
tle in a barren Alexandrian-encyclopedia way. They are scholarly in-
trospective observers, We have the insight and natural certainty of the

naïve, of Christ's children, of fools, of the third sons in fairy stories. They are aridly commercial, financial, distributive; We represent real production, the soil. They are bourgeois-respectable or perverted; We are folk-simple, or else consciously bohemian so as to break up Their system and morale—there is also a suggestion of the prodigal son, of being reborn through sin. They represent the sterile city, We the fertile country; I want to emphasize this, the surprisingly *rural* character of most of Auden's earliest poems, because so far as I know everyone has emphasized the opposite. They are white-collar workers, executives, or idlers—those who neither "make" nor "do"; We are scientists, explorers, farmers, manual laborers, aviators, fighters and conspirators—the real makers and doers. Auden gets Science over on Our side by his constant use of it both for insight and images, by his admiration of, preoccupation with, the fertile adventurous side of it; he leaves Them only the decadent complexity of Jeans or "psychological" economics.

Since Auden has had to reject Tradition, he sets up a new tradition formed of the available elements (available because rejected, neglected, or misinterpreted) of the old. There are hundreds of examples of this process (particularly when it comes to appropriating old writers as Our ancestors); the process is necessary partly to reassure oneself, partly to reassure one's readers, who otherwise would have to reject Our position because accepting it necessitates rejecting too much else. One can see this working even in the form of Auden's early poetry: in all the Anglo-Saxon imitation; the Skeltonics; the Hopkins accentual verse, alliteration, assonance, consonance; the Owen rhymes; the use of the fairy story, parable, ballad, popular song—the folk tradition They have rejected or collected in Childs. Thus Auden has selected his own ancestors, made from the disliked or misprized his own tradition.

In *The Orators* Auden shows, by means of the regular Mendelian inheritance chart, that one's "true ancestor" may be neither a father nor a mother, but an uncle. (His true ancestor wasn't the Tradition, but the particular elements of it most like himself.) This concept is extremely useful to Auden in (1) family, (2) religious, and (3) political relations. (1) By this means he acquires a different and active type of family relationship to set up against the inertia of the ordinary bourgeois womanized family. (2) God is addressed and thought of as Uncle instead of Father: God as Uncle will help revolutionary Us just as naturally and appropriately as God as Father would help his legitimate sons, the Enemy. This Uncle has a Christlike sacrificial-hero representative on earth, who is surrounded with a great deal of early-Christian, secret-service paraphernalia. This hero is confused or identified with (3) the political leader, a notably unpolitical sort of fantasy Hitler, who seems to have strayed into politics with his worshippers only because he lives in an unreligious age. There is hardly more politics in early Auden than in G. A. Henty; what one gets is mostly religion, hero worship, and Adventure, combined with the odd Lawrence-Nazi folk mysticism that serves as a false front for the real politics behind it—which Auden doesn't treat.

When Auden occasionally prays to this Uncle he asks in blunt definite language for definite things: it is a personal, concrete affair. In his later poetry Auden is always praying or exhorting, but only to some abstract eclectic Something-or-Other, who is asked in vague exalted language for vague exalted abstractions. Once Auden wanted evils removed by revolutionary action, and he warned *(it is later than you think)*. Today—when he is all ends and no means, and sees everything in the long run—he exhorts *(we all know how late it is, but with Love and Understanding it is not too late for us to . . .)* or prays *(Thou knowest—O save us!)*. Most of this belongs to the bad half of what Burke calls secular prayer: the attempt, inside any system, to pray away, exhort away, legislate away evils that are not incidental but essential to the system. Auden used to satirize the whole "change of heart" point of view; "do not speak of a change of heart," he warned. He had a deceived chorus sing vacantly: "Revolutionary worker / I get what you mean. / But what you're needing / 'S a revolution within." He came to scoff, he remained to pray: for a general moral improvement, a spiritual rebirth, Love. Remembering some of the incredible conclusions to the later poems—*Life must live*, Auden's wish to *lift an affirming flame*—the reader may object that this sort of thing is sentimental idealism. But sentimental idealism is a necessity for someone who, after rejecting a system as evil, finally accepts it— even with all the moral reservations and exhortations possible. The sentimentality and idealism, the vague abstraction of such prayers and exhortations, is a *sine qua non*: we can fool ourselves into praying for some vague general change of heart that is going to produce, automatically, all the specific changes that even we could never be foolish enough to pray for. When Auden prays for anything specific at all; when he prays against the organization of the world that makes impossible the moral and spiritual changes he prays for, it will be possible to take the prayer as something more than conscience- and face-saving sublimation, a device ideally suited to make action un-urgent and its nature vague.

Swift believed—to quote Empson—that "everything spiritual

and valuable has a gross and revolting parody, very similar to it, with the same name." Similarly, everything spiritual and valuable has a sentimental idealistic parody; and——by a horrible variant of Gresham's law——this parody replaces it with stupid people, discredits it with cleverer people. (The reactionary intellectual's immediate revulsion toward anything that even smells of "progress" or "humanitarianism" is an example of the operation of this law.) Auden's desire to get away from the negativism typical of so much modernist poetry has managed to make the worst sections of his latest lyrics not much more than well-meaning gush. These sentimental parodies are far more dangerous than any gross ones could possibly be. If we have wicked things to say, and say them badly, not even the Girl Guides are injured; but if we say badly what is "spiritual and valuable," we not only spoil it, but help to replace or discredit the already expressed good that we wish to preserve. Let me quote Auden against himself: "And what was livelihood / Is tallness, strongness / Words and longness, / All glory and all story / Solemn and not so good."

Just how did Auden manage to change from almost Communist to quite liberal? He did *not* switch over under stress of circumstance; long before any circumstances developed he was making his Progress by way of an old and odd route: mysticism. In Auden's middle period one finds a growing preoccupation with a familiar cluster of ideas: All power corrupts; absolute power corrupts absolutely. Government, a necessary evil, destroys the governors. All action is evil; the will is evil; life itself is evil. The only escape lies in the avoidance of action, the abnegation of the will. I don't mean that Auden wholly or practically accepted all this——who does? But he was more or less fascinated by such ideas (completely opposed to Marxism; fairly congenial with a loose extension of psychoanalysis), and *used* them: If all government is evil, why should we put our trust in, die for, a choice of evils? If all action is evil, how can we put our faith in doing anything? If the will itself is evil, why select, plan, do? Life is evil; surely the contemplation of ideal ends is better than the willing and doing of the particular, so-often-evil means.

The reader may object that the method of change I suggest is too crude. But let me quote against him the changer: "The windiest militant trash / Important Persons shout / Is not so crude as our wish . . ." What is the mechanism of most changes of attitude?——the search for any reasons that will justify our believing what it has become necessary for us to believe. How many of us can keep from chorusing with Bolingbroke, *God knows, my son, by what bypaths and indirect crook'd ways I met this*—position? Marxism was too narrow, tough, and materialistic for the Essential Auden, who would far rather look dark with Heraclitus than laugh with Democritus. Auden's disposition itself (Isherwood says that if Auden had his way their plays would be nothing but choruses of angels); the fact that he was never a consistent or orthodox Marxist; the constant pressure of a whole society against any dangerous heresy inside it; Auden's strong "medical" inclinations, his fundamental picture of society as diseased, willing itself to be diseased (a case to be sympathized with, treated, and talked to à la Groddeck); his increasing interest in metaphysics and religion; the short-range defeatism, the compensatory long-range optimism that kept growing during the interminable defeat of the thirties—these, and more, made Auden's change inevitable.

But let me return to We and They, the early Auden. We are Love; They are hate and all the terrible perversions of love. There is an odd ambivalent attitude toward homosexuality: in Us it is a quite natural relationship shading off into comradeship (like Greek homosexuality in Naomi Mitchison), in Them it is just another decadent perversion. The reader can see this plainly in *The Dog beneath the Skin*: the Cozy Corner, where Jimmy "sent them crazy in his thick white socks," belongs to Them; We have the vague virtuous relationship between Alan and Francis, which the reader rates very high, since he is forced to compare it with Alan's relations with Miss Iris Crewe and Miss Lou Vipond. Such cultural homosexuality is an alienation more or less forced upon certain groups of Auden's society by the form of their education and the nature of their social and financial conditions. Where the members of a class and a sex are taught, in a prolonged narcissistic isolation, to hero-worship themselves—class and sex; where—to a different class—unemployment is normal, where one's pay is inadequate or impossible for more than one; where children are expensive liabilities instead of assets; where women are business competitors; where most social relationships have become as abstract, individualistic, and mobile as the relations of the labor market, homosexuality is a welcome asset to the state, one of the cheapest and least dangerous forms of revolution. One gets no such analysis in the early Auden, though a real uneasiness about Our condition is plain in the allegorical *Letter to a Wound*, implicit in the Airman's kleptomania. A contempt for women sometimes breaks out in little half-sublimated forms; "there is something peculiarly horrible about the idea of women pilots," writes the Airman, whose love for E. has not managed to give him any prejudice in her sex's favor.

Sometimes this contempt is openly expressed. "All of the women and most of the men / Shall work with their hands and not think again" is the early Auden's lyrical premonition of the ideal State of the future. Words fail me here; this is not tactics, not sense, and certainly not Marxism: compare Engels's contempt at Dühring's ingenuous belief that the Ideal State would have professional porters. All this is related to a Lawrence–Hitler–*Golden Bough* folk mysticism—complete with Führer, folk, blood, intuition, "the carved stone under the oaktree"—which crops up constantly; it is partly literary, partly real. What is wrong with it is too plain to say; what is right about it—the insistence on a real society, the dislike of the weird isolation and individualism, the helpless rejection, forced on so many of the members of our own society—may be worth mentioning. Auden has forgotten the good with the bad, and now takes the isolation of the individual—something that would have seemed impossible to almost any other society, that is a tragic perversion of ours—as necessary, an absolute that can only be accepted.

We are health, They are disease; everything Auden gets from Freud and Groddeck is used to put Them into the category of patients, of diseased sufferers who unconsciously will their own disease. This makes Our opposition not only good for Them but necessary— Our violence is the surgeon's violence, Their opposition is the opposition of madmen to psychiatrists. We are Life, They are Death. The death wish is the fundamental motive for all Their actions, Auden often says or implies; if They deny it, he retorts, "Naturally you're not *conscious* of it."

These earliest poems are soaked in Death: as the real violence of revolutionary action and as a very comprehensive symbol. Death is Their necessary and desired conclusion; often poems are written from Their increasingly desperate point of view. Death belongs to Us as martyrs, spies, explorers, tragic heroes—with a suggestion of scapegoat or criminal—who die for the people. It belongs to Us because We, Their negation, have been corrupted by Them, and must ourselves be transcended. But, most of all, it is a symbol for *rebirth*: it is only through death that We can leave the old for good, be finally reborn. I have been astonished to see how consistently most of the important elements of ritual (purification, rebirth, identification, etc.) are found in the early poems; their use often seems unconscious. The most common purification rituals (except that of purification by fire) are plain. There is purification through decay: physical and spiritual, the rotting away of the machines and the diseased perversions of the men. There

are constant glaciers, ice, northern exploration—enough to have made
Cleanth Brooks consider the fundamental metaphorical picture of the
early poems that of a new ice age. There is purification by water: in
the second poem in *On This Island* a sustained flood metaphor shifts
into parent-child imagery. There is some suggestion of purification
through sin. There is mountain climbing: from these cold heights
one can see differently, free of the old perspectives; one returns, like
Moses, with new insights. This is akin to the constantly used parable
of the fairy-tale search, the hero's dangerous labors or journey. And
the idea of rebirth is plainest of all, extending even to the common
images of ontogenetic or phylogenetic development; of the fetus,
newborn infant, or child; of the discontinuities of growth. The *uncle*
is so important because he is a new ancestor whom We can identify
ourselves with (Auden recommends "ancestor worship" of the true
ancestor, the Uncle); by this identification We destroy our real parents,
our Enemy ancestry, thus finally abolishing any remaining traces of
Them in us. These ideas and their extensions are worth tracing in de-
tail, if one had the space. Here is a quotation in which rebirth through
death is extremely explicit; seasonal rebirth and the womb of the
new order are packed in also. Auden writes that love

> Needs death, death of the grain, our death,
> Death of the old gang; would leave them
> In sullen valley where is made no friend,
> The old gang to be forgotten in the spring,
> The hard bitch and the riding-master.
> Stiff underground; deep in clear lake
> The lolling bridegroom, beautiful, there.

I want my treatment of Auden's early position to be suggestive
rather than exhausting, so I shall not carry it any further; though I
hate to stop short of all the comic traits Auden gives the Enemy,
wretched peculiarities as trivial as saying *I mean* or having a room
called the Den. The reader can do his own extending or filling in by
means of a little unusually attractive reading: Auden's early poems.
My own evaluation of Auden's changes in position has been fairly
plain in my discussion. There are some good things and some fantas-
tic ones in Auden's early attitude; if the reader calls it a muddle I
shall acquiesce, with the remark that the later position might be con-
sidered a more rarefied muddle. But poets rather specialize in mud-
dles—and I have no doubt which of the muddles was better for

Auden's poetry: one was fertile and usable, the other decidedly is not. Auden sometimes seems to be saying with Henry Clay, "I had rather be right than poetry"; but I am not sure, then, that he is either.

II

In considering Auden's earliest poems one finds little to say about peculiar kinds of rhetoric, but a great deal to say about a peculiar language. (The opposite is true of the late poems.) One sees how effective the best of the early poems are—how concrete, startling, and thoroughly realized their texture is; but one finds, on analysis, that they are astonishingly unrhetorical, that the tough magical effects that enchant one are not being accomplished by any elaborate rhetoric, but by a great variety of causes, the most noticeable of which is the language—a concrete, laconic, and eccentric variant of ordinary English. (It is derived, probably, from the extension of certain tendencies in Hopkins, Joyce, and Anglo-Saxon.) Even when Auden is not using this private language, his regular speech is tougher and terser because of it. I offer a list of some of its more important characteristics: (1) The frequent omission of articles and demonstrative adjectives. (2) The frequent omission of subjects—especially *I, you, he,* etc. (3) The frequent omission of *there* and similar introductory words. (4) The frequent omission of coordinate conjunctions, subordinating conjunctions, conjunctive adverbs, etc. Even prepositions are sometimes omitted. (5) The frequent omission of relative pronouns. (6) The frequent omission of auxiliary verbs. (7) Constant inversion, consciously effective changes of the usual word order. (8) Unusual punctuation: a decided underpunctuation is common. (9) To denote habitual action, verbals are regularly preferred to nouns. (10) The scarcity of adverbs, adjectives, or any words that can possibly be dispensed with. On the other hand, there are enormous numbers of verbs, verbals, and nouns. The result is a very strong speech. (11) Constant parataxis, often ungrammatical. In these poems Auden is willing to stretch or break most rules of grammar or syntax. (12) The use of dangling participles and other dangling modifiers. (13) A sort of portmanteau construction—common to the Elizabethans—in which a qualifying phrase may refer both to what comes before and to what comes after. (14) Repetition or partial repetition of words; this is allied to the use of like-sounding or similarly constructed words. (15) The use of absolute constructions. (16) The constant use of alliteration, assonance, consonance, etc. (17) The use of, normally uncoordinate elements as coordinates. (18) The use of unusual or unusually abrupt appositions. (19) The occasional use of archaic words or constructions. (20) Frequent ambiguity—usually effective, sometimes merely confusing. (21) Constant ellipses, sometimes enormous ones; similarly, there are frequent jumps in logic where one must make out a meaning without much help from the syntax. (22) The use of very long parallel constructions, generally elliptical; the elements may even be separated by periods. (23) The wide (sometimes very wide) separation of modifiers from what they modify. (24) The use of a homogeneous and somewhat specialized vocabulary. (25) The use of one part of speech for another: adjective for adverb, adverb for adjective, verb or preposition for noun, etc. (26) The insertion into a sentence of elements which have no orthodox syntactical relationship to any part of the sentence.

These are most of the more important characteristics. It is a list that obviously gives the reader no idea of the effect or value of the language; I hope that he will look up examples and minor characteristics himself—I have no space for them, nor for any thorough evaluation of the language and its effects. It seems to me generally successful; at its best, magnificent. It is easy to condemn it as an eccentric limitation of language; I am going to defend it as a creative extension. One can show, I think, that much of the early poems' strength and goodness—often original enough to seem positively magical—exist because of this language or because of its effect on Auden's regular language, and could not have been attained otherwise. The language fits what he has to say (or generates new and fitting things to say). It is original, not merely odd; it is "constructive," not merely *Transition* breaking-of-rules for breaking-of-rules' sake. Let me invoke for it the protecting aegis of the Elizabethans. (If the language of the early poems is unfamiliar to the reader, I beg him not to make any judgments on these remarks merely from my list of characteristics.)

In Auden's later poems the language becomes weaker. It is relatively passive and abstract; full of adverbs, adjectives, intransitive verbs, it seems pale and feeble by the side of his magnificently verb-y early speech. But the rhetoric becomes stronger. In the late poems there is a system of rhetorical devices so elaborate that Auden might list it under *Assets*, just as a firm lists its patents. I shall analyze a good many of these devices; and I shall sometimes give a good many examples of them, since I need to show that they are typical, and since I want the reader to appreciate the full weight and range of their use.

How much the texture of poetry depends on the poet's extreme sensitivity to different levels or ranges of words, to the juxtaposition, sometimes shocking and sometimes almost imperceptible, of words from different universes or way stations of discourse, can hardly be exaggerated; though if it can, reading Auden is the way to do it. Everyone recognizes such extreme cases as the Elizabethans' *gross and full of bread* formula and the Orators' Favorite—the insertion of a concrete word in an abstract context; but many of the nicer cases go unpraised and unanalyzed, though not unfelt. One of Auden's most thoroughly exploited rhetorical formulas (rhetoricians ought to distinguish it with his name) is an inversion of the Orators' Favorite: a surprisingly abstract word is put into a concrete "poetic" context—in general, unexpectedly abstract critical "nonpoetic" words, taken from relatively abstract technical "nonpoetic" universes of discourse, are substituted for their expected and concrete sisters. The consistent use of this device is one of the things that has got Auden's poetry attacked as relaxed or abstract. The device, like its opposite, is a variety of Effect by Incongruity. Here are some examples—a few from many; most of them will be rather obvious, since the less obvious depend too much on a largish context or established tone to be convenient for quotation:

The beauty's set cosmopolitan smile; love's fascinating biased hand; the baroque frontiers, the surrealist police; the shining neutral summer; the tree's clandestine tide; a new imprudent year; the small uncritical islands; and the indigenous figure on horseback / On the bridle-path down by the lake; the genteel dragon; the rare ambiguous monster; the luscious lateral blossoming of woe; weep the non-attached angels; their whorled unsubtle ears; the first voluptuous rectal sins; the band / Makes its tremendous statements; the hot incurious sun; and so on. In one stanza occur *the effusive welcome of the piers, the luxuriant life of the steep stone valleys,* and *the undiscriminating sea.* These last three are not very effective; I chose them to show how the method can degenerate into abstraction. The reader will have noticed that this device is often an inversion of the *gross and full of bread* formula, with the *and* omitted.

This sort of thing is not Auden's discovery, any more than accentual verse was Hopkins's; but its bureaucratization, its systematic use as a major principle of rhetoric, is new, I think. It is the opposite of poetic diction, where the abstract is thought of as the necessary and proper language of poetry; here the effect depends on the opposite idea, on the fact that the context of the poem (*ground* in relation to the expression's *figure*) is still concrete.

Another of Auden's usual formulas is the *juxtaposition of disparate coordinates*: this includes the Elizabethan adjective-formula and the extension of it to three or four not regularly coordinate terms. One finds many examples of the first (or of its common Shakespearean application to two nouns): *remote and hooded; nude and fabulous epochs; your unique and moping station; the noise and policies of summer; dumb and violet; deaf to prophecy or China's drum; the flutes and laughter of the happily diverted; the stoves and resignations of the frozen plains.* Here are some examples of the second: *the enchanted, the world, the sad;* (spoken of the sea) *the citiless, the corroding, the sorrow; the friend, the rash, the enemy / The essayist, the able; cold, impossible, ahead; the melting friend, the aqueduct, the flower; an illness, a beard, Arabia found in a bed, / Nanny defeated, money; were they or he / The physician, bridegroom, and incendiary?* See how beautifully a variation of the device can describe Civilization As We Know It:

> Certainly our city—with the byres of poverty down to
> The river's edge, the cathedral, the engines, the dogs;
>   Here is the cosmopolitan cooking
>   And the light alloys and the glass . . .

When Auden began to use the capitalized personified abstraction, he was extremely conscious of what he was doing, and meant for the reader to realize that: the use is different and exciting, a virtuoso performance meant to make the reader exclaim, "Why, he got away with it after all." One finds such things as *ga-ga Falsehood; Scandal praying with her sharp knees up; Lust . . . muttering to his fuses in a tunnel, "Could I meet here with Love, / I would hug him to death."* But Auden was like someone who keeps showing how well he can hold his liquor until he becomes a drunkard. At first he made all sorts of ingenious variations: he made capitalized personified abstractions out of verbs, adverbs, pronouns, or whole phrases. But at last even his ingenuity disappears; he is like a man who will drink canned heat, rubbing alcohol, anything. There is a thirteen-line menagerie where I Will, I Know, I Am, I Have Not, and I Am Loved peer idiotically from behind their bars; nearby, gobbling peanuts, throng the Brothered-One, the Not-Alone, the Just, the Happy-Go-Lucky, the Filthy, hundreds of We's and They's and Their's and Our's and Me's, the Terrible Demon, the Lost People, the Great, the Old Masters, and the Unexpected; they feel Love and Hate and Lust and Things; above them hover all sorts of tutelary deities: the Present, the Past, the Future, the Just City, the Good Place, Fate, Pride, Charity, Success, Knowledge, Wisdom, Violence, Life and Art and Salvation and Matter and the Nightmare, Form, the State, Democracy, Authority, Duality, Business, Collective Man, the Generalized Life, the Meaning of Knowing, the Flower of the Ages, and Real Estate. Reading *Another Time* is like attending an Elks' Convention of the Capital Letters; all my examples come from it, and I had not even begun to exhaust the supply. (There are not a tenth as many in his previous book of poems.) The reader must manage for himself a list of noncapitalized personified abstractions; experience has taught me that all this is a squeamish business, a pilgrimage through some interminable Vegetarians' Cafeteria.

The terrible thing about such rhetorical devices, about any of the mechanisms and patented insights that make up so much of any style, is that they are habit-forming, something the style demands in ever-increasing quantities. We learn subtle variations or extensions we once would have thought impossible or nonexistent; but we constantly permit ourselves excesses, both in quantity and quality, that once would have appalled us. That is how styles—and more than styles—degenerate. Stylistic rectitude, like any other, is something that has to be worked at all the time, a struggle—like sleeping or eating or living—that permits only temporary victories; and nothing makes us more susceptible to a vice than the knowledge that we have already overcome it. (The fact that one once used an argument somehow seems to give one the right to ignore it.)

Everyone must have noticed all the *the*'s in Auden's middle and late poems: *the this, the that, the other*—all the thousands of categories into which beings are flung. (Compare this with the early poems, where *the*'s are as far as possible omitted.) The bases of classification are thoroughly unsystematic, whatever comes to hand in need. The device is a convenient shorthand, shortcut, in which the type or trait is used as the unit of analysis: it is a useful method for handling the immense quantities and qualities of difference that everyone sees everywhere today—especially Auden, who took the world for his province without much hesitation. (The constant use of this method helps explain why Auden, in the plays, gets efficient observed types, but no characters.) There is plenty of journalism, fact as *summum bonum,* in Auden; his *the* method has an illusive effect of merely pointing to the Facts, a reality effective in itself. But Auden has far more than the good journalistic sense of the typical or immediately differentiating detail; his differentiating characteristics seem at their best conclusive. Let me finish with the rueful commonplace that he has exploited this method for all it is worth. In his later verse one finds the most mechanical or exaggerated examples: poems that are mere masques of abstractions, gatherings not of the clans but of the classes.

Auden depends a good deal on periphrasis: *the neat man / To their east who ordered Gorki to be electrified; the naughty life-forcer in the Norfolk jacket; that lean hard-bitten pioneer* (there follow fourteen lines: Dante); *the German who / Obscure in gas-lit London, brought* (there follow fifty lines about Marx); etc. It is easy for the rhetorical heightening this represents—the substitution of an elegant or surprising allusiveness for the proper noun—to become a vice; not so easy, however, in didactic or expository verse, where a little formal gilding comforts the yawning traveler.

Auden fairly early began to use words like *lovely, marvelous, wonderful, lucky, wicked* (words that are all weight and no "presentation"; that are all attitude of subject and no description of object; that approach as a limit the semanticists' *meaningless emotional noises*) in a peculiarly sophisticated sense. Their use is highly conscious, and implies quite definitely an attitude that it is hard to state definitely, but that I shall paraphrase as: *How well I know such words as these are looked down on, by any schoolboy even, as simple-silly, naïve, wholly inadequate. Yet you and I know that all the most cunningly chosen figures, all the "objective" terms, all the "presentation," are in the end quite as inadequate—that real representation, especially of the states such words point at, is impossible. You know how much better I could do; but certainly that better would not be good enough; this time I shan't even try, the* lovely *is something we can tacitly consent to, an indulgent and shared secret. Besides, how much of the charm, the real freshness of the experience such a word retains; and there is a real shock about it, too, an undoubted rhetorical effectiveness about its lack either of rhetoric or effectiveness, here in the midst of so much of both.*

A good deal of the "early romanticism" in Auden has a vague root in some such attitude as this. I hope the tone of my paraphrase doesn't seem to deny its real and precarious effectiveness; this is one of the dangerous devices of decadence, but not less charming for that. The use of such words later degenerated into oblivious sentimentality; the same end was waiting for Auden's *love-dove rhymes*, which at first were small jokes that, in their contexts at the end of poems, had a deliberate and pathetic conclusiveness.

One of the conscious devices of the late poems is the use of a simile blunt, laconic, and prosaic enough to be startling: Housman *kept tears like dirty postcards in a drawer*; in Rimbaud *the rhetorician's lie / Burst like a pipe*. There are *the rooks / Like agile babies; Terrible Presences that like farmers have purpose and knowledge.* Desire *like a policedog is unfastened; a phrase goes packed with meaning like a van.* As if to show how much on order this device is, Auden once uses it three times in five lines: poets are *encased in talent like a uniform . . . amaze us like a thunderstorm . . . dash forward like hussars.* This device is allied to the surprising and compressed metaphor, where no explanation is furnished, but where one is required—of the reader: *the beast of vocation, the bars of love, the stool of madness,* etc. And Auden will often insert slang or colloquialisms in an elevated or abstract context: he says in an idealistic sonnet about the Composer, *only your notes are pure contraption*; one finds *an invite with gilded edges; the identical and townee smartness; ga-ga Falsehood; the sexy airs of summer; lucky to love the new pansy railway*; and so on. All this is merely a special case of the insertion of the concrete word in the abstract context, which itself is a special case of Effect by Incongruity. These last are too common in any poet to need quotation here.

I now come to some formidable machinery which I am going to overwhelm with the even more formidable title of: The Bureaucratization of Perspective by Incongruity. Auden, who has a quick eye and an enormous range (of interests, information, and insight), was at the start plunged into the very blood of the world, the Incongruous; and he found even a drop of that blood, like Fafnir's, enough to make us see (the word is ambiguous here, standing for both perception and insight) what we could not possibly see without it. He began to make his poems depend on perspective by incongruity very much more than other modern poetry does; and he made them depend very much less on violence, forced intensity, emotional heightening, etc. But—if I may bureaucratize my own metaphor—so ingenious and conscious a mind was thoroughly dissatisfied with the random application of any drop or two of blood from that disreputable old dragon, the world. Why not rationalize the whole process? Why not mass together incongruities in a sort of blood bank, as ready as money, available for unlimited use in any emergency? Why not *synthesize* the Incongruous? and then (independent of natural sources, your warehouses groaning with the cheap blood poured out, in ever-increasing quantities, by that monopoly-creating secret) why not flood the world's markets, retire on the unlimited profits of the unlimited exploitation of— Incongruity?

I have been so extravagantly and mechanically incongruous because Auden has been; he has bureaucratized his method about as completely—and consequently as disastrously—as any efficiency expert could wish. It is a method that can be applied to any material: a patented process guaranteed to produce insights in any quantities. The qualities, unfortunately, cannot be guaranteed. The law of diminishing returns sets in very quickly; the poet's audience (one of the members of which is the poet) is as easily fatigued for incongruity as for an odor, and the poet has to supply larger and larger quantities that have less and less effect. The reader has seen in my earlier quotations many examples of Auden's use of this method; there exist enough examples for several generations of critics; I shall take the space for only one, a certain kind of spatial metaphor Auden uses for people.

Freud is a *climate, weather*. The *provinces* of Yeats's body revolted; *the squares of his mind were empty, / Silence invaded the suburbs, / The current of his feeling failed*. Matthew Arnold is a *dark disordered city*, completely equipped with *square, boulevard, slum, prison, forum, haphazard alleys, mother-farms, and a father's fond-chastising sky*—all this in twelve packed lines. Let me quote a poem, "Edward Lear," and italicize the unexpected or incongruous effects the poet and I want noticed. In some story a child keeps repeating, "I want to see the *weels* go round"; I hope no child will need to make such a remark here.

Left by his friend to breakfast alone on the white
Italian shore, his *Terrible Demon* arose
Over his shoulder; he wept to himself in the night,
A *dirty* landscape-painter who *hated his nose*.

The legions of cruel inquisitive *They*
Were *so many and big like dogs*; he was upset
By *Germans and boats*; affection was *miles away*:
But *guided by tears* he successfully *reached his Regret*.

How prodigious the welcome was. *Flowers took his hat*
And *bore him off* to *introduce him to the tongs*;
The demon's *false nose* made the *table laugh*; a *cat*
Soon had him waltzing madly, let him squeeze her hand;
Words pushed him to the piano to sing comic songs;

And children swarmed to him *like settlers*. He *became a land*.

I shan't insult the reader with comment—though I should like to mention the dangling participle I couldn't italicize. No one could miss seeing how mechanical, how consciously *willed*, such a rhetorical process is; in italicizing these words I have done no one an injustice— they have already been italicized by the poet. And now my list of quotations comes to a magnificent climax, with a conceit in which Auden sees Man as two pages of English countryside. But—two pages! I shall have to conclude weakly, with a bare reference to *New Year Letter*.

This collection of lists must by now have suggested a generalization to the reader: that in his later poems Auden depends to an extraordinary extent on *devices*. I could now add to my lists the device of—lists; but I will leave to the reader the pleasure of discovering that Auden not only imitates Joyce, Whitman, et cetera, but even parodies a list of Chaucer's. Another extended device, not precisely rhetorical, has a decided effect on the rhetorical texture of a poem. It is what might be called the *set piece*: a poem conscientiously restricted to some appropriated convention. This may even arrive at its limit, the parody; in any case, the interplay between prototype and "copy" is consistently and consciously effective—if the reader does not realize that the poem depends upon the relations to a norm of deviations from a norm, the poem will be badly misunderstood. The poem exists on two levels, like counterpoint—that is, like a counterpoint in which one of the levels has to be supplied by the hearer. Auden, who has an acute sense of the special function and convention of a poem, and no trace of the delusion that a single poem can serve as a model for the poet's poems or for Poetry, often tries for these limited successes. When he writes a popular song, it is always a pleasure to see critics discovering that he is "influenced by popular songs"; which is like finding that Eliot's poems in French are "influenced by the French language," or like finding Tchaikovsky's *Mozartiana* "influenced by Mozart." Today we are not good at convention, and delight in nothing so much as demanding sermons from stones, books from brooks—from every poem the more-than-what-it-gives that is precisely what its convention precludes it from giving; if we are poets we even try to furnish the *more than*. Auden has eight or ten types of set pieces; the reader will remember most of them, so there is no need for another list. (A good deal of the incidental effectiveness of *New Year Letter*, even, comes from this source.) Another favorite and very noticeable device is the long, mechanically worked-out conceit.

Auden's effective rhetorical use of abstract diction sometimes degenerates, in the later poems, into the flatness and vagueness, the essayistic deadness, of bad prose. (Let me emphasize, however, that the relatively abstract—what most poets would reject or fear—is one of the principal sources of Auden's effectiveness.) *The major cause of our collapse / Was a distortion in the human plastic by luxury produced* is bad enough; later Rimbaud is *from lyre and weakness estranged*—I am surprised Auden didn't finish the list with *the fair sex*; finally there is *If he succeeded, why, the Generalized Life / Would become impossible, the monolith / Of State be broken, and prevented / The cooperation of avengers.* With *Imperialism's face / And the international wrong* we have left poetry for editorials; and *the Hitlerian monster* is like a parody of Churchill—if I am not making an Irish bull.

But this degeneration into abstraction was inescapable for Auden, the reflection of his whole development. Auden's development, to a critic who knows his work well, has so much causal unity, fits together so logically and becomingly, that the critic can hardly bear to break up the whole into fragments of analysis, and feels like saying with Schopenhauer: All this is a single thought. It was *necessary* for Auden to develop and depend upon all this rhetorical machinery, because his poetry, his thought itself, was becoming increasingly abstract, public, and prosaic. These rhetorical devices constitute a quasi-scientific method by which you can make rhetorically effective *any* material, by which even the dead or half living can be galvanized into a sort of animation. (The method is much better suited to didactic or expository poetry than to lyric poetry: so *New Year Letter* is much more successful than Auden's latest lyrics—he is working with a congenial subject and a congenial method.) The earliest poems do not need and do not have such a rhetoric.

Auden wished to make his poetry better organized, more logical, more orthodox, more accessible, and so on; with these genuinely laudable intentions, going in the right direction from his early work, he has managed to run through a tremendous series of changes so fast that his lyric poetry has almost been ruined. If I may speak in the loose figurative language that fits such feelings: this late technique and material seem appropriated, not earned—an empty rootless *goes after* without the *comes before* necessary to give it meaning. Many of the early poems seem produced by Auden's whole being, as much unconscious as conscious, necessarily made just as they are; the best of them have shapes (just as driftwood or pebbles do) that seem the direct representation of the forces that produced them. Most of the later poems represent just as directly the forces that produced *them*: the head, the head, the top of the head; the correct, reasoning, idealistic, sentimental Intelligence. Nietzsche has this terrible sentence: *Euripides as a poet is essentially an echo of his own conscious knowledge*. It is hard not to apply the judgment to most of Auden's latest poetry.

How conscious, rational, controlled is poetry? can poetry afford to be? Our answers are bad: the half-knowledge we keep comes mostly from personal experience—which differs—and is terribly corrupted by our desires. (Imagine trying to reconcile Winters's testimony with that of Dylan Thomas.) But I think one can safely say that Auden's later method is far too conscious and controlled; too Socratic, too Alexandrian—to borrow from Nietzsche again. This rational intelligence guides and selects, it does not produce and impose; we make our poetry, but we make it what we can, not what we wish. Freud has taught everyone what happens to us when we impose on ourselves unacceptable or unbearable restrictions. Poetry—which represents the unconscious (or whatever you want to call it) as well as the conscious, our lives as well as our thoughts; and which has its true source in the first and not the second—is just as easily and fatally perverted. The sources of poetry—which I, like you, don't know much about, except that they are delicate and inexplicable, and open or close for no reason we can see—are not merely checked, but dried up, by too rigorous supervision.

Auden has been successful in making his poetry more accessible; but the success has been entirely too expensive. Realizing that the best poetry of the twenties was too inaccessible, we can will our poetry into accessibility—but how much poetry will be left when we finish? Our political or humanitarian interests may make us wish to make our poetry accessible to large groups; it is better to try to make the groups accessible to the poetry, to translate the interests into political or humanitarian activity. The best of causes ruins as quickly as the worst; and the road to Limbo is paved with writers who have done everything—I am being sympathetic, not satiric—for the very best reasons. All this is a problem that disquiets most poets today; to write as good and plain a poem as you can, and to find it over the heads of most of your readers, is enough to make anyone cry. The typical solution of the twenties (modern poetry is necessarily obscure; if the reader can't get it, let him eat Browning) and the typical solution of the political poetry of the thirties (poetry must be made available to the People or it is decadent escapism; poetry is Public Speech—to use

MacLeish's sickening phrase, so reminiscent of the public prayer of the Pharisees) were inadequate simplicities, absurd half-truths. A classically rational and absurd solution is that of Winters and his school, whose willed and scrupulously limited talking-down has resulted in a kind of moral baby-talk. Auden's more appealing solution has worked out much better; it is too conscious, too thin, too merely rational: we should distrust it just as we distrust any Rational (or Rationalized) Method of Becoming a Saint. I am not going to try to tell the reader what the solution should be, but I can tell him where to find it: in the work of the next first-rate poet. An essay like this may seem an ungrateful return for all the good poetry Auden has written; and I feel embarrassed at having furnished—even in so limited an article—so much Analysis and so little Appreciation. But analyses, even unkind analyses of faults, are one way of showing appreciation; and I hope at another time to try another way.

[1941/TBC]

From the Kingdom

of Necessity

MANY OF THE PEOPLE who reviewed *Lord Weary's Castle* felt
that it was as much of an event as Auden's first book; no one younger
than Auden has written better poetry than the best of Robert Lowell's,
it seems to me. Anyone who reads contemporary poetry will read it;
perhaps people will understand the poetry more easily, and find it
more congenial, if they see what the poems have developed out of,
how they are related to each other, and why they say what they say.

Underneath all these poems "there is one story and one story
only"; when this essential theme or subject is understood, the unity of
attitudes and judgments underlying the variety of the poems becomes
startlingly explicit. The poems understand the world as a sort of con-
flict of opposites. In this struggle one opposite is that cake of custom
in which all of us lie embedded like lungfish—the statis or inertia of
the stubborn self, the obstinate persistence in evil that is damnation.
Into this realm of necessity the poems push everything that is closed,
turned inward, incestuous, that blinds or binds: the Old Law, imperi-
alism, militarism, capitalism, Calvinism, Authority, the Father, the
"proper Bostonians," the rich who will "do everything for the poor ex-
cept get off their backs." But struggling within this like leaven, falling
to it like light, is everything that is free or open, that grows or is will-
ing to change: here is the generosity or openness or willingness that
is itself salvation; here is "accessibility to experience"; this is the
realm of freedom, of the Grace that has replaced the Law, of the per-
fect liberator whom the poet calls Christ.

Consequently the poems can have two possible movements or organizations: they can move from what is closed to what is open, or from what is open to what is closed. The second of these organizations—which corresponds to an "unhappy ending"—is less common, though there are many good examples of it: "The Exile's Return," with its menacing *Voi ch'entrate* that transforms the exile's old home into a place where even hope must be abandoned; the harsh and extraordinary "Between the Porch and the Altar," with its four parts each ending in constriction and frustration, and its hero who cannot get free of his mother, her punishments, and her world even by dying, but who sees both life and death in terms of her, and thinks at the end that, sword in hand, the Lord "watches me for Mother, and will turn / The bier and baby-carriage where I burn."

But normally the poems move into liberation. Even death is seen as liberation, a widening into darkness: that old closed system Grandfather Arthur Winslow, dying of cancer in his adjusted bed, at the last is the child Arthur whom the swanboats once rode through the Public Garden, whom now "the ghost of risen Jesus walks the waves to run / Upon a trumpeting black swan / Beyond Charles River and the Acheron / Where the wide waters and their voyager are one." (Compare the endings of "The Drunken Fisherman" and "Dea Roma.") "The Death of the Sheriff" moves from closure—the "ordered darkness" of the homicidal sheriff, the "loved sightless smother" of the incestuous lovers, the "unsearchable quicksilver heart / Where spiders stare their eyes out at their own / Spitting and knotted likeness"—up into the open sky, to those "light wanderers" the planets, to the "thirsty Dipper on the arc of night." Just so the cold, blundering, iron confusion of "Christmas Eve Under Hooker's Statue" ends in flowers, the wild fields, a Christ "once again turned wanderer and child." In "Rebellion" the son seals "an everlasting pact / With Dives to *contract* / The world that *spreads* in pain"; but at last he rebels against his father and his father's New England commercial theocracy, and "the world *spread* / When the clubbed flintlock broke my father's brain." The italicized words ought to demonstrate how explicitly, at times, these poems formulate the world in the terms that I have used.

"Where the Rainbow Ends" describes in apocalyptic terms the wintry, Calvinist, capitalist—Mr. Lowell has Weber's unconvincing belief in the necessary connection between capitalism and Calvinism—dead end of God's covenant with man, a frozen Boston where even the cold-blooded serpents "whistle at the cold." (The poems often use cold as a plain and physically correct symbol for what is constricted or static.) There "the scythers, Time and Death, / Helmed locusts, move upon the tree of breath," of the spirit of man; a bridge curves over Charles River like an ironic parody of the rainbow's covenant; both "the wild ingrafted olive and its root / Are withered" [these are Paul's terms for the Judaism of the Old Law and the Gentile Christianity grafted upon it]; "every dove [the Holy Ghost, the bringer of the olive leaf to the Ark] is sold" for a commercialized, legalized sacrifice. The whole system seems an abstract, rationalized "graph of Revelations," of the last accusation and judgment brought against man now that "the Chapel's sharp-shinned eagle shifts its hold / On serpent-Time, the rainbow's epitaph." This last line means what the last line in "The Quaker Graveyard"—"The Lord survives the rainbow of His will"—means; both are inexpressibly menacing, since they show the covenant as something that binds only us, as something abrogated merely by the passage of time, as a closed system opening not into liberation but into infinite and overwhelming possibility; they have something of the terror, but none of the pity, of Blake's "Time is the mercy of Eternity."

Then the worshipper, like a victim, climbs to the altar of the terrible I AM, to breathe there the rarefied and intolerable ether of his union with the divinity of the Apocalypse; he despairs even of the wings that beat against his cheek: "What can the dove of Jesus give / You now but wisdom, exile?" When the poem has reached this point of the most extreme closure, when the infinite grace that atones and liberates is seen as no more than the acid and useless wisdom of the exile, it opens with a rush of acceptant joy into: "Stand and live, / The dove has brought an olive branch to eat." The dove of Jesus brings to the worshipper the olive branch that shows him that the flood has receded, opening the whole earth for him; it is the olive branch of peace and reconciliation, the olive branch that he is "to eat" as a symbol of the eaten flesh of Christ, of atonement, identification, and liberation. Both the old covenant and the new still hold, nothing has changed: here as they were and will be—says the poem—are life and salvation.

Mr. Lowell's Christianity has very little to do with the familiar literary Christianity of *as if*, the belief in the necessity of belief; and it is a kind of photographic negative of the faith of the usual Catholic convert, who distrusts freedom as much as he needs bondage, and who sees the world as a liberal chaos which can be ordered and redeemed only by that rigid and final Authority to Whom men submit without question. Lowell reminds one of those heretical enthusiasts, often disciplined and occasionally sanctified or excommunicated, who are more at home in the Church Triumphant than in the church of this world, which is one more state. A phrase like Mr. Lowell's "St. Peter, the distorted key" is likely to be appreciated outside the church and overlooked inside it, *ad maiorem gloriam* of Catholic poetry. All Mr. Lowell's earliest poems would seem to suggest that he was, congenitally, the ideal follower of Barth or Calvin: one imagines him, a few years ago, supporting neither Franco nor the loyalists, but yearning to send a couple of clippers full of converted minutemen to wipe out the whole bunch—human, hence deserving. (I wish that he could cast a colder eye on minutemen; his treatment of the American Revolution is in the great tradition of Marx, Engels, and Parson Weems.) Freedom is something that he has wished to escape into, by a very strange route. In his poems the Son is pure liberation from the incestuous, complacent, inveterate evil of established society, of which the Law is a part—although the Father, Jehovah, has retained both the violence necessary to break up this inertia and a good deal of the menacing sternness of Authority as such, just as the poems themselves have. It is interesting to compare the figure of the Uncle in early Auden, who sanctifies rebellion by his authority; the authority of Mr. Lowell's Christ is sanctified by his rebellion or liberation.

Anyone who compares Mr. Lowell's earlier and later poems will see this movement from constriction to liberation as his work's ruling principle of growth. The grim, violent, sordid constriction of his earliest poems—most of them omitted from *Lord Weary's Castle*—seems to be temperamental, the Old Adam which the poet grew from and only partially transcends; and a good deal of what is excessive in the extraordinary rhetorical machine of a poem like "The Quaker Graveyard at Nantucket," which first traps and then wrings to pieces the helpless reader—who rather enjoys it—is gone from some of his later poems, or else dramatically justified and no longer excessive. "The Quaker Graveyard" is a baroque work, like *Paradise Lost*, but all the *extase* of baroque has disappeared—the coiling violence of its rhetoric, the harsh and stubborn intensity that accompanies all its verbs and verbals, the clustering stresses learned from accentual verse, come from a man contracting every muscle, grinding his teeth together till his shut eyes ache. Some of Mr. Lowell's later work moved, for a while, in the direction of the poem's quiet contrast-section, "Walsingham"; the denunciatory prophetic tone disappeared, along with the savagely satiric effects that were one of the poet's weaknesses. Some of the later poems depend less on rhetorical description and more on dramatic speech; their wholes have escaped from the hypnotic bondage of the details. Often the elaborate stanzas have changed into a novel sort of dramatic or narrative couplet, run-on but with heavily stressed rhymes. A girl's nightmare, in the late "Katherine's Dream," is clear, open, and speech-like, compared to the poet's own descriptive meditation in an earlier work like "Christmas at Black Rock."

Mr. Lowell has a completely unscientific but thoroughly historical mind. It is literary and traditional as well; he can use the past so effectively because he thinks so much as it did. He seems to be condemned both to read history and to repeat it. His present contains the past—especially Rome, the late Middle Ages, and a couple of centuries of New England—as an operative skeleton just under the skin. (This is rare among contemporary poets, who look at the past more as Blücher is supposed to have looked at London: "What a city to sack!") War, Trade, and Jehovah march side by side through all Mr. Lowell's ages: it is the fundamental likeness of the past and present, and not their disparity, which is insisted upon. "Cold / Snaps the bronze toes and fingers of the Christ / My father fetched from Florence, and the dead / Chatters to nothing in the thankless ground / His father screwed from Charlie Stark and sold / To the selectmen." Here is a good deal of the history of New England's nineteenth century in a sentence.

Of New England Mr. Lowell has the ambivalent knowledge one has of one's damned kin. The poems are crowded with the "fearful Witnesses" who "fenced their gardens with the Redman's bones"; the clippers and the slavers, their iron owners, and their old seamen knitting at the asylum; the Public Garden "where / The bread-stuffed ducks are brooding, where with tub / And strainer the mid-Sunday Irish scare / The sun-struck shallows for the dusky chub"; the faith "that made the Pilgrim Makers take a lathe / To point their wooden steeples lest the Word be dumb." Here his harshest propositions flower out of facts. But some of his earlier satires of present-day politics and its continuation have a severe crudity that suggest Michael Wigglesworth rewriting the "Horatian Ode"; airplanes he treats as Allen Tate does, only more so—he gives the impression of having encountered them in Mother Shipton. But these excesses were temporary; what is permanently excessive is a sort of obstinate violence or violent obstinacy of temperament and perception—in a day when poets long to be irresistible forces, he is an immovable object.

Mr. Lowell's period pieces are notable partly for their details—which are sometimes magically and professionally illusionary—and partly for the empathy, the historical identification that underlie the details. These period pieces are intimately related to his adaptations of poems from other languages; both are valuable as ways of getting a varied, extensive, and alien experience into his work. Dismissing these adaptations as misguided "translations" is like dismissing "To Celia" or *Cathay*, and betrays an odd dislike or ignorance of an important and traditional procedure of poets.

Mr. Lowell is a thoroughly professional poet, and the degree of intensity of his poems is equaled by their degree of organization. Inside its elaborate stanzas the poem is put together like a mosaic: the shifts of movement, the varied pauses, the alternation in the length of sentences, and the counterpoint between lines and sentences are the outer form of a subject matter that has been given a dramatic, dialectical internal organization; and it is hard to exaggerate the strength and life, the constant richness and surprise of metaphor and sound and motion, of the language itself. The organization of the poems resembles that of a great deal of traditional English poetry—especially when compared to that type of semi-imagist modern organization in which the things of a poem seem to marshal themselves like Dryden's atoms—but often this is complicated by stream-of-consciousness, dream, or dramatic-monologue types of structure. This makes the poems more difficult, but it is worth the price—many of the most valuable dramatic effects can hardly be attained inside a more logical or abstract organization. Mr. Lowell's poetry is a unique fusion of modernist and traditional poetry, and there exist side by side in it certain effects that one would have thought mutually exclusive; but it is essentially a post- or anti-modernist poetry, and as such is certain to be influential.

This poet is wonderfully good at discovering powerful, homely, grotesque, but exactly appropriate particulars for his poems. "Actuality is something brute," said Peirce. "There is no reason in it. I instance putting your shoulder against a door and trying to force it open against an unseen, silent, and unknown resistance." The things in Mr. Lowell's poems have, necessarily, been wrenched into formal shape, organized under terrific pressure, but they keep to an extraordinary degree their stubborn, unmoved toughness, their senseless originality and contingency: no poet is more notable for what, I have read, Duns Scotus calls *haeccitas*—the contrary, persisting, and singular thinginess of every being in the world; but this detailed factuality is particularly effective because it sets off, or is set off by, the elevation and rhetorical sweep characteristic of much earlier English poetry. Mr. Lowell is obviously a haptic rather than a visual type: a poem like "Colloquy in Black Rock" has some of the most successful kinaesthetic effects in English. It is impossible not to notice the weight and power of his lines, a strength that is sometimes mechanical or exaggerated, and sometimes overwhelming. But because of this strength the smooth, calm, and flowing ease of a few passages, the flat and colloquial ease of others, have even more effectiveness than they ordinarily would have: the dead mistress of Propertius, a black nail dangling from a finger, Lethe oozing from her nether lip, in the end can murmur to the "apple-sweetened Anio":

> . . . Anio, you will please
> Me if you whisper upon sliding knees:
> "Propertius, Cynthia is here:
> She shakes her blossoms when my waters clear."

Mr. Lowell, at his best and latest, is a dramatic poet: the poet's generalizations are usually implied, and the poem's explicit generalizations are there primarily because they are dramatically necessary—it is not simply the poet who means them. He does not present themes or generalizations but a world; the differences and similarities between it and ours bring home to us themes, generalizations, and the poet himself. It is partly because of this that atheists are vexed by his Catholic views (and Catholics by his heretical ones) considerably less than they normally would be.

But there are other reasons. The poet's rather odd and imaginative Catholicism is thoroughly suitable to his mind, which is so traditional, theocentric, and anthropomorphic that no images from the sciences, next to none from philosophy, occur in his poems. Such a Catholicism is thoroughly suited to literature, since it *is* essentially literary, anthropomorphic, emotional. It is an advantage to a poet to have a frame of reference, terms of generalization, which are themselves human, affective, and effective as literature. *Bodily Changes in Fear, Rage, Pain, and Hunger* may let the poet know more about the anger of Achilles, but it is hard for him to have to talk about adrenaline and the thalamus; and when the arrows of Apollo are transformed into a "lack of adequate sanitary facilities," everything is lost but understanding. (This helps to explain the dependence of contemporary poetry on particulars, emotions, things—its generalizations, where they are most effective, are fantastic, though often traditionally so.)

Naturally the terms of scientific explanation cannot have these poetic and emotional effects, since it is precisely by the exclusion of such effects that science has developed. (Many of the conclusions of the sciences are as poetic as anything in the world, but they have been of little use to poets—how can you use something you are delighted never to have heard of?) Mr. Lowell's Catholicism represents effective realities of human behavior and desire, regardless of whether it is true, false, or absurd; and, as everyone must realize, it is possible to tell part of the truth about the world in terms that are false, limited, and fantastic—else how should we have told it? There is admittedly no "correct" or "scientific" view of a great many things that a poet writes about, and he has to deal with them in dramatic and particular terms, if he has forgone the advantage of pre-scientific ideologies like Christianity or Marxism. Of course it seems to me an advantage that he can well forgo; I remember writing about contemporary religious poems, "It is hard to enjoy the ambergris for thinking of all those suffering whales," and most people will feel this when they encounter a passage in Mr. Lowell's poetry telling them how Bernadette's miraculous vision of Our Lady "puts out reason's eyes." It does indeed.

It is unusually difficult to say which are the best poems in *Lord Weary's Castle*: several are realized past changing, successes that vary only in scope and intensity—others are poems that almost any living poet would be pleased to have written. But certainly some of the best things in the book are "Colloquy in Black Rock," "Between the Porch and the Altar," the first of the two poems that compose "The Death of the Sheriff," and "Where the Rainbow Ends"; "The Quaker Graveyard at Nantucket" and "At the Indian-Killer's Grave" have extremely good parts; some other moving, powerful, and unusual poems are "Death from Cancer," "The Exile's Return," "Mr. Edwards and the Spider," and "Mary Winslow"—and I hate to leave entirely unmentioned poems like "After the Surprising Conversions," "The Blind Leading the Blind," "The Drunken Fisherman," and "New Year's Day."

When I reviewed Mr. Lowell's first book I finished by saying, "Some of the best poems of the next years ought to be written by him." The appearance of *Lord Weary's Castle* makes me feel less like Adams or Leverrier than like a rainmaker who predicts rain and gets a flood which drowns everyone in the county. One or two of these poems, I think, will be read as long as men remember English.

[1947/PA]

Poets, Critics, and Readers

PEOPLE OFTEN ASK ME: "Is there any poet who makes his living writing poetry?" and I have to say: "No." The public has an unusual relationship to the poet: it doesn't even know that he is there. Our public is a rich and generous one; if it knew that the poet was there, it would pay him for being there. As it is, poets make their living in many ways: by being obstetricians, like William Carlos Williams; or directors of Faber and Faber, like T. S. Eliot; or vice-presidents of the Hartford Accident and Indemnity Company, like Wallace Stevens. But most poets, nowadays, make their living by teaching. Kepler said, "God gives every animal a way to make its living, and He has given the astronomer astrology"; and now, after so many centuries, He has given us poets students. But what He gives with one hand He takes away with the other: He has taken away our readers.

Yet the poet can't help looking at what he has left, his students, with gratitude. His job may be an impossible one—there are three impossible tasks, said Freud: to teach, to govern, and to cure—but what is there so grateful as impossibility? and what is there better to teach, more nearly impossible to teach, than poems and stories? As Lord Macaulay says: "For how can man live better / Than facing fearful odds / For the poems of his fathers—"

I seem to have remembered it a little wrong, but it's a natural error. And, today, when we get people to read poems—to read very much of anything—naturally and joyfully, to read it not as an unnatural rightness but as a natural error: what people always have done, always will do—we do it against fearful odds. I can't imagine a better way for the poet to make his living. I certainly can't imagine his making his living by writing poems—I'm not *that* imaginative. I'm used to things as they are.

But there is a passage in Wordsworth that I read, always, with a rueful smile. He is answering the question, *Why write in verse?* He gives several reasons. His final reason, he writes, "is all that is *necessary* to say upon this subject." Here it is, all that it is *necessary* to say upon this subject: "Few persons will deny, that of two descriptions, either of passions, manners, or characters, each of them equally well executed, the one in prose and the other in verse, the verse will be read a hundred times where the prose is read once."

One sees sometimes, carved on geology buildings: *O Earth, what changes thou hast seen!* When a poet finishes reading this passage from Wordsworth, he thinks in miserable awe: *O Earth, what changes thou hast seen!* Only a hundred and fifty years ago *this* is what people were like. Nowadays, of course, the prose will be read a thousand times where the verse is read once. And this seems to everybody only natural; the situation Wordsworth describes seems unnatural, improbable, almost impossible. What Douglas Bush writes is true: we live in "a time in which most people assume that, as an eminent social scientist once said to me, 'Poetry is on the way out.' " To most of us, verse, any verse, is so uncongenial, so exhaustively artificial, that I have often thought that a man could make his fortune by entirely eliminating from our culture verse of any kind: in the end there would *be* no more poems, only prose translations of them. This man could begin by publishing his Revised Standard Version of *Mother Goose*: without rhyme, meter, or other harmful adulterants; with no word of anything but honest American prose, prose that cats and dogs can read.

A friend of mine once took a famous Italian scholar on a tour of New Haven. She specialized in objects of art and virtue—samplers, figureheads, paintings of women under willows, statues of General Washington—but no matter what she showed him, the man would only wave his hand in the air and exclaim: *Ridickalus!* And shouldn't we feel so about things like *Mother Goose?*

Early to bed and early to rise
Makes a man healthy, wealthy, and wise.

Ridickalus! Why say it like a rocking horse? why make it jingle so? and *wise*—who wants to be wise?

> Which sibling is the well-adjusted sibling?
> The one that gets its sleep.

That is the way the modern *Mother Goose* will put it. I don't expect the modern *Mother Goose* to be especially popular with little children, who have not yet learned not to like poetry; but it is the parents who buy the book.

Isn't writing verse a dying art, anyway, like blacksmithing or buggymaking? Well, not exactly: poets are making as many buggies as ever—good buggies, fine buggies—they just can't get anybody much to ride in them. As for blacksmithing: I read the other day that there are twice as many blacksmith shops in the United States as there are bookstores. Something has gone wrong with that comparison too. No, I'm doing what poets do, complaining; and if I exaggerate a little when I complain, why, that's only human—surely you want me to exaggerate a little, in my misery. Goethe says, when he is talking about slum children: "No person ever looks miserable who feels that he has the right to make a demand on you." This right is not anything that anyone can confer upon himself; it is the public, society, all of us, that confer this right. If the poet looks miserable, it is because we have made him feel that he no longer has the right to make a demand on us. It is no longer a question of what he wants, or of what he ought to be given—he takes what he gets, and complains about getting it, and he hears the echo of his complaint, and then the silence settles around him, a little darker, a little deeper.

What does he want? To be read. Read by whom? critics? men wise enough to tell him, when they have read the poem, what it is and ought to be, what its readers feel and ought to feel? Well, no. A writer cannot learn about his readers from his critics: they are different races. The critic, unless he is one in a thousand, reads to criticize; the reader reads to read.

Freud talks of the "free-floating" or "evenly-hovering" attention with which the analyst must listen to the patient. Concentration, note-taking, listening with a set—a set of pigeonholes—makes it difficult or impossible for the analyst's unconscious to respond to the patient's; takes away from the analyst the possibility of learning from the patient what the analyst doesn't already know; takes away from him all those random guesses or intuitions or inspirations which come out of nowhere—and come, too, out of the truth of the patient's being. But this is quite as true of critics and the poems that are *their* patients: when one reads as a linguist, a scholar, a New or Old or High or Low critic, when one reads the poem *as a means to an end*, one is no longer a pure reader but an applied one. The true reader "listens like a three years' child: / The Mariner hath his will." Later on he may write like a sixty-three-year-old sage, but he knows that in the beginning, unless ye be converted, and become as little children, ye shall not enter into the kingdom of art. Hofmannsthal says, with awful finality: "The world has lost its innocence, and without inno- cence no one creates or enjoys a work of art"; but elsewhere he says more hopefully, with entire and not with partial truth, that each of us lives in an innocence of his own which he never entirely loses.

Is there a public for poetry that is still, in this sense of the word, innocent? Of course, there are several publics for poetry—small, be- nighted, eccentric publics—just as there are publics for postage stamps and cobblers' benches; but this is such a disastrous change from the days of *Childe Harold* and *In Memoriam* and *Hiawatha*, when the public for poetry was, simply, the reading public, that you can see why poets feel the miserable astonishment that they feel. The better-known poets feel it more than the lesser-known, who—poor things—lie under the table grateful for crumbs, pats, kicks, anything at all that will let them be sure they really exist, and are not just a dream someone has stopped dreaming. A poet like Auden says that no- body reads him except poets and young men in cafeterias—his de- scription of the young men is too repellent for me to repeat it to you.

Literally, Auden is wrong: we read Auden, this is no cafeteria; but, figuratively, Auden is right—the poet's public's gone. Frederick the Great translated Voltaire, and trembled as the poet read the trans- lation; Elizabeth—Elizabeth the First—and Henry the Eighth and Richard the Lion-hearted wrote good poems and read better; and I cannot resist quoting to you three or four sentences from Frans Bengtsson's novel *The Long Ships*, to show you what things were like at the court of Harald Bluetooth, King of Denmark in the year 1000. A man gets up from a banquet table: "His name was Björn Asbrandsson, and he was a famous warrior, besides being a great poet to boot ... Although he was somewhat drunk, he managed to impro- vise some highly skilful verses in King Harald's honor in a meter known as *töglag*. This was the latest and most difficult verse-form that the Icelandic poets had invented, and indeed the poem was so artfully contrived that little could be understood of its content.

Everybody, however, listened with an appearance of understanding, for any man who could not understand poetry would be regarded as a poor specimen of a warrior; and King Harald praised the poet and gave him a gold ring."

Auden is a descendant of just such poets as this one; but if Auden, when he next visits the University of your state, makes up an incomprehensible poem, in a difficult new meter, in honor of the President of the University, will all its football players pretend they understand the poem, so as not to be thought poor specimens of football players? and will the President give Auden a gold ring?

In the days when his readers couldn't read, the poet judged his public by his public: the gold ring or the scowl the king gave him was as concrete as the labored, triumphant faces of his hearers. But nowadays King Harald and his warriors are represented by a reviewer, next year, in *The New York Times*; a critic, nine years later, in *The Sewanee Review*. "Ah, better to sing my songs to a wolf pack on the Seeonee than to a professor on the *Sewanee*!" the poet blurts, baring his teeth; but then—what choice has he?—he lets the Reality Principle do its worst, and projects or extends or extrapolates a critic or two, a dozen reviewers, into the Public; into Posterity. Critics, alas! are the medium through which the poet darkly senses his public. Nor is it altogether different for the public: Harald and his Vikings, lonely in their split-levels, do not even remember the days when, as they listened, they could look into one another's faces and know without looking what they would find there. Now they too look into the *Times*; wish that they could replace that scowl with a gold ring, that gold ring with a scowl; reconstruct from the exclamations on dust jackets, quotations in advertisements, the fierce smiles on the faces of the warriors.

So if we are to talk about the poet and his poems and his public, what each is to the others, we must spend much of our time—too much of our time—talking about his critics. Criticism is necessary, I suppose; I know. Yet criticism, to the poet, is no necessity, but a luxury he can ill afford. Conrad cried to his wife: "I don't want criticism, I want praise!" And it is praise, blame, tears, laughter, that writers want; when Columbus comes home he needs to be cheered for finding a new way to India, not interned while the officials argue about whether it is Asia, Africa, or Antarctica that he has discovered. Really, of course, it's America—and if they agreed about it this would be helpful to Columbus; he could say to himself, in awe: "So it was America I discovered!" But how seldom the critics do agree! A gray writer seems black to his white critics, white to his black critics: the same poem will seem incomprehensible modernistic nonsense to Robert Hillyer, and a sober, old-fashioned, versified essay to the critics of some little magazine of advanced tastes. Ordinary human feeling, the most natural tenderness, will seem to many critics and readers rank sentimentality, just as a kind of nauseated brutality (in which the writer's main response to the world is simply to vomit) will seem to many critics and readers the inescapable truth. We live in a time in which Hofmannsthal's "Good taste is the ability continuously to counteract exaggeration" will seem to most readers as false as it seems tame. "Each epoch has its own sentimentality," Hofmannsthal goes on, "its specific way of overemphasizing strata of emotion. The sentimentality of the present is egotistic and unloving; it exaggerates not the feeling of love but that of the self."

Everyone speaks of the "negative capability" of the artist, of his ability to lose what self he has in the many selves, the great self of the world. Such a quality is, surely, the first that a critic should have; yet who speaks of the negative capability of the critic? how often are we able to observe it? The commonest response to the self of a work of art is the critic's assertion that he too has a self. What he writes proves it. I once saw, in an essay by a psychoanalyst, the phrase *the artist and his competitor, the critic.* Where got he that truth? Out of an analysand's mouth? I do not know; but that it is an important and neglected truth I do know. All mediators become competitors: the exceptions to this rule redeem their kind.

Critics disagree about almost every quality of a writer's work; and when some agree about a quality, they disagree about whether it is to be praised or blamed, nurtured or rooted out. After enough criticism the writer is covered with lipstick and bruises, and the two are surprisingly evenly distributed. There is *nothing* so plain about a writer's books, to some critics, that its opposite isn't plain to others. Kafka is original? Not at all, according to Edmund Wilson. A fine critic of poetry, Ezra Pound, writes: "In [the writer So-and-So] you have an embroidery of language, a talk *about* the matter, not presentation; you have grace, richness of language, etc., as much as you like, but you have nothing that isn't replaceable by something else, no ornament that wouldn't have done just as well in some other connection, or that for which some other figure of rhetoric or fancy couldn't have served, or which couldn't have been distilled from literary antecedents." About whom is Pound speaking? About Shakespeare. Anyone who has read at all widely has come across thousands of such judgments, and it is easy for him to sympathize with the artist when the artist murmurs: "We wish to learn from our critics, but it is hard for us even to recover from them. A fool's reproach has an edge like a razor, and his brother's praise is small consolation. Critics are like bees: one sting lasts longer than a dozen jars of honey."

The best thing ever said about criticism—I am not, now, speaking as a critic—was said, as is often the case, by Goethe: "Against criticism we can neither protect nor defend ourselves; we must act in despite of it, and gradually it resigns itself to this." The great Goethe suffered just as we little creatures do, and he spoke about it, as we don't, in imperishable sentences: "All great excellence in life or art, at its first recognition, brings with it a certain pain arising from the strongly felt inferiority of the spectator; only at a later period, when we take it into our own culture, and appropriate as much of it as our capacities allow, do we learn to love and esteem it. Mediocrity, on the other hand, may often give us unqualified pleasure; it does not disturb our self-satisfaction, but rather encourages us with the thought that we are as good as another . . . Properly speaking, we learn only from those books we cannot judge. The author of a book that I am competent to criticize would have to learn from me." Goethe says over and over: "Nothing is more terrible than ignorance in action . . . It is a terrible thing when fools thrive at the expense of a superior man." You and I will agree—and then we will have to decide whether we're being thriven at the expense of, or thriving. Goethe says in firm doggerel: "However clear and simple be it / Finder and doer alone may see it." No, Goethe didn't have too much use for critics, since he thought that critics weren't of too much use.

And why am I quoting all this to you? have critics hurt me so that I want to pull down the temple upon their heads, even if I too perish in the ruins?—for I too am a critic. No, it's not that; critics have done their best for me, and their best has been, perhaps, only too good; when I myself criticize, I am willing for you to believe what I say; but I am trying to explain why it is that critics are of so little use to writers, why it is that they are such a poor guide to the opinions of the next age—and I am explaining in an age which has an unprecedented respect for, trust in, criticism.

All of us have read pieces of criticism—many pieces of criticism—which seem worthy both of delighted respect and cautious trust. All of us have read criticism in which the critic takes it for granted that what he writes about comes first, and what he writes comes second—takes it for granted that he is writing as a reader to other readers, to be of use to them; criticism in which the critic works, as far as he is able, in the spirit of Wordsworth's "I have endeavored to look steadily at my subject." All of us have some favorite, exceptional critic who might say, with substantial truth, that he has not set up rigid standards to which a true work of art must conform, but that he has tried instead to let the many true works of art—his experience of them—set up the general expectations to which his criticism of art conforms; that he has tried never to see a work of art as mere raw material for criticism, data for generalization; that he has tried never to forget the difference between creating a work of art and criticizing a work of art; and that he has tried, always, to remember what Proust meant when he said, about writers like Stendhal, Balzac, Hugo, Flaubert, the great creators called "romantics": "The classics have no better commentators than the 'romantics.' The romantics are the only people who really know how to read the classics, because they read them as they were written, that is to say, 'romantically,' and because if one would read a poet or a prose writer properly one must be, not a scholar, but a poet or a prose writer." It might be put a little differently: if one would read a poet or a prose writer properly one must be, not a scholar or a poet or a prose writer, but a reader: someone who reads books as they were written, that is to say, "romantically." Proust's grandmother was not a poet or a prose writer, but she read Madame de Sévigné properly. To be, as she was, a reader, is a lofty and no longer common fate.

The best poetry critic of our time, T. S. Eliot, has said about his criticism: "I see that I wrote best about poets whose work had influenced my own, and with whose poetry I had become thoroughly familiar, long before I desired to write about them, or had found the occasion to do so . . . The best of my literary criticism . . . is a by-product of my private poetry-workshop." But perhaps something of this sort is always true: perhaps true criticism is something, like sincerity or magnanimity, that cannot be aimed at, attained, directly; that must always be, in some sense, a by-product, whether of writing or reading, of a private poetry-workshop or a private reading-room.

We all realize that writers are inspired, but helpless and fallible beings, who know not what they write; readers, we know from personal experience, are less inspired but no less helpless and fallible beings, who half the time don't know what they're reading. Now, a critic is half writer, half reader: just as the vices of men and horses met in centaurs, the weaknesses of readers and writers meet in critics. A good critic—we cannot help seeing, when we look back at any other age—is a much rarer thing than a good poet or a good novelist. Unless you are one critic in a hundred thousand, the future will quote you only as an example of the normal error of the past, what everybody was foolish enough to believe then. Critics are discarded like calendars; yet, for their year, with what trust the world regards them!

Art is long, and critics are the insects of a day. But while he survives, it is the work of art he criticizes which is the critic's muse, or daemon, or guardian angel: it is a delight to the critic to think that sometimes, in moments of particular good fortune, some poem by Rilke or Yeats or Wordsworth has hovered above him, whispering what to say about it in his ear. And, in the moments of rash ambition which can come even to such humble—rightly humble—things as critics, the critic can imagine some reader, in the midst of his pleasure at a poem or story the critic has guided him to, being willing to think of some paragraph of the critic's work in terms of a sentence of Goethe's: "There is a sensitive empiricism that ultimately identifies itself with the object and thereby becomes genuine theory."

In other moments the critic can imagine the reader's thinking of him in terms of a paragraph that Proust once wrote. That miraculous writer and great critic, distressed at someone's having referred to Sainte-Beuve as one of the "great guides," exclaimed: "Surely no one ever failed so completely as did he in performing the functions of a guide? The greater part of his *Lundis* are devoted to fourth-rate writers, and whenever, by chance, he does bring himself to speak of somebody really important, of Flaubert, for instance, or Baudelaire, he immediately atones for what grudging praise he may have accorded him by letting it be understood that he writes as he does about them simply because he wants to please men who are his personal friends . . . As to Stendhal, the novelist, the Stendhal of *La Chartreuse*, our 'guide' laughs out of court the idea that such a person ever existed, and merely sees in all the talk about him the disastrous effects of an attempt (foredoomed to failure) to foist Stendhal on the public as a novelist . . . It would be fun, had I not less important things to do, to 'brush in' (as Monsieur Cuvillier Fleury would have said), in the manner of Sainte-Beuve, a 'picture of French literature in the nineteenth century,' in such a way that not a single great name would appear and men would be promoted to the position of outstanding authors whose books today have been completely forgotten."

A portion of any critic, as he reads these sentences, turns white; and if another portion whispers, "Ah, but *you* needn't be afraid; certainly *you're* not as bad a critic as Sainte-Beuve," it is not a sentence to bring the color back into his cheeks, unless he blushes easily.

Wordsworth said, as Proust said after him, that "every writer, in so far as he is great and at the same time *original,* has the task of creating the taste by which he is to be enjoyed: so is it, so will it continue to be." But *taste,* he goes on to say, is a vicious and deluding word. (And surely he is right; surely we should use, instead, a phrase like *imaginative judgment.*) Using such a word as *taste* helps to make us believe that there is some passive faculty that responds to the new work of art, registering the work's success or failure; but actually the new work must call forth in us an active power analogous to that which created it—the reader "cannot proceed in quiescence, he cannot be carried like a dead weight," he must "exert himself" to feel, to sympathize, and to understand. *"There,"* as Wordsworth says, "lies the true difficulty." He is right: *there* lies the difficulty for us, whether we are critics or readers; so is it, so will it continue to be.

You may say, "Of course this is true of great and original talents, but how does it apply to the trivial, immature, and eccentric writers with whom our age, like any other, is infested?" It applies only in this way: some of these trivial, immature, and eccentric writers *are* our great and original talents. The readers of Wordsworth's age said, "Of course what he says is true of great and original talents, but it is absurd when applied to a trivial and eccentric creature like Wordsworth"; and the critics of Wordsworth's age, applying the standards of the age more clearly, forcibly, and self-consciously, could condemn him with a more drastic severity. The readers read to read, the critics read to judge—both were wrong, but the critics were more impressively and rigorously and disastrously wrong, since they confirmed most readers in their dislike of Wordsworth and scared most of the others out of their liking.

We all see that the writer cannot afford to listen to critics when they are wrong—though how is he, how are we, to know when they are wrong? Can he afford to listen to them when they are right?—though how is he, how are we, to know when they are right? and right for this age or right for the next?* The writer cannot afford to question his own essential nature; must have, as Marianne Moore says, "the courage of his peculiarities." But often it is this very nature, these very peculiarities—originality always seems peculiarity, to begin with—that critics condemn. There must be about the writer a certain

*"When the great innovation appears, it will almost certainly be in a muddled, incomplete, and confusing form. To the discoverer himself it will be only half-understood; to everybody else it will be a mystery. For any speculation which does not at first glance look crazy, there is no hope."—F. L. Dyson, *Innovation in Physics*

spontaneity or naïveté or somnambulistic rightness: he must, in some sense, move unquestioning in the midst of his world—at his question all will disappear.

And if it is slighter things, alterable things which the critics condemn, should the poet give in, alter them, and win his critics' surprised approval? "No," says Wordsworth, "where the understanding of an author is not convinced, or his feelings altered, this cannot be done without great injury to himself: for his own feelings are his stay and support, and, if he set them aside in this one instance, he may be induced to repeat this act till his mind shall lose all confidence in itself, and become utterly debilitated. To this it may be added that the critic ought never to forget that he is himself exposed to the same errors as the Poet." Let me repeat this: we ought never to forget that the critic is himself exposed to the same errors as the poet. We all know this— yet, in a deeper sense, we don't know it. We all realize that the poet's beliefs are, first of all, *his*: our books show how his epoch, his childhood, his mistresses, and his unconscious produced the beliefs; we know, now, the "real" reasons for his believing what he believed. Why do we not realize what is equally true (and equally false)?—that the critic's beliefs are, first of all, *his*; that we can write books showing how his epoch, his childhood, his mistresses, and his unconscious produced the beliefs; that we can know, now, the "real" reasons for his believing what he believed. The work of criticism is rooted in the unconscious of the critic just as the poem is rooted in the unconscious of the poet. I have had the pleasure and advantage of knowing many poets, many critics, and I have not found one less deeply neurotic than the other.

When the critic is also an artist—a T. S. Eliot—we find it easier to remember all this, and to distrust him; but when the critic is an Irving Babbitt—that is to say, a man who, tenanted by all nine of the muses, still couldn't create a couplet—we tend to think of his beliefs as somehow more objective. "Surely," we feel, "a man with so little imagination couldn't be making up something—couldn't be *inspired*." We are wrong. Criticism is the poetry of prosaic natures (and even, in our time, of some poetic ones); there is a divinity that inspires the most sheeplike of scholars, the most tabular of critics, so that the man too dull to understand *Evangeline* still can be possessed by some theory about *Evangeline*, a theory as just to his own being as it is unjust to *Evangeline*'s. The man is entitled to his inspiration; and yet . . . if only he would leave out *Evangeline*! If only he could secede from Literature, and set up some metaliterary kingdom of his own!

The poet *needs* to be deluded about his poems—for who can be sure that it is delusion? In his strongest hours the public hardly exists for the writer: he does what he ought to do, has to do, and if afterwards some Public wishes to come and crown him with laurel crowns, well, let it! if critics wish to tell people all that he isn't, well, let them—he knows what he is. But at night when he can't get to sleep it seems to him that it is what he is, his own particular personal quality, that he is being disliked for. It is this that the future will like him for, if it likes him for anything; but will it like him for anything? The poet's hope is in posterity, but it is a pale hope; and now that posterity itself has become a pale hope . . .

The writer—I am still talking about the writer-not-yet-able-to-go-to-sleep—is willing to have his work disliked, if it's bad; is ready to rest content in dislike, if it's good. But which is it? *He* can't know. He thinks of all those pieces of his that he once thought good, and now thinks bad; how many of his current swans will turn out to be just such ducklings? All of them? If he were worse, would people like him better? If he were better, would people like him worse? If—

He says to himself, "Oh, go to sleep!" And next morning, working at something the new day has brought, he is astonished at the night's thoughts—he does what he does, and lets public, critics, posterity worry about whether it's worth doing. For to tell the truth, the first truth, the poem is a love affair between the poet and his subject, and readers come in only a long time later, as witnesses at the wedding . . .

But what would the ideal witnesses—the ideal public—be? What would an ideal public do? Mainly, essentially, it would just read the poet; read him with a certain willingness and interest; read him imaginatively and perceptively. It needs him, even if it doesn't know that; he needs it, even if he doesn't know that. It and he are like people in one army, one prison, one world: their interests are great and common, and deserve a kind of declaration of dependence. The public might treat him very much as it would like him to treat it. It has its faults, he has his; but both "are, after all," as a man said about women, "the best things that are offered in that line." The public ought not to demand the same old thing from the poet whenever he writes something very new, nor ought it to complain, *The same old thing!* whenever he writes something that isn't very new; and it ought to realize that it is not, unfortunately, in the writer's power to control what he writes: something else originates and controls it, whether you call that something else the unconscious or Minerva or the Muse.

The writer writes what he writes just as the public likes what it likes; he can't help himself, it can't help itself, but each of them has to try: most of our morality, most of our culture are in the trying.

We readers can be, or at least can want to be, what the writer himself would want us to be: a public that reads a *lot*—that reads widely, joyfully, and naturally; a public whose taste is formed by acquaintance with the good and great writers of many ages, and not simply acquaintance with a few fashionable contemporaries and the fashionable precursors of those; a public with broad general expectations, but without narrow particular demands, that the new work of art must satisfy; a public that reads with the calm and ease and independence that come from liking things in themselves, for themselves.

This is the kind of public that the poet would like; and if it turned out to be the kind of public that wouldn't like him, why, surely that is something he could bear. It is not his poems but poetry that he wants people to read; if they will read Rilke's and Yeats's and Hardy's poems, he can bear to have his own poems go unread forever. He *knows* that their poems are good to read, and that's something he necessarily can't know about his own; and he knows, too, that poetry itself is good to read—that if you cannot read poetry easily and naturally and joyfully, you are cut off from much of the great literature of the past, some of the good literature of the present. Yet the poet could bear to have people cut off from all that, if only they read widely, naturally, joyfully in the rest of literature: much of the greatest literature, much of the greatest poetry, even, is in prose. If people read this prose—read even a little of it—generously and imaginatively, and felt it as truth and life, as a natural and proper joy, why, that would be enough.

A few months ago I read an interview with a critic; a well-known critic; an unusually humane and intelligent critic. The interviewer had just said that the critic "sounded like a happy man," and the interview was drawing to a close; the critic said, ending it all: "I read, but I don't get time to read at whim. All the reading I do is in order to write or teach, and I resent it. We have no TV, and I don't listen to the radio or records, or go to art galleries or the theater. I'm a completely negative personality."

As I thought of that busy, artless life—no records, no paintings, no plays, no books except those you lecture on or write articles about—I was so depressed that I went back over the interview looking for some bright spot, and I found it, one beautiful sentence: for a moment I had left the gray, dutiful world of the professional critic, and was back in the sunlight and shadow, the unconsidered joys, the unreasoned sorrows, of ordinary readers and writers, amateurishly reading and writing "at whim." The critic said that once a year he read *Kim*; and he read *Kim*, it was plain, at whim: not to teach, not to criticize, just for love—he read it, as Kipling wrote it, just because he liked to, wanted to, couldn't help himself. To him it wasn't a means to a lecture or an article, it was an end; he read it not for anything he could get out of it, but for itself. And isn't this what the work of art demands of us? The work of art, Rilke said, says to us always: *You must change your life*. It demands of us that we too see things as ends, not as means—that we too know them and love them for their own sake. This change is beyond us, perhaps, during the active, greedy, and powerful hours of our lives; but during the contemplative and sympathetic hours of our reading, our listening, our looking, it is surely within our power, if we choose to make it so, if we choose to let one part of our nature follow its natural desires. So I say to you, for a closing sentence: *Read at whim! read at whim!*

[*1959/SHS*]

Fifty Years
of American Poetry

IN 1910 AMERICAN POETRY was a bare sight. We were not, like Canada or New Zealand, a province without a national poetry of its own. There had been good American poets—but how few, and already how far in the past! Whitman and Dickinson, the two greatest and most decidedly American, seemed to owe both their greatness and their Americanness to their own entire originality and eccentricity. Three other genuinely American poets, Melville, Emerson, and Thoreau, had written good poems, most of them less notably un-English than Whitman's and Dickinson's. But the American poets who were admired most during the nineteenth century, who seemed most plainly the center of American poetry, and who fitted into the regular tradition of English poetry as plainly as Whitman and Dickinson did not, were Longfellow, Lowell, Whittier, and Bryant. There had been a gap of thirty or forty years, from the seventies until 1910, during which almost no good American poetry had been written. If in 1912 someone had predicted that during the next fifty years American poetry would be the best and most influential in the English language, and that the next generation of poets would be American classics, men who would establish once and for all the style and tone of American poetry, his prediction would have seemed fantastic. Yet all this is literally true of the generation of American poets that included Frost, Stevens, Eliot, Pound, Williams, Marianne Moore, Ransom. When we read the poems of these poets and of the Irishman Yeats, we realize that the whole center of gravity of poetry in English had shifted west of England.

It is worth our while, then, to look hard at the American poetry of the last fifty years. I'll try not to theorize about movements and tendencies but to stick to the poets and their poems; as Goethe says, "Theories are as a rule impulsive reactions of an overhasty understanding which would like to have done with phenomena and therefore substitutes for them images, concepts, or often even just words." I have written out for you the opinions of a devoted reader of this poetry; often I have summarized or quoted from what I have already written about a poet.

When you read Edwin Arlington Robinson's poems, you are conscious of a mind looking seriously at a world with people in it and expressing itself primarily in terms of these human beings it has observed and created. Robinson's steady human sympathy is accompanied by a steady hatred of the inhuman world that people have made for themselves, the world of business and greed and hypocritical morality; he felt for the America of the end of the century the same gloomy despair that Henry Adams and Mark Twain felt, asking it:

> Are you to pay for what you have
> With all you are?

You see his qualities at their rare best in "Mr. Flood's Party," at their ordinary best in "Eros Turannos," "George Crabbe," "The Clerks." He is far better when he is reserved and prosaic than when he is poetic; his poetic rhetoric is embarrassingly threadbare and commonplace, as when he writes about his own lost belief:

> I can hear it only as a bar
> Of lost, imperial music, played when fair
> And angel fingers wove, and unaware,
> Dead leaves to garlands where no roses are.

Such rhetoric is accompanied, characteristically, by an emptily antithetical, quibbling, riddling paradoxicalness. Robinson wrote a great deal of poetry and only a few good poems; and yet there is a somber distinction and honesty about him—he is a poet you respect.

If Edgar Lee Masters's *Spoon River Anthology* seems to us, today, more a part of literary history than of living poetry, still it is a surprisingly live part, a "Main Street" through whose mud the old buggies and the new horseless carriages are still pushing. It tells the historical truth of the late-nineteenth- and early-twentieth-century

towns of the Middle West—the struggle of greed and puritanical-
ness and provinciality with innocent radicalism and idealism and
culture—directly in terms of the people who embodied them; it is a
kind of "Ironies of Circumstance" told by an honest muckraker. Its
whole is more effective than any of its parts; and the poems' prosaic
effects are always better than their poetic effects, since Masters's
rhetoric, his whole idea of what a poetic effect is, is commonplace—
he is either sincerely prosaic or ingenuously poetic. His work has less
distinction than Robinson's; and yet his style and tone are his own, the
poems plainly come out of the life they describe. He writes:

> The earth keeps some vibration going
> There in your heart, and that is you.

Such a vibration is still going in some of the poems.

Carl Sandburg's poems, generally, are improvisations whose
wording is approximate; they do not have the exactness, the guaran-
teeing sharpness and strangeness of a real style. Sandburg is a color-
ful, appealing, and very American writer, so that you long for his lit-
tle vignettes or big folk editorials, with their easy sentimentality and
easy idealism, to be made into finished works of art; but he sings
songs more stylishly than he writes them, says his poems better than
they are written—it is marvelous to hear him say "The People, Yes,"
but it is not marvelous to read it as a poem. Probably he is at his best
in slight pieces like "Grass" or "Losers," or in such folkish inventions
as:

> tell me why a hearse horse snickers
> hauling a lawyer's bones.

The oddest and most imaginative of these poets is Vachel
Lindsay. He has the innocent, desperate eccentricity of the artist in a
world with no room for, no patience with, artists; you could die for
what you believed, Lindsay said, and no one would notice or care, but
if you had the nerve to go broke time after time, they would notice.
Nowadays when a poet with one privately printed book can have his
next three years taken care of by a Guggenheim fellowship, a *Kenyon
Review* fellowship, and the Prix de Rome, it is hard to remember
what chances the poet took in that small-town world, how precari-
ously hand to mouth his existence was. And yet in one way the old
days were better; Lindsay after a while, by luck and skill, got far more

readers than any poet could get today. His rhetoric with its wild, queer charm (half vaudeville and half grammar-school pageant, dreamed by a provincial Blake) and his almost childlike imagination produced a good many poems that we make allowances for and complacently enjoy; but at his best—in "Bryan, Bryan, Bryan, Bryan," in "A Negro Sermon: Simon Legree," and in "Daniel"—the poems are truly imagined and written; they have a rightness all their own. In "Bryan, Bryan, Bryan, Bryan," for instance, you find a real aesthetic distance, an unexpected objectivity and historical truth that go along with the consciously exaggerated and audacious phrases. What other writer, in the smiling expectation of his reader's smile, has ever called his sweetheart and himself "fairy Democrats"? The rest of literature, the rest of the world were for Lindsay a kind of secondhand shop from which he could get, cheap, the properties of his poems; but he had more sheer imagination, sheer objective command than most of his contemporaries, so that several of his poems are perfected as almost none of theirs are.

Robert Frost, along with Stevens and Eliot, seems to me the greatest of the American poets of this century. Frost's virtues are extraordinary. No other living poet has written so well about the actions of ordinary men; his wonderful dramatic monologues or dramatic scenes come out of a knowledge of people that few poets have had, and they are written in a verse that uses, sometimes with absolute mastery, the rhythms of actual speech. It is hard to overestimate the effect of this exact, spaced-out, prosaic movement, whose objects have the tremendous strength—you find it in Hardy's best poems—of things merely put down and left to speak for themselves. (Though Frost has little of Hardy's self-effacement, his matter-of-fact humility; Frost's tenderness, sadness, and humor are adulterated with vanity and a hard complacency.) Frost's seriousness and honesty; the bare sorrow with which, sometimes, things are accepted as they are, neither exaggerated nor explained away; the many, many poems in which there are real people with their real speech and real thought and real emotions—all this, in conjunction with so much subtlety and exactness, such classical understatement and restraint, makes the reader feel that he is not in a book but a world, and a world that has in common with his own some of the things that are most important in both. I don't need to praise anything so justly famous as Frost's observation of and empathy with everything in Nature from a hornet to a hillside; and he has observed his own nature, one person's random or consequential chains of thoughts and feelings and perceptions, quite as well. The least crevice of the good poems is saturated with imagination, an imagination that expresses itself in the continual wit and humor and particularity of what is said, and in the hand-hewn or hand-polished texture of its saying. And when you remember that Frost has written "The Witch of Coös," "Home Burial," "A Servant to Servants," "Directive," "Neither Out Far Nor In Deep," "Provide, Provide," "Acquainted with the Night," "After Apple-Picking," "Mending Wall," "The Most of It," "An Old Man's Winter Night," "To Earthward," "Stopping by Woods on a Snowy Evening," "Spring Pools," "The Lovely Shall Be Choosers," "Design," "Desert Places"— these and "The Fear," "The Pauper Witch of Grafton," "The Gift Outright," "The Need of Being Versed in Country Things," and a dozen or two dozen more as good—when you remember this you are astonished, almost as you are with Yeats and Rilke, that one man could have written so *many* good poems.

How little Frost's poems seem performances, no matter how brilliant or magical, how little things made primarily of words, and how much things made out of lives and the world that the lives inhabit! In Frost's poems men are not only the glory and jest and riddle of the world but also the habit of the world, its strange ordinariness, its ordinary strangeness, and they too trudge down the ruts along which the planets move in their courses. Frost is that rare thing, a complete or representative poet, and not one of the brilliant partial poets who do justice, far more than justice, to a portion of reality, and leave the rest of things forlorn. When you know Frost's poems, you know surprisingly well what the world seemed to one man. The grimness and awfulness and untouchable sadness of things, both in the world and in the self, have justice done to them in the poems—the limits which existence approaches and falls back from have seldom been stated with such bare composure—but no more justice than is done to the tenderness and love and delight; and everything in between is represented somewhere too, some things willingly and often and other things only as much—in Marianne Moore's delicate phrase—"as one's natural reticence will allow." To have the distance from the most awful and most nearly unbearable parts of the poems to the most tender, subtle, and loving parts, a distance so great; to have this whole range of being treated with so much humor and sadness and composure, with such plain truth; to see that a man can still include, connect, and make humanly understandable or un-understandable so *much*— this is one of the freshest and oldest of joys, a joy strong enough to make us say, with the Greek poet, that many things in this world are wonderful, but of all these the most wonderful is man.

Athens was called the education of Hellas; from 1912 till 1922 Ezra Pound could have been called the education of poetry. (I once read all the issues of *Poetry* printed during those years, and what stood out most was one poet, Yeats, and one critic, Pound.) His advice to poets could be summed up in a sentence: Write like speech—and *read French poetry!* He had needed his own advice; his earliest work was a sort of anthology of romantic sources—Browning, early Yeats, the *fin-de-siècle* poets, Villon and the troubadours (in translations or adaptations that remind one of Swinburne's and Rossetti's), Heine. His own variety of modernist poetry, though influenced by Laforgue and Corbière, was partly a return to the fresh beginnings of romantic practices, from their diluted and perfunctory ends; partly an extension to their limits of some of the most characteristic obsessions of romanticism, for instance, its passion for "pure" poetry, for putting everything in terms of sensation and emotion, with logic and generalizations excluded; and partly an adaptation of the exotic procedures of Chinese poetry, those silks that swathe a homely heart. Much of Pound's earlier poetry was a sort of bohemian *vers de société*; Pound's best work before the *Cantos,* with the exception of some parts of *Mauberly,* consists of adaptations of Chinese and Latin poetry. The best poems in *Cathay* are marvelous in their crystalline clearness, in the way their words stand out in delicate lucid pure being; Pound's style at its best is always a part of—in Pound's words—"the radiant world where one thought cuts through another with clean edge, a world of moving energies . . . the glass under water, the form that seems a form seen in a mirror." This style comes to us, mostly, in beautiful fragments or adaptations; it is surprising that a poet of Pound's extraordinary talents should have written so few good poems all his own.

Most of Pound's life has been spent on the *Cantos.* Many writers have felt, like Pound: Why not invent an art form that will permit me to put all my life, all my thoughts and feelings about the universe, directly into a work of art? But the trouble is, when they've invented it, it isn't an art form. The *Cantos* are a "form" that permits Pound, much of the time, not even to try to write poetry; but since he is a poet, a wonderful one, he sometimes still writes it. The *Cantos* are less a "poem containing history" than a heap containing poetry, history, recollections, free associations, obsessions. Form, as Kenneth Burke says, is a satisfied expectation; in much of the *Cantos* it is only our expectation of disorder, of an idiosyncratic hodgepodge, that is satisfied. Some of the lines have an easy elegance, a matter-of-fact reality; the bare look and motion of the words, sometimes, is a delight.

A great deal of the *Cantos* is interesting in the way an original soul's indiscriminate notes on books and people, countries and centuries, are interesting; all these fragmentary citations and allusions remind you that if you had read exactly the books Pound has read, known exactly the people Pound has known, and felt about them exactly as Pound has felt, you could understand the *Cantos* pretty well. Gertrude Stein was most unjust to Pound when she called that ecumenical alluder a village explainer: he can hardly *tell* you anything (unless you know it already), much less explain it. He makes notes on the margin of the universe; to tell how just or unjust a note is, you must know that portion of the text yourself. Some of the poetry is clearly beautiful, some of the history live: Pound can pick out, make up, a sentence or action that resurrects a man or a time. Many of Pound's recollections are as engaging as he is; his warmth, delight, disinterestedness, honest indignation help to make up for his extraordinary misuse of extraordinary powers, for everything that makes the *Cantos* a *reductio ad absurdum* of genius. His obsessions, at their worst, are a moral and intellectual disaster and make us ashamed for him:

> Democracies electing their sewage
> till there is no clear thought about holiness
> a dung flow from 1913
> and, in this, their kikery functioned, Marx, Freud and the American
> > beaneries
> Filth under filth . . .

What is worst in Pound and what is worst in the age have conspired to ruin the *Cantos* and have not succeeded. I cannot imagine any future that will think the whole of it a good poem, a finished work of art; but, then as now, scholars will process it, anthologies present a few of its beauties, readers dig through all that blue clay for more than a few diamonds.

At the bottom of Wallace Stevens's poetry there is wonder and delight, the child's or animal's or savage's—man's—joy in his own existence, and thankfulness for it. He is the poet of well-being: "One might have thought of sight, but who could think / Of what it sees, for all the ill it sees?" This sigh of awe, of wondering pleasure, is underneath all these poems that show us the "celestial possible," everything that has not yet been transformed into the infernal impossibilities of our everyday earth. Stevens is full of the natural or Aristotelian virtues; he is, in the terms of Hopkins's poem, all windhover and no Jesuit. There is about him, under the translucent glazes, a Dutch solidity and weight; he sits surrounded by all the good things of this earth, with rosy cheeks and fresh clear blue eyes, eyes not going out to you but shining in their place, like fixed stars. If he were an animal he would be, without a doubt, that rational, magnanimous, voluminous animal, the elephant.

His best poems are the poetry of a man fully human—of someone sympathetic, disinterested, both brightly and deeply intelligent; the poems see, feel, and think with equal success; they treat with mastery that part of existence which allows of mastery, and experience the rest of it with awe or sadness or delight. Minds of this quality of genius, of this breadth and delicacy of understanding, are a link between us and the past, since they are, for us, the past made living; and they are our surest link with the future, since they are the part of us which the future will know. Many of the poems look grayly out at

> . . . the immense detritus of a world
> That is completely waste, that moves from waste
> To waste, out of the hopeless waste of the past
> Into a hopeful waste to come.

But more of the poems see the unspoilable delights, the inexhaustible interests of existence.

Stevens did what no other American poet has ever done, what few poets have ever done: wrote some of his best and newest and strangest poems during the last year or two of a very long life. These are poems from the other side of existence, the poems of someone who sees things in steady accustomedness, as we do not, and who sees their accustomedness, and them, as about to perish. Many of the poems' qualities come naturally from age, so that they are appropriately and legitimately different from other people's poems, from Stevens's own younger poems. The poems are calmly exact, grandly plain, as though they themselves had suggested to Stevens his "Be orator but with an accurate tongue / And without eloquence"; and they seem strangely general and representative, so that we could say of them, of Stevens, what Stevens himself says "To an Old Philosopher in Rome":

> . . . each of us
> Behold himself in you, and hears his voice
> In yours, master and commiserable man . . .

How much of our existence is in that "master and commiserable man"! Poems like these, in their plainness and human rightness, remind me most of a work of art superficially very different, Verdi's *Falstaff.* Both are the products of men at once very old and beyond the dominion of age; such men seem to have entered into (or are able to create for us) a new existence, a world in which everything is enlarged and yet no more than itself, transfigured and yet beyond the need of transfiguration.

Stevens has an extraordinarily original imagination, one that has created for us, so to speak, many new tastes and colors and sounds, many real, half-real, and nonexistent beings. He has spoken, always, with the authority of someone who thinks of himself as a source of interest, of many interests. He has never felt it necessary to appeal to us, make a hit with us, nor does he try to sweep us away, to overawe us; he has written as if poems were certain to find, or make, their true readers. Throughout half this century of the common man, this age in which each is like his sibling, Stevens has celebrated the hero, the capacious, magnanimous, excelling man; has believed, with obstinacy and good humor, in all the heights which draw us toward them, make us like them, simply by existing. In an age when almost everybody sold man and the world short, he never did, but acted as if joy *were* "a word of our own," as if nothing excellent were alien to us.

William Carlos Williams is as magically observant and mimetic as a good novelist. He reproduces the details of what he sees with surprising freshness, clarity, and economy; and he sees just as extraordinarily, sometimes, the forms of this earth, the spirit moving behind the letters. His quick transparent lines have a nervous and contracted strength, move as jerkily and intently as a bird. Sometimes they have a marvelous delicacy and gentleness, a tact of pure showing; how well he calls into existence our precarious, confused, partial looking out at the world—our being-here-looking, just looking! And if he is often pure presentation, he is often pure exclamation, and delights in yanking something into life with a galvanic imperative or interjection. All this proceeds from the whole bent of his nature: he prefers a clear, active, intense confusion to any "wise passiveness," to any calm and clouded two-sidedness.

He has a boyish delight and trust in Things: there is always on his lips the familiar, pragmatic, American "These are the facts"—for he is the most pragmatic of writers and so American that the adjective itself seems inadequate; one exclaims in despair and delight: He is the America of poets. His imagist-objectivist background and bias have helped his poems by their emphasis on truthfulness, exactness, concrete presentation; but they have harmed the poems by their underemphasis on organization, logic, narrative, generalization. The materials of Williams's unsuccessful poems have as much reality as the brick one stumbles over on the sidewalk; but how little has been done to them!—the poem is pieces or, worse still, a piece. But sometimes just enough, exactly as little as is necessary, has been done; and in these poems the Nature of the edge of the American city—the weeds, clouds, and children of vacant lots—and its reflection in the minds of its inhabitants exist for good.

Anyone would apply to Williams such adjectives as outspoken, warmhearted, generous, fresh, sympathetic, enthusiastic, spontaneous, impulsive, emotional, observant, curious, rash, courageous, undignified, unaffected, humanitarian, experimental, empirical, liberal, secular, democratic. One is rather embarrassed at the necessity of calling him original; it is like saying that a Cheshire cat smiles. He is even less logical than the average poet—he is an intellectual in neither the good nor the bad sense of the word—but loves abstractions for their own sake and makes accomplished, characteristic, inveterate use of them, exactly as if they were sensations or emotions. Both generalizations and particulars are handled with freshness and humor and imagination, with a delicacy and fantasy that are especially charming in so vigorous, realistic, and colloquial a writer. He is full of homely shrewdness and common sense, of sharply intelligent comments dancing cheek-to-cheek with prejudices and random eccentricity; he is someone who, sometimes, does see what things are like, and he is able to say what he sees more often than most poets, since his methods permit (indeed encourage) him to say anything at all without worrying: *Can* one say such things in poetry? in this particular poem?

Williams's poetry is more remarkable for its empathy, its muscular and emotional identification with its subjects, than any modern poetry except Rilke's. His knowledge of plants and animals, our brothers and sisters in the world, is surprising for its range and intensity; and he sets them down in the midst of the real weather of the world, so that the reader is full of an innocent lyric pleasure just in being out in the open, in feeling the wind tickling his skin. At first people were introduced into the poems mainly as overheard or overlooked landscape; they spread. Williams has the knowledge of people one expects, and often does not get, from doctors; a knowledge one does not expect, and very seldom gets, from contemporary poets. Williams's attitude toward his people is particularly admirable; he has neither that condescending, impatient, pharisaical dismissal of the illiterate mass of mankind, nor that manufactured, mooing awe for an equally manufactured Little or Common Man, that disfigures so much contemporary writing.

Williams's ability to rest (or at least to thrash happily about) in contradictions, doubts, and general guesswork, without ever climbing aboard any of the monumental certainties that go perpetually by, perpetually on time—this ability may seem the opposite of Whitman's gift for boarding every certainty and riding off into every infinite, but the spirit behind them is the same. Williams's range (it is roughly *Paterson*, that microcosm which he has half discovered, half invented) is narrower than Whitman's, and yet there too one is reminded of Whitman: Williams has much of the freeness of an earlier America, though it is a freedom haunted about by desperation and sorrow. The little motto one could invent for him—"In the suburbs, there one feels free"—is particularly ambiguous when one considers that those suburbs of his are overshadowed by, are a part of, the terrible industrial landscape of northeastern New Jersey. But the ambiguity is one that Williams himself not only understands but insists upon: if his poems are full of what is clear, delicate, and beautiful, they are also full of what is coarse, ugly, and horrible. There is no optimistic blindness in Williams, though there is a fresh gaiety, a stubborn or invincible joyousness: in his best poems, and in the first and best parts of *Paterson*, the humor and sadness and raw absurdity of things, and the things themselves, exist in startling reality.

In John Crowe Ransom's best poems every part is subordinated to the whole, and the whole is accomplished with astonishing exactness and thoroughness. Their economy, precision, and restraint give the poems, sometimes, an original yet impersonal perfection; and Ransom's feel for the exact convention of a particular poem, the exact demands of a particular situation, has resulted in poems different from each other and everything else, as unified, individualized, and unchangeable as nursery rhymes. In Ransom the contradictions of existence are clear, exactly contradictory, not fused in arbitrary overall emotion; one admires the clear, sharp, Mozartian lightness of texture of the best poems. And sometimes their phrasing is magical— light as air, soft as dew, the real old-fashioned enchantment. The poems satisfy our nostalgia for the past, yet themselves have none. They are the reports (written by one of the most elegant and individual war correspondents who ever existed) of our world's old war between power and love, between those who efficiently and practi-

cally know and those who are "content to feel / What others under-
stand." And these reports of battles are, somehow, bewitching: disen-
chantment and enchantment are so beautifully and inextricably min-
gled in them that we accept everything with sad pleasure, and smile
at the poems' foreknowing, foredefeated, half-acceptant pain. For in
the country of the poems wisdom is a poor butterfly dreaming that it
is Chuang-tzu, and not an optimistic bird of prey; and the greatest sin-
gle subject of the romantics, pure potentiality, is treated with a clas-
sical grace and composure.

Most writers become overrhetorical when they are insisting on
more emotion than they actually feel; Ransom is perpetually insisting,
by his detached, mock-pedantic, wittily complicated tone, that he is
not feeling much at all, not half so much as he really should be feel-
ing—and this rhetoric becomes overmannered, too protective, only
when there is not much emotion for him to pretend not to be feeling,
and he keeps on out of habit. Ransom has the personal seriousness
that treats the world as it seems to him, not the solemnity that treats
the really important things, the world as everybody knows it is. His
poems are full of an affection that cannot help itself for an innocence
that cannot help itself—for the stupid travelers lost in the maze of the
world, for the clever travelers lost in the maze of the world. The
poems are not a public argument but personal knowledge, personal
feeling; and their virtues are the "merely" private virtues—their
characters rarely vote, rarely even kill one another, but often fall in
love.

Ransom's poems profess their limitations so candidly, almost as
a principle of style, that it is hardly necessary to say they are not
poems of the largest scope or the greatest intensity. But they are some
of the most original poems ever written, just as Ransom is one of the
best, most original, and most sympathetic poets alive; it is easy to see
that his poetry will always be cared for, since he has written poems
that are perfectly realized and occasionally almost perfect—poems
that the hypothetical generations of the future will be reading page
by page with Wyatt, Campion, Marvell, and Mother Goose.

And then there is Eliot. During the last thirty or forty years
Eliot has been so much the most famous and influential of American
poets that it seems almost absurd to write about him, especially when
everybody else already has: when all of you can read me your own ar-
ticles about Eliot, would it have really been worthwhile to write you
mine? Yet actually the attitude of an age toward its Lord Byron—in
this case, a sort of combination of Lord Byron and Dr. Johnson—is al-

ways surprisingly different from the attitude of the future. Won't the future say to us in helpless astonishment: "But did you actually believe that all those things about objective correlatives, classicism, the tradition, applied to *his* poetry? Surely you must have seen that he was one of the most subjective and daemonic poets who ever lived, the victim and helpless beneficiary of his own inexorable compulsions, obsessions? From a psychoanalytical point of view he was far and away the most interesting poet of your century. But for you, of course, after the first few years, his poetry existed undersea, thousands of feet below that deluge of exegesis, explication, source listing, scholarship, and criticism that overwhelmed it. And yet how bravely and personally it survived, its eyes neither coral nor mother-of-pearl but plainly human, full of human anguish! Think of the magical rightness of 'Prufrock,' one of the most engaging and haunting and completely accomplished poems that ever existed. Or take the continuation of it, that mesmeric subjective correlative *The Waste Land*, which Eliot would have written about the Garden of Eden, but which your age thought its own realistic photograph. And if none of the poets of your age—except perhaps for your greatest, Yeats—could write a really good play, still, how genuinely personal, what a subjective therapeutic success *Murder in the Cathedral* and *The Family Reunion* are! And if none of the poets of your age could write a long poem that compares with the best of their short poems, still, how wonderful the *Four Quartets* are: a long poem by a good poet that (as neither the *Cantos* nor *The Bridge* nor *Paterson* does) brings an intelligent man's own world view into an organized and thoughtful whole. If the reasons you gave were often the wrong reasons, the poet and the poems you loved were the right poet and the right poems; so far as Eliot is concerned, your age can be satisfied with itself."

Marianne Moore has as careful and acute an eye as anybody alive, and almost as good a tongue. The reader relishes in her poems a fineness and strangeness and firmness of discrimination that he is not accustomed to. Her poems are notable for their wit and particularity and observation; a knowledge of "prosaic" words that reminds one of "Comus"; a texture that will withstand any amount of rereading; a restraint and delicacy that make many more powerful poems seem obvious. Their forms have the lacy, mathematical extravagance of snowflakes, seem as arbitrary as the prohibitions in fairy tales; difficulty is the chief technical principle of her poetry, almost. What intelligence vibrates in the sounds, the rhythms, the pauses, in all the minute particulars that make up the body of the poem! The tone of her poems, often, is enough to give the reader great pleasure, since it is a tone of imagination and precision and intelligence, of irony and forbearance, of unusual moral penetration—is plainly the voice of a person of good taste and good sense and good will, of a genuinely human being. It is the voice, too, of a natural, excessive, and magnificent eccentric. In some of her poems she has discovered both a new sort of subject (a queer many-headed one) and a new sort of connection and structure for it, so that she has widened the scope of poetry; if poetry, like other organisms, wants to convert into itself everything that is, she has helped it to. She has shown us that the world is more poetic than we thought.

She has great limitations—her work is one long triumph of them. How often she has written about Things (hers are aesthetic-moral, not commercial-utilitarian—they persist and reassure); or Plants (how can anything bad happen to a plant?); or Animals with holes, a heavy defensive armament, or a massive and herbivorous placidity superior to either the dangers or temptations of aggression! Because so much of our own world is evil, she has transformed the Animal Kingdom, that amoral realm, into a realm of good; her consolatory, fabulous bestiary is more accurate than, but is almost as arranged as, any medieval one. The poems say, sometimes, to the beasts: "You reassure me and people don't, except when they are like you—but really they are always like you"; and it is wonderful to have it said so, and for a moment to forget, behind the animals of a darkening landscape, their dark companions.

Some of her poems have the manners or manner of ladies who learned a little before birth not to mention money, who neither point nor touch, and who scrupulously abstain from the mixed, live vulgarity of life. "You sit still if, whenever you move, something jingles," Pound quotes an officer of the old school as saying. There is the same aristocratic abstention behind the restraint, the sitting still as long as it can, of this poetry. "The passion for setting people right is in itself an afflictive disease. / Distaste that takes no credit to itself is best," she says in an early poem: and says, broadly and fretfully for her, "We are sick of the earth, / sick of the pig-sty, wild geese and wild men." One feels like quoting against her own "As if a death-mask could replace / Life's faulty excellence," and blurting that life masks have their disadvantages too. We are uncomfortable—or else too comfortable—in a world in which feeling, affection, charity are so entirely divorced from sexuality and power, the bonds of the flesh. In the world of her poems there are many thoughts, things, animals, sentiments, moral insights; but money and passion and power, the brute fact that *works*, whether or not correctly, whether or not precisely— the whole Medusa-face of the world: these are gone.

A good deal of Marianne Moore's poetry is specifically (and changingly) about armor, weapons, protection, places to hide; and she is not only conscious that this is so, but after a while writes poems about the fact that it is so. As she says, "armor seems extra," but it isn't; and when she writes about "another armored animal," about another "thing made graceful by adversities, conversities," she does so with the sigh of someone who has come home. Sometimes she writes about armor and wears it, the most delicately chased, live-seeming scale-armor anybody ever put together: armor hammered out of fern seed, woven from the silk of invisible cloaks—for it is almost, though not quite, as invisible as it pretends to be, and is when most nearly invisible most nearly protecting. And yet in the long run she has learned to put no trust in armor and says, "Pig-fur won't do, I'll wrap / myself in salamander-skin like Prester John," the "inextinguishable salamander" who "revealed / a formula safer than / an armorer's: the power of relinquishing / what one would keep," and whose "shield was his humility." And "What Are Years" begins: "All are naked, none are safe," and speaks of overcoming our circumstances by accepting them; just as "Nevertheless" talks not about armor, not about weapons, but about what is behind or above them both:

> The weak overcomes its
> menace, the strong over-
> comes itself. What is there
> like fortitude? What sap
> went through that little thread
> to make the cherry red!

Just so the poet overcomes herself, when she says at last: "What is more precise than precision? Illusion." There is so much of a life concentrated into, objectified on, the poet's hard, tender, serious pages, there is such wit and truth and moral imagination inhabiting this small space, that we are surprised at possibility, and marvel all over again at the conditions of human making and being. What Marianne Moore's best poetry does, I can say best in her own words: it "comes into and steadies the soul," so that the reader feels himself "a life prisoner, but reconciled."

E. E. Cummings persisted so boldly and stubbornly, for a whole career, in his own extraordinary individuality, that it is hard for his readers to believe that he is gone. No one else has ever made avant-garde, experimental poems so attractive to both the general and the special reader; since the early twenties, Cummings has been more widely imitated and more easily appreciated than any other modernist poet. His fairy godmother, after giving him several armfuls of sensibility, individuality, and rhetorical skill, finished by saying: "And best of all, everyone will forgive you everything, my son." Just as he persisted in the interests with which he began—his disposition was unchanging—so he persisted in the development of the style with which he began, and worked out the most extraordinary variations, inversions, and extrapolations of the romantic rhetoric of his earliest poems. His rhetoric was as skillful, approached as nearly to the limit of every last possibility, as the acts of the circus performers or burlesque comedians he felt an admiring kinship for. Many a writer has spent his life putting his favorite words in all the places they belong; but how many, like Cummings, have spent their lives putting their favorite words in all the places they don't belong, thus discovering many effects that no one had even realized were possible? As Cummings said, "Every man is wonderful / and a formula"; often this is true of Cummings himself, so that you get tired of the hundredth application of the formula—but often it is from that very formula, worked out into a fantastic new one, that Cummings has derived an effect of wonderful originality.

Language is a world of signs, and of prescribed relations between the signs, that stand for the things in the natural world and *their* relations. But there are all sorts of impossible, unprescribed relations between words that seem to stand for something, have quasi-denotations, vague or contradictory but exciting meanings. And since we feel that words and their prescribed relations don't fully or satisfactorily describe the world, that there is a disorder or meta-order in the world to which ordered words are inadequate, we sympathize with the contradictory or impossible order of words, and try to feel what it must stand for. The round-square may be impossible, but we believe in it because it is impossible. Cummings is a very great expert in all these, so to speak, illegal syntactical devices: his misuse of parts of speech, his use of negative prefixes, his word coining, his systematic relation of words that grammar and syntax don't permit us to relate—all this makes him a magical bootlegger or moonshiner of language, one who intoxicates us on a clear liquor no government has legalized with its stamp.

The accomplished body of Conrad Aiken's work—which has been at once respected and neglected—is something you read with consistent pleasure, but without the astonished joy that you feel for the finest poetry, which is always extraordinary. It is peculiarly hard to say what is lacking in Aiken's work, since he has written poems that come as close to being good poems, without ever quite being so, as any I know. Isaac Babel said about style: "A phrase is born into the world good and bad at the same time. The secret lies in a slight, almost invisible twist. The lever should rest in your hand, getting warm, and you can turn it once, not twice." Aiken has kept his hand on the lever all his life, and he has turned it over and over and over. He is a kind of Midas: everything that he touches turns to verse; so that reading his poems is like listening to Delius—one is experiencing an unending undifferentiating wash of lovely sounds—or like watching an only moderately interesting, because almost entirely predictable, kaleidoscope. Aiken's diluted world is a world where everything blurs into everything else, where the accomplished, elegiac, nostalgic verse turns everything into itself, as the diffused Salon photography of the first years of this century turned everything into Salon photographs.

Another respected but somewhat neglected poet is Allen Tate. But the best of his harshly formed, powerful poems are far more individual, unusual, than even the best of Aiken's. Perhaps they are read less than they are admired because of their lack of charm, of human appeal and human sympathy, and because of their tone of somewhat forbidding authority; but the neglect of poems as good as "Mother and Son," "The Cross," and "The Mediterranean" will surely be temporary.

Robinson Jeffers has taken an interesting and unusual part of the world and has described it, narrated some overpowering events that have occurred in it, with great—but crude and approximate—power. He celebrates the survival of the fittest, the war of all against all, but his heart goes out to animals rather than to human beings, to minerals rather than to animals, since he despises the bonds and qualifications of existence. Because of all this, his poems do not have the exactness and concision of the best poetry; his style and temperament, his whole world view, are to a surprising extent a matter of simple exaggeration. The motto of his work is "More! more!"—but as Tolstoy says, "A wee bit omitted, overemphasized, or exaggerated in poetry, and there is no contagion"; and Frost, bearing him out, says magnificently: "A very little of anything goes a long way in a work of art."

Archibald MacLeish first employed his delicate lyric gift upon more easily and immediately attractive versions of poems like Eliot's, Pound's, and Apollinaire's; the smoothly individual style that he developed makes such a poem as "And You, Andrew Marvell" beautiful in just the way that a Georgia O'Keeffe painting is beautiful. In his later work he began to make overpowering general demands upon this limited and specific talent. The directly impressive rhetoric of a play like *J.B.* is akin to the rhetoric of the most cultivated and effective television programs: the play, like so much of MacLeish's later work, is the "public speech" of an authoritative public figure who is controlling the responses of a mass audience. MacLeish's work suffers, characteristically, from something akin to the "metaphysical pathos": it is almost more conscious of the impressiveness of what it says than of what it says.

Hart Crane's *The Bridge* does not succeed as a unified work of art, partly because some of its poems are bad or mediocre, and partly because Crane took for his subject an ambiguous failure and tried to treat it as a mystical triumph: it is as if Fitzgerald had tried to make an ecstatic patriotic success out of Gatsby's world by showing, with real rhetorical magnificence, how the Brooklyn Bridge joins West Egg to the American continent. Actually Crane had some of Fitzgerald's understanding of, feeling for, the worst changes in the United States, but instead of making these into a controlling image—as Fitzgerald did in his valley of ashes, his deserted mansion with its scrawled obscenity on the front steps—Crane tried to transcend them by means of the contradictory "positive" image of the bridge. And yet how wonderful parts of *The Bridge* are! "Van Winkle" is one of the clearest and freshest and most truly American poems ever written; "The Dance," "Harbor Dawn," "The Tunnel," and "To Brooklyn Bridge," if they are in part rhetorical failures, are in part magical successes. Crane's poetry is hurt most by rhetoric and sentimentality— his automatic ecstatic mysticism, often of a Whitmanesque kind, is a form of sentimentality—and yet it is helped sometimes by the rhetorical risks Crane takes: if sometimes we are bogged down in lines full of "corymbulous," "hypogeum," "plangent," "irrefragably," "glozening," "tellurian," "conclamant," sometimes we are caught up in the soaring rapture of something unprecedented, absolutely individual. Remember the beautifully imaginative, haunting sympathy of "Black Tambourine"; the composed magic of "Repose of Rivers"; the serious exact interest, the organized concision, of "National Winter Garden"; the mesmeric rhetoric of "Voyages II," one of the most beautiful of all those poems in which love, death, and sleep "are fused for an instant in one floating flower." All these poems have the clear freshness (both young in itself and, somehow, in the America from which it came) of Crane at his inspired, astonishing, and attractive best.

Elizabeth Bishop's *Poems* seems to me one of the best books an American poet has written, one that the future will read almost as it will read Stevens and Moore and Ransom. Her poems are quiet, truthful, sad, funny, most marvelously individual poems; they have a sound, a feel, a whole moral and physical atmosphere, different from anything else I know. They are honest, modest, minutely observant, masterly; even their most complicated or troubled or imaginative effects seem, always, personal and natural, and as unmistakable as the first few notes of a Mahler song, the first few patches of a Vuillard interior. Her best poems—poems like "The Man-Moth," "The Fish," "The Weed," "Roosters," "The Prodigal Son," "Faustina, or Rock Roses," "The Armadillo"—remind one of Vuillard or even, sometimes, of Vermeer. The poet and the poems have their limitations; all exist on a small scale, and some of the later poems, especially, are too detailedly and objectively descriptive. But the more you read her poems, the better and fresher, the more nearly perfect they seem; at least half of them are completely realized works of art.

Robert Penn Warren's narrative and dramatic gifts seem to me greater than his lyric gifts, though he has written lyrics as memorable as "Original Sin" and "Pursuit"; he is at his best in one of the only good long poems of our century, *Brother to Dragons*. It is a terrible but sometimes very touching poem, one of extraordinary immediacy, strength, and scope. The poem's traumatic subject is Original Sin, but there is no Saviour left to save anybody in the poem; the consoling veil of religion and art and philosophy is gone, leaving us raw nature, raw morality, and the saving grace, the shaky grace, of custom. Cruel sometimes, crude sometimes, obsessed sometimes, *Brother to Dragons* has its touches of tender inconsequence, of forbearance and magnanimity. Some of Warren's wrenching historical understanding, his rhetoric, and his moralizing are hard for us to accept; but there is a wonderful amount of life in the poem—of human beings who, in the end, are free both of Warren's rhetoric and moralizing and of our own.

Theodore Roethke's poems began under glass (his greenhouse poems give you the live feel of a special world) and moved underground, underwater, out into the growing universe of roots and slugs, of all the "lewd, tiny, careless lives that scuttled under stones." One is struck by what the world of his poems is full of or entirely lacking in; plants and animals, soil and weather, sex, ontogeny, and the unconscious swarm over the reader, but he looks in vain for hydrogen bombs, world wars, Christianity, money, ordinary social observations, his everyday moral doubts. Many poets are sometimes childish; Roethke, uniquely, is sometimes babyish, though he is a powerful Donatello baby who has love affairs, and whose marshlike unconscious is continually celebrating its marriage with the whole wet dark underside of things. He is a thoroughly individual but surprisingly varied poet: if we were to read aloud four or five of his best poems ("Dolor," "My Papa's Waltz," "Frau Bauman, Frau Schmidt, and Frau Schwartze," "I Knew a Woman," and "Meditations of an Old Woman" or one of the poems from *Praise to the End!*), we should see to our astonishment that each is in a decidedly different style; instead of conquering and living in one country, Roethke has led expeditions into several and has won notable victories in each. His best large poems are not, perhaps, as thoroughly satisfying as the best small ones. Certainly the long poems in *Praise to the End!* are partially or superficially successful, but do they mean enough? Are not the parts (except where these are derived from a formula, so that they can be duplicated or replaced too easily) better than the whole? Don't such poems tend to have impressive "positive" endings of a certain rhetorical insincerity? "Meditations of an Old Woman" is a more directly meaningful adaptation of this *Praise to the End!* type of long poem; it is interestingly influenced by the *Four Quartets*, just as some of Roethke's later poems are overpoweringly influenced by Yeats. Roethke is a forceful, delicate, and original poet whose poetry is still changing.

As these accounts must have reminded you, good American poets are surprisingly individual and independent; they have little of the member-of-the-Academy, official-man-of-letters feel that English or continental poets often have. When American poets join literary political parties, doctrinaire groups with immutable principles, whose poems themselves are manifestoes, the poets are ruined by it. We see this in the beatniks, with their official theory that you write a poem by putting down anything that happens to come into your head; this iron spontaneity of theirs makes it impossible for even a talented beatnik to write a good poem except by accident, since it eliminates the selection, exclusion, and concentration that are an essential part of writing a poem. Besides, their poems are as direct as true works of art are indirect: ironically, these conscious social manifestoes of theirs, these bohemian public speeches, make it impossible for the artist's unconscious to operate as it normally does in the process of producing a work of art.

This doctrinaire directness is as noticeable in the beatniks' opposites, the followers of Yvor Winters. These poets have—if I may invent a parable—met an enchanter who has said to them: "You have all met an enchanter who has transformed you into obscure romantic animals, but you can become clear and classical and human again if you will only swallow these rules." The poets swallow them, and from that moment they are all Henry Wadsworth Longfellow, a wax one; from that moment they wander, grave weighing shades, through a landscape each leaf of which rhymes, and scans, and says softly: "And the moral of *that* is . . ."

Does the Muse come to men with a ruler, a pair of compasses, and a metronome? Is it all right to say anything, no matter how commonplace and pompous and cliché, as long as you're sober, and say what the point is, and see that it scans? The worst thing about such planned poems as these is that they are so unnaturally silly: this is a learned imbecility, a foolishness of the schools; and ordinary common sense, ordinary human nature, will dismiss it with Johnson's "Clear your mind of cant," or with his "Sir, a man might write such stuff forever, if he would *abandon* his mind to it."

There is another, larger group of poets who, so to speak, come out of Richard Wilbur's overcoat. The work of these academic, tea-party, creative-writing-class poets rather tamely satisfies the rules or standards of technique implicit in what they consider the "best modern practice," so that they are very close to one another, very craftsman-like, never take chances, and produce (extraordinarily) a pretty or correctly beautiful poem and (ordinarily) magazine verse. Their poems are without personal force—come out of poems, not out of life; are, at bottom, social behavior calculated to satisfy a small social group of academic readers, editors, and foundation executives.

Earlier in this century there was a tradition of feminine verse—roughly, an Elizabeth Barrett Browning tradition—which produced many frankly romantic and poetic poems, most of them about love or nature. Elinor Wylie was the most crystalline and superficially metaphysical of these writers, and Edna St. Vincent Millay the most powerful and most popular. (One thinks with awe and longing of this real and extraordinary popularity of hers: if only there were *some* poet—Frost, Stevens, Eliot—whom people still read in canoes!) Millay seems to me at her best in a comparatively quiet and unpretentious poem like "The Return"; two later poets in this tradition,

Léonie Adams and Louise Bogan, have produced (in poems like "The Figure Head" and "Henceforth, from the Mind") poems more delicately beautiful than any of Millay's or Wylie's. I have already written about two poets in a very different tradition, Marianne Moore and Elizabeth Bishop, who seem to me the best woman poets since Emily Dickinson; an extraordinarily live, powerful, and original poet, Eleanor Taylor, is a fitting companion of theirs; and I am sorry to have no space in which to write about such individual poets as Adrienne Rich and Katherine Hoskins.

I should like, if I had room, to write about such interesting and intelligent poets as John Berryman, Howard Nemerov, and Delmore Schwartz; such charming, individual, or forceful poets as W. D. Snodgrass, James Wright, Theodore Weiss, James Dickey, and Louis Simpson; and such respected poets as Mark Van Doren, Horace Gregory, Yvor Winters, Stanley Kunitz, Babette Deutsch, Richard Eberhart, Muriel Rukeyser, Louis Untermeyer, and John Peale Bishop. Instead let me finish by writing about Karl Shapiro, Richard Wilbur, and Robert Lowell.

Karl Shapiro's poems are fresh and young and rash and live; their hard clear outlines, their flat bold colors create a world like that of a knowing and skillful neoprimitive painting, without any of the confusion or profundity of atmosphere, of aerial perspective, but with notable visual and satiric force. The poet early perfected a style, derived from Auden but decidedly individual, which he has not developed in later life but has temporarily replaced with the clear Rilke-like rhetoric of his Adam and Eve poems, the frankly Whitmanesque convolutions of his latest work. His best poems—poems like "The Leg," "Waitress," "Scyros," "Going to School," "Cadillac"—have a real precision, a memorable exactness of realization, yet they plainly come out of life's raw hubbub, out of the disgraceful foundations, the exciting and disgraceful surfaces of existence. Both in verse and in prose Shapiro loves, partly out of indignation and partly out of sheer mischievousness, to tell the naked truths or half-truths or quarter-truths that will make anybody's hair stand on end; he is always crying: "But he hasn't any clothes on!" about an emperor who is half the time surprisingly well dressed.

Petronius spoke of the "studied felicity" of Horace's poetry, and I can never read one of Richard Wilbur's books without thinking of this phrase. His impersonal, exactly accomplished, faintly sententious skill produces poems that, ordinarily, compose themselves into a little too regular a beauty—there is no eminent beauty without a certain strangeness in the proportion; and yet "A Baroque Wall-Fountain in the Villa Sciarra" is one of the most marvelously beautiful, one of the most nearly perfect poems any American has written, and poems like "A Black November Turkey" and "A Hole in the Floor" are the little differentiated, complete-in-themselves universes that true works of art are. Wilbur's lyric calling-to-life of the things of this world—the things, rather than the processes or the people—specializes in both true and false happy endings, not by choice but by necessity; he obsessively sees, and shows, the bright underside of every dark thing. What he says about his childhood is true of his maturity:

> In my kind world the dead were out of range
> And I could not forgive the sad or strange
> In beast or man.

This compulsion limits his poems; and yet it is this compulsion, and not merely his greater talent and skill, that differentiates him so favorably from the controlled, accomplished, correct poets who are common nowadays.

More than any other poet Robert Lowell is the poet of shock: his effects vary from crudity to magnificence, but they are always surprising and always his own—his style manages to make even quotations and historical facts a personal possession. His variant of Tolstoy's motto, "Make it strange," is "Make it grotesque"—largely grotesque, grandly incongruous. The vivid incongruity he gives the things or facts he uses is so decided that it amounts to a kind of wit; in his poetry fact is a live stumbling block that we fall over and feel to the bone. But it is life that he makes into poems instead of, as in Wilbur, the things of life. In Wilbur the man who produces the poems is somehow impersonal and anonymous, the composed conventional figure of The Poet; we know well, almost too well, the man who produces Lowell's poems. The awful depths, the plain absurdities of his own actual existence in the prosperous, developed, disastrous world he and we inhabit are there in the poems. Most poets, most good poets even, no longer have the heart to write about what is most terrible in the world of the present: the bombs waiting beside the rockets, the hundreds of millions staring into the temporary shelter of their television sets, the decline of the West that seems less a decline than the fall preceding an explosion. Perhaps because his own existence seems to him in some sense as terrible as the public world—his private world hangs over him as the public world hangs over others—he does not forsake the headlined world for the refuge of one's private joys and decencies, the shaky garden of the heart; instead, as in his wonderful poem about Boston Common, he sees all these as the lost paradise of the childish past, the past that knew so much but still didn't *know.* In *Life Studies* the pathos of the local color of the past—of the lives and deaths of his father and mother and grandfather and uncle, crammed full of their own varied and placid absurdity—is the background that sets off the desperate knife-edged absurdity of the jailed conscientious objector among gangsters and Jehovah's Witnesses, the private citizen returning to his baby, older now, from the mental hospital. He sees things as being part of history; if you say about his poor detailedly eccentric, trust-fund Lowells, "But they *weren't,*" he can answer, "They are now."

Lowell has always had an astonishing ambition, a willingness to learn what past poetry was and to compete with it on its own terms. In many of his early poems his subjects have been rather monotonously wrenched into shape, organized under a terrific unvarying pressure; in the later poems they have been allowed, in comparison, to go on leading their own lives. (He bullied his early work, but his own vulnerable humanity has been forced in on him.) The particulars of all the poems keep to an extraordinary degree their stubborn toughness, their senseless originality and contingency; but the subject matter and peculiar circumstances of Lowell's best work—for instance, "Falling Asleep over the Aeneid," "For the Union Dead," "Mother Marie Therese," "Ford Madox Ford," "Skunk Hour"—justify the harshness and violence, the barbarous immediacy, that seem arbitrary in many of the others. He is a poet of great originality and power who has, extraordinarily, developed instead of repeating himself. His poems have a wonderful largeness and grandeur, exist on a scale that is unique today. You feel before reading any new poem of his the uneasy expectation of perhaps encountering a masterpiece.

[*1963/TBC*]

A JARRELL
GALLERY

Introduction to a Poetry Roundup

When anyone reads and writes about a great many books of poetry—
and I am reviewing twice as many as usual, since the spring issue
was all Wallace Stevens—he is uneasy at liking so few of the books.
He feels, just as the poets and their readers feel, that he should like
many more: it seems only right, only human. And yet really he should
be uneasy at liking as many as he does. Posterity won't. Our age's
eight or ten great, twenty or twenty-five good, forty or fifty talented
poets—what has posterity to do with these illusions of ours? As little
as we have to do with the illusions of 1855; those poets whose names
we do not recognize, whose poems we have never even seen. Whether
we live in the Athens of Pericles or the England of Elizabeth I, there
is one law we can be sure of: there are only a few good poets alive. And
there follows from it another law, about critics: if a man likes a great
many contemporary poets, he is, necessarily, a bad critic.

But even if all this is true—and it seems to me unarguably
true—saying so doesn't make me feel any better about not liking
more of the books. Somewhere in the depths of my being, as in yours,
there is something that keeps saying, *Praise, praise*; part of me wants
to take as its rule of life, of criticism even, *Love, or be silent*; when I
can write in dazzled bliss about Hardy or Yeats or Whitman or
Hopkins or Frost or Eliot or Dickinson or Stevens or Moore or Thomas
or Auden or Williams or Ransom or such—when I can quote, or ad-
mire, or appreciate, beautiful or witty or moving poems by Pound or

Lawrence or Graves or Lowell or Stephens or Bridges or Muir or Elizabeth Bishop or Owen or Tate or MacNeice or Warren or Shapiro or Katherine Hoskins or Roethke or such, I feel that I am behaving as man (who shudders in awe, and delights most in that shudder) behaves when he is truly man; and when I tell you what troubles me about MacLeish, and that Edith Sitwell isn't a very good poet, I feel that I'm only behaving like the Devil, that accuser, that Spirit who Denies. Disliking what is bad is only the other face of liking what is good; but what a dark, dank, grudging, graceless face, one endeared neither to gods nor men! And the good, in poetry, is always a white blackbird, an abnormal and unlikely excellence; all that deserves our respect in ordinary life—the consistent, adequate, responsible norm of behavior—gains only our indifference, here. It is unpleasant, discouraging, unnatural to have to go on saying, about each shining new blackbird: *But it's black*; I do it, but I hate doing it.

On Emily Dickinson

Fifty-three years after the death of Queen Victoria, it has become possible to read Emily Dickinson's poems as she wrote them, and not as her guides, relatives, and friends wished that she had written them: Thomas H. Johnson and the Belknap Press of the Harvard University Press have brought out in three big volumes, noted, chronologically arranged, and accurate to the last variant, misspelling, and grammatical error, *The Poems of Emily Dickinson*. Now and then—I know I shouldn't admit this—I am glad of what the people did to the poems: for instance, *signed away / What portion of me I / Could make assignable*, in the poem that begins *I heard a fly buzz when I died*; but usually Emily Dickinson's own ways are better, even when there is a dash every second word and an exclamation point every third. This is, truly, a marvelous book: the reader finishes speechless, and laughing, and shaking his head in helpless wonder. He has read some great poems, and some good ones, and some arch and silly and *terrible* ones, poems that would make a bureau blush; all the absolutes and intensives and eccentricities of an absolutely intense eccentric have passed over him like a train of avalanches, and left him a couple of hundred feet deep in Knowledge.

On Modernism

Modernist poetry—the poetry of Pound, Eliot, Crane, Tate, Stevens, Cummings, MacLeish, et cetera—appears to be and is generally considered to be a violent break with romanticism; it is actually, I believe, an extension of romanticism, an end product in which most of the tendencies of romanticism have been carried to their limits. Romanticism—whether considered as the product of a whole culture or, in isolation, as a purely literary phenomenon—is necessarily a process of extension, a vector; it presupposes a constant experimentalism, the indefinite attainment of "originality," generation after generation, primarily by the novel extrapolation of previously exploited processes. (Neoclassicism, in theory at least, is a static system.) All these romantic tendencies are exploited to their limits; and the movement which carries out this final exploitation, apparently so different from earlier stages of the same process, is what we call modernism. Then, at last, romanticism is confronted with an impasse, a critical point, a genuinely novel situation that it can meet successfully only by contriving genuinely novel means—that is, means which are not romantic; the romantic means have already been exhausted.

———

It is the end of the line. Poets can go back and repeat the ride; they can settle in attractive, atavistic colonies along the railroad; they can repudiate the whole system, à la Yvor Winters, for some neoclassical donkey caravan of their own. But Modernism As We Knew It— the most successful and influential body of poetry of this century— is dead. Compare a 1940 issue of *Poetry* with a 1930 issue. Who could have believed that modernism would collapse so fast? Only someone who realized that modernism is a limit which it is impossible to exceed. How can poems be written that are more violent, more disorganized, more obscure, more—supply your own adjective—than those that have already been written? But if modernism could go no further, it was equally difficult for it to stay where it was: how could a movement completely dynamic in character, as "progressive" as the science and industrialism it accompanied, manage to become static or retrogressive without going to pieces?

———

Today, for the poet, there is an embarrassment of choices: young poets can choose—do choose—to write anything from surrealism to imitations of Robert Bridges; the only thing they have no choice about is making their own choice. The Muse, forsaking her sterner laws, says to everyone: "Do what you will."

———

Auden was so influential because his poetry was the only novel and successful reaction away from modernism; and a few years later Dylan Thomas was so influential—in England—because his poetry was the only novel and successful reaction away from Auden. But his semi-surrealist experimentalism could be as good as it was, and as influential as it was, only in a country whose poets had never carried modernism to the limits of its possibilities. No one can understand these English developments if he forgets that, while we were having the modernism of Pound, Stevens, Williams, Moore, Eliot, Tate, Crane, Cummings, and all the rest, England was having the modernism of the Sitwells.

On the Roots of Fiction

A baby asleep but about to be waked by hunger sometimes makes little sucking motions: he is dreaming that he is being fed, and manages by virtue of the dream to stay asleep. He may even smile a little in satisfaction. But the smile cannot last for long—the dream fails, and he wakes. This is, in a sense, the first story; the child in his "impotent omnipotence" is like us readers, us writers, in ours.

On André Malraux and the Nature of Criticism

The critic of art often does all that he can to make the ways of art inevitable, saying without any smile: "Certainly no representational painting of the first importance could be produced *now*; certainly no diatonic composition of the first importance could be produced *now.*" Schönberg said that there were a great many good pieces still to be composed in the key of C major, and his sentence is as inspiring to me, as a human being, as is Cromwell's: "I beseech you, in the bowels of Christ, believe that you may be mistaken!"

What I am saying is very obvious, and if anything is obvious enough it seems almost to give us the right to ignore it. Analysts of society or art regularly neglect what is, for the parts of it their explanation is able to take account of, and then go on the assumption that their explanation is all that there is. (If the methods of some discipline deal only with, say, what is quantitatively measurable, and something is not quantitatively measurable, then the thing does not exist for that discipline—after a while the lower right-hand corner of the inscription gets broken off, and it reads *does not exist*.) But if some-one has a good enough eye for an explanation he finally sees nothing inexplicable, and can begin every sentence with that phrase dearest to all who professionally understand: *It is no accident that* . . . We should love explanations well, but the truth better; and often the truth is that there *is* no explanation, that so far as we know it is an accident that . . . The motto of the city of Hamburg is: *Navigare necesse est, vivere no necesse.* A critic might say to himself: For me to know *what* the work of art is, is necessary; for me to explain *why* it is what it is, is not always necessary nor always possible.

––––

The artist and Nature, as Malraux conceives them, are almost exactly like Henry James and that innocent bystander who gives James the germ of one of his stories. "Just outside Rye the other day," the man begins, "I met a—" "Stop! stop!" cries James. "Not a word more or you'll spoil it!"

On Robert Frost

The responsibility and seriousness of Frost's best work—his worst work has an irresponsible conceit, an indifference to everything but himself, that appalls one—are nowhere better manifested than in the organization of these poems: an organization that, in its concern for any involution or ramification that really belongs to its subject, and in its severity toward anything else, expresses that absorption into a subject that is prior even to affection. The organization of Frost's poems is often rather simple or—as people say—"old-fashioned." But, as people ought to know, very complicated organizations are excessively rare in poetry, although in our time a very complicated disorganization has been excessively common; there is more successful organization in "Home Burial" or "The Witch of Coös"—one feels like saying, in indignant exaggeration—than in the *Cantos* and *The Bridge* put together.

On John Crowe Ransom

The most important thing to notice about this treatment, the rhetor-ical machinery of the poems, is that it is not a method of forcing in-tensity, of creating a factitious or at least arbitrary excitement, as most modern rhetoric is. Instead of listening through the hands, with closed eyes, as one is sucked deeper and deeper into the maelstrom, one listens with one's eyes open and one's head working about as well as it usually works. Most writers become overrhetorical when they are insisting on more emotion than they actually feel or need to feel; Ransom is just the opposite. He is perpetually insisting, by his detached, mock-pedantic, wittily complicated tone, that he is not feeling much at all, not half so much as he really should be feeling—and this rhetoric becomes overmannered, too protective, when there is not much emotion for him to pretend not to be feeling, and he keeps on out of habit. Ransom developed this rhetorical machinery—tone, phrasing, properties, and all the rest—primarily as a way of handling sentiment or emotion without ever seeming sentimental or overemotional; as a way of keeping the poem at the proper aesthetic distance from its subject; and as a way for the poem to extract from its subject, no matter how unpleasant or embarrassing, an unembarrassed pleasure. He was writing in an age in which the most natural feeling of tenderness, happiness, or sorrow was likely to be called sentimental; consequently he needed a self-protective rhetoric as the most brutal or violent of poets did not—such a poet, on being told that some poem of his was a delirium of pointless violence, had only to reply, with a satisfied smile, "Yes, isn't it?" One can say, *very* crudely, that Ransom's poems are produced by the classical, or at worst semiclassical, treatment of romantic subjects.

———

Ransom seems in his poems, as most modern poets do not, sympathetic and charming, full of tenderness and affection, wanting the light and sorry for the dark—moral and condemning only when he has to be, not because he wants to be; loving neither the sterner vices nor the sterner virtues.

On Ivan Turgenev

There are greater writers than Turgenev, better books than *A Sportsman's Sketches,* as long as we are not reading it; but for as long as we read, it is beyond comparison.

On Rudyard Kipling

If you compare one of the best of Kipling's early stories ("Without Benefit of Clergy," say) with some of the best of his late stories, you realize that the late stories are specialized in their moral and human attitudes—in their subject matter, even—in a way in which the early story is not. The early story's subject is a general subject that will repay any amount of general skill or general talent: you can imagine a greater writer's rewriting "Without Benefit of Clergy" and making a much better story out of it. But this is precisely what you cannot imagine with Kipling's later stories: Chekhov and Tolstoy and Turgenev together couldn't improve " 'They' " or " 'Wireless,' " since in each a highly specialized subject has received an exactly appropriate, extraordinarily skilled and talented treatment. These later stories of Kipling's don't compete, really, with "Gusev" and *The Death of Ivan Ilych* and *A Sportsman's Sketches*, but have set up a kingdom of their own, a little off to the side of things, in which they are incomparable: their reader feels, "You can write better stories than Kipling's, but not better Kipling stories." This kingdom of theirs is a strange, disquieting, but quite wonderful place, as if some of the Douanier Rousseau's subjects had been repainted by Degas. If we cannot make the very greatest claims for the stories, it would be absurd not to make great ones: as long as readers enjoy style and skill, originality and imagination—in a word, genius—they will take delight in Kipling's stories.

On Franz Kafka

One can imagine—perhaps with badly concealed pleasure—cutting *Remembrance of Things Past, Ulysses, The Magic Mountain*: fifty or a hundred pages of place names, of Dublin details, of debates between Naphta and Settembrini, never would be missed. And we can say of these great or extremely good novels, "This part is successful, that less so, that scarcely at all so." But who would have the courage to declare part of *The Castle* unnecessary or unsuccessful? Its most grudging reader could hardly refuse it the epithet "perfect of its kind"; K. and the assistants will last as long as Alice or Gulliver or that traveler who called himself Noman.

———

Indeed, Kafka's whole method is rooted in the immense complication of our whole society. The perfect calm, the dispassionate rigor, that might be called either scientific or classical, clothe an insight too profound ever to be blinded by indignation. In Kafka there is an unexampled extension of the methods of comedy to the material of tragedy. K. is seeking for salvation, for truth, Joseph K. for justice, for his very life; their search is presented with the utmost possible concern and intensity; and yet Kafka's method of treatment, his whole attitude, make us see at the same time that the details are somehow comic, that the whole, looked at in one way, is itself comic. It is absurd not to call the world evil, and it is impossible to take the condemnation seriously: either laughter or tears are impossibly inadequate, we have for it only the stare we give Medusa's head.

On Anthologies

This is so much the age of anthologies that it is surprising that poets still waste their time on books of verse, instead of writing anthologies in the first place. If you are about to print a book of poems, don't: make up a few names and biographical sketches with which to punctuate your manuscript, change its title to *Poems of Democracy,* and you will find yourself transformed from an old pumpkin, always in the red, to a shiny black new coach. For the average reader knows poetry mainly from anthologies, just as he knows philosophy mainly from histories of philosophy or textbooks: the *Complete Someone*—hundreds or thousands of small-type, double-column pages of *poetry,* without one informing repentant sentence of ordinary prose—evokes from him a start of that savage and unreasoning timidity, that *horror vacui,* with which he stares at the lemmas and corollaries of Spinoza's *Ethics.* Those cultural entrepreneurs, the anthologists, have become figures of melancholy and deciding importance for the average reader of poetry, a man of great scope and little grasp, who still knows what he likes—in the anthologies.

And yet if you ask, "What do I need to become an anthologist?" it is difficult to answer, as one would like to: "Taste." Zeal and a publisher seem the irreducible and, usually, unexceeded minimum. The typical anthologist is a sort of Gallup Poll with connections—often astonishing ones; it is hard to know whether he is printing a poem because he likes it, because his acquaintances tell him he ought to, or because he went to high school with the poet. But certainly he is beyond good or evil, and stares over his herds of poets like a patriarch, nodding or pointing with a large industrial air.

On Walter de la Mare

De la Mare is a hopeless romantic? Yes; but whose Law is it that a hopeless romantic cannot write good poetry? Reading de la Mare, one often has a sense of delicate and individual boredom, and wishes him a better writer than he is; but the man who would wish him a *different* writer would wish the Great Snowy Owl at the zoo a goose, so as to eat it for Christmas.

———

De la Mare's world is neither the best nor the worst but the most enchanted of all possible worlds. It assures us that if reality is not necessarily what we should like it to be, it is necessarily what we feel it to be: to be is to be *felt*. In the "clear grave dark" universe of these poems Falstaff and a ghost are ontologically equal, and both of them are ontologically superior to you, reader, unless you appeal to de la Mare a good deal more than there is any reason to suppose you do. Unfortunately, this criterion is a thoroughly accidental one; if de la Mare happened to develop a taste for science, a whole new category of reality would suddenly come into being.

———

When he writes in the grand manner it is with a certain innocence, as children act out an execution; he is genuinely unassuming, a mouse in a corner, and never thinks to tell you, as better but vainer poets do: "Now I am going to be humble."

On E. E. Cummings

That the poems are extravagantly, professedly modernist, experimental, avant-garde, is an additional attraction: the reader of modern poetry—especially the inexperienced or unwilling reader—feels toward them the same gratitude that the gallery-goer feels when, his eyes blurred with corridors of analytical cubism, he comes into a little room full of the Pink and Blue periods of Picasso.

———

One is bewildered by the complacency with which the poet accepts himself and his, and rejects or doesn't even notice the existence of the rest of the world. One of his poems lives along the line like

Pope's spider, but hides at the heart of its sensitivity a satisfied inac-
cessibility to experience—for experience is, after all, what is different
from oneself. He has hidden his talent under a flower, and there it has
gone on reproducing, by parthenogenesis, poem after poem after poem.

———

In fact, as soon as the reader lowers the demands he makes on
art—pretends that it is, at best, no more than a delightful or ecstatic
or ingenious diversion—the best poems become a thorough pleasure.
For Mr. Cummings is a fine poet in the sense in which Swinburne is
one; but in the sense in which we call Hardy and Yeats and Proust and
Chekhov poets, great poets, he is hardly a poet at all. Marshal
Zhdanov said, delighting me: *There is a great big hole in the founda-
tions of Soviet music*; well, there is a great big moral vacuum at the
heart of E. E. Cummings's poetry. As Louise Bogan has written, with
summary truth: "It is this deletion of the tragic that makes
Cummings's joy childish and his anger petulant." What delights and
amuses and disgusts us he has represented; but all that is heartbreak-
ing in the world, the pity and helplessness and love that were called,
once, the tears of things, the heart of heartlessness—these hardly
exist for him.

On Marianne Moore

She not only can, but must, make poetry out of everything and any-
thing: she is like Midas, or like Mozart choosing unpromising themes
for the fun of it, or like one of those princesses whom wizards force
to manufacture sheets out of nettles.

———

Miss Moore has great limitations—her work is one long tri-
umph of them; but it was sad, for so many years, to see them and
nothing else insisted upon, and Miss Moore neglected for poets who
ought not to be allowed to throw elegies in her grave. I have read
that several people think So-and-So the greatest living woman poet;
anybody would dislike applying so clumsy a phrase to Miss Moore—
but surely she is. Her poems, at their unlikely best, seem already im-
mortal, objects that have endured their probative millennia in bar-
rows; she has herself taken from them what time could take away, and
left a skeleton the years can only harden. People have complained
about the poems, in the words of the poems: "Why dissect destiny

with instruments which are more specialized than the tissues of destiny itself?" But nothing is more specialized than destiny. Other people have objected, "They are so small." Yes, they are as small as those animals which save the foolish heroes of fairy tales—which can save only the heroes, because they are too small not to have been disregarded by everyone else.

On Marianne Moore's "In Distrust of Merits"

Miss Moore thinks of the war in blindingly moral terms. We are fighting "that where there was death there may be life." This is true, in a sense; but the opposite is true in a more direct sense. She writes at the climax of her poem, "If these great patient / dyings—all these agonies / and woundbearings and bloodshed / can teach us how to live, these dyings were not wasted"; and she is certain that they were not wasted, and ends the poem with "Beauty is eternal / and dust is for a time." (The armies and the peoples died, and it meant that Beauty is eternal.) Since Pharaoh's bits were pushed into the jaws of the kings, these dyings—patient or impatient, but dyings—have happened, by the hundreds of millions; they were all wasted. They taught us to kill others and to die ourselves, but never how to live. Who is "taught to live" by cruelty, suffering, stupidity, and that occupational disease of soldiers, death? The moral equivalent of war! Peace, our peace, is the moral equivalent of war. If Miss Moore had read a history of the European "colonization" of our planet (instead of natural histories full of the quaint animals of those colonies) she would be astonished at nothing in the last world war, or in this one, or in the next. She should distrust us and herself, but not at the eleventh hour, not because of the war (something incommensurable, beside which all of us are good): she should have distrusted the peace of which our war is only the extrapolation. It is the peace of which we were guilty. Miss Moore's seeing what she sees, and only now, betrays an extraordinary but common lack of facts, or imagination, or *something*. But how honest and lovable—how genuinely careless about herself and caring about the rest of the world—Miss Moore seems in this poem, compared to most of our poets, who are blinder to the war than they ever were to the peace, who call the war "this great slapstick," and who write (while everyone applauds) that *they* are not going to be foolish enough to be "war poets." How could they be? The real war poets are always war poets, peace or any time.

First Review of Robert Graves

Robert Graves's poems are pleasant, rather interesting, nicely constructed, noticeably his own; he is agreeably sensible and able; so it is really unpleasant to decide that he is not a good poet, that even his best poems just miss. There is too much comment, fancy, anecdote; one thinks, "Sensible! rather witty! nicely put!" but never how moving or extraordinary or *right*.

On Allen Tate

Men like Mr. Tate have denounced the evils of what they call finance-capitalism; they have denounced the scientists and industrialists who, discarding art, religion, and philosophy as meaningless luxuries, have tried to throw away half our culture. But they are themselves eager to sacrifice the scientific, mathematical, and technical half of European culture, in order to return to the good society (traditional, theological, based on property, the "primary medium through which man expressed his moral nature") that is the womb from which the rest of us have struggled to get free.

On James Stephens's "Egan O Rahilly"

Someone, Michelangelo I think, said that you should be able to roll a good statue downhill without having the arms and legs break off; this poem could be rolled downhill, and hammered red-hot, and dropped in cold water, and nothing would happen except that the hammer would break and the water boil away.

On Roy Campbell

If the damned, blown willy-nilly around the windy circle of hell, enjoyed it and were proud of being there, they would sound very much as he sounds.

On The Collected Poems of Wallace Stevens

Back in the stacks, in libraries; in bookcases in people's living rooms; on brick-and-plank bookshelves beside studio couches, one sees big books in dark bindings, the *Collected Poems* of the great poets. Once, long ago, the poems were new: the book went by post—so many horses and a coach—to a man in a country house, and the letter along with it asked him to describe, evaluate, and fix the place in English literature, in 12,000 words, by January 25, of the poems of William Wordsworth. And the man did.

It is hard to remember that this is the way it was; harder to remember that this is the way it is. The *Collected Poems* still go out—in this century there have been Hardy's and Yeats's and Frost's and Eliot's and Moore's, and now Stevens's—and the man who is sent them still treats them with rough, or rude, or wild justice; still puts them in their place, appreciates their virtues, says, *Just here thou ail'st*, says, *Nothing I can say will possibly* ... and mails the essay off.

It all seems terribly queer, terribly risky; surely, by now, people could have thought of some better way? Yet is it as different as we think from what we do to the old *Poems* in the dark bindings, the poems with the dust on them? Those ruins we star, confident that we are young and they, they are old—they too are animals no one has succeeded in naming, young things nothing has succeeded in aging; beings to which we can say, as the man in Kafka's story says to the corpse: "What's the good of the dumb question you are asking?" They keep on asking it; and it is only our confidence and our innocence that let us believe that describing and evaluating them, fixing their places—in however many words, by whatever date—is any less queer, any less risky.

———

Ordinarily this poet's thought moves (until "The Rock") in unrhymed iambic pentameter, in a marvelously accomplished Wordsworthian blank verse—or, sometimes, in something akin to Tennyson's bland lissome adaptation of it. If someone had predicted to Pound, when he was beginning his war on the iambic foot; to Eliot, when he was first casting a cold eye on post-Jacobean blank verse; to both, when they were first condemning generalization in poetry, that in forty or fifty years the chief—sometimes, I think in despair, the only—influence on younger American poets would be this generalizing, masterful, scannable verse of Stevens's, wouldn't both have laughed in confident disbelief? And how many of the youngest English poets seem to want to write like Cowper! A great revolution is hardest of all on the great revolutionists.

On José Garcia Villa

Once upon a time, in Manila or Guadalajara, as he sat outside a convent wall and listened to the nuns preparing a confection called Angels' Milk, a little boy decided to go to New York City and become a great poet. There he wrote a book called, charmingly, *Have Come, Am Here*; after he had read the reviews of it he telegraphed to his parents, *Vici*, and said to himself, in his warm, gentle, Southern way: "What critics these mortals be!" For Edith Sitwell had said that he was "a poet with a great, even an astounding, and perfectly original gift . . . no poet now writing is more so"; Mark Van Doren had spoken of his "purest and most natural gifts . . . his power to say, quietly, the most astonishing and exalted things"; Marianne Moore had said, "Final wisdom encountered in poem after poem." Babette Deutsch wrote that his poetry was "as singular as the work of Emily Dickinson or Hopkins"; Conrad Aiken wrote that he was "the most important new poet in America in a decade"—Irwin Edman, in a generation.

For there to be great poets there must be great audiences too: the poet, sure of his, wrote *Volume Two*. He wrote a poem made of 476 commas, a poem made of 132 repetitions of the letter *O*, and a poem—called "The Emperor's New Sonnet," naturally—made of nothing at all. He wrote eighty Aphorisms like "LOVE-KNOW / LOVE-DO"; like "Imperil, me—*Mohammedan, rose!*" For a hundred and fifty pages he put a comma between each word and the next; as he says, "The result is a lineal pace of quiet dignity and movement." For instance:

> Pale, vermouth, ultraviolet,
> And, tender, lambs, astray,
> But, if, these, keep, love, beautiful,
> Sweet, heavens, yes.

> If, they, keep, love, beautiful,
> Wych-tree, wych-bird,
> Any, living, whyless, do,
> In, that, living, kingdom, fire.

This is a typical passage. But so is any passage. One reads a poem and asks oneself, *Isn't this the poem before?*—but when one goes back and reads that, one asks oneself, *Isn't this the poem before?* But it is time for the end of my story: imagine Miss Sitwell and Mr. Van Doren and

Miss Deutsch; imagine them somewhere in *Volume Two*, turning its commas slowly over on their tongues, and thinking a little complacently, a little drowsily, but with perfect truth: "If it hadn't been for *my* encouragement Mr. Villa would never have gone on to write 'The Emperor's New Sonnet.' "

I wish that I had had the wit to invent this story, a parable of the way in which critics can guide and encourage the poet to the fullest realization of his powers—but in these matters art limps trembling behind reality. I thought of calling a fairy tale of this kind *The Perfect Fool*, but then it occurred to me that it would be better to call it *The Perfect Fools*.

On Stephen Spender

That a poem beginning *I think continually of those who were truly great* should ever have been greeted with anything but helpless embarrassment makes me ashamed of the planet upon which I dwell.

————

It isn't Mr. Spender but a small, simple—determinedly simple—part of Mr. Spender that writes the poems; the poet is a lot smarter man than his style allows him to seem. (If he were as soft and sincere and sentimental as most of his poems make him out to be, the rabbits would have eaten him for lettuce, long ago.)

On W. H. Auden

ANOTHER TIME

Auden at the beginning was oracular (obscure, original), bad at organization, neglectful of logic, full of astonishing or magical language, intent on his own world and his own forms; he has changed continuously toward organization, plainness, accessibility, objectivity, social responsibility. He has gone in the right direction, and a great deal too far. *Another Time* is Auden's eighteenth century; rational, didactic, social, full of abstractions, comment, light verse—the forms are automatic, the language is plain or formally rhetorical. Now, in too many of the poems, we see not the will, but the understanding, trying to do the work of the imagination (I use these charming fictions for convenience's sake); they are moral, rational, manufactured, written by the top of the head for the top of the head. The mechanical operation of the fancy produces too many of the light poems. Auden has lost the quick animal certainty of his daemon, his "gift": the good poems are magnificently and carefully right, the bad ones full of effects that have almost the wrongness of a fallacy.

THE DOUBLE MAN

In 1931 Pope's ghost said to me, "Ten years from now the leading young poet of the time will publish, in *The Atlantic Monthly*, a didactic epistle of about nine hundred tetrameter couplets." I answered absently, "You are a fool"; and who on this earth would have thought him anything else? But he was right: the decline and fall of modernist poetry—if so big a swallow, and a good deal of warm weather, make a summer—were nearer than anyone could have believed. The poetry which came to seem during the twenties the norm of all poetic performance—experimental, lyric, obscure, violent, irregular, determinedly antagonistic to didacticism, general statement, science, the public—has lost for the young its once obsessive attraction; has evolved, in Auden's latest poem, into something that is almost its opposite. *New Year Letter* (which, with many notes and a few lyrics, forms *The Double Man*) is a happy compound of the *Essay on Man* and the *Epistle to Dr. Arbuthnot*, done in a version of Swift's most colloquial couplets. Pope might be bewildered at the ideas, and make fun of, or patronizingly commend, the couplets; but he would relish the Wit, Learning, and Sentiment—the last becoming, as it so often does, plural and Improving; and the Comprehending Generality, Love of Science, and Social Benevolence might warm him into the murmur, "Well enough for such an age." How fast the world changes! and poetry with it! What he would have said of the more characteristic glories of "Gerontion," the *Cantos*, or *The Bridge*, I leave to the reader's ingenuity.

THE AGE OF ANXIETY

The Age of Anxiety is the worst thing Auden has written since *The Dance of Death*; it is the equivalent of Wordsworth's "Ecclesiastical Sonnets." The man who, during the thirties, was one of the five or six best poets in the world has gradually turned into a rhetoric mill grinding away at the bottom of Limbo, into an automaton that keeps making little jokes, little plays on words, little rhetorical engines, as compulsively and unendingly and uneasily as a neurotic washes his hands.

THE SHIELD OF ACHILLES

Auden has become the most professional poet in the world; there is a matter-of-course mastery behind the elaborate formality, the colloquial matter-of-factness, of these last two books—after reading "Under Sirius" another poet is likely to feel, "Well, back to my greeting cards." But to be the most professional poet in the world is not necessarily to be the best: Minerva says, "But *you* don't need *me.*" Auden is using extraordinary skill in managing a sadly reduced income.

———

One is delighted at the slower and drier excellence that has replaced the somewhat flashy and ambiguous excellence of what Auden wrote during the later part of the thirties, the earlier part of the forties; but has Auden ever again written quite so well as he was writing at the beginning of the thirties, in *Poems* and *Paid on Both Sides?* He wrote, then, some of the strongest, strangest, and most original poetry that anyone has written in this century; when old men, dying in their beds, mumble something unintelligible to the nurse, it is some of those lines that they will be repeating.

On William Bacon Evans's
Chorus of Bird Voices, Sonnets, Battle-Dore,
Unconventional Verse, etc.

Mr. Evans's title is almost enough of a review for his book. While ailing in Syria, he wrote a song for every species of North American bird (I am no ornithologist, but there *can't* be any more of the damn things); it has seldom been better done. This is poetry which instructs its writer and entertains its reader (the functions of poetry, I have read); a missionary could hardly be more harmlessly employed. Mr. Evans is an amiable, unpretentious, and tolerant person—he apparently dislikes nothing but cigarettes—and won my heart immediately: more than I can say for most of the poets I am reviewing. But then, Mr. Evans is no poet.

On Horace Gregory

Everyone is familiar with the romanticism of the far away and long ago; but what is today a more popular kind goes almost unrecognized—the exoticism of the ticker tape, let me call it. Crane said that poetry must assimilate the machine, metropolitan existence; this sort of romanticism *exploits* the machine, and considers intrinsically valuable the showily topical and megalopolitan terms it translates everything into. Mr. Gregory (a mouse from Twenty-third Street) tells you that Macbeth embezzled, the market fell, his life insurance went to the banks; this is the strategy, intensive and extensive, of his most typical poems. "Ticker tape / on private yachts: ring them up on the cash register / cable them" will show how concentrated and willful such imagery often becomes. Unfortunately, the modernity of its terms does not guarantee the truth or even the modernity of an insight. Imagine a writer of the nineties who conscientiously put everything in the latest metropolitan terms—bicycles, incandescent lamps, streetcars—and you will see how much power, in themselves, such things keep after a generation. This whole fashion of writing (and it has been enormously fashionable) rests on a variant of the old fallacy that there are classes of words or objects which are themselves poetic. The romantics had failed before, had to escape from, the modern world: they had employed, as much as possible, "poetic" words and objects; what they rejected as anti-poetic—the mechanical, the sordid, the prosaic—was perhaps a sure means to success? A fortuitous collocation of the anti-poetic (plus, for emotion or profundity, the same old romantic and sentimental excesses) was too many poets' solution of the problem of how to express the modern world. It was a mistake, of course; to the Muse of Poetry—a neutral monist from way back—Crane's burnt match skating in a urinal is just another primrose by the river's brim.

On Isabella Gardner

Miss Gardner is very different: to her the world is a costume party for which she has just breathlessly overdressed herself, and these poems are her starry, tinselly, gold-leafy entrance into it.

On Ezra Pound

CANTOS LII—LXXI

Early in his life Mr. Pound met with strong, continued, and unintelligent opposition. If people keep opposing you when you are right, you think them fools; and after a time, right or wrong, you think them fools simply because they oppose you. Similarly, you write true things or good things, and end by thinking things true or good simply because you write them. For Mr. Pound, both circumstance and predisposition made the process inescapable. His friends and disciples were eager to encourage him in his worst excesses; and modernist poets or critics hated, by caviling at the work of their talented fellow, to expose him to the jeers of the academic masses, who already condemned indiscriminately all that he had done.

———

Half of *Cantos LII–LXXI* is a personal, allusive, and wildly eccentric retelling of Chinese history, full of names, dates, quotations, ideograms, abbreviations, underlinings, and slang. Everything is seen as through a glass darkly, the glass being Mr. Pound: 1766 B.C. talks exactly like A.D. 1735, and both exactly like Ezra Pound. To the old complaint "All Chinamen look alike," Mr. Pound makes one add, "And talk alike, and act alike—and always did." Little of the intrinsic interest of the events manages to survive the monotonous didacticism of the account. The rest of the book is more interesting, since it consists mostly of quotations—intelligent, informative, or just odd— from John Adams, its subject. (On the dust jacket New Directions twice insists that Pound's subject is John Quincy Adams—a queer mistake to make; whoever made it must have found Pound's style too entrancing ever to determine what he was writing about.)

SECTION: ROCK-DRILL. 85–95 DE LOS CANTARES
Many writers have felt, like Pound: Why not invent an art form that will permit me to put all my life, all my thoughts and feelings about the universe, directly into a work of art? But the trouble is, when they've invented it it isn't an art form.

On Elizabeth Bishop

She is morally so attractive, in poems like "The Fish" or "Roosters," because she understands so well that the wickedness and confusion of the age can explain and extenuate other people's wickedness and confusion, but not, for you, your own; that morality, for the individual, is usually a small, personal, statistical, but heartbreaking or heartwarming affair of omissions and commissions the greatest of which will seem infinitesimal, ludicrously beneath notice, to those who govern, rationalize, and deplore.

———

Sometimes when I can't go to sleep at night I see the family of the future. Dressed in three-tone shorts-and-shirt sets of disposable Papersilk, they sit before the television wall of their apartment, only their eyes moving. After I've looked a while I always see—otherwise I'd die—a pigheaded soul over in the corner with a book; only his eyes are moving, but in them there is a different look.

Usually it's Homer he's holding—this week it's Elizabeth Bishop. Her *Poems* seems to me one of the best books an American poet has ever written: the people of the future (the ones in the corner) will read her just as they will read Dickinson or Whitman or Stevens, or the other classical American poets still alive among us. I have been reading most of Elizabeth Bishop's poems—two-thirds were printed in *North and South,* a book long out of print—for ten years; I've read my many favorites many hundreds of times, and they seem better and fresher, more nearly perfect, than they ever did. They are quiet, truthful, sad, funny, most marvelously individual poems; they have a sound, a feel, a whole moral and physical atmosphere, different from anything else I know. And I don't know of any other poet with so high a proportion of good poems: at least half are completely realized works of art. They are honest, modest, minutely observant, masterly; even their most complicated or troubled or imaginative effects seem, always, personal and natural, and as unmistakable as the first few notes of a Mahler song, the first few patches of a Vuillard interior. (The poems are like Vuillard or even, sometimes, Vermeer.) Occasionally you meet someone and feel in astonished joy: "Well, this is what people ought to be like"; this is what poems ought to be like.

On Josephine Miles

These seem easily different from anybody else's poems, but hardly distinguishable from one another; their language, tone, and mechanism of effect have a relishingly idiosyncratic and monotonous regularity, as if they were the diary some impressionable but unimpassioned monomaniac had year by year been engraving on the side of a knitting needle.

On Marshall Schacht

Someone praises these poems by speaking of their "deceptive simplicity": it is this deceived and conscious "simplicity" of form and content which serves Mr. Schacht for a style—that is, instead of a style— so that he reminds one of those carefully humble, awkward, sincere persons, full of hesitations, *wells,* and *you knows,* half *jeune fille,* half Grandma Moses, whose lives are one long moral victory over their suffering and inattentive friends.

On Alan Ross

Alan Ross has written almost the worst line I ever saw in a poem: "But the *Zeitgeist* had a kind of *ethos.*"

On Sports Cars

People love cars. Looking at them driving off fast in every direction, a Thoreau or Emerson might ask: "From what are they all escaping?" The answer is, "Themselves"; if only they'd stayed home and cultivated those selves they wouldn't need to escape from them. "It is because our own eyes are so dull that the chromium on our cars shines so," the Thoreau or Emerson would continue. All this is one of those demeaning truths to which we say, "It's so. It's so," and walk away muttering, "Thank God *something* shines!" Nor should the word "escape" frighten us: most selves are good things to escape from—happy the man who has become, for a moment, selfless!

On the Music Criticism of B. H. Haggin

And yet not one of these unfavorable essays is as notable as any of twenty or thirty favorable ones: moving and serious evocations of masterpieces, of composers and musicians at their greatest—essays full of a real forgetfulness of self, of anything at all but their subjects, that make one remember Goethe's "In the face of the great superiority of another person there is no means of safety but love."

All Mr. Haggin's unfavorable pieces seem necessary and useful: taste has to be maintained (or elevated, if it's at too low a level to make maintenance bearable), and there is no other way of doing it.

———

This sort of admission of error, of change, makes us trust a critic as nothing else but omniscience could.

———

Haggin has the shameless honesty of the true critic——he couldn't lie to you if he tried.

On the Twentieth Century

Most of us know, now, that Rousseau was wrong: that man, when you knock his chains off, sets up the death camps. Soon we shall know everything the eighteenth century didn't know, and nothing it did, and it will be hard to live with us.

THE
REST OF IT

The Age of Criticism

THERE IS A SUBJECT that I cannot do justice to, but would like to treat even unjustly—a subject readers and novelists and poets often talk about, but almost never write about: our age of criticism. Perhaps I ought only to talk or, at most, write a verse satire about it; one can say anything in verse and no one will mind. I wish that you would treat what I am going to write as if it were verse or talk, a conversation-with-no-one about our age of criticism. It is only a complaint, perhaps more false than true—partial, and full of exaggerations and general impressions; but it is a complaint that people do make, and may at least relieve their feelings and mine. And I will try to spare other people's by using no names at all.

The common reader does not know that it is an age of criticism, and for him it is not. He reads (seldomer and seldomer now) historical novels, the memoirs of generals, whatever is successful; good books, sometimes—good books too are successful. He cannot tell the book editor of the Chicago *Tribune* from Samuel Johnson, and is neither helped nor hindered by criticism—to him a critic is a best-seller list, only less so. Such a reader lives in a pleasant, anarchic, oblivious world, a world as democratic, almost, as the warm dark depths below, where nobody reads anything but newspapers and drugstore books and comic books and the *Reader's Digest* at the dentist's. This common reader knows what he likes, but is uncomfortable when other people do not read it or do not like it—for what people read and like is good: that is what *good* means.

On the slopes above (as a fabulist might put it) live many races of animals: the most numerous are the members of Book Clubs and the dwellers in the Land of Book Reviews. These find out from their leaders weekly, monthly, what they ought to read, what they ought to like; and since, thank goodness, that is almost always what they would have read and liked anyway, without the help of the reviewers, they all live in unity and amity. It is the country of King Log, the fabulist would say: thousands of logs lie booming on the hillside, while their subjects croak around them; if you shut your eyes it is hard to tell who reads, who writes, and who reviews . . . Nearby one finds readers of scholarly journals, readers of magazines of experiment, readers of magazines of verse. But highest of all, in crevices of the naked rock, cowering beneath the keen bills of the industrious storks, dwell our most conscious and, perhaps, most troubled readers; and for these—cultivated or academic folk, intellectuals, "serious readers," the leaven of our queer half-risen loaf—this is truly an age of criticism. It is about them and their Stork-Kings that I am going to talk for the rest of this article.

Four times a year (six if they read *Partisan Review*) these people read or try to read or wish that they had read large magazines called literary quarterlies. Each of these contains several poems and a piece of fiction—sometimes two pieces; the rest is criticism.

The rest is criticism. The words have a dull uneasy sound; they lie on the spirit with a heavy weight. There has never been an age in which so much good criticism has been written—or so *much* bad; and both of them have become, among "serious readers," astonishingly or appallingly influential. I am talking as a reader of the criticism of the last few years to other readers of it, and am assuming that we recognize its merits and services, which are great; I myself can and do read the magazines that I have been talking about, and they seem to me the best magazines that we have—the magazines which enjoy attacking them are almost ludicrously inferior to them. But, I think, they print far too much criticism, and far too much of the criticism that they print is of a kind that is more attractive to critics and to lovers of criticism than it is to poets and fiction writers and to lovers of poetry and fiction. Criticism *does* exist, doesn't it, for the sake of the plays and stories and poems it criticizes? Much of this criticism does not; much of it gives a false idea of the nature and use of criticism, a false idea of the variety and importance of critics.

Some of this criticism is as good as anyone could wish: several of the best critics alive print most of their work in such magazines as these. Some more of this criticism is intelligent and useful—it sounds as if it had been written by a reader for readers, by a human being for human beings. But a great deal of this criticism might just as well have been written by a syndicate of encyclopedias for an audience of International Business Machines. It is not only bad or mediocre, it is *dull*; it is, often, an astonishingly graceless, joyless, humorless, long-winded, niggling, blinkered, methodical, self-important, cliché-ridden, prestige-obsessed, almost-autonomous criticism. Who *can* believe that either readers or writers are helped by most of the great leaden articles on Great or currently fashionable writers—always the same fifteen or twenty, if the critic can manage it—which encounter us as regularly as the equinoxes and the solstices? I have heard intelligent and cultivated people complain more times than I can remember, "I can hardly *read* the quarterlies any more"; and I once heard Elizabeth Bishop say, "After I go through one of the literary quarterlies I don't feel like reading a poem for a week, much less like writing one." Many other people have felt so; and for weeks or months or years afterwards they have neither read poems nor written them, but have criticized. For—one begins to see—an age of criticism is not an age of writing, nor an age of reading: it is an age of criticism. People still read, still write—and well; but for many of them it is the act of criticism which has become the representative or Archetypal act of the intellectual.

Critics may still be rather negligible figures in comparison to the composers and painters they write about; but when they write about writers, what a difference! A novelist, a friend of mine, one year went to a Writers' Conference; all the other teachers were critics, and each teacher had to give a formal public lecture. My friend went to the critics' lectures, but the critics didn't go to his; he wasn't surprised; as he said, "You could tell they knew I wasn't really literary like them." Recently I went to a meeting at which a number of critics discussed what Wordsworth had said about writing poetry. It was interesting to me to see how consciously or unconsciously patronizing they were to—poor Wordsworth, I almost wrote. They could see what he had meant, confused as he was, layman that he was; and because he had been, they supposed they must admit, a great poet, it did give what he had to say a wonderful documentary interest, like Nelson's remarks at Trafalgar. But the critics could not help being conscious of the difference between themselves, and Wordsworth, and my friend: *they* knew how poems and novels are put together, and Wordsworth and my friend didn't, but had just put them together. In the same way, if a pig wandered up to you during a bacon-judging contest, you would say impatiently, "Go away, pig! What do you know about bacon?"

It is no wonder that, in some of the places where critics are most concentrated, and their influence most overpowering, people write less and less. (By *write* I mean *write stories, poems, or plays.*) Some boys at a large and quite literary college I visited were telling me how much trouble they have getting poems and stories for the college's magazine. "There are only four or five we can depend on much," the editor said sadly; "everybody else that's any good writes criticism." I suppose I should have said to him, "Make the magazine criticism"; after all, isn't that the way you run a literary magazine?—but I hadn't the heart to.

These days, when an ambitious young intellectual finishes college, he buys himself a new typewriter, rents himself a room, and settles down to write . . . book reviews, long critical articles, explications. "As for living, our servants can do that for us," said Villiers de l'Isle Adam; and in the long run this gets said not only of living but also of writing stories and poems, which is almost as difficult and helpless and risky as living. Why stick one's neck out so far for so little? It is hard to write even a competent naturalistic story, and when you have written it what happens?—someone calls it a competent naturalistic story. Write another "Horatian Ode," and you will be praised as "one of the finest of our minor poets." No, as anyone can see, it is hardly worthwhile being a writer unless you can be a great one; better not sell your soul to the Muse till she has shown you the critical articles of 2100. Unless you are one of a dozen or so writers you will have a life like Trigorin's; he said that they would put on his tombstone that he had been a fine writer, *but not so good as Turgenev*—and sure enough, if you go and look on his tombstone that is what is there. Our Trigorins can hardly fail to see that, in serious critical circles, the very recognition of their merit dismisses it and them; there is written on their hearts in little red letters, "It's only me." I never remember hearing *anybody* say of a critic, "He's all right, but he's no Saint-Beuve"; but substitute *Dante* or some such O.K. name for *Saint-Beuve*, and there are very few writers about whom the statement hasn't been made. When the first book of one of the best of living poets was published, one of the best of living critics said about it only that it was "grating," and lacked the sweetness of the *Divine Comedy.* So it did; the poet might have replied with the same truth that his critic lacked Matthew Arnold's yellow kid gloves.

Critics can easily infect their readers (though usually less by pre-cept than example) with the contempt or fretful tolerance which they feel for "minor" works of art. If you work away, with sober, methodical, and industrious complication, at the masterpieces of a few great or fashionable writers, you after a while begin to identify yourself with these men; your manner takes on the authority your subject matter has unwittingly delegated to you, and when—returned from the peaks you have spent your life among, picking a reluctant way over those Parnassian or Castalian foothills along whose slopes herdboys sit playing combs—you are required to judge the competitions of such artists, you do so with a certain reluctance. Everybody has observed this in scholars, who feel that live authors, as such, are self-evidently inferior to dead ones; though a broad-minded scholar will look like an X-ray machine at such a writer as Thomas Mann, and feel, relenting: "He's as good as dead." This sort of thing helps to make serious criticism as attractive as it is to critics: they live among the great, and some of the greatness comes off on them. No wonder poor poets become poor critics, and count themselves blest in their bargain; no wonder young intellectuals become critics before, and not after, they have failed as artists. And sometimes—who knows?—they might not have failed; besides, to have failed as an artist may be a respectable and valuable thing.

———

Some of us write less; all of us, almost, read less—the child at his television set, the critic or novelist in the viewplate of the set, grayly answering questions on topics of general interest. Children have fewer and fewer empty hours, and the eight-year-old is discouraged from filling them with the books written for his brother of ten; nor is anyone at his school surprised when he does not read very much or very well—it is only "born readers" who do that.

But if we read less and less—by *we*, this time, I mean the cultivated minority—a greater and greater proportion of what we read is criticism. Many a man last read *Moby Dick* in the eleventh grade, *The Brothers Karamazov* in his freshman year in college; but think of all the articles about them he's read since! It is no use to tell such a reader, "Go read *Moby Dick*"; he would only answer, "I've read it," and start out on the latest book about Melville. And imagine how he would look at you if you told him to read, say, *Kim*. In such a case, whether he has or hasn't read it doesn't matter: he knows that he doesn't need to. It is criticism, after all, which protects us from the bad or unimportant books that we would otherwise have to read; and during the time we have saved we can read more of the criticism which protects us. I imagine, in gray hours, a generation which will have read a few masterpieces, a few thousand criticisms of these, and almost nothing else but—as the generation will say apologetically—"trash." It is an Alexandrian notion, but in many ways we *are* Alexandrian; and we do not grow less so with the years. I was told recently two awful and delightful instances of the specialization, the dividing into categories, of people's unlucky lives. A student at Harvard, taking his final examinations for a Ph.D. in English, was asked to make a short criticism of some contemporary book he had read and liked. This was the first question to give him any trouble—he had been particularly good on Middle English; he said after a while, "I don't believe I've read any contemporary books—at least not since I've been in college." Another student, taking *his* final examinations at Princeton, was asked to summarize Tennyson's "Ulysses." He did. "How does this treatment of Ulysses compare with that in the *Divine Comedy*?" someone asked. The student said that he didn't know, he hadn't read the *Divine Comedy.* "How does Tennyson's Ulysses compare with the one in the *Odyssey*?" someone else asked. The student said that he didn't know, he hadn't read the *Odyssey.* Both students were scolded and passed, and their professors came home to tell me the stories.

These men were indeed specialists in English. And yet, reader, aren't many intellectuals almost as great specialists in Important— that is to say, currently fashionable—books? Many of the intellectuals whom one hears discussing books certainly do not seem to have read widely or enthusiastically. Talking with an excellent critic and historian of ideas—a professor, too, à la Matthew Arnold—I asked him whether his students read much. He said, "My students! I can't get my colleagues to read anything!" Of course he was exaggerating; I felt that he was exaggerating very much; but it troubled me to remember the conversation at the literary parties at which he and I had occasionally met. Here people talked about few books, perhaps, but the books they talked about were the same: it was like the Middle Ages. And—this was like the Middle Ages too—they seemed more interested in the books' commentators than in the books; though when the books were Great, this was not always so. If you talked about the writings of some minor American novelist or short-story writer or poet—by *minor,* here, I mean anybody but the immediately fashionable six or eight—your hearer's eyes began to tap their feet almost before you had finished a sentence. (I have to admit that if you talked about such writers' unfortunate lives, and not their unfortunate writings, this didn't happen: lives, however minor, keep their primitive appeal.) But if you talked about what the ten-thousandth best critic in the country had just written, in the last magazine, about the next-worse critic's analysis of *The Ambassadors*, their eyes shone, they did not even interrupt you. There are few things more interesting to people of this sort than what a bad critic says of a bad criticism of a fashionable writer; what a good critic says of good criticism of him is equally interesting, if it is equally difficult, complicated, or novel.

If, at such parties, you wanted to talk about *Ulysses* or *The Castle* or *The Brothers Karamazov* or *The Great Gatsby* or Graham Greene's last novel—Important books—you were at the right place. (Though you weren't so well off if you wanted to talk about *Remembrance of Things Past*. Important, but too long.) But if you wanted to talk about Turgenev's novelettes, or *The House of the Dead*, or *Lavengro*, or *Life on the Mississippi*, or *The Old Wives' Tale*, or *The Golovlyov Family*, or Cunninghame Graham's stories, or Saint-Simon's memoirs, or *Lost Illusions*, or *The Beggar's Opera*, or *Eugen Onegin*, or *Little Dorrit*, or the *Burnt Njal Saga*, or *Persuasion*, or *The Inspector-General*, or *Oblomov*, or *Peer Gynt*, or *Far from the Madding Crowd*, or *Out of Africa*, or the *Parallel Lives*, or *A Dreary Story*, or *Debits and Credits*, or *Arabia Deserta*, or *Elective Affinities*, or *Schweik*, or—or any of a thousand good or interesting but Unimportant books, you couldn't expect a very ready knowledge or sympathy from most of the readers there. They had looked at the big sights, the current sights, hard, with guides and glasses; and those walks in the country, over unfrequented or thrice-familiar territory, all alone—those walks from which most of the joy and good of reading come—were walks that they hadn't gone on very often. And unless they were poets or poetry-critics, or of the minority that still is fond of poems, they weren't likely to know much poetry. Nothing would surprise the readers of another age more than the fact that to most of us literature is primarily fiction. It still surprises visitors from another culture: a Colombian student of mine, marveling at it, said, "In my country businessmen, quite a good many of them, write poetry; and when the maid cleans my room, she often picks up one of my poetry books and reads in it." When he said this I remembered that the critic and historian of ideas I spoke of had said to me, in a tone he would not have used for prose: "Now about *Paterson*—what do you think of it? Is it really much good?" I amused myself by trying to imagine Dr. Johnson asking Christopher Smart this about Gray's *Elegy*.

Many of the critics one reads or meets make an odd impression about reading, one that might be given this exaggerated emblematic form: "Good Lord, you don't think I *like* to read, do you? Reading is serious business, not something you fool around with in your spare time." Such critics read, pencil in hand, the books they have to read for an article, have to read for basic literary conversation—although most of these last, they are glad to think, they got through long ago. Readers, real readers, are almost as wild a species as writers; most critics are so domesticated as to seem institutions—as they stand there between reader and writer, so different from either, they remind one of the Wall standing between Pyramus and Thisbe. And some of *their* constant readers are so serious, responsible, and timid about reading a great work that they start out on it with a white hunter, native bearers, and a $10,000 policy they bought from the insurance-machine at the airport. The critics got back, but who knows whether they will be able to?

To the question "Have you read 'Gerontion'?"—or some other poem that may seem difficult to people—I've several times heard people reply: "Well, not really—I've *read* it, but I've never read a thorough analysis of it, or really gone through it systematically." And one critic will say of another critic's analysis of a book like *Moby Dick*: "Mr. Something has given us the first thorough [or *systematic*] reading of *Moby Dick* that we have had." After people had leafed through it for so long, it's at last been read! Yet, often, how plain and actual the poem or story itself seems, compared to those shifting and contradictory and all-too-systematic "readings" that veil it as clouds veil the rocks of a mountain. Luckily, we can always seek refuge from the analyses in the poem itself—*if we like poems better than we like analyses.* But poems, stories, new-made works of art, are coming to seem rather less congenial and important than they once did, both to literary and not-so-literary readers. So far as the last are concerned, look at the lists of best-sellers, the contents of popular magazines—notice how cheerful and beefy *Time* is when it's reviewing a biography, how grumpy and demanding it gets as soon as it's reviewing a serious novel. And look at the literary quarterlies, listen to the conversation of literary people: how much of it is criticism of criticism, talk about talk about books!

People realize that almost all fiction or poetry is bad or mediocre—it's the nature of things. Almost all criticism is bad or mediocre too, but it's harder for people to tell; and even common-place criticism can seem interesting or important simply because of its subject matter. An English statesman said that he liked the Order of the Garter because there was *no damned merit involved*; there is no damned inspiration involved in the writing of criticism, generally, and that is what the literary magazines like about it—there is an inexhaustible, unexceptionable, indistinguishable supply. They are not interested in being wildcat drillers for oil, but had rather have a hydroelectric plant at Niagara Falls. This was always the policy of *The Criterion*, their immediate ancestor: it gave a bare token representation to the literature of the twenties and thirties, and used up its space on criticism, much of it by J. Middleton Murry, John Gould Fletcher, and other Faithful Contributors.

A friend said to me one day, after he had opened his mail: "Whenever I have a story published, I get two or three letters asking me to write reviews." It isn't any different with poets. A young critic—one who makes his living by teaching, as most serious young critics do—could say in practical justification of his work: "If you're a critic the magazines *want* you to write for them, they *ask* you to write for them—there's all that space just waiting to be filled with big articles, long reviews. Look at this quarterly: 2½ pages of poems, 11 of a story, 134 of criticism. My job depends on my getting things printed. What chance have *I* got to get in those 13½ pages? Me for the 134!" So he might speak. But the chances are that it has never even occurred to the young critic to write a story or a poem. New critic is but old scholar writ large, as a general thing: the same gifts which used to go into proving that the Wife of Bath was really an aunt of Chaucer's named Alys Persë now go into proving that all of Henry James's work is really a Swedenborgian allegory. Criticism will soon have reached the state of scholarship, and the most obviously absurd theory—if it is maintained intensively, exhaustively, and professionally—will do the theorist no harm in the eyes of his colleagues.

But one must remember (or remain a child where criticism is concerned) that a great deal of the best and most sensible criticism of any age *is necessarily absurd*. Hundreds of examples will occur to anybody: Goethe and Schiller thought so little of Hölderlin that after a while they wouldn't even answer his letters. "Ah, but *we* wouldn't have been so foolish as Goethe and Schiller," we always feel; "you won't catch *us* making that mistake." And you don't: we love Hölderlin. But some duckling we have never spared a smile for is *our* Hölderlin, and half the swans we spent our Sundays feeding bread crumbs to will turn out to have been Southeys. And just as we will have been wrong about such people, so all of our critics will have been wrong: it's their *métier*, isn't it?—it always has been. It is easy to nod to all this as a truism, but it is hard to feel it as a truth. To feel it is to be fortified in the independence and humility that we as readers ought to have.

Once critics wrote as best they could, like anybody else—they knew no better; but today many of them have a language and style as institutionalized as those of sociologists. They have managed to develop this style in fifteen or twenty years—one finds only its crude beginnings in the *Hound and Horn* and *The Dial*; the critics of those days may have sounded superior and difficult to the readers of those days, but to us, now, they seem endearingly amateurish and human and informal, so that one looks at some essay and thinks, smiling, "That was certainly the *Paul et Virginie* stage of Kenneth Burke." Who had perfected, then, that strange sort of Law French which the critic now can set up like a Chinese Wall between himself and the lay (i.e., boreable) reader? The first generation wrote distinguishably well; the second writes indistinguishably ill; who knows how the third will write? Academic or scholarly writing has some bad qualities, and the writing of Superior Intellectuals has others: the style that I am describing almost combines the two. It is a style, a tone, that is hard to picture: if the two bears that ate the forty-two little children who said to Elisha, "Go up, thou baldhead"—if they, after getting their Ph.D.'s from the University of Göttingen, had retired to Atta Troll's Castle and written a book called *A Prolegomena to Every Future Criticism of Finnegans Wake*, they might have written so.

This style partly is a result of the difficult or once-difficult position of such critics (and of such intellectuals in general) in both our universities and our general literary culture. Sociologists went in for jargon, psychologists for graphs and statistics, mostly because they knew that physicists and chemists and biologists did not think sociology and psychology sciences; English professors did the same thing for the same reason; and the critics in the universities probably felt a similar need to show the scholars who looked down on them that criticism is just as difficult and just as much of a science as "English." But the literary quarterlies are also "little magazines," revolutionary organs of an oppressed or neglected class; their contributors, by using a style which insists upon their superiority to the society that disregards them, both protect themselves and punish their society.

One can understand why so many critics find it necessary to worry and weary their readers to death, in the most impressive way possible; if they themselves understood, they might no longer find it necessary. Or so one thinks—but one is naïve to think it: this style or tone of theirs is a spiritual necessity, and how can they give it up without finding something to put in its place? What began in need has been kept and elaborated in love. And I don't want them put out of their misery, I am only crying to them out of mine. May one of them say to the others, soon: "Brothers, *do* we want to sound like the *Publications of the Modern Language Association*, only worse? If we don't set things straight for ourselves, others will set them straight for us—or worse still, others won't, and things will go on as they are going on until one day even you and I won't be able to read each other, for sheer boredom."

Of course I do not mean that critics should all go out and try to have Styles, or that we should judge them by the way they write—though an absolutely bad writer is at least relatively incapable of distinguishing between good and bad in the writing that he criticizes. It is his reading that we judge a critic by, not his writing. The most impressive thing about the good critic is the fact that he *does* respond to the true nature and qualities of a work of art—not always, but often. But to be impressed by this you must be able to see these qualities when they are pointed out to you: that is, you have to be under favorable circumstances almost as good a reader as the critic is under less favorable ones. Similarly, the most impressive thing about the bad critic is his methodical and oblivious contempt for unfashionable masterpieces, his methodical and superstitious veneration for fashionable masterpieces and their reflections; but to be properly impressed with this you must have responded to the works themselves, and not to their reputations. There is a Critical Dilemma which might be put in this form: To be able to tell which critics are reliable guides to literature, you must know enough about literature not to need guides. (This is a less-than-half-truth, but a neglected one.) What we need, it might seem, is somebody who can tell us not which are the good and bad writers, but which are the good and bad critics; and half the critics I know are also trying to supply this need. In literature it is not that we have a labyrinth without a clue; the clues themselves have become a worse labyrinth, a perfect Navy Yard of great coiling hawsers which we are supposed to pay out behind us on our way into the darkness of—oh, "To His Coy Mistress," or whatever it is we're reading.

It is easier for the ordinary reader to judge among poems or stories or plays than it is for him to judge among pieces of criticism. Many bad or commonplace works of art never even succeed in getting him to notice them, and there *are* masterpieces which can shake even the Fat Boy awake. Good critics necessarily disagree with some of the reader's dearest convictions—unless he is a Reader among readers—and they are likely to seem offensive in doing so. But the bad or commonplace critic can learn very easily (as easily as a preacher or politician, almost) which are the right people to look down on or up to, and what are the right things to write for any occasion, the things his readers will admire and agree with almost before he has written them. And he can write in an impressive and authoritative way; can use a definitive tone, big words, great weighty sentences. Clinching References—the plagues of Egypt couldn't equal all the references to Freud and Jung and Marx and myths and existentialism and neo-Calvinism and Aristotle and St. Thomas that you'll sometimes see in one commonplace article. ("If he knows all these things how can he be wrong about a little thing like a poem?" the reader may well feel.) It is perpetually tempting to the critic to make his style and method so imposing to everyone that nobody will notice or care when he is wrong. And if the critic is detailedly and solemnly enthusiastic about the great, and rather silent and condescending about the small, how *can* he go very badly wrong? make a complete fool of himself? But taking the chance of making a complete fool of himself—and, sometimes, doing so—is the first demand that is made upon any real critic: he *must* stick his neck out just as the artist does, if he is to be of any real use to art.

———

The essential merit of a critic, then, is one that it is hard for many of his readers to see. Critics have a wonderfully imposing look, but this is only because they are in a certain sense impostors: the judges' black gowns, their positions and degrees and qualifications, their professional accomplishments, methods, styles, distinctions—all this institutional magnificence hides from us the naked human beings who do the judging, the fallible creatures who are what the accidents of birth and life have left them. If, as someone says, we ought not to forget that a masterpiece is something written by a man sitting alone in a room before a sheet of paper, we ought not to forget that a piece of criticism is produced in the same way: we have no substitute for these poor solitary human souls who do the writing, the criticizing and, also, the reading of poems and stories and novels. (I did recently meet a Scandinavian social scientist who said that after "an extension of the statistical methods of public opinion polls," this would no longer be true.) It is easy for readers and critics to forget this: "Extraordinary advances in critical method," writes an innocent anthologist, "make the inspection of a poem today by a first-rate critic as close and careful as a chemical analysis." As close and as careful, perhaps, but more delightfully unpredictable: for these are chemists who, half the time, after the long weeks of analysis are over, can't even agree whether what they were analyzing was bread or beer. An *Encyclopedia of Pseudo-Sciences* might define critical method as *the systematic (q.v.) application of foreign substances to literature; any series of devices by which critics may treat different works of art as much alike as possible.* It is true that a critical method can help us neither to read nor to judge; still, it is sometimes useful in pointing out to the reader a few gross discrete reasons for thinking a good poem good— and it is invaluable, almost indispensable, in convincing a reader that a good poem is bad, or a bad one good. (The best critic who ever lived could not *prove* that the *Iliad* is better than "Trees"; the critic can only state his belief persuasively, and hope that the reader of the poem will agree—but *persuasively* covers everything from a sneer to statistics.)

We do not become good critics by reading criticism and, secondarily, the "data" or "raw material" of criticism: that is, poems and stories. We become good critics by reading poems and stories and by living; it is reading criticism which is secondary—if it often helps us a great deal, it often hinders us more: even a good critic or reader has a hard time recovering from the taste of the age which has produced him. Many bad critics are bad, I think, because they have spent their life in card indexes; or if they have not, no one can tell. If works of art were about card indexes the critic could prepare for them in this way, but as it is he cannot. An interesting book about recent criticism was called *The Armed Vision*; the title and a few of the comments on the qualities of the ideal modern critic suggested that he would rather resemble one of those robots you meet in science-fiction stories, with a microscope for one eye, a telescope for the other, and the mechanical brain at Harvard for a heart.

Everybody understands that poems and stories are written by memory and desire, love and hatred, daydreams and nightmares—by a being, not a brain. But they are read just so, judged just so; and some great lack in human qualities is as fatal to the critic as it is to the novelist. Someone asked Eliot about critical method, and he replied: "The only method is to be very intelligent." And this is of course only a beginning: there have been many very intelligent people, but few good critics—far fewer than there have been good artists, as any history of the arts will tell you. "Principles" or "standards" of excellence are either specifically harmful or generally useless; the critic has nothing to go by except his experience as a human being and a reader, and is the personification of empiricism. A Greek geometer said that there is no royal road to geometry—there is no royal, or systematic, or impersonal, or rational, or safe, or sure road to criticism. Most people understand that a poet is a good poet because he does well some of the time; this is true of critics—if we are critics we can see this right away for everybody except ourselves, and everybody except ourselves can see it right away about *us*. But many critics have the bearing of people who are right all the time, and most of us like this: it makes them look more like our fathers.

Real criticism demands of human beings an almost inhuman disinterestedness, one which they adopt with reluctance and maintain with difficulty: the real critic must speak ill of friends and well of enemies, ill of agreeable bad works and well of less agreeable good ones; must admire writers whom his readers will snicker at him for admiring, and dislike writers whom it will place him among barbarians to dislike. For it is the opinion he offers with trepidation, thinking: "Nobody will believe it, and I hardly see how it can be so; but it seems so to me"—it is this opinion that may be all the next age will value him for; though in all probability it will value him for nothing—critics had better make the best of their own age, for few of them ever survive to the next. Criticism demands of the critic a terrible nakedness: a real critic has no one but himself to depend on. He can never forget that all he has to go by, finally, is his own response, the self that makes and is made up of such responses—and yet he must regard that self as no more than the instrument through which the work of art is seen, so that the work of art will seem everything to him and his own self nothing: the good critic has, as Eliot says, a great "sense of fact." Real critics do some of the time see what is there, even when—especially when—it is not what they want to be there. The critic must in this sense get away from his self-as-self; and he must as much as he can, for as long as he can, train and expose and widen this self, get rid of all that he can see as merely self—prejudices and disabilities and predilections—without ever losing the personal truth of judgment that his criticism springs from. (In the end the critic disappears, like the rest of us, in the quicksand of his own convictions.) Real criticism demands not only unusual human qualities but an unusual combination and application of these: it is no wonder that even real critics are just critics, most of the time. So much of our society is based, necessarily, on lies, equivocations, glossings-over; a real critic, about a part of this society, tries to tell only the truth. When it is a pleasant truth—

and it often is—reader and writer and critic are a joy to one another; but when the critic comes to the reader's house and tells him, causelessly and senselessly and heartlessly, that the book he is married to isn't everything she should be—ah, then it's a different affair!

But I have been talking of a "real critic" who would have a very short half-life, one who may never have been on sea or land; let me talk instead about good ordinary ones—viable ones, as a Modern Critic would say. What *is* a critic, anyway? So far as I can see, he is an extremely good reader—one who has learned to show to others what he saw in what he read. He is always many other things too, but these belong to his accident, not his essence. Of course, it is often the accident and not the essence that we read the critic for: pieces of criticism are frequently, though not necessarily, works of art of an odd anomalous kind, and we can sympathize with someone when he says lovingly about a critic, as Empson says about I. A. Richards, that we get more from *him* when he's wrong than we do from other people when they're right. I myself have sometimes felt this way about Empson; and the reader surely has his favorites too, writers to whom he goes for style and wit and sermons, informal essays, aesthetics, purple passages, confessions, aphorisms, wisdom—a thousand things. (One occasionally encounters intellectual couples for whom some critic has taken the place of the minister they no longer have.) Critics—I admit it very willingly—are often useful and wonderful and a joy to have around the house; *but* they're the bane of our age, because our age so fantastically overestimates their importance and so willingly forsakes the works they are writing about for them. We are brought into the world by specialists, borne out of it by specialists: more and more people think of the critic as an indispensable middle man between writer and reader, and would no more read a book alone, if they could help it, than have a baby alone. How many of us seem to think that the poem or story is in some sense "data" or "raw material" which the critic cooks up into understanding, so that we say, "I'd just never *read* 'We Are Seven' till I got So-and-So's analysis of it for Christmas!" But the work of art is as done as it will ever get, and all the critics in the world can't make its crust a bit browner; they may help *us*, the indigent readers, but they haven't done a thing to it. Around the throne of God, where all the angels read perfectly, there are no critics— there is no need for them.

Critics exist simply to help us with works of art—isn't that true? Once, taking to a young critic, I said as a self-evident thing, "Of course, criticism's necessarily secondary to the works of art it's about."

He looked at me as if I had kicked him, and said: "Oh, that's not *so!*" (I had kicked him, I realized.) And recently I heard a good critic, objecting to most of the criticism in the quarterlies, say what *real* criticism did: what it did, as he put it, was almost exactly what people usually say that religion, love, and great works of art do. Criticism, which began by humbly and anomalously existing for the work of art, and was in part a mere by-product of philosophy and rhetoric, has by now become, for a good many people, almost what the work of art exists for: the animals come up to Adam and Eve and are named—the end crowns the work.

There is an atmosphere or environment, at some of the higher levels of our literary culture, in which many people find it almost impossible not to write criticism and almost impossible to write anything else, if they pay much attention to the critics. For these fond mothers not only want the artist to be good, they want him to be great; and not simply great, but great in just the way he should be: they want him to be exactly the same as, only somehow entirely different from, the *Divine Comedy*. If the reader says, "It's always been that way," I'll answer, "Of course, of course. But critics are so much better armed than they used to be in the old days: they've got tanks and flame-throwers now, and it's harder to see past them to the work of art—in fact, magnificent creatures that they are, it's hard to *want* to see past them. Can't you imagine an age in which critics are like paleontologists, an age in which the last bone that the youngest critic has wired together is already hundreds of years old? Scholars are like that now. And critics are already like conductors, and give you *their* 'Lear,' *their* 'Confidence Man,' *their* 'Turn of the Screw.' It's beginning to frighten me a little; do we really *want* it to be an Age of Criticism?"

———

Ben Jonson called one of his poems "A Fit of Rhyme against Rhyme," and perhaps I should have called this article "A Fit of Criticism against Criticism." But of course I'm complaining not just about criticism and the literary quarterlies, but about the age; and that's only fair—what is an age but something to complain about? But if the age, the higher literary levels of it, doesn't wish to be an age of criticism, and an increasingly Alexandrian one at that, it needs to care more for stories and novels and poems and plays, and less for criticism; it needs to read more widely, more independently, and more joyfully; and it needs to say to its critics: "Write so as to be of some use to a reader—a reader, that is, of poems and stories, not of criticism. Vary a little, vary a little! Admit what you can't conceal, that criticism is no more than (and no less than) the helpful remarks and the thoughtful and disinterested judgment of a reader, a loving and experienced and able reader, but only a reader. And remember that works of art are never data, raw material, the crude facts that you critics explain or explain away. Remember that you can never be more than the staircase to the monument, the guide to the gallery, the telescope through which the children see the stars. At your best you make people see what they might never have seen without you; but they must always forget you in what they see."

Since I have complained of the style and method of much of the criticism that we read, I ought to say now that I know my own are wrong for this article. An article like this ought, surely, to avoid satire; it ought to be documented and persuasive and sympathetic, much in sorrow and hardly at all in anger—the reader should not be able to feel the wound for the balm. And yet a suitable article might not do any more good than this sort: people have immediate and irresistible reasons for what they do, and cannot be much swayed by helpful or vexing suggestions from bystanders. But if because of an article like this, or because of the better one that I hope someone else will write, a few people read a story instead of a criticism, write a poem instead of a review, pay no attention to what the most systematic and definitive critic says against some work of art they love—if that happens, the articles will have been worth writing.

[1952/PA]

On Preparing
to Read Kipling

MARK TWAIN SAID that it isn't what they don't know that hurts people, it's what they do know that isn't so. This is true of Kipling. If people don't know about Kipling they can read Kipling, and then they'll know about Kipling: it's ideal. But most people already do know about Kipling—not very much, but too much: they know what isn't so, or what might just as well not be so, it matters so little. They know that, just as Calvin Coolidge's preacher was against sin and the Snake was for it, Kipling was for imperialism; he talked about the white man's burden; he was a crude popular—immensely popular— writer who got popular by writing "If," and "On the Road to Mandalay," and *The Jungle Book*, and stories about India like Somerset Maugham, and children's stories; he wrote, "East is East and West is West and never the twain shall meet"; he wrote, "The female of the species is more deadly than the male"—or was that Pope? *Somebody* wrote it. In short: Kipling was someone people used to think was wonderful, but we know better than that now.

People certainly didn't know better than that then. "Dear Harry," William James begins. (It is hard to remember, hard to believe, that anyone ever called Henry James *Harry*, but if it had to be done, William James was the right man to do it.) "Last Sunday I dined with Howells at the Childs', and was delighted to hear him say that you were both a friend and an admirer of Rudyard Kipling. I am ashamed to say that I have been ashamed to write of that infant phenomenon, not knowing, with your exquisitely refined taste, how you might be affected by him and fearing to *jar.* [It is wonderful *to have the engineer / Hoist with his own petard.*] The more rejoiced am I at this, but why didn't you say so ere now? He's more of a Shakespeare than anyone yet in this generation of ours, as it strikes me. And seeing the new effects he lately brings in in *The Light That Failed,* and that Simla Ball story with Mrs. Hauksbee in the *Illustrated London News,* makes one sure now that he is only at the beginning of a rapidly enlarging career, with indefinite growth before him. Much of his present coarseness and jerkiness is youth only, divine youth. But *what* a youth! Distinctly the biggest literary phenomenon of our time. He has such human entrails, and he takes less time to get under the heart-strings of his personages than anyone I know. On the whole, bless him.

"All intellectual work is the same,—the artist feeds the public on his own bleeding insides. Kant's *Kritik* is just like a Strauss waltz, and I felt the other day, finishing *The Light That Failed,* and an ethical address to be given at Yale College simultaneously, that there was no *essential* difference between Rudyard Kipling and myself as far as that sacrificial element goes."

It surprises us to have James take Kipling so seriously, without reservations, with Shakespeare—to treat him as if he were Kant's *Kritik* and not a Strauss waltz. (Even Henry James, who could refer to "the good little Thomas Hardy"—who was capable of applying to the Trinity itself the adjective *poor*—somehow felt that he needed for Kipling that coarse word *genius,* and called him, at worst, "the great little Kipling.") Similarly, when Goethe and Matthew Arnold write about Byron, we are surprised to see them bringing in Shakespeare—are surprised to see how unquestioningly, with what serious respect, they speak of Byron, as if he were an ocean or a new ice age: "our soul," wrote Arnold, "had *felt* him like the thunder's roll." It is as though mere common sense, common humanity, required this of them: the existence of a world figure like Byron demands (as the existence of a good or great writer does not) that any inhabitant of the world treat him somehow as the world treats him. Goethe knew that Byron "is a child when he reflects," but this did not prevent him from treating Byron exactly as he treated that other world figure Napoleon.

An intelligent man said that the world felt Napoleon as a weight, and that when he died it would give a great *oof* of relief. This is just as true of Byron, or of such Byrons of their days as Kipling and Hemingway: after a generation or two the world is tired of being their pedestal, shakes them off with an *oof*, and then—hoisting onto its back a new world figure—feels the penetrating satisfaction of having made a mistake all its own. Then for a generation or two the Byron lies in the dust where we left him: if the old world did him more than justice, a new one does him less. "If he was so good as all that why isn't he still famous?" the new world asks—if it asks anything. And then when another generation or two are done, we decide that he wasn't altogether a mistake people made in those days, but a real writer after all—that if we like *Childe Harold* a good deal less than anyone thought of liking it then, we like *Don Juan* a good deal more. Byron *was* a writer, people just didn't realize the sort of writer he was. We can feel impatient with Byron's world for liking him for the wrong reasons, and with the succeeding world for disliking him for the wrong reasons, and we are glad that our world, the real world, has at last settled Byron's account.

Kipling's account is still unsettled. Underneath, we still hold it against him that the world quoted him in its sleep, put him in its headlines when he was ill, acted as if he were God; we are glad that we have Hemingway instead, to put in *our* headlines when his plane crashes. Kipling is in the dust, and the dust seems to us a very good place for him. But in twenty or thirty years, when Hemingway is there instead, and we have a new Byron-Kipling-Hemingway to put in our news programs when his rocket crashes, our resistance to Hemingway will have taken the place of our resistance to Kipling, and we shall find ourselves willing to entertain the possibility that Kipling *was* a writer after all—people just didn't realize the sort of writer he was.

There is a way of traveling into this future—of realizing, now, the sort of writer Kipling was—that is unusually simple, but that people are unusually unwilling to take. The way is: to read Kipling as if one were not prepared to read Kipling; as if one didn't already know about Kipling—had never been told how readers do feel about Kipling, should feel about Kipling; as if one were setting out, naked, to see something that is there naked. I don't entirely blame the reader if he answers: "Thanks very much; if it's just the same to you, I'll keep my clothes on." It's only human of him—man is the animal that wears clothes. Yet aren't works of art in some sense a way of doing without clothes, a means by which reader, writer, and subject are able for once to accept their own nakedness? the nakedness not merely of the "naked truth," but also of the naked wishes that come before and after that truth? To read Kipling, for once, not as the crudely effective, popular writer we know him to be, but as, perhaps, the something else that even crudely effective, popular writers can become, would be to exhibit a magnanimity that might do justice both to Kipling's potentialities and to our own. Kipling did have, at first, the "coarseness and jerkiness" and mannered vanity of youth, human youth; Kipling did begin as a reporter, did print in newspapers the *Plain Tales from the Hills* which ordinary readers—and, unfortunately, most extraordinary ones—do think typical of his work; but then for half a century he kept writing. Chekhov began by writing jokes for magazines, skits for vaudeville; Shakespeare began by writing *Titus Andronicus* and *The Two Gentlemen of Verona,* some of the crudest plays any crudely effective, popular writer has ever turned out. Kipling is neither a Chekhov nor a Shakespeare, but he is far closer to both than to the clothing-store-dummy-with-the-solar-topee we have agreed to call Kipling. Kipling, like it or not, admit it or not, was a great genius; and a great neurotic; and a great professional, one of the most skillful writers who have ever existed—one of the writers who have used English best, one of the writers who most often have made other writers exclaim, in the queer tone they used for the exclamation: "Well, I've got to admit it really is *written.*" When he died and was buried in that foreign land England, that only the Anglo-Indians know, I wish that they had put above his grave, there in *their* Westminster Abbey: "It really was *written.*"

Mies van der Rohe said, very beautifully: "I don't want to be interesting, I want to be good." Kipling, a great realist but a greater inventor, could have said that he didn't want to be realistic, he wanted to get it right: that he wanted it not the way it did or—statistics show—does happen, but the way it really would happen. You often feel about something in Shakespeare or Dostoevsky that nobody ever said such a thing, but that it's just the sort of thing people would say if they could—is more real, in some sense, than what people do say. If you have given your imagination free rein, let things go as far as they want to go, the world they made for themselves while you watched can have, for you and later watchers, a spontaneous finality. Some of Kipling has this spontaneous finality; and because he has written so many different kinds of stories—no writer of fiction of comparable genius has depended so much, for so long, on short stories alone—you end dazzled by his variety of realization: so many plants, and so many of them dewy!

If I had to pick one writer to invent a conversation between an animal, a god, and a machine, it would be Kipling. To discover what, if they ever said, the dumb would say—this takes real imagination; and this imagination of what isn't is the extension of a real knowledge of what is, the knowledge of a consummate observer who took no notes, except of names and dates: "If a thing didn't stay in my memory I argued it was hardly worth writing out." Knowing what the peoples, animals, plants, weathers of the world look like, sound like, smell like, was Kipling's *métier*, and so was knowing the words that could make someone else know. You can argue about the judgment he makes of something, but the thing is there. When as a child you first begin to read, what attracts you to a book is illustrations and conversations, and what scares you away is "long descriptions." In Kipling illustration and conversation and description (not long description; read, even the longest of his descriptions is short) have merged into a "toothsome amalgam" which the child reads with a grown-up's ease, and the grown-up with a child's wonder. Often Kipling writes with such grace and command, such a combination of experienced mastery and congenital inspiration, that we repeat with Goethe: "Seeing someone accomplishing arduous things with ease gives us an impression of witnessing the impossible." Sometimes the arduous thing Kipling is accomplishing seems to us a queer, even an absurd thing for anyone to wish to accomplish. But don't we have to learn to consent to this, with Kipling as with other good writers?—to consent to the fact that good writers just don't have good sense; that they are going to write it their way, not ours; that they are never going to have the objective, impersonal rightness they should have, but only the subjective, personal wrongness from which we derived the idea of the rightness. The first thing we notice about *War and Peace* and *Madame Bovary* and *Remembrance of Things Past* is how wonderful they are; the second thing we notice is how much they have wrong with them. They are not at all the perfect work of art we want—so perhaps Ruskin was right when he said that the person who wants perfection knows nothing about art.

Kipling says about a lion cub he and his family had on the Cape: "He dozed on the stoep, I noticed, due north and south, looking with slow eyes up the length of Africa"; this, like several thousand such sentences, makes you take for granted the truth of his "I made my own experiments in the weights, colors, perfumes, and attributes of words in relation to other words, either as read aloud so that they may hold the ear, or, scattered over the page, draw the eye." His words range from gaudy effectiveness to perfection; he is a professional magician but, also, a magician. He says about stories: "A tale from which pieces have been raked out is like a fire that has been poked. One does not know that the operation has been performed, but everyone feels the effect." (He even tells you how best to rake out the pieces: with a brush and Chinese ink you grind yourself.) He is a kind of Liszt—so isn't it just empty bravura, then? Is Liszt's? Sometimes; but sometimes bravura is surprisingly full, sometimes virtuosos are surprisingly plain: to boil a potato perfectly takes a chef home from the restaurant for the day.

Kipling was just such a potato boiler: a professional knower of professionals, a great trapeze artist, cabinetmaker, prestidigitator, with all the unnumbered details of others' guilds, crafts, mysteries, techniques at the tip of his fingers—or, at least, at the tip of his tongue. The first sentences he could remember saying as a child had been haltingly translated into English "from the vernacular" (that magical essential phrase for the reader of Kipling!) and just as children feel that it is they and not the grown-ups who see the truth, so Kipling felt about many things that it is the speakers of the vernacular and not the sahibs who tell the truth; that there are many truths that, to be told at all, take the vernacular. From childhood on he learned—to excess or obsession, even—the vernaculars of earth, the worlds inside the world, the many species into which place and language and work divide man. From the species which the division of labor produces it is only a step to the animal species which evolutionary specialization produces, so that Kipling finds it easy to write stories about animals; from the vernaculars or dialects or cants which place or profession produces (Kipling's slogan is, almost, "The cant *is* the man") it is only a step to those which time itself produces, so that Kipling finds it easy to write stories about all the different provinces of the past, or the future (in "As Easy as A.B.C."), or Eternity (if his queer institutional stories of the bureaucracies of Heaven and Hell are located there). Kipling was no Citizen of the World, but like the Wandering Jew he had lived in many places and known many peoples, an uncomfortable stranger repeating to himself the comforts of earth, all its immemorial contradictory ways of being at home.

Goethe, very winningly, wanted to have put on his grave a sentence saying that he had never been a member of any guild, and was an amateur until the day he died. Kipling could have said, "I never saw the guild I wasn't a member of," and was a professional from the day he first said to his ayah, in the vernacular—not being a professional myself, I don't know what it was he said, but it was the sort of thing a man would say who, from the day he was sixteen till the day he was twenty-three, was always—"luxury of which I dream still!"—shaved by his servant before he woke up in the morning.

This fact of his life, I've noticed, always makes hearers give a little shiver; but it is all the mornings when no one shaved Kipling before Kipling woke up, because Kipling had never been to sleep, that make me shiver. "Such night-walkings" were "laid upon me through my life," Kipling writes, and tells you in magical advertising prose how lucky the wind before dawn always was for him. You and I should have such luck! Kipling was a professional, but a professional possessed by both the Daemon he tells you about, who writes some of the stories for him, and the demons he doesn't tell you about, who write some others. Nowadays we've learned to call part of the unconscious *it* or *id*; Kipling had not, but he called this Personal Demon of his *it*. (When he told his father that *Kim* was finished his father asked: "Did *it* stop, or you?" Kipling "told him that it was It.") "When your Daemon is in charge," Kipling writes, "do not try to think consciously. Drift, wait, and obey." He was sure of the books in which "my Daemon was with me . . . When those books were finished they said so themselves with, almost, the water-hammer click of a tap turned off." (Yeats said that a poem finishes itself with a click like a closing box.) Kipling speaks of the "doom of the makers": when their Daemon is missing they are no better than anybody else; but when he is there, and they put down what he dictates, "the work he gives shall continue, whether in earnest or jest." Kipling even "learned to distinguish between the peremptory motions of my Daemon, and the 'carry-over' of induced electricity, which comes of what you might call mere 'frictional' writing." We always tend to distrust geniuses about genius, as if what they say didn't arouse much empathy in us, or as if we were waiting till some more reliable source of information came along; still, isn't what Kipling writes a colored version of part of the plain truth?—there is plenty of supporting evidence. But it is interesting to me to see how thoroughly Kipling manages to avoid any subjective guilt, fallible human responsibility, so that he can say about anything in his stories either: "Entirely conscious and correct, objectively established, independently corroborated, the experts have testified, the professionals agree, it is the consensus of the authorities at the Club," or else: "I had nothing to do with it. I know nothing about it. *It* did it. The Daemon did it all." The reader of Kipling—this reader at least—hates to give all the credit to the Professional or to the Daemon; perhaps the demons had something to do with it too. Let us talk about the demons.

One writer says that we only notice what hurts us—that if you went through the world without hurting anyone, nobody would even know you had been alive. This is quite false, but true, too: if you put it in terms of the derivation of the Principle of Reality from the primary Principle of Pleasure, it does not even sound shocking. But perhaps we only notice a sentence if it sounds shocking—so let me say grotesquely: Kipling was someone who had spent six years in a concentration camp as a child; he never got over it. As a very young man he spent seven years in an India that confirmed his belief in concentration camps; he never got over this either.

As everybody remembers, one of Goya's worst engravings has underneath it: *I saw it*. Some of Kipling has underneath: *It is there*. Since the world is a necessary agreement that it isn't there, the world answered: *It isn't,* and told Kipling what a wonderful imagination he had. Part of the time Kipling answered stubbornly: *I've been there* (*I am there* would have been even truer) and part of the time he showed the world what a wonderful imagination he had. Say *Fairy tales!* enough to a writer and he will write you fairy tales. But to our *Are you telling me the truth or are you reassuring yourself?*—we ask it often of any writer, but particularly often of Kipling—he sometimes can say truthfully: *Reassuring you*; we and Kipling have interests in common. Kipling knew that "every nation, like every individual, walks in a vain show—else it could not live with itself"; Kipling knew people's capacity not to see: "through all this shifting, shouting brotheldom the pious British householder and his family bored their way back from the theatres, eyes-front and fixed, as though not seeing." But he himself had seen, and so believed in, the City of Dreadful Night, and the imperturbable or delirious or dying men who ran the city; this City outside was the duplicate of the City inside; and when the people of Victorian Europe didn't believe in any of it, except as you believe in a ghost story, he knew that this was only because they didn't *know*— he knew. So he was obsessed by—wrote about, dreamed about, and stayed awake so as not to dream about—many concentration camps, of the soul as well as of the body; many tortures, hauntings, hallucinations, deliria, diseases, nightmares, practical jokes, revenges, monsters, insanities, neuroses, abysses, forlorn hopes, last chances, extremities of every kind; these and their sweet opposites. He feels the convalescent's gratitude for mere existence, that the world is what the world was: how blue the day is, to the eye that has been blinded! Kipling praises the cessation of pain and its more blessed accession, when the body's anguish blots out for a little "Life's grinning face . . .

the trusty Worm that dieth not, the steadfast Fire also." He praises
man's old uses, home and all the ways of home: its Father and Mother,
there to run to if you could only wake; and praises all our dreams of
waking, our fantasies of return or revenge or insensate endurance. He
praises the words he has memorized, that man has made from the si-
lence; the senses that cancel each other out, that man has made from
the senselessness; the worlds man has made from the world; but he
praises and reproduces the sheer charm of—few writers are so purely
charming!—the world that does not need to have anything done to it,
that is simply there around us as we are there in it. He knows the joy
of finding exactly the right words for what there are no words for; the
satisfactions of sentimentality and brutality and love too, the "ex-
quisite tenderness" that began in cruelty. But in the end he thanks
God most for the small drugs that last—is grateful that He has not
laid on us "the yoke of too long Fear and Wonder," but has given us
Habit and Work: so that his Seraphs waiting at the Gate praise God

> Not for any miracle of easy Loaves and Fishes
> But for doing, 'gainst our will, work against our wishes,
> Such as finding food to fill daily emptied dishes . . .

praise him

> Not for Prophecies or Powers, Visions, Gifts, or Graces
> But the unregardful hours that grind us in our places
> With the burden on our backs, the weather in our faces.

"Give me the first six years of a child's life and you can have the
rest" are the first words of *Something of Myself,* Kipling's reticent and
revealing autobiography. The sentence exactly fits and exactly doesn't
fit. For the first six years of his life the child lived in Paradise, the in-
ordinately loved and reasonably spoiled son of the best of parents;
after that he lived in the Hell in which the best of parents put him,
and paid to have him kept: in "a dark land, and a darker room full of
cold, in one wall of which a woman made naked fire . . . a woman
who took in children whose parents were in India." The child did not
see his parents again for the next six years. He accepted the Hell as
"eternally established . . . I had never heard of Hell, so I was intro-
duced to it in all its terrors . . . I was regularly beaten . . . I have known
a certain amount of bullying, but this was calculated torture—reli-
gious as well as scientific . . . Deprivation from reading was added to

my punishments . . . I was well beaten and sent to school through the streets of Southsea with the placard 'Liar' between my shoulders . . . Some sort of nervous breakdown followed, for I imagined I saw shadows and things that were not there, and they worried me more than the Woman . . . A man came down to see me as to my eyes and reported that I was half-blind. This, too, was supposed to be 'showing-off,' and I was segregated from my sister—another punishment—as a sort of moral leper."

At the end of the six years the best of parents came back for their leper ("She told me afterwards that when she first came up to my room to kiss me goodnight, I flung up an arm to guard off the cuff I had been trained to expect"), and for the rest of their lives they continued to be the best and most loving of parents, blamed by Kipling for nothing, adored by Kipling for everything: "I think I can truthfully say that those two made up for me the only public for whom then I had any regard whatever till their deaths, in my forty-fifth year."

My *best of parents* cannot help sounding ironic, yet I do not mean it as irony. From the father's bas-reliefs for *Kim* to the mother's "There's no Mother in Poetry, my dear," when the son got angry at her criticism of his poems—from beginning to end they are bewitching; you cannot read about them without wanting to live with them; they were the best of parents. It is *this* that made Kipling what he was: if they had been the worst of parents, even fairly bad parents, even ordinary parents, it would all have made sense, Kipling himself could have made sense out of it. As it was, his world had been torn in two and he himself torn in two: for under the part of him that extenuated everything, blamed for nothing, there was certainly a part that extenuated nothing, blamed for everything—a part whose existence he never admitted, most especially not to himself. He says about some of the things that happened to him during those six years: "In the long run these things and many more of the like drained me of any capacity for real, personal hatred for the rest of my life." To admit from the unconscious something inadmissible, one can simply deny it, bring it up into the light with a *No*; Kipling has done so here—the capacity for real, personal hatred, real, personal revenge, summary fictional justice, is plain throughout Kipling's work. Listen to him tell how he first began to write. He has just been told about Dante: "I bought a fat, American-cloth-bound notebook and set to work on an *Inferno*, into which I put, under appropriate tortures, all my friends and most of the masters." (Why only *most?* Two were spared, one for the Father and one for the Mother.) Succinct and reticent as *Something of Myself* is, it has room for half a dozen scenes in which the help-less Kipling is remorselessly, systematically, comprehensively humil-iated before the inhabitants of his universe. At school, for instance: "H——then told me off before my delighted companions in his best style, which was acid and contumelious. He wound up with a few general remarks about dying as a 'scurrilous journalist' . . . The tone, matter, and setting of his discourse were as brutal as they were meant to be—brutal as the necessary wrench on the curb that fetches up a too-flippant colt." Oh, necessary, entirely necessary, we do but tor-ture in education! one murmurs to these methodical justifications of brutality as methodical, one of authority's necessary stages. Here is another master: "Under him I came to feel that words could be used as weapons, for he did me the honor to talk at me plentifully . . . One learns more from a good scholar in a rage than from a score of lucid and laborious drudges; and to be made the butt of one's companions in full form is no bad preparation for later experiences. I think this 'approach' is now discouraged for fear of hurting the soul of youth, but in essence it is no more than rattling tins or firing squibs under a colt's nose. I remember nothing save satisfaction or envy when C—— broke his precious ointments over my head." Nothing? Better for Kipling if he had remembered—not remembering gets rid of noth-ing. Yet who knows? he may even have felt—known that he felt— "nothing save satisfaction and envy," the envying satisfaction of iden-tification. As he says, he was learning from a master to use words as weapons, but he had already learned from his life a more difficult les-son: to know that, no matter how the sick heart and raw being rebel, it is all for the best; in the past there were the best of masters and in the future there will be the best of masters, if only we can wait out, bear out, the brutal present—the incomprehensible present that some-day we shall comprehend as a lesson.

The scene changes from England to India, school to Club, but the action—passion, rather—is the same: "As I entered the long, shabby dining-room where we all sat at one table, everybody hissed. I was innocent enough to ask: 'What's the joke? Who are they hissing?' 'You,' said the man at my side. 'Your damn rag has ratted over the Bill.' It is not pleasant to sit still when one is twenty while all your universe hisses you." One expects next a sentence about how customary and salutary hissing is for colts, but for once it doesn't come; and when Kipling's syntax suffers as it does in this sentence, he is remembering something that truly is not pleasant. He even manages somewhat to justify, somehow to justify, his six years in Hell: the devils' inquisitions, after all, "made me give attention to the lies I soon found it necessary to tell; and this, I presume, is the foundation of literary effort . . . Nor was my life an unsuitable preparation for my future, in that it demanded constant wariness, the habit of observation and attendance on moods and tempers; the noting of discrepancies between speech and action; a certain reserve of demeanor; and automatic suspicion of sudden favors." I have seen writers called God's spies, but Kipling makes it sound as if they were just spies—or spies on God. If only he could have blamed God—his Gods—a little consciously, forgiven them a little unconsciously! could have felt that someone, sometimes, doesn't *mean* something to happen! But inside, and inside stories, everything is meant.

After you have read Kipling's fifty or seventy-five best stories you realize that few men have written this many stories of this much merit, and that very few have written more and better stories. Chekhov and Turgenev are two who immediately come to mind; and when I think of their stories I cannot help thinking of what seems to me the greatest lack in Kipling's. I don't know exactly what to call it: a lack of dispassionate moral understanding, perhaps—of the ability both to understand things and to understand that there is nothing to do about them. (In a story, after all, there is always something you *can* do, something that a part of you is always trying to make you do.) Kipling is a passionate moralist, with a detailed and occasionally profound knowledge of part of things; but his moral spectrum has shifted, so that he can see far down into the infra-red, but is blind for some frequencies normal eyes are sensitive to. His morality is the one-sided, desperately protective, sometimes vindictive morality of someone who has been for some time the occupant of one of God's concentration camps, and has had to spend the rest of his life justifying or explaining out of existence what he cannot forget. Kipling tries so hard to celebrate and justify true authority, the work and habit and wisdom of the world, because he feels so bitterly the abyss of pain and insanity that they overlie, and can do—even will do—nothing to prevent.

Kipling's morality is the morality of someone who has to prove that God is not responsible for part of the world, and that the Devil is. If Father and Mother were not to blame for anything, yet what did happen to you could happen to you—if God is good, and yet the concentration camps exist—then there has to be *someone* to blame, and to punish too, some real, personal source of the world's evil. (He finishes "At the End of the Passage" by having someone quote: "There may be Heaven, there must be Hell. / Meanwhile there is our life here. Well?" In most of his stories he sees to it that our life here is Heaven and Hell.) But in this world, often, there is nothing to praise but no one to blame, and Kipling can bear to admit this in only a few of his stories. He writes about one source of things in his childhood: "And somehow or other I came across a tale about a lion-hunter in South Africa who fell among lions who were all Freemasons, and with them entered into a conspiracy against some wicked baboons. I think that, too, lay dormant until the Jungle Books began to be born." In Chekhov or Turgenev, somehow or other, the lions aren't really Freemasons and the baboons aren't really wicked. In Chekhov and Turgenev, in fact, most of the story has disappeared from the story: there was a lion hunter in South Africa, and first he shot the lions, and then he shot the baboons, and finally he shot himself; and yet it wasn't *wicked*, exactly, but human—very human.

Kipling had learned too well and too soon that, in William James's words: "The normal process of life contains moments as bad as any of those which insane melancholy is filled with, moments in which radical evil gets its innings and takes its solid turn. The lunatic's visions of horror are all drawn from the material of daily fact. Our civilization is founded on the shambles, and each individual existence goes out in a lonely spasm of helpless agony. If you protest, my friend, wait till you arrive there yourself!" Kipling had arrived there early and returned there often. One thinks sadly of how deeply congenial to this torturing obsessive knowledge of Kipling's the First World War was: the death and anguish of Europe produced some of his best and most terrible stories, and the death of his own son, his own anguish, produced "Mary Postgate," that nightmarish, most human and most real daydream of personal revenge. The world *was* Hell and India underneath, after all; and he could say to the Victorian, Edwardian Europeans who had thought it all just part of his style: "You wouldn't believe me!"

Svidrigaylov says: "We are always thinking of eternity as an idea that cannot be understood, something immense. But why must it be? What if, instead of all this, you suddenly find just a little room there, something like a village bath-house, grimy, and spiders in every corner, and that's all eternity is . . . I, you know, would certainly have made it so deliberately." Part of Kipling would have replied to this with something denunciatory and Biblical, but another part would have blurted eagerly, like somebody out of *Kim*: "Oah yess, that is dam-well likely! Like a dak-bungalow, you know." It is an idea that would have occurred to him, down to the last *deliberately*.

But still another part of Kipling would suddenly have seen—he might even later have written it down, according to the dictates of his Daemon—a story about a boy who is abandoned in a little room, grimy, with spiders in every corner, and after a while the spiders come a little nearer, and a little nearer, and one of them is Father Spider, and one of them is Mother Spider, and the boy is their Baby Spider. To Kipling the world was a dark forest full of families: so that when your father and mother leave you in the forest to die, the wolves that come to eat you are always Father Wolf and Mother Wolf, your real father and real mother, and you are—as not even the little wolves ever quite are—their real son. The family romance, the two families of the Hero, have so predominant a place in no other writer. Kipling never said a word or thought a thought against his parents, "both so entirely comprehending that except in trivial matters we had hardly need of words"; few writers have made authority so tender, beautiful, and final—have had us miserable mortals serve better masters; *but* Kipling's Daemon kept bringing Kipling stories in which wild animals turn out to be the abandoned Mowgli's real father and mother, a heathen Lama turns out to be the orphaned Kim's real father— and Kipling wrote down the stories and read them aloud to his father and mother.

This is all very absurd, all very pathetic? Oh yes, that's very likely; but, reader, down in the darkness where the wishes sleep, snuggled together like bats, you and I are Baby Spider too. If you think *this* absurd you should read Tolstoy—all of Tolstoy. But I should remark, now, on something that any reader of Kipling will notice: that though he can seem extraordinarily penetrating or intelligent—inspired, even—he can also seem very foolish or very blind. This is a characteristic of the immortals from which only we mortals are free. They oversay everything. It is only ordinary readers and writers who have ordinary common sense, who are able to feel about things what an ordinarily sensible man should. To another age, of course, our ordinary common sense will seem very very common and ordinary, but not sense, exactly: sense never lasts for long; instead of having created our own personal daydream or nightmare, as the immortals do, we merely have consented to the general daydream or nightmare which our age accepted as reality—it will seem to posterity only sense to say so, and it will say so, before settling back into a common sense of its own.

In the relations of mortals and immortals, yesterday's and today's posterities, there is a certain pathos or absurdity. There is a certain absurdity in my trying to persuade you to read Kipling sympathetically—who are *we* to read or not read Kipling sympathetically? part of me grunts. Writing about just which writers people are or are not attracted to, these years—who was high in the nineteenth, who's low in the twentieth—all the other stock-market quotations of the centuries, makes me feel how much such things have to do with history, and how little with literature. The stories themselves are literature. While their taste is on my tongue, I can't help feeling that virtue is its own reward, that good writing will take care of itself. It is a feeling I have often had after reading all of an author: that there it is. I can see that if I don't write this about the stories, plenty of other writers will; that if you don't read the stories, plenty of other readers will. The man Kipling, the myth Kipling is over; but the stories themselves—Kipling—have all the time in the world. The stories—some of them—can say to us with the calm of anything that has completely realized its own nature: "Worry about yourselves, not us. *We're* all right."

And yet, I'd be sorry to have missed them, I'd be sorry for you to miss them. I have read one more time what I've read so often before, and have picked for you what seem—to a loving and inveterate reader, one ashamed of their faults and exalted by their virtues—fifty of Kipling's best stories.

[*1961/SHS*]

The Taste of the Age

WHEN WE LOOK AT THE AGE in which we live—no matter what age it happens to be—it is hard for us not to be depressed by it. The taste of the age is, always, a bitter one. "What kind of a time is this when one must envy the dead and buried!" said Goethe about his age; yet Matthew Arnold would have traded his own time for Goethe's almost as willingly as he would have traded his own self for Goethe's. How often, after a long day witnessing elementary education, School Inspector Arnold came home, sank into what I hope was a Morris chair, looked round him at the Age of Victoria, that Indian Summer of the Western World, and gave way to a wistful, exacting, articulate despair!

Do people feel this way because our time is worse than Arnold's, and Arnold's than Goethe's, and so on back to Paradise? Or because forbidden fruits—the fruits forbidden us by time—are always the sweetest? Or because we can never compare our own age with an earlier age, but only with books about that age?

We say that somebody doesn't know what he is missing; Arnold, pretty plainly, didn't know what he was having. The people who live in a Golden Age usually go around complaining how yellow everything looks. Maybe we too are living in a Golden or, anyway, Gold-Plated Age, and the people of the future will look back at us and say ruefully: "We never had it so good." And yet the thought that they will say this isn't as reassuring as it might be. We can see that Goethe's and Arnold's ages weren't as bad as Goethe and Arnold thought them: after all, they produced Goethe and Arnold. In the same way, our times may not be as bad as we think them: after all, they have produced us. Yet this too is a thought that isn't as reassuring as it might be.

A Tale of Two Cities begins by saying that the times were, as always, "the best of times, the worst of times!" If we judge by wealth and power, our times are the best of times; if the times have made us willing to judge by wealth and power, they are the worst of times. But most of us still judge by more: by literature and the arts, science and philosophy, education. (Really we judge by more than these: by love and wisdom; but how are we to say whether our own age is wiser and more loving than another?) I wish to talk to you for a time about what is happening to the audience for the arts and literature, and to the education that prepares this audience, here in the United States.

In some ways this audience is improving, has improved, tremendously. Today it is as easy for us to get *Falstaff* or *Boris Godunov* or *Ariadne auf Naxos,* or Landowska playing *The Well-Tempered Clavichord*, or Fischer-Dieskau singing *Die Schöne Müllerin,* or Richter playing Beethoven's piano sonatas, as it used to be to get Mischa Elman playing *Humoresque.* Several hundred thousand Americans bought Toscanini's recording of Beethoven's Ninth Symphony. Some of them played it only to show how faithful their phonographs are; some of them played it only as the stimulus for an hour of random, homely rumination. But many of them really listened to the records—and, later, went to hear the artists who made the records—and, later, bought for themselves, got to know and love, compositions that a few years ago nobody but musicologists or musicians of the most advanced tastes had even read the scores of. That there are sadder things about the state of music here, I know; still, we are better off than we were twenty-five or thirty years ago. Better off, too, so far as the ballet is concerned: it is our good fortune to have had the greatest influence on American ballet the influence of the greatest choreographer who ever lived, that "Mozart of choreographers" George Balanchine.

Here today the visual arts are—but I don't know whether to borrow my simile from the Bible, and say *flourishing like the green bay tree,* or to borrow it from Shakespeare and say *growing like a weed.* We are producing paintings and reproductions of paintings, painters and reproductions of painters, teachers and museum directors and gallery-goers and patrons of the arts, in almost celestial quantities. Most of the painters are bad or mediocre, of course—this is so, necessarily, in any art at any time—but the good ones find shelter in numbers, are bought, employed, and looked at like the rest. The people of the past rejected Cézanne, Monet, Renoir, the many great painters they did not understand; by liking and encouraging, without exception, all the painters they do not understand, the people of the present have made it impossible for this to happen again.

Our society, it turns out, can use modern art. A restaurant, today, will order a mural by Miró in as easy and matter-of-fact a spirit as, twenty-five years ago, it would have ordered one by Maxfield Parrish. The president of a paint factory goes home, sits down by his fireplace—it *looks* like a chromium aquarium set into the wall by a wall-safe company that has branched out into interior decorating, but there is a log burning in it, he calls it a fireplace, let's call it a fireplace too—the president sits down, folds his hands on his stomach, and stares relishingly at two paintings by Jackson Pollock that he has hung on the wall opposite him. He feels at home with them; in fact, as he looks at them he not only feels at home, he feels as if he were back at the paint factory. And his children—if he has any—his children cry for Calder. He uses thoroughly advanced, wholly non-representational artists to design murals, posters, institutional advertisements: if we have the patience (or are given the opportunity) to wait until the West has declined a little longer, we shall all see the advertisements of Merrill Lynch, Pierce, Fenner, and Smith illustrated by Jean Dubuffet.

This president's minor executives may not be willing to hang a Kandinsky in the house, but they will wear one, if you make it into a sport shirt or a pair of swimming trunks; and if you make it into a sofa, they will lie on it. They and their wives and children will sit on a porcupine, if you first exhibit it at the Museum of Modern Art and say that it is a chair. In fact, there is nothing, nothing in the whole world that someone won't buy and sit in if you tell him that it is a chair: the great new art form of our age, the one that will take anything we put in it, is the chair. If Hieronymus Bosch, if Christian Morgenstern, if the Marquis de Sade were living at this hour, what chairs they would be designing!

Our architecture is flourishing too. Even colleges have stopped rebuilding the cathedrals of Europe on their campuses; and a mansion, today, is what it is not because a millionaire has dreamed of the Alhambra, but because an architect has dreamed of the marriage of Frank Lloyd Wright and a silo. We Americans have the best factories anyone has ever designed; we have many schools, post offices, and public buildings that are, so far as one can see, the best factories anyone has ever designed; we have many delightful, or efficient, or extraordinary houses. The public that lives in the houses our architects design—most houses, of course, are not designed, but just happen to a contractor—this public is a broad-minded, tolerant, adventurous public, one that has triumphed over inherited prejudice to an astonishing degree. You can put a spherical plastic gas tower on aluminum stilts, divide it into rooms, and quite a few people will be willing to crawl along saying, "Is this the floor? Is this the wall?"—to make a down payment, and to call it home. I myself welcome this spirit, a spirit worthy of Captain Nemo, of Rossum's Universal Robots, of the inhabitants of the Island of Laputa; when in a few years some young American airmen are living in a space satellite partway to the moon, more than one of them will be able to look around and think: "It's a home just like Father used to make," if his father was an architect.

But in the rest of the arts, the arts that use words—

But here you may interrupt me, saying: "You've praised or characterized or made fun of the audience for music, dancing, painting, furniture, and architecture, yet each time you've talked only about the crust of the pie, about things that apply to hundreds of thousands, not to hundreds of millions. Most people don't listen to classical music at all, but to rock-and-roll or hillbilly songs or some album named *Music to Listen to Music By*; they've never seen any ballet except a television ballet or some musical comedy's last echo of *Rodeo*. When they go home they sit inside chairs like imitation-leather haystacks, chairs that were exhibited not at the Museum of Modern Art but at a convention of furniture dealers in High Point; if they buy a picture they buy it from the furniture dealer, and it was the furniture dealer who painted it; and their houses are split-level ranch-type rabbit warrens. Now that you've come to the 'arts that use words,' are you going to keep on talking about the unhappy few, or will you talk for a change about the happy many?"

I'll talk about the happy many; about the hundreds of millions, not the hundreds of thousands. Where words and the hundreds of thousands are concerned, plenty of good things happen—though to those who love words and the arts that use them, it may all seem far from plenty. We do have good writers, perhaps more than we deserve—and good readers, perhaps fewer than the writers deserve. But when it comes to tens of millions of readers, hundreds of millions of hearers and viewers, we are talking about a new and strange situation; and to understand why this situation is what it is, we need to go back

in time a little way, back to the days of Matthew Arnold and Queen
Victoria.

I I

We all remember that Queen Victoria, when she died in 1901, had
never got to see a helicopter, a television set, penicillin, an electric re-
frigerator; yet she *had* seen railroads, electric lights, textile machin-
ery, the telegraph—she came about midway in the industrial and
technological revolution that has transformed our world. But there are
a good many other things, of a rather different sort, that Queen
Victoria never got to see, because she came at the very beginning of
another sort of half-technological, half-cultural revolution. Let me
give some examples.

If the young Queen Victoria had said to the Duke of Wellington:
"Sir, the Bureau of Public Relations of Our army is in a deplorable
state," he would have answered: "What is a Bureau of Public
Relations, ma'am?" When he and his generals wanted to tell lies, they
had to tell them themselves; there was no organized institution set up
to do it for them. But of course Queen Victoria couldn't have made any
such remark, since she too had never heard of public relations. She
had never seen, or heard about, or dreamed of an advertising agency;
she had never seen—unless you count Barnum—a press agent; she
had never seen a photograph of a sex slaying in a tabloid—had never
seen a tabloid. People gossiped about her, but not in gossip columns;
she had never heard a commentator, a soap opera, a quiz program.
Queen Victoria—think of it!—had never heard a singing commercial,
never seen an advertisement beginning: *Science says . . .* and if she *had*
seen one she would only have retorted: "And what, pray, does the
Archbishop of Canterbury say? What does dear good Albert say?"

When some comedian or wit—Sydney Smith, for example—
told Queen Victoria jokes, they weren't supplied him by six well-paid
gag writers, but just occurred to him. When Disraeli and Gladstone
made speeches for her government, the speeches weren't written for
them by ghostwriters; when Disraeli and Gladstone sent her lovingly
or respectfully inscribed copies of their new books, they had written
the books themselves. There they were, with the resources of an em-
pire at their command, and they wrote the books themselves! And
Queen Victoria had to read the books herself: nobody was willing—
or able—to digest them for her in *Reader's Digest,* or to make movies
of them, or to make radio or television programs of them, so that she

could experience them painlessly and effortlessly. In those days people chewed their own food or went hungry; we have changed all that.

Queen Victoria never went to the movies and had an epic costing eight million dollars injected into her veins—she never went to the movies. She never read a drugstore book by Mickey Spillane; even if she had had a moral breakdown and had read a Bad Book, it would just have been *Under Two Flags* or something by Marie Corelli. She had never been interviewed by, or read the findings of, a Gallup Poll. She never read the report of a commission of sociologists subsidized by the Ford Foundation; she never Adjusted herself to her Group, or Shared the Experience of her Generation, or breathed a little deeper to feel herself a part of the Century of the Common Man—she *was* a part of it for almost two years, but she didn't know that that was what it was.

And all the other people in the world were just like Queen Victoria.

Isn't it plain that it is all *these* lacks that make Queen Victoria so old-fashioned, so finally and awfully different from us, rather than the fact that she never flew in an airplane, or took insulin, or had a hydrogen bomb dropped on her? Queen Victoria in a DC-7 would be Queen Victoria still—I can hear her saying to the stewardess: "We do not wish Dramamine"; but a Queen Victoria who listened every day to *John's Other Wife, Portia Faces Life,* and *Just Plain Bill*—that wouldn't be Queen Victoria at all!

There has been not one revolution, an industrial and technological revolution, there have been two; and this second, cultural revolution might be called the Revolution of the Word. People have learned to process words too—words, and the thoughts and attitudes they embody: we manufacture entertainment and consolation as efficiently as we manufacture anything else. One sees in stores ordinary old-fashioned oatmeal or cocoa; and, side by side with it, another kind called Instant Cocoa, Instant Oats. Most of our literature—I use the word in its broadest sense—is Instant Literature: the words are short, easy, instantly recognizable words, the thoughts are easy, familiar, instantly recognizable thoughts, the attitudes are familiar, already-agreed-upon, instantly acceptable attitudes. And if all this is true, can these productions be either truth or—in the narrower and higher sense—literature? The truth, as everybody knows, is sometimes complicated or hard to understand; is sometimes almost unrecognizably different from what we expected it to be; is sometimes difficult or, even, impossible to accept. But literature is necessarily mixed up with truth, isn't it?—our truth, truth as we know it; one can almost define literature as the union of a wish and a truth, or as a wish modified by a truth. But this Instant Literature is a wish reinforced by a cliché, a wish proved by a lie: Instant Literature—whether it is a soap opera, a Broadway play, or a historical, sexual best-seller—tells us always that life is not only what we wish it, but also what we think it. When people are treating him as a lunatic who has to be humored, Hamlet cries: "They fool me to the top of my bent"; and the makers of Instant Literature treat us exactly as advertisers treat the readers of advertisements—humor us, flatter our prejudices, pull our strings, show us that they know us for what they take us to be: impressionable, emotional, ignorant, somewhat weak-minded Common Men. They fool us to the top of our bent—and if we aren't fooled, they dismiss us as *a statistically negligible minority.*

An advertisement is a wish modified, if at all, by the Pure Food and Drug Act. Take a loaf of ordinary white bread that you buy at the grocery. As you eat it you know that you are eating it, and not the blotter, because the blotter isn't so bland; yet in the world of advertisements little boys ask their mother not to put any jam on their bread, it tastes so good without. This world of the advertisements is a literary world, of a kind: it is the world of Instant Literature. Think of some of the speeches we hear in political campaigns—aren't they too part of the world of Instant Literature? And the first story you read in *The Saturday Evening Post,* the first movie you go to at your neighborhood theater, the first dramatic program you hear on the radio, see on television—are these more like Grimm's tales and *Alice in Wonderland* and *The Three Sisters* and *Oedipus Rex* and Shakespeare and the Bible, or are they more like political speeches and advertisements?

The greatest American industry—why has no one ever said so?—is the industry of using words. We pay tens of millions of people to spend their lives lying to us, or telling us the truth, or supplying us with a nourishing medicinal compound of the two. All of us are living in the middle of a dark wood—a bright Technicolored forest—of words, words, words. It is a forest in which the wind is never still: there isn't a tree in the forest that is not, for every moment of its life and our lives, persuading or ordering or seducing or overawing us into buying this, believing that, voting for the other.

And yet, the more words there are, the simpler the words get. The professional users of words process their product as if it were baby food and we babies: all we have to do is open our mouths and swallow. Most of our mental and moral food is quick-frozen, pre-digested, spoon-fed. E. M. Forster has said: "The only thing we learn from spoon-feeding is the shape of the spoon." Not only is this true—pretty soon, if anything doesn't have the shape of that spoon we won't swallow it, we can't swallow it. Our century has produced some great and much good literature, but the habitual readers of Instant Literature cannot read it; nor can they read the great and good literature of the past.

If Queen Victoria had got to read the *Reader's Digest*—awful thought!—she would have loved it; and it would have changed her. Everything in the world, in the *Reader's Digest*—I am using it as a convenient symbol for all that is like it—is a palatable, timely, ultimately reassuring anecdote, immediately comprehensible to everybody over, and to many under, the age of eight. Queen Victoria would notice that Albert kept quoting, from Shakespeare—that the Archbishop of Canterbury kept quoting, from the Bible—things that were very different from anything in the *Reader's Digest*. Sometimes these sentences were not reassuring but disquieting, sometimes they had big words or hard thoughts in them, sometimes the interest in them wasn't human, but literary or divine. After a while Queen Victoria would want Shakespeare and the Bible—would want Albert, even—digested for her beforehand by the *Reader's Digest*. And a little further on in this process of digestion, she would look from the *Reader's Digest* to some magazine the size of your palm, called *Quick* or *Pic* or *Click* or *The Week in TV*, and a strange half-sexual yearning would move like musk through her veins, and she would—

But I cannot, I will not say it. You and I know how she and Albert will end: sitting before the television set, staring into it, silent; and inside the set, there are Victoria and Albert, staring into the television camera, silent, and the master of ceremonies is saying to them: "No, I think you will find that *Bismarck* is the capital of North Dakota!"

But for so long as she still reads, Queen Victoria will be able to get the Bible and Shakespeare—though not, alas! Albert—in some specially prepared form. Fulton Oursler or Fulton J. Sheen or a thousand others are always rewriting the Bible; there are many comic-book versions of Shakespeare; and only the other day I read an account of an interesting project of rewriting Shakespeare "for students":

Philadelphia, Pa. Feb. 1 (AP)
Two high school teachers have published a simplified version of Shakespeare's *Julius Caesar* and plan to do the same for *Macbeth*. Their goal is to make the plays more understandable to youth.

The teachers, Jack A. Waypen and Leroy S. Layton, say if the Bible can be revised and modernized why not Shakespeare? They made 1,122 changes in *Julius Caesar* from single words to entire passages. They modernized obsolete words and expressions and substituted "you" for "thee" and "thou."

Shakespeare had Brutus say in Act III, Scene I:

> *Fates, we will know your pleasures;*
> *That we shall die, we know; 'tis but the time*
> *And drawing days out, that men stand upon.*

In the Waypen-Layton version, Brutus says:

> *We will soon know what Fate decrees for us.*
> *That we shall die, we know. It's putting off*
> *The time of death that's of concern to men.*

Not being Shakespeare, I can't find a comment worthy of this, this project. I am tempted to say in an Elizabethan voice: "Ah, wayward Waypen, lascivious Layton, lay down thine errant pen!" And yet if I said this to them they would only reply earnestly, uncomprehendingly, sorrowfully: "Can't you give us some *con*structive criticism, not *de*structive? Why don't you say *your* errant pen, not *thine*? And *lascivious*! Mr. Jarrell, if you *have* to talk about that type subject, don't say *lascivious* Layton, say *sexy* Layton!"

Even Little Red Riding Hood is getting too hard for children, I read. The headline of the story is CHILD'S BOOKS BEING MADE MORE SIMPLE; the story comes from New York, is distributed by the International News Service, and is written by Miss Olga Curtis. Miss Curtis has interviewed Julius Kushner, the head of a firm that has been publishing children's books longer than anyone else in the country. He tells Miss Curtis:

" 'Non-essential details have disappeared from the 1953 Little Red Riding Hood story. Modern children enjoy their stories better stripped down to basic plot—for instance, Little Red Riding Hood meets wolf, Little Red Riding Hood escapes wolf. [I have a comment: the name Little Red Riding Hood seems to me both long and nonessential—why not call the child Red, and strip the story down to

Red meets wolf, Red escapes wolf? At this rate, one could tell a child all of Grimm's tales between dinner and bedtime.]

" 'We have to keep up with the mood of each generation,' Kushner explained. 'Today's children like stories condensed to essentials, and with visual and tactile appeal as well as interesting content.'

"Modernizing old favorites, Kushner said, is fundamentally a matter of simplifying. Kushner added that today's children's books are intended to be activity games as well as reading matter. He mentioned books that make noises when pressed, and books with pop-up three-dimensional illustrations as examples of publishers' efforts to make each book a teaching aid as well as a story."

As one reads one sees before one, as if in a vision, the children's book of the future: a book that, pressed, says: *I'm your friend*; teaches the child that Crime Does Not Pay; does not exceed thirty words; can be used as a heating pad if the electric blanket breaks down; and has three-dimensional illustrations dyed with harmless vegetable coloring matter and flavored with pure vanilla. I can hear the children of the future crying: "Mother, read us another vanilla book!"

But by this time you must be thinking, as I am, of one of the more frightening things about our age: that much of the body of common knowledge that educated people (and many uneducated people) once had, has disappeared or is rapidly disappearing. Fairy tales, myths, proverbs, history—the Bible and Shakespeare and Dickens, the *Odyssey* and *Gulliver's Travels*—these and all the things like them are surprisingly often things that most of an audience won't understand an allusion to, a joke about. These things were the ground on which the people of the past came together. Much of the wit or charm or elevation of any writing or conversation with an atmosphere depends upon this presupposed, easily and affectionately remembered body of common knowledge; because of it we understand things, feel about things, as human beings and not as human animals.

Who teaches us all this? Our families, our friends, our schools, society in general. Most of all, we hope, our schools. When I say *schools* I mean grammar schools and high schools and colleges—but the first two are more important. Most people still don't go to college, and those who do don't get there until they are seventeen or eighteen. "Give us a child until he is seven and he is ours," a Jesuit is supposed to have said; the grammar schools and high schools of the United States have a child for ten years longer, and then he is— whose? Shakespeare's? Leroy S. Layton's? The *Reader's Digest's*?

When students at last leave high school or go on to college, what are they like?

III

College teachers continually complain about their students' "lack of preparation," just as, each winter, they complain about the winter's lack of snow. Winters don't have as much snow as winters used to have: things are going to the dogs and always have been. The teachers tell one another stories about The Things Their Students Don't Know—it surprises you, after a few thousand such stories, that the students manage to find their way to the college. And yet, I have to admit, I have as many stories as the rest; and, veteran of such conversations as I am, I am continually being astonished at the things my students don't know.

One dark, cold, rainy night—the sort of night on which clients came to Sherlock Holmes—I read in a magazine that winters don't have as much snow as winters used to have; according to meteorologists, the climate *is* changing. Maybe the students are changing too. One is always hearing how much worse, or how much better, schools are than they used to be. But one isn't any longer going to grammar school, or to high school either; one isn't, like Arnold, a school inspector; whether one believes or disbelieves, blames or praises, how little one has to go on! Hearing one child say to another: "What does E come after in the alphabet?" makes a great, and perhaps unfair, impression on one. The child may not be what is called a random sample.

Sitting in my living room by the nice warm fire, and occasionally looking with pleasure at the rain and night outside—how glad I was that I wasn't in them!—I thought of some other samples I had seen just that winter, and I wasn't sure whether they were random, either. That winter I had had occasion to talk with some fifth-grade students and some eighth-grade students; I had gone to a class of theirs; I had even gone caroling, in a truck, with some Girl Scouts and their Scoutmistress, and had been dismayed at all the carols I didn't know—it was a part of my education that had been neglected.

I was not dismayed at the things the children hadn't known, I was overawed; there were very few parts of their education that had not been neglected. Half the fifth-grade children—you won't, just as I couldn't, believe this—didn't know who Jonah was; only a few had ever heard of King Arthur. When I asked an eighth-grade student about King Arthur she laughed at my question, and said: "Of course I know who King Arthur was." My heart warmed to her *of course*. But she didn't know who Lancelot was, didn't know who Guinevere was; she had never heard of Sir Galahad. I realized with a pang the truth of the line of poetry that speaks of "those familiar, now unfamiliar knights that sought the Grail." I left the Knights of the Round Table for history: she didn't know who Charlemagne was.

She didn't know who Charlemagne was! And she had never heard of Alexander the Great; her class had "had Rome," but she didn't remember anything about Julius Caesar, though she knew his name. I asked her about Hector and Achilles: she had heard the name Hector, but didn't know who he was; she had never heard of "that other one."

I remembered the college freshman who, when I had asked her about "They that take the sword shall perish with the sword," had answered: "It's Shakespeare, I think"; and the rest of the class hadn't even known it was Shakespeare. Nobody in the class had known the difference between faith and works. And how shocked they had all been—the Presbyterians especially—at the notion of predestination!

But all these, except for the question of where E comes in the alphabet, had been questions of literature, theology, and European history; maybe there *are* more important things for students to know. The little girl who didn't know who Charlemagne was had been taught, I found, to conduct a meeting, to nominate, and to second nominations; she had been taught—I thought this, though far-fetched, truly imaginative—the right sort of story to tell an eighteen-months-old baby; and she had learned in her Domestic Science class to bake a date pudding, to make a dirndl skirt, and from the remnants of the cloth to make a drawstring carryall. She could not tell me who Charlemagne was, it is true, but if I were an eighteen-months-old baby I could go to her and be sure of having her tell me the right sort of story. I felt a senseless depression at this; and thought, to alleviate it, of the date pudding she would be able to bake me.

I said to myself about her, as I was getting into the habit of saying about each new eighth-grade girl I talked to: "She must be an exception"; pretty soon I was saying: "She *must* be an exception!" If I had said this to her teacher she would have replied: "Exception indeed! She's a nice, normal, well-adjusted girl. She's one of the drum majorettes and she's Vice-President of the Student Body; she's had two short stories in the school magazine and she made her own formal for the Sadie Hawkins dance. She's an *exceptionally* normal girl!" And what could I have answered? "But she doesn't know who Charlemagne was"? You can see how ridiculous that would have sounded.

How many people cared whether or not she knew who Charlemagne was? How much good would knowing who Charlemagne was ever do her? Could you make a dirndl out of Charlemagne? make, even, a drawstring carryall? There was a chance—one chance in a hundred million—that someday, on a quiz program on the radio, someone would ask her who Charlemagne was. If she knew the audience would applaud in wonder, and the announcer would give her a refrigerator; if she didn't know the audience would groan in sympathy, and the announcer would give her a dozen cartons of soap powder. Euclid, I believe, once gave a penny to a student who asked: "What good will studying geometry do me?"—studying geometry made *him* a penny. But knowing who Charlemagne was would in all probability never make her a penny.

Another of the eighth-grade girls had shown me her Reader. All the eighth-grade students of several states use it; it is named *Adventures for Readers*. It has in it, just as Readers used to have in them, *The Man Without a Country* and *The Legend of Sleepy Hollow* and *Evangeline*, and the preface to *Adventures for Readers* says about their being there: "The competition of movies and radios has reduced the time young children spend with books. It is no longer supposed, as it once was, that reading skills are fully developed at the end of the sixth grade . . . Included are *The Man Without a Country, The Legend of Sleepy Hollow*, and *Evangeline*. These longer selections were once in every eighth-grade reading book. They have disappeared because in the original they are far too difficult for eighth grade readers. Yet, they are never presented for other years. If they are not read in the eighth grade, they are not read at all. In their simplified form they are once more available to young people to become a part of their background and experience."

I thought that in the next edition of *Adventures for Readers* the editors would have to substitute for the phrase *the competition of movies and radios*, the phrase *the competition of movies, radios, and television*: I thought of this thought for some time. But when I thought of Longfellow's being *in the original* far too difficult for eighth-grade students, I—I did not know what to think. How much more difficult everything is than it used to be!

I remembered a letter, one about difficult writers, that I had read in the *Saturday Review*. The letter said: "I have been wondering when somebody with an established reputation in the field of letters would stand tiptoe and slap these unintelligibles in the face. Now I hope the publishers will wake up and throw the whole egotistical, sophist lot of them down the drain. I hope that fifty years from now nobody will remember that Joyce or Stein or James or Proust or Mann ever lived."

I knew that such feelings are not peculiar to our own place or age. Once while looking at an exhibition of Victorian posters and paintings and newspapers and needlework, I had read a page of the London *Times*, printed in the year 1851, that had on it a review of a new book by Alfred Tennyson. After several sentences about what was wrong with this book, the reviewer said: "Another fault is not particular to *In Memoriam*; it runs through all Mr. Tennyson's poetry— we allude to his obscurity." And yet the reviewer would not have alluded to Longfellow's obscurity; those Victorians for whom everything else was too difficult still understood and delighted in Longfellow. But Tennyson had been too obscure for some of them, just as Longfellow was getting to be too obscure for some of us, as our "reading skills" got less and less "fully developed."

This better-humored writer of the London *Times* had not hoped that in fifty years nobody would remember that Tennyson had ever lived; and this is fortunate, since he would not have got his wish. But I thought that the writer to *The Saturday Review* might well get, might already be getting, a part of his wish. How many people there were all around him who did not remember—who indeed had never learned—that Proust or James or Mann or Joyce had ever lived! How many of them there were, and how many more of their children there were, who did not remember—who indeed had never learned—that Jonah or King Arthur or Galahad or Charlemagne had ever lived! And in the end all of us would die, and not know, then, that anybody had ever lived: and the writer to the *Saturday Review* would have got not part of his wish but all of it.

And if, in the meantime, some people grieved to think of so much gone and so much more to go, they were the exception. Or, rather, the exceptions: millions and millions—tens of millions, even—of exceptions. There were enough exceptions to make a good-sized country; I thought, with pleasure, of walking through the streets of that country and having the children tell me who Charlemagne was.

I decided not to think of Charlemagne any more, and turned my eyes from my absurd vision of the white-bearded king trying to learn to read, running his big finger slowly along under the words . . . My samples weren't really random, I knew; I was letting myself go, being exceptionally unjust to that exceptionally normal girl and the school that had helped to make her so. She was being given an education suitable for the world she was to use it in; my quarrel was not so much with her education as with her world, and our quarrels with the world are like our quarrels with God: no matter how right we are, we are wrong. But who wants to be right all the time? I thought, smiling; and said goodbye to Charlemagne with the same smile.

Instead of thinking, I looked at *The New York Times Book Review*; there in the midst of so many books, I could surely forget that some people don't read any. And after all, as Rilke says in one of his books, we are—some of us are—*beaten at / By books as if by perpetual bells*; we can well, as he bids us, *rejoice / When between two books the sky shines to you, silent*. In the beginning was the Word, and man has made books of it.

I read quietly along, but the review I was reading was continued on page 47; and as I was turning to page 47 I came to an advertisement, a two-page advertisement of the Revised Standard Version of the Bible. It was a sober, careful, authorized sort of advertisement, with many testimonials of clergymen, but it was, truly, an advertisement. It said:

"In these anxious days, the Bible offers a practical antidote for sorrow, cynicism, and despair. But the King James version is often difficult reading.

"If *you* have too seldom opened your Bible because the way it is written makes it hard for you to understand, the Revised Standard Version can bring you an exciting new experience.

"Here is a Bible so enjoyable you find you pick it up twice as often . . ."

Tennyson and Longfellow and the Bible—what *was* there that wasn't difficult reading? And a few days before that I had torn out of the paper—I got it and read it again, and it was hard for me to read it—a Gallup Poll that began: "Although the United States has the highest level of formal education in the world, fewer people here read books than in any other major democracy." It didn't compare us with minor autocracies, which are probably a lot worse. It went on to say that "fewer than one adult American in every five was found to be reading a book at the time of the survey. [Twenty years ago, 29 percent were found to be reading a book; today only 17 percent are.] In England, where the typical citizen has far less formal schooling than the typical citizen here, nearly three times as many read books. Even among American college graduates fewer than half read books."

It went on and on; I was so tired that, as I read, the phrase *read books* kept beating in my brain, and getting mixed up with Charlemagne: compared to other major monarchs, I thought sleepily, fewer than one-fifth of Charlemagne reads books. I read on as best I could, but I thought of the preface to *Adventures for Readers*, and the letter to the *Saturday Review*, and the advertisement in *The New York Times Book Review*, and the highest level of formal education in the world, and they all went around and around in my head and said to me an advertisement named *Adventures for Non-Readers*:

"In these anxious days, reading books offers a practical antidote to sorrow, cynicism, and despair. But books are often, in the original, difficult reading.

"If *you* have too seldom opened books because the way they are written makes them hard for you to understand, our Revised Standard Versions of books, in their simplified, televised form, can bring you an exciting new experience.

"Here are books so enjoyable you find you turn them on twice as often."

I shook myself; I was dreaming. As I went to bed the words of the eighth-grade class's teacher, when the class got to *Evangeline*, kept echoing in my ears: "We're coming to a long poem now, boys and girls. Now don't be babies and start counting the pages." I lay there like a baby, counting the pages over and over, counting the pages.

[*1958/SHS*]

Against
Abstract Expressionism

A DEVIL'S ADVOCATE OPPOSES, as logically and forcibly as he can, the canonization of a new saint. What he says is dark, and serves the light. The devil himself, if one can believe Goethe, is only a sort of devil's advocate. Here I wish to act as one for abstract expressionism.

Continued long enough, a quantitative change becomes qualitative. The latest tradition of painting, abstract expressionism, seems to me revolutionary. It is not, I think, what it is sometimes called: the purified essence of that earlier tradition which has found a temporary conclusion in painters like Bonnard, Picasso, Matisse, Klee, Kokoschka. It is the specialized, intensive exploitation of one part of such painting, and the rejection of other parts and of the whole.

Earlier painting is a kind of metaphor: the world of the painting itself, of the oil-and-canvas objects and their oil-and-canvas relations, is one that stands for—that has come into being because of—the world of flesh-and-blood objects and their flesh-and-blood relations, the "very world, which is the world / Of all of us,—the place where, in the end, / We find our happiness or not at all." The relation between the representing and the represented world sometimes is a direct, mimetic one; but often it is an indirect, far-fetched, surprising relation, so that it is the difference between the subject and the painting of it that is insisted upon, and is a principal source of our pleasure. In the metaphors of painting, as in those of poetry, we are awed or dazed to find things superficially so unlike, fundamentally so like; superficially so like, fundamentally so unlike. Solemn things are painted gaily; overwhelmingly expressive things—the Flagellation, for instance—painted inexpressively; Vollard is painted like an apple, and an apple like the Fall; the female is made male or sexless (as in Michelangelo's *Night*), and a dreaming, acquiescent femininity is made to transfigure a body factually masculine (as in so many of the nude youths on the ceiling of the Sistine Chapel). Between the object and its representation there is an immense distance: within this distance much of painting lives.

All this sums itself up for me in one image. In Georges de La Tour's *St. Sebastian Mourned by St. Irene* there is, in the middle of a dark passage, a light one: four parallel cylinders diagonally intersected by four parallel cylinders; they look like a certain sort of wooden fence, as a certain sort of cubist painter would have painted it; they are the hands, put together in prayer, of one of St. Irene's companions. As one looks at what has been put into—withheld from—the hands, one is conscious of a mixture of emotion and empathy and contemplation; one is moved, and is unmoved, and is something else one has no name for, that transcends either affect or affectlessness. The hands are truly like hands, yet they are almost more truly unlike hands; they resemble (as so much of art resembles) the symptomatic gestures of psychoanalysis, half the expression of a wish and half the defense against the wish. But these parallel cylinders of La Tour's— these hands at once oil-and-canvas and flesh-and-blood; at once dynamic processes in the virtual space of the painting, and spiritual gestures in the "very world" in which men are martyred, are mourned, and paint the mourning and the martyrdom—these parallel cylinders are only, in an abstract expressionist painting, four parallel cylinders: they are what they are.

You may say, more cruelly: "If they are part of such a painting, by what miracle have they remained either cylindrical or parallel? In this world bursting with action and accident—the world, that is, of abstract expressionism—are they anything more than four homologous strokes of the paintbrush, inclinations of the paint bucket; the memory of four gestures, and of the four convulsions of the Unconscious that accompanied them? . . . We need not ask—they are what they are: four oil-and-canvas processes in an oil-and-canvas continuum; and if, greatly daring, we venture beyond this world of the painting itself, we end only in the painter himself. A universe has been narrowed into what lies at each end of a paintbrush."

But ordinarily such painting—a specialized, puritanical reduction of earlier painting—is presented to us as its final evolution, what it always ought to have been and therefore "really" was. When we are told (or, worse still, shown) that painting "really" is "nothing but" this, we are being given one of those definitions which explain out of existence what they appear to define, and put a simpler entity in its place. If this is all that painting is, why, what painting was was hardly painting. Everyone has met some of the rigorously minded people who carry this process of reasoning to its conclusion, and value Piero della Francesca and Goya and Cézanne only in so far as their paintings are, in adulterated essence, the paintings of Jackson Pollock. Similarly, a few centuries ago, one of those mannerist paintings in which a Virgin's face is setting after having swallowed alum must have seemed, to a contemporary, what a Donatello Virgin was "really" intended to be, "essentially" was.

The painting before abstract expressionism might be compared to projective geometry: a large three-dimensional world of objects and their relations, of lives, emotions, significances, is represented by a small cross section of the rays from this world, as they intersect a plane. Everything in the cross section has two different kinds of relations: a direct relation to the other things in the cross section, and an indirect—so to speak, transcendental—relation to what it represents in the larger world. And there are also in the small world of the picture process many absences or impossible presences, things which ought to be there but are not, things which could not possibly be there but are. The painter changes and distorts, simplifies or elaborates the cross section; and the things in the larger world resist, and are changed by, everything he does, just as what he has done is changed by their resistance. Earlier painters, from Giotto to Picasso, have dealt with two worlds and the relations between the two: their painting is a heterogeneous, partly indirect, many-leveled, extraordinarily complicated process. Abstract expressionism has kept one part of this process, but has rejected as completely as it could the other part and all the relations that depend on the existence of this other part; it has substituted for a heterogeneous, polyphonic process a homogeneous, homophonic process. One sees in abstract expressionism the terrible aesthetic disadvantages of directness and consistency. Perhaps painting can do without the necessity of imitation; can it do without the possibility of distortion?

As I considered some of the phrases that have been applied to abstract expressionism—revolutionary; highly non-communicative; non-representational; uncritical; personal; maximizing randomness; without connection with literature and the other arts; spontaneous;

exploiting chance or unintended effects; based on gesture; seeking a direct connection with the Unconscious; affirming the individual; rejecting the external world; emphasizing action and the process of making the picture—it occurred to me that each of them applied to the work of a painter about whom I had just been reading. She has been painting only a little while, yet most of her paintings have already found buyers, and her friends hope, soon, to use the money to purchase a husband for the painter. She is a chimpanzee at the Baltimore Zoo. Why should I have said to myself, as I did say: "I am living in the first age that has ever bought a chimpanzee's paintings"? It would not have occurred to me to buy her pictures—it would not have occurred to me even to get her to paint them; yet in the case of action painting, is it anything but unreasoning prejudice which demands that the painter be a man? Hath not an ape hands? Hath not an animal an Unconscious, and quite a lot less Ego and Superego to interfere with its operations?

I reminded myself of this as, one Saturday, I watched on Channel 9 a chimpanzee painting; I did not even say to myself, "I am living in the first age that has ever televised a chimpanzee painting." I watched him (since he was dressed in a jumper, and named Jeff, I judged that he was a male) dispassionately. His painting, I confess, did not interest me; I had seen it too many times before. But the way in which he painted it! He was, truly, magistral. He did not look at his model once; indeed, he hardly looked even at the canvas. Sometimes his brush ran out of paint and he went on with the dry brush—they had to remind him that the palette was there. He was the most active, the most truly sincere, painter that I have ever seen; and yet, what did it all produce?—nothing but that same old abstract expressionist painting . . .

I am joking. But I hope it is possible to say of this joke what Goethe said of Lichtenberg's: "Under each of his jokes there is a problem." There is an immense distance between my poor chimpanzee's dutiful, joyful paintings and those of Jackson Pollock. The elegance, force, and command of Pollock's best paintings are apparent at a glance—are, indeed, far more quickly and obviously apparent than the qualities of a painter like Chardin. But there is an immense distance, too, between Pollock's paintings and Picasso's; and this not entirely the result of a difference of native genius. If Picasso had limited himself to painting the pictures of Jackson Pollock—limited himself, that is, to the part of his own work that might be called abstract expressionism—could he have been as great a painter as he is?

I ask this as a typical, general question; if I spoke particularly I should of course say: If Picasso limited himself in anything he would not be Picasso: he loves the world so much he wants to steal it and eat it. Pollock's anger at things is greater than Picasso's, but his appetite for them is small; is neurotically restricted. Much of the world—much, too, of the complication and contradiction, the size and depth of the essential process of earlier painting—is inaccessible to Pollock. It has been made inaccessible by the provincialism that is one of the marks of our age.

As I go about the world I see things (people; their looks and feelings and thoughts; the things their thoughts have made, and the things that neither they nor their thoughts had anything to do with making: the whole range of the world) that, I cannot help feeling, Piero della Francesca or Bruegel or Goya or Cézanne would paint if they were here now—could not resist painting. Then I say to my wife, sadly: "What a pity we didn't live in an age when painters were still interested in the world!" This is an exaggeration, of course; even in the recent past many painters have looked at the things of this world and seen them as marvelously as we could wish. But ordinarily, except for photographers and illustrators—and they aren't at all the same— the things of our world go unseen, unsung. All that the poet must do, Rilke said, is praise: to look at what is, and to see that it is good, and to make out of it what is at once the same and better, is to praise. Doesn't the world need the painter's praise any more?

Malraux, drunk with our age, can say about Cézanne: "It is not the mountain he wants to realize but the picture." All that Cézanne said and did was not enough to make Malraux understand what no earlier age could have failed to understand: that to Cézanne the realization of the picture necessarily involved the realization of the mountain. And whether we like it or not, notice it or not, the mountain is still there to be realized. Man and the world are all that they ever were—their attractions are, in the end, irresistible; the painter will not hold out against them long.

[1957/KA]

An Unread Book

A MAN ON A PARK BENCH has a lonely final look, as if to say: "Reduce humanity to its ultimate particles and you end here; beyond this single separate being you cannot go." But if you look back into his life you cannot help seeing that he is separated off, not separate—is a later, singular stage of an earlier plural being. All the tongues of men were baby talk to begin with: go back far enough and which of us knew where he ended and Mother and Father and Brother and Sister began? The singular subject in its objective universe has evolved from that original composite entity—half subjective, half objective, having its own ways and laws and language, its own life and its own death—the family.

The Man Who Loved Children knows as few books have ever known—knows specifically, profoundly, exhaustively—what a family is: if all mankind had been reared in orphan asylums for a thousand years, it could learn to have families again by reading *The Man Who Loved Children*. Tolstoy said that "each unhappy family is unhappy in a way of its own"—a way that it calls happiness; the Pollits, a very unhappy family, are unhappy in a way almost unbelievably their own. And yet as we read we keep thinking: "How can anything so completely itself, so completely different from me and mine, be, somehow, me and mine?" The book has an almost frightening power of remembrance; and so much of our earlier life is repressed, forgotten, both in the books we read and the memories we have, that this seems friendly of the book, even when what it reminds us of is terrible. A poem says, "O to be a child again, just for tonight!" As you read *The Man Who Loved Children* it is strange to have the wish come true.

When you begin to read about the Pollits you think with a laugh, "They're wonderfully plausible." When you have read fifty or a hundred pages you think with a desperate laugh, or none, that they are wonderfully implausible—implausible as mothers and fathers and children, in isolation, *are* implausible. There in that warm, dark, second womb, the bosom of the family, everything is carried far past plausibility: a family's private life is as immoderate and insensate, compared to its public life, as our thoughts are, compared to our speech. (O secret, satisfactory, shameless things! things that, this side of Judgment Day, no stranger ever will discover.) Dostoevsky wrote: "Almost every reality, even if it has its own immutable laws, nearly always is incredible as well as improbable. Occasionally, moreover, the more real, the more improbable it is." Defending the reality of his own novels, he used to say that their improbable extremes were far closer to everyday reality than the immediately plausible, statistical naturalism of the books everyone calls lifelike; as a proof he would read from newspaper clippings accounts of the characters and events of a Dostoevsky novel. Since Christina Stead combines with such extremes an immediately plausible naturalism, she could find her own newspaper clippings without any trouble; but the easiest defense of all would be simply for her to say, "Remember?" We do remember; and, remembering, we are willing to admit the normality of the abnormal—are willing to admit that we never understand the normal better than when it has been allowed to reach its full growth and become the abnormal.

II

Inside the Pollit family the ordinary mitigated, half-appreciative opposition of man and woman has reached its full growth. Sam and his wife Henny are no longer on speaking terms; they quarrel directly, but the rest of the time one parent says to a child what the child repeats to the other parent. They are true opposites: Sam's blue-eyed, white-gold-haired, pale fatness is closer to Henny's haggard saffron-skinned blackness than his light general spirit is to her dark particular one. The children lean to one side of the universe or the other and ask for understanding: "Sam's answers were always to the point, full of facts; while the more one heard of Henny's answer, the more intriguing it was, the less was understood. Beyond Sam stood the physical world, and beyond Henny—what?"

Like Henny herself are Henny's *treasure drawers*, a chaos of laces, ribbons, gloves, flowers, buttons, hairpins, pots of rouge, bits of mascara, foreign coins, medicines (Henny's own "aspirin, phenacetin, and pyramidon"); often, as a treat, the children are allowed to *look in the drawers*. "A musky smell always came from Henrietta's room, a combination of dust, powder, scent, body odors that stirred the children's blood, deep, deep." At the center of the web of odors is their *Mothering, Moth, Motherbunch*, "like a tall crane in the reaches of the river, standing with one leg crooked and listening. She would look fixedly at her vision and suddenly close her eyes. The child watching (there was always one) would see nothing but the huge eyeball in its glove of flesh, deep-sunk in the wrinkled skull-hole, the dark circle round it and the eyebrow far above, as it seemed, while all her skin, unrelieved by brilliant eye, came out in its real shade, burnt olive. She looked formidable in such moments, in her intemperate silence, the bitter set of her discolored mouth with her uneven slender gambler's nose and scornful nostrils, lengthening her sharp oval face, pulling the dry skinfolds. Then when she opened her eyes there would shoot out a look of hate, horror, passion, or contempt."

To the children she is "a charming, slatternly witch; everything that she did was right, right, her right: she claimed this right to do what she wished because of all her sufferings, and all the children believed in her rights." She falls in a faint on the floor, and the accustomed children run to get pillows, watch silently "the death-like face, drawn and yellow under its full black hair," the "poor naked neck with its gooseflesh." She is nourished on "tea and an aspirin"; "tea, almost black, with toast and mustard pickles"; a "one-man curry" of "a bit of cold meat, a hard-boiled egg, some currants, and an onion"— as her mother says, "All her life she's lived on gherkins and chilies and Worcestershire sauce . . . She preferred pickled walnuts at school to candy." She sews, darns, knits, embroiders. School had taught her only three things: to play Chopin ("there would steal through the listening house flights of notes, rounded as doves, wheeling over housetops in the sleeping afternoon, Chopin or Brahms, escaping from Henny's lingering, firm fingers"), to paint watercolors, and to sew. It is life that has taught her to give it "her famous *black look*"; to run through once again the rhymes, rituals, jokes, sayings, stories—inestimable stones, unvalued jewels—that the children beg her for; to drudge at old tasks daily renewed; to lie and beg and borrow and sink deeper into debt; to deal the cards out for the game she cheats at and has never won, an elaborate two-decked solitaire played "feverishly, until her mind was a darkness, until all the memories and the ease had long since drained away . . . leaving her sitting there, with blackened eyes, a yellow skin, and straining wrinkles." Marriage, that had found Henny a "gentle, neurotic creature wearing silk next to the skin and expecting to have a good time at White House receptions," has left her "a thin, dark scarecrow," a "dirty cracked plate, that's just what I am." In the end, her black hair swiftly graying, she has turned into "a dried-up, skinny, funny old woman" who cries out, "I'm an old woman, your mother's an old woman"; who cries out, "Isn't it rotten luck? Isn't every rotten thing in life rotten luck?"

All Henny's particularities, peculiarities, sum themselves up into a strange general representativeness, so that she somehow stands for all women. She shares helplessly "the natural outlawry of womankind," of creatures who, left-handed, sidelong in the right-handed, upright world of men, try to get around by hook or by crook, by a last weak winning sexual smile, the laws men have made for them. Henny "was one of those women who secretly sympathize with all women against all men; life was a rotten deal, with men holding all the aces." Women, as people say, *take everything personally*—even Henny's generalizations of all existence are personal, and so living. As she does her "microscopic darning," sometimes a "small mouse would run past, or even boldly stand and inquisitively stare at her. Henny would look down at its monstrous pointed little face calmly and go on with her work." She accepts the "sooty little beings" as "house guests" except when she wakes to smell the "musky penetrating odor of their passage"; or when she looks at one and sees that it is a pregnant mother; or when the moralist her husband says that mice bring germs, and obliges her to kill them. She kills them; "nevertheless, though she despised animals, she felt involuntarily that the little marauder was much like herself, trying to get by." Henny is an involuntary, hysterical moralist or none; as her creator says, "Henny was beautifully, wholeheartedly vile: she asked no quarter and gave none to the foul world." And yet, and so, your heart goes out to her, because she is miserably what life has made her, and makes her misery her only real claim on existence. Her husband wants to be given credit for everything, even his mistakes—especially his mistakes, which are always well-meaning, right-minded ones that in a better world would be unmistaken. Henny is an honest liar; even Sam's truths are ways to get his own way.

But you remember best about Henny what is worst about Henny: her tirades. These are too much and (to tell the truth) too many for us; but if anything so excessive is to be truthfully represented, that is almost inevitable. These tirades are shameful, insensate, and interminable, including and exaggerating all that there is; looking at the vile world, her enemy, Henny cries: "Life is nothing but rags and tags, and filthy rags at that. Why was I ever born?" Before long the reader has impressed upon his shrinking flesh the essential formula of Henny's rhetoric. A magnifying word like *great* is followed by an intensive like *vile, filthy, rotten, foul*: Henny's nose has been shoved into the filth of things, so that she sees them magnified, consummately foul, as Swift saw the bodies and the physiological processes of the people of Brobdingnag. At the "mere sight of the great flopping monster" her stepdaughter, Henny cries out: "She's that Big-Me all over again. Always with her eyes glued to a book. I feel like snatching the rotten thing from her and pushing it into her eyes, her great lolling head . . . She crawls, I can hardly touch her, she reeks with her slime and filth—she doesn't notice! I beat her until I can't stand—she doesn't notice! When I fall on the floor, she runs and gets a pillow and at that I suppose she's better than her murderer of a father who lets me lie there."

The girl sewing a fine seam, the watercolor painter, the piano player has stepped from the altar into the filth of marriage and childbearing and child rearing; and forever after she can tell the truth about it—the naked, physiological, excremental truth—only in physiological, excremental terms. It is women who must clean up the mess men make, the mess everything makes; the hag Henny stares out at "the darn muck of existence," the foul marsh above which the dwellings of men rise on precarious stilts, and screams at it her daemonic tirades. She knows. Whatever men say, women know; as an old woman says chuckling, an accessory to the fact: "Life's dirty, isn't it, Louie, eh? Don't you worry what they say to you, we're all dirty." Sometimes even Henny absently consents to it: "she looked vaguely about, sniffing that familiar smell of fresh dirtiness which belongs to mankind's extreme youth, a pleasant smell to mothers."

When Henny is "defenseless, in one of those absences of hatred, aimless lulls that all long wars must have," she looks at us "strangely, with her great, brown eyes," and even her husband's "heart would be wrung with their unloving beauty." Our own hearts are wrung by Henny, when, "beginning to cry like a little girl, and putting the fold of her dressing gown to her face," she cries, "Ai, ai";

when she feels "a curious, dull, but new sensation," and awakening from "a sort of sullen absence . . . knew what was happening: her heart was breaking. That moment, it broke for good and all"; when, no longer able to "stand any of this life any longer," in a sort of murderous delirium she beats her favorite child "across the head, screaming at him, 'Die, die, why don't you all die and leave me to die or to hang; fall down, die; what do I care?' "—while her son, "not thinking of defending himself," cries "brokenly, in a warm, pleading voice, 'Mother, don't, don't, Mother, Mother, Mother, Mother, Mother, don't, please, please, Mother, Mother' "; when her love affair—an affair like a piece of dirty newspaper—reaches its abject public end; when, a few days after death, "the image of Henny started to roam . . . the window curtains flapped, the boards creaked, a mouse ran, and Henny was there, muttering softly to herself, tapping a sauce pan, turning on the gas. The children were not frightened. They would say, laughing, somewhat curious, 'I thought I heard Mothering,' and only Ernie or Tommy . . . would look a bit downcast; and perhaps Chappy missed her, that queer, gypsylike, thin, tanned, pointed face with big black eyes rolling above him"; and when, last of all, the storms of July thunder above her grave, and "it was as if Henny too had stormed, but in another room in the universe, which was now under lock and key."

III

There is something grand and final, indifferent to our pity, about Henny: one of those immortal beings in whom the tragedy of existence is embodied, she looks unseeingly past her mortal readers. The absurdity and hypocrisy of existence are as immortal in her husband Sam.

All of us can remember waking from a dream and uselessly longing to go back into the dream. In Sam the longing has been useful: he has managed to substitute for everyday reality an everyday dream, a private work of art—complete with its own language, customs, projects, ideology—in which, occasionally pausing for applause, he goes on happily and foolishly and self-righteously existing. As he reads about Henny the reader feels, in awe, how terrible it must be to be Henny; as he reads about Sam he blurts, "Oh, please don't let me be like Sam!" Sam is more than human; occasionally he has doubts, and is merely human for a moment—so that our laughter and revulsion cease, and we uneasily pity him—but then the moment is over and he is himself again.

Often Henny, in defeated misery, plunges to rock bottom, and gropes among the black finalities of existence; up above, in the holy light, the busy Sam, "painting and scraping and singing and jigging from the crack of dawn," clambers happily about in the superstructure of life. There among his own children, his own speeches, his own small zoo, pond, rockery, aquaria, museum ("What a world of things he had to have to keep himself amused!"), the hobbyist, naturalist, bureaucrat, democrat, moralist, atheist, teetotaler, ideologue, sermonizer, sentimentalist, prude, hypocrite, idealist Sam can say, like Kulygin: "I am satisfied, I am satisfied, I am satisfied!" If he had not been married he would not have remembered that he was mortal. Sam "was naturally lighthearted, pleasant, all generous effusion and responsive emotion . . . Tragedy itself could not worm its way by any means into his heart. Such a thing would have made him ill or mad, and he was all for health, sanity, success, and human love."

Sam's vanity is ultimate: the occasional objectivity or common decency that makes us take someone else's part, not our own, is impossible for Sam, who is right because he is Sam. It is becoming for Sam to love children so (Henny says in mockery, "The man who loves children!" and gives the book its title), since he himself is partly an adult and partly a spoiled child in his late thirties; even his playing with words, the grotesque self-satisfying language he makes for himself, is the work of a great child, and exactly right for children. After he has had to live among adults for eight months, he seems sobered and commonplace; but at home among the children, he soon is Sam again. At home "the children listened to every word he said, having been trained to him from the cradle." He addresses them "in that low, humming, cello voice and with that tender, loving face he had when beginning one of his paeans or dirges"; his speech has "a low insinuating humming that enchanted the sulky ear-guards and got straight to their softened brains." The children listen openmouthed; but Sam's mouth is open wider still, as he wonders at himself. "Were not his own children happy, healthy, and growing like weeds, merely through having him to look up to and through knowing that he was always righteous, faithful, and understanding?" It is wonderful to him that he orginates independently the discoveries of the great: "The theory of the expanding universe . . . it came to me by myself . . . And very often I have an idea and then find months, years later, that a man like our very great Woodrow Wilson or Lloyd George or Einstein has had it too."

Kim was the Little Friend of all the World; Sam is its Little

Father. He wishes that he "had a black baby too. A tan or Chinese one—every kind of baby. I am sorry that the kind of father I can be is limited." A relative objects, to his not sending the children to Sunday school, "When they grow up they will have nothing to believe in." Sam replies: "Now they believe in their poor little Dad: and when they grow up they'll believe in Faraday, Clerk Maxwell, and Einstein." Their poor little Dad is for the Pollit children a jealous God, one who interferes with everything they do and still is not satisfied, but imports children from outside the family so that he can interfere with *them.* He makes each of the children tell him what the others are doing "in the secrecy of their rooms or the nooks they had made their own. With what surprise and joy he would seize on all this information of his loving spies, showing them traits of character, drawing a moral conclusion from everything!" Sam loves and enjoys the children, the children admire and enjoy Sam; and yet there is nothing too awful for him to do to them and feel that he is right to do to them—the worst things are so mean and petty, are full of such selfishness and hypocrisy, are so *impossible,* that even as you believe you cry, "It's unbelievable!"

We can bear to read about Sam, a finally exasperating man, only because he is absolutely funny and absolutely true. He is so entirely real that it surprises the reader when an occasional speech of his—for instance, some of his *Brave New World* talk about the future—is not convincing. Perhaps different parts of his speech have different proportions of imagination and fancy and memory: it doesn't seem that the same process (in Christina Stead, that is) has produced everything. But Sam is an Anglo-Saxon buffoon, hypocrite, quite as extraordinary as the most famous of Dostoevsky's or Saltykov-Shchedrin's Slavic ones. Sam asks for everything and with the same breath asks to be admired for never having asked for anything; his complete selfishness sees itself as a complete selflessness. When he has been out of work for many months, it doesn't bother him: "About their money, as about everything, he was vague and sentimental. But in a few months he would be earning, and in the meantime, he said, 'It was only right that the mother too should fend for her offspring.' " One morning there are no bananas. "Sam flushed with anger. 'Why aren't there any bananas? I don't ask for much. I work to make the Home Beautiful for one and all, and I don't even get bananas. Everyone knows I like bananas. If your mother won't get them, why don't some of you? Why doesn't anyone think of poor little Dad?' He continued, looking in a most pathetic way round the table, at the abashed children, 'It isn't much. I give you kids a house and a wonderful playground of nature and fish and marlin and everything, and I can't even get a little banana.' " Sam moralizes, rationalizes, anything whatsoever: the children feel that they have to obey, *ought* to obey, his least whim. There is an abject reality about the woman Henny, an abject ideality about the man Sam; he is so idealistically, hypocritically, transcendentally masculine that a male reader worries, "Ought I to be a man?"

Every family has words and phrases of its own; that ultimate family, the Pollits, has what amounts to a whole language of its own. Only Sam can speak it, really, but the children understand it and mix phrases from it into their ordinary speech. (If anyone feels that it is unlikely for a big grown man to have a little language of his own, let me remind him of that great grown man Swift.) Children's natural distortions of words and the distortions of Artemus Ward and Uncle Remus are the main sources of this little language of Sam's. As we listen to Sam talking in it, we exclaim in astonished veneration, "It's so!" Many of the words and phrases of this language are so natural that we admire Christina Stead for having invented them at the same instant at which we are thinking, "No, nobody, not even Christina Stead, could have made *that* up!"——they have the uncreated reality of any perfect creation. I quote none of the language: a few sentences could show neither how marvelous it is nor how marvelously it expresses Sam's nature, satisfies his every instinct. When he puts his interminable objections and suggestions and commands into the joke terms of this unctuous, wheedling, insinuating language——what a tease the wretch is!——it is as if to make the least disagreement on the part of the children a moral impossibility.

His friend Saul says to Sam: "Sam, when you talk, you know you create a world." It is true; and the world he creates is a world of wishes or wish-fantasies. What Freud calls the primary principle, the pleasure principle, is always at work in that world—the claims of the reality principle, of the later ego, have been abrogated. It is a world of free fantasy: "Sam began to wonder at himself: why did he feel free? He had always been free, a free man, a free mind, a freethinker."

Bismarck said: "You can do anything with children if you will only play with them." All Bismarck's experience of mankind has been concentrated into knowledge, and the knowledge has been concentrated into a single dispassionate sentence. Sam has, so to speak, based his life on this sentence; but he has taken literally the *children* and *play* that are figurative in Bismarck's saying. Children are damp clay which Sam can freely and playfully manipulate. Yet even there he prefers "the very small boys" and "the baby girls"; the larger boys, the girls of school age, somehow cramp his style. (His embryonic love affair is an affair not with a grown-up but with the child-woman Gillian.) He reasons and moralizes mainly to force others to accept his fantasy, but the reasoning and moralizing have become fantastic in the process.

In psychoanalytical textbooks we read of the mechanism of denial. Surely Sam was its discoverer: there is no reality—except Henny—stubborn enough to force Sam to recognize its existence if its existence would disturb his complacency. We feel for Sam the wondering pity we feel for a man who has put out his own eyes and gets on better without them. To Sam everything else in the world is a means to an end, and the end is Sam. He is insensate. So, naturally, he comes out ahead of misunderstanding, poverty, Henny, anything. Life itself, in Johnson's phrase, *dismisses him to happiness*: " 'All things work together for the good of him that loves the Truth,' said the train to Sam as it rattled down towards the Severn, 'all things—work—together—for the good—of him—that loves—the TRUTH!' "

Sam is one of those providential larger-than-life-size creations, like Falstaff, whom we wonder and laugh at and can't get enough of; like Queen Elizabeth wanting to see Falstaff in love, we want to see Sam in books called *Sam at School, Sam in the Arctic, Grandfather Sam*. About him there is the grandeur of completeness: beyond Sam we cannot go. Christina Stead's understanding of him is without hatred; her descriptions of his vilest actions never forget how much fun it is to be Sam, and she can describe Sam's evening walk with his child in sentences that are purely and absolutely beautiful: "Pale as a candle flame in the dusk, tallow-pale, he stalked along, holding her hand, and Louie looked up and beyond him at the enfeebled stars. Thus, for many years, she had seen her father's head, a ghostly earth flame against the heavens, from her little height. Sam looked down on the moon of her face; the day-shine was enough still to light the eyeballs swimming up to him."

IV

A description of Louie ought to begin with *Louie knew she was the ugly duckling*. It is ugly ducklings, grown either into swans or into remarkably big, remarkably ugly ducks, who are responsible for most works of art; and yet how few of these give a truthful account of what it was like to be an ugly duckling!—it is almost as if the grown, successful swan had repressed most of the memories of the duckling's miserable, embarrassing, magical beginnings. (These memories are deeply humiliating in two ways: they remind the adult that he once was more ignorant and gullible and emotional than he is; and they remind him that he once *was*, potentially, far more than he is.) Stumbling through creation in awful misery, in oblivious ecstasy, the fat, clumsy, twelve- or thirteen-year-old Louie is, as her teacher tells her, one of those who "will certainly be famous." We believe this because the book is full of the evidence for it: the poems and plays Louie writes, the stories she tells, the lines she quotes, the things she says. The usual criticism of a novel about an artist is that, no matter how real he is as a man, he is not real to us as an artist, since we have to take on trust the works of art he produces. We do not have to take on trust Louie's work, and she is real to us as an artist.

Someone in a story says that when you can't think of anything else to say you say, "Ah, youth, youth!" But sometimes as you read about Louie there *is* nothing else to say: your heart goes out in homesick joy to the marvelous inconsequential improbable reaching-out-to-everything of the duckling's mind, so different from the old swan's mind, that has learned what its interests are and is deaf and blind to the rest of reality. Louie says, "I wish I had a Welsh grammar." Sam says, "Don't be an idiot! What for?" Louie answers: "I'd like to learn Welsh or Egyptian grammar; I could read the poetry Borrow talks about and I could read *The Book of the Dead*."

She starts to learn *Paradise Lost* by heart ("Why? She did not know really"); stuffs the little children full of La Rochefoucauld; in joyful amazement discovers that *The Cenci* is about her father and herself; recites,

> A yellow plum was given me and in return a topaz fair I gave,
> No mere return for courtesy but that our friendship might outlast
> the grave,

indignantly insisting to the grown-ups that it *is* Confucius; puts as a motto on her wall, *By my hope and faith, I conjure thee, throw not away the hero in your soul*; triumphantly repeats to that little tyrant of her fields, Sam-the-Bold:

> The desolator desolate,
> The tyrant overthrown;
> The arbiter of other's fate,
> A suppliant for his own!

Louie starts out on her own *Faust,* a "play, called *Fortunatus,* in which a student, sitting alone in his room in the beaming moon, lifts his weary head from the book and begins by saying,

> The unforgotten song, the solitary song,
> The song of the young heart in the age-old world,
> Humming on new May's reeds transports me back
> To the vague regions of celestial space . . ."

For the teacher whom she loves Louie creates "a magnificent project, the Aiden cycle . . . a poem of every conceivable form and also every conceivable meter in the English language," all about Miss Aiden. She copies the poems into an out-of-date diary, which she hides; sometimes she reads them to the children in the orchard "for hours on end, while they sat with rosy, greedy faces upturned, listening." As Henny and Sam shriek at each other downstairs, Louie tells the children, lying loosely in bed in the warm night, the story of *Hawkins, the North Wind.* Most of Louie's writings are so lyrically funny to us that as we laugh we catch our breath, afraid that the bubble will break. At *Hawkins,* a gruesomely satisfying story different from any story we have read before, we no longer laugh, nor can we look down at the storyteller with a grown-up's tender, complacent love for a child: the story is dark with Louie's genius and with Christina Stead's.

Best of all is *Tragos: Herpes Rom (Tragedy: The Snake-Man).* Louie writes it, and the children act it out, for Sam's birthday. It is written in a new language Louie has made up for it; the language maker Sam says angrily, "Why isn't it in English?" and Louie replies, "Did Euripides write in English?" Not only is the play exactly what Louie would have written, it is also a work of art in which the relations between Louie and her father, as she understands them, are expressed with concentrated, tragic force. Nowhere else in fiction, so far as I know, is there so truthful and satisfying a representation of the works of art the ugly duckling makes up, there in the morning of the world.

Louie reads most of the time—reads, even, while taking a shower: "her wet fingers pulped the paper as she turned." Her life is accompanied, *ostinato,* by *always has her nose stuck in a book . . . learn to hold your shoulders straight . . . it will ruin your eyes.* Louie "slopped liquids all over the place, stumbled and fell when carrying buckets, could never stand straight to fold the sheets and tablecloths from the wash without giggling or dropping them in the dirt, fell over invisible creases in rugs, was unable to do her hair neatly, and was always leopard-spotted yellow and blue with old and new bruises . . . She ac-knowledged her unwieldiness and unhandiness in this little world, but she had an utter contempt for everyone associated with her, father, stepmother, even brothers and sister, an innocent contempt which she never thought out, but which those round her easily recognized." The Louie who laconically holds her scorched fingers in the candle flame feels "a growling, sullen power in herself . . . She went up to bed in-sulted again. 'I will repay,' she said on the stairs, halting and looking over the banisters, with a frown." When the world is more than she can bear she screams her secret at it: " 'I'm the ugly duckling, you'll see,' shrieked Louie."

Most of the time she knows that she is better and more intelli-gent than, different from, the other inhabitants of her world; but the rest of the time she feels the complete despair—the seeming to one-self wrong, *all* wrong, about everything, *everything*—that is the other, dark side of this differentness. She is a force of nature, but she is also a little girl. Heartbroken when her birthday play is a shameful fail-ure, like so much of her life at home, Louie "began to squirm and, un-consciously holding out one of her hands to Sam, she cried, 'I am so miserable and poor and rotten and so vile [the words *rotten* and *vile* are natural, touching reminiscences of Henny's tirade style] and melodramatic, I don't know what to do. I don't know what to do. I can't bear the daily misery . . .' She was bawling brokenly on the tablecloth, her shoulders heaving and her long hair, broken loose, plastered over her red face. 'No wonder they all laugh at me,' she bellowed. 'When I walk along the street, everyone looks at me, and whispers about me, because I'm so messy. My elbows are out and I have no shoes and I'm so big and fat and it'll always be the same. I can't help it, I can't help it . . . They all laugh at me: I can't stand it any more . . .' Coming to the table, as to a jury, she asked in a firmer voice, but still crying, 'What will become of me? Will life go on like this? Will I always be like this?' She appealed to Sam, 'I have always been like this: I can't live and go on being like this?' "

And Sam replies: "Like what? Like what? I never heard so much idiotic drivel in my born days. Go and put your fat head under the shower."

To Louie the world is what won't let her alone. And the world's interferingness is nothing to Sam's: Sam—so to speak—wakes her up and asks her what she's dreaming just so as to be able to make her dream something different, and then tells her that not every little girl is lucky enough to have a Sam to wake her up. To be let alone! is there any happiness that compares with it, for someone like Louie? Staying with her mother's relatives in the summer, she feels herself inexplicably, miraculously given a little space of her own—is made, for a few weeks, a sort of grown-up by courtesy. And since Louie has "a genius for solitude," she manages to find it even at home. Henny may scold her and beat her, but Henny does leave her alone ("It is a rotten shame, when I think that the poor kid is dragged into all our rotten messes"), and Louie loves her for it—when Sam talks to Louie about her real mother, Louie retorts, "Mother is my mother," meaning Henny.

At school Louie "was in heaven, at home she was in a torture chamber." She never tells anyone outside "what it is like at home . . . no one would believe me!" To the ordinary misery of differentness is added the misery of being the only one who sees the endless awful war between Henny and Sam for what it is: "Suddenly she would think, *Who can see aught good in thee / Soul-destroying misery?* and in this flash of intelligence she understood that her life and their lives were wasted in this contest and that the quarrel between Henny and Sam was ruining their moral natures." It is only Louie who tries to do anything about it all: with a young thing's fresh sense and ignorance and courage she tries to save the children and herself in the only way that she knows—what she does and what she can't quite make herself do help to bring the book to its wonderful climax. It is rare for a novel to have an ending as good as its middle and beginning: the sixty or seventy pages that sum up *The Man Who Loved Children,* bring the action of the book to its real conclusion, are better than even the best things that have come before.

As he looks at Louie, Sam "can't understand what on earth caused this strange drifting nebula to spin." By the time we finish the book we have been so thoroughly in sympathy and in empathy with Louie that we no longer need to understand—we are used to being Louie. We think about her, as her teacher thinks: "It's queer to know everything and nothing at the same time." Louie knows, as she writes in her diary, that "everyday experience which is misery degrades me"; she mutters aloud, "If I did not know I was a genius, I would die: why live?"; a stranger in her entirely strange and entirely familiar family, she cries to her father: "I know something, I know there are people not like us, not muddleheaded like us, better than us." She knows that soon she will have escaped into the world of the people better than us, the great objective world better than Shakespeare and Beethoven and Donatello put together—didn't they all come out of it?

Louie is a potentiality still sure that what awaits it in the world is potentiality, not actuality. That she is escaping from some Pollits to some more Pollits, that she herself will end as an actuality among actualities, an accomplished fact, is an old or middle-aged truth or half-truth that Louie doesn't know. As Louie's story ends she has gone for a walk, "a walk around the world"; she starts into the future accompanied by one of those Strauss themes in which a whole young orchestra walks springily off into the sunshine, as though going away were a final good.

V

As you read *The Man Who Loved Children* what do you notice first? How much life it has, how natural and original it is; Christina Stead's way of seeing and representing the world is so plainly different from anyone else's that after a while you take this for granted, and think cheerfully, "Oh, she can't help being original." The whole book is different from any book you have read before. What other book represents—tries to represent, even—a family in such conclusive detail?

Aristotle speaks of the pleasure of recognition; you read *The Man Who Loved Children* with an almost ecstatic pleasure of recognition. You get used to saying, "Yes, that's the way it is"; and you say many times, but can never get used to saying, "I didn't know *anybody* knew that." Henny, Sam, Louie, and the children—not to speak of some of the people outside the family—are entirely real to the reader. This may not seem much of a claim: every year thousands of reviewers say it about hundreds of novels. But what they say is conventional exaggeration—reality is rare in novels.

Many of the things of the world come to life in *The Man Who Loved Children*: the book has an astonishing sensory immediacy. Akin to this is its particularity and immediacy of incident; it is full of small, live, characteristic, sometimes odd or grotesque details that are at once surprising enough and convincing enough to make the reader feel, "No, nobody could have made that up." And akin to these on a larger scale are all the "good scenes" in the book: scenes that stand out in the reader's memory as in some way remarkable—as representing something, summing something up, with real finality. There is an extraordinary concentration of such scenes in the pages leading up to the attempted murder and accomplished suicide that is the climax of the book: Ernie's lead, Louie's play, Louie's breakdown after it, Ernie's money box, Ernie's and Louie's discoveries before Miss Aiden comes,

Miss Aiden's visit, Henny's beating of Ernie, the end of Henny's love affair, Henny's last game of solitaire, the marlin, Sam and the bananas, the last quarrel. That these scenes come where they do is evidence of Christina Stead's gift for structure; but you are bewildered by her regular ability to make the scenes that matter most the book's best-imagined and best-realized scenes.

Without its fairly wide range of people and places, attitudes and emotions, *The Man Who Loved Children* might seem too concentrated and homogeneous a selection of reality. But the people outside the Pollit household are quite varied: for instance, Louie's mother's family, Sam's and Henny's relatives, some of the people at Singapore, Henny's Bert Anderson, the "norphan" girl, Louie's friend Clare. There are not so many places—Washington, Ann Arbor, Harpers Ferry, Singapore—but each seems entirely different and entirely alive. As he reads about Louie's summers the reader feels, "So this is what Harpers Ferry looks like to an Australian!" European readers are used to being told what Europe looks like to an American or Russian of genius; we aren't, and we enjoy it. (Occasionally Christina Stead has a kind of virtuoso passage to show that she is not merely a foreign visitor, but a real inhabitant of the United States; we enjoy, and are amused at, it.) Because *The Man Who Loved Children* brings to life the variety of the world outside the Pollit household, the happenings inside it—terrible as some of them are—do not seem depressing or constricted or monotonous to the reader: "within, a torment raged, day and night, week, month, year, always the same, an endless conflict, with its truces and breathing spaces; out here were a dark peace and love." And, too, many of the happenings inside the family have so much warmth and habitual satisfaction, are so pleasant or cozy or funny, are so *interesting*, that the reader forgets for a moment that this wonderful playground is also a battlefield.

Children-in-families have a life all their own, a complicated one. Christina Stead seems to have remembered it in detail from her childhood, and to have observed it in detail as an adult. Because of this knowledge she is able to imagine with complete realism the structures, textures, and atmosphere of one family's spoken and unspoken life. She is unusually sensitive to speech styles, to conversation structures, to everything that makes a dialogue or monologue a sort of self-propagating entity; she knows just how family speech is different from speech outside the family, children's speech different from adults'. She gives her children the speeches of speakers to whom a word has the reality of a thing: a thing that can be held wrong side up, played with like a toy, thrown at someone like a toy. Children's speechways—their senseless iteration, joyous nonsense, incremental variation, entreaties and insults, family games, rhymes, rituals, proverbs with the force of law, magical mistakes, occasional uncannily penetrating descriptive phrases—are things Christina Stead knows as well as she knows the speechways of families, of people so used to each other that half the time they only half say something, imply it with a family phrase, or else spell it out in words too familiar to be heard, just as the speaker's face is too familiar to be seen. The book's household conversations between mother and child, father and child, are both superficially and profoundly different from any conversation in the world outside; reading such conversations is as satisfying as being given some food you haven't tasted since childhood. (After making your way through the great rain forest of the children's speech, you come finally to one poor broomstick of a tree, their letters: all the children—as Ernie says, laughing—"start out with 'Dear Dad, I hope you are well, I am well, Mother is well,' and then they get stuck.") The children inherit and employ, or recognize with passive pleasure, the cultural scraps—everything from Mozart to *Hiawatha*—that are a part of the sounds the grown-ups make. Father and Mother are gods but (it is strange!) gods who will sometimes perform for you on request, taking part in a ritual, repeating stories or recitations, pretending to talk like a Scot or a Jew or an Englishman—just as, earlier, they would pretend to be a bear.

Christina Stead knows the awful eventfulness of little children's lives. That grown-ups seldom cry, scream, fall, fight each other, or have to be sent to bed seems very strange to someone watching children: a little child pays its debt to life penny by penny. Sam is able to love a life spent with children because he himself has the insensate busyness of a child. Yet, wholly familiar as he is, partly childlike as he is, to the children he is monstrous—not the singular monster that he is to us, but the ordinary monster that any grown-up is to you if you weigh thirty or forty pounds and have your eyes two feet from the floor. Again and again the reader is conscious of Christina Stead's gift for showing how different *anything* is when looked at from a really different point of view. Little Evie, "fidgeting with her aunt's great arm around her, seemed to be looking up trustfully with her brown eyes, but those deceptive eyes were full of revolt, mistrust, and dislike"; she averts her gaze from her aunt's "slab cheeks, peccary skin . . . the long, plump, inhuman thigh, the glossy, sufficient skirt, from everything powerful, coarse, and proud about this great unmated mare . . . 'Oh,' thought Evie to herself, 'when I am a lady with a baby, I won't have all those bumps, I won't be so big and fat, I will be a lit-tle woman, thin like I am now and not fat in front or in the skirt.' "

One of the most obvious facts about grown-ups, to a child, is that they have forgotten what it is like to be a child. The child has not yet had the chance to know what it is like to be a grown-up; he be-lieves, even, that being a grown-up is a mistake he will never make— when *he* grows up he will keep on being a child, a big child with power. So the child and grown-up live in mutual love, misunder-standing, and distaste. Children shout and play and cry and want candy; grown-ups say *Ssh!* and work and scold and want steak. There is no disputing tastes as contradictory as these. It is not just Mowgli who was raised by a couple of wolves; any child is raised by a couple of grown-ups. Father and Mother may be nearer and dearer than anyone will ever be again—still, they are members of a different species. God is, I suppose, what our parents were; certainly the giant or ogre of the stories is so huge, so powerful, and so stupid because that is the way a grown-up looks to a child.

Grown-ups forget or cannot believe that they seem even more unreasonable to children than children seem to them. Henny's oldest boy, Ernie (to whom money is the primary means of understanding and changing the world; he is a born economic determinist, someone with absolute pitch where money is concerned), is one of Christina Stead's main ways of making us remember how mistaken and hypo-critical grown-ups seem to children. Ernie feels that he sees the world as it is, but that grown-ups are no longer able to do this: their ratio-nalization of their own actions, the infinitely complicated lie they have agreed to tell about the world, conceals the world from them. The child sees the truth, but is helpless to do anything about it.

The Pollit children are used to the terrible helplessness of a child watching its parents war. There over their heads the Sun and the Moon, God the Father and the Holy Virgin, are shouting at each other, striking each other—the children contract all their muscles, try not to hear, and hear. Sometimes, waked in darkness by the familiar sounds, they lie sleepily listening to their parents; hear, during some lull in the quarrel, a tree frog or the sound of the rain.

Ernie feels the same helpless despair at the poverty of the fam-ily; thinking of how *many* children there already are, he implores, "Mothering, don't have another baby!" (Henny replies, "You can bet your bottom dollar on that, old sweetness.") But he does not really un-derstand what he is saying: later on, he and the other children look uncomprehendingly at Henny, "who had again queerly become a large woman, though her hands, feet, and face remained small and narrow." One night they are made to sleep downstairs, and hear Henny screaming hour after hour upstairs; finally, at morning, she is silent. "They had understood nothing at all, except that Mother had been angry and miserable and now she was still; this was a blessed relief." Their blank misunderstanding of what is sexual is the opposite of their eager understanding of what is excremental. They thrill to the inexplicably varying permissiveness of the world: here they are being allowed to laugh at, as a joke, what is ordinarily not referred to at all, or mentioned expediently, in family euphemisms!

The book is alive with their fights, games, cries of "You didn't kiss me!"—"Look, Moth, Tommy kissed you in the glass!" But their great holidays so swiftly are gone: the "sun was going down, and Sunday-Funday was coming to an end. They all felt it with a kind of misery: with such a fine long day and so many things to do, how could they have let it slip past like this?" And summer vacation is the same: the indefinite, almost infinite future so soon is that small, definite, disregarded thing, the past!

On a winter night, with nothing but the fire in the living room to warm the house, the child runs to it crying, "Oo, gee whiz, is it cold; jiminy, I'm freezing. Moth, when are we going to get the coal?" (Anyone who remembers his childhood can feel himself saying those sentences—those and so many more of the book's sentences.) And as the child grows older, how embarrassing the parent is, in the world outside: "Louie looked stonily ahead or desperately aside." And, home again, the parent moralizes, sermonizes—won't he *ever* stop talking?—to the child doing its homework, writing, writing, until finally the parent reads over the child's shoulder what is being written on the page of notebook paper: *Shut up, shut up, shut up, shut up . . .* The book follows the children into the cold beds they warm, goes with them into their dreams: when you read about Louie's hard-soft nightmare or the horseman she hears when she wakes in the middle of the night, you are touching childhood itself.

VI

There is a bewitching rapidity and lack of self-consciousness about Christina Stead's writing; she has much knowledge, extraordinary abilities, but is too engrossed in what she is doing ever to seem conscious of them, so that they do not cut her off from the world but join her to it. How literary she makes most writers seem! Her book is very human, and full of humor of an unusual kind; the spirit behind it doesn't try to be attractive and is attractive. As you read the book's climactic and conclusive pages you are conscious of their genius and of the rightness of that genius: it is as though at these moments Christina Stead's mind held in its grasp the whole action, the essential form, of *The Man Who Loved Children*.

Say that you read: "As Henny sat before her teacup and the steam rose from it and the treacherous foam gathered, uncollectible round its edge, the thousand storms of her confined life would rise up before her, thinner illusions on the steam. She did not laugh at the words 'a storm in a teacup.' " You feel an astonished satisfaction at the swift and fatal conclusiveness, the real poetry—the concentration of experience into a strange and accurate, resonant image—of such a passage. Doesn't one feel the same satisfaction with, wonder at, some of the passages I have already quoted? But quotation gives no idea of what is most important in Christina Stead's style, its simple narrative power—she tells what happens so that it happens, and to you. The direct immediate life of most of her sentences is in extraordinary contrast to the complicated uneasy life of others; as her content varies, her style varies. Ordinary styles have the rhythmical and structural monotony of a habit, of something learned and persisted in. A style like Christina Stead's, so remarkable for its structural variety, its rhythmical spontaneity, forces you to remember that a style can be a whole way of existing, so that you exist, for the moment, in perfect sympathy with it: you don't read it so much as listen to it as it sweeps you along—fast enough, often, to make you feel a blurred pleasure in your own speed. Often a phrase or sentence has the uncaring unconscious authority—how else could you say it?—that only a real style has. But few such styles have the spontaneity of Christina Stead's; its own life carries it along, here rapid and a little rough, here good-humoredly, grotesquely incisive, here purely beautiful—and suddenly, without ever stopping being natural, it is grand.

Her style is live enough and spontaneous enough to be able to go on working without her; but, then, its life is mechanical. When her style is at its worst you have the illusion that, once set in motion, it can rattle along indefinitely, narrating the incidents of a picaresque, Pollit-y universe with an indiscriminate vivacity that matches theirs. (You remember, then, that where everybody's somebody, nobody's anybody—that Christina Stead is, on her father's side, a Pollit.) But, normally, you listen to "the breeze, still brittle, not fully leaved"; see a mountain graveyard, "all grass and long sights"; have a child raise to you its "pansy kitten-face"; see a ragged girl fling out her arms in "a gesture that somehow recalled the surf beating on a coast, the surf of time or of sorrows"; see that in the world outside "clouds were passing over, swiftly staining the garden, the stains soaking in and leaving only bright light again." You read: "Bonnie stayed upstairs sobbing, thinking she had a broken heart, until she heard soft things like the hands of ghosts rubbing her counterpane and soft ghostly feet unsteadily shifting on her rug; and, looking up, she saw Evie and Isabel staring at her with immense rabbit eyes. In a little crockery voice, Isabel asked, 'What are you crying for?' " Louie's dying uncle tells her the story of *Pilgrim's Progress*; "and occasionally he would pause, the eyes would be fixed on her, and suddenly he would smile with his long dark lips; the face would no longer be the face of a man dying of consumption, with its burning eyes, but the ravishment of love incarnate, speaking through voiceless but not secret signs to the child's nature." Sometimes one of her long descriptive sentences lets you see a world at once strange and familiar, Christina Stead's and your own: the romantic Louie looks out at the shabby old Georgetown of the 1930s and sees "the trees of the heath round the Naval Observatory, the lamplight falling over the wired, lichened fence of the old reservoirs, the mysterious, long, dim house that she yearned for, the strange house opposite, and below, the vapor-blue city of Washington, pale, dim-lamped, under multitudinous stars, like a winter city of Africa, she thought, on this night at this hour." As you look at the landscapes—houses and yards and trees and birds and weathers—of *The Man Who Loved Children*, you see that they are alive, and yet you can't tell what has made them come to life—not the words exactly, not even the rhythm of the words, but something behind both: whatever it is that can make the landscapes live and beautiful, but that can make Ernie sobbing over his empty money box, and Henny beginning to cry, "Ugh-ugh," with her face in her hands, more beautiful than any landscape.

VII

Christina Stead can perfectly imitate the surface of existence—and, what is harder, recognize and reproduce some of the structures underneath that surface, and use these to organize her book. You especially notice, in her representation of life, two structural processes: (1) A series of similar events, of increasing intensity and importance, that leads to a last event which sums up, incarnates, all the events that have come before. It is easy to recognize and hard to make up such an event; Christina Stead has an uncanny ability to imagine an event that will be the necessary but surprising sum of the events before it. (2) A series of quantitative changes that leads to a qualitative change: that is, a series of events leading to a last qualitatively different event that at once sums up and contradicts the earlier events, and is the beginning of a new series. And Christina Stead depends almost as much on the conflict of opposites—for instance, of Sam with Henny, the male principle with the female principle, the children with the grown-ups, the ugly duckling with the ducks. She often employs a different principle of structure, the principle that a different point of view makes everything that is seen from that point of view different. Her book continually shows the difference between children's and adults' points of view, between men's and women's, between Henny's relatives' and Sam's relatives', between Sam's and anybody else's, between Louie's and anybody else's, between Henny's and anybody else's—when Henny comes home from shopping and tells what happened on the trip, the people and events of the story seem to the children part of a world entirely different from their own, even if they have been along with Henny on the trip. A somewhat similar principle of organization is the opposition between practice and theory, between concrete fact and abstract rationalization, between what people say things are and what they are. And Christina Stead, like Chekhov, is fond of having a character tell you what life is, just before events themselves show you what it is.

The commonest and most nearly fundamental principle of organization, in serial arts like music and literature, is simply that of repetition; it organizes their notes or words very much as habit organizes our lives. Christina Stead particularly depends on repetition, and particularly understands the place of habit in our lives. If she admits that the proverb is true—*Heaven gives us habits to take the place of happiness*—she also admits that the habits *are* happiness of a sort, and that most happiness, after all, is happiness of a sort; she could say with Yeats that in Eden's Garden "no pleasing habit ends."

Her book, naturally, is full of the causal structures in terms of which we explain most of life to ourselves. Very different from the book's use of these is its use of rhythm as structure, atmosphere as structure: for instance, the series of last things that leads up to Henny's suicide has a dark finality of rhythm and atmosphere that prepares for her death as the air before a thunderstorm prepares for the thunderstorm. Kenneth Burke calls form the satisfaction of an expectation; *The Man Who Loved Children* is full of such satisfactions, but it has a good deal of the deliberate disappointment of an expectation that is also form.

A person is a process, one that leads to death: in *The Man Who Loved Children* the most carefully worked-out, conclusive process is Henny. Even readers who remember themselves as ugly ducklings (and take a sort of credulous, incredulous delight in Louie) will still feel their main humanness identify itself with Henny: the book's center of gravity, of tragic weight, is Henny. She is a violent, defeated process leading to a violent end, a closed tragic process leading to a conclusion of all potentiality, just as Louie is an open process leading to a "conclusion" that is pure potentiality. As the book ends, Henny has left, Louie is leaving, Sam stays. Sam is a repetitive, comic process that merely marks time: he gets nowhere, but then he doesn't want to get anywhere. Although there is no possibility of any real change in Sam, he never stops changing: Sam stays there inside Sam, getting less and less like the rest of mankind and more and more like Sam, Sam squared, Sam cubed, Sam to the *n*th. A man who repeats himself is funny; a man who repeats himself, *himself,* HIMSELF, is funnier. The book dignifies Henny in death, dismisses Sam with: *And he lived happily ever after.* The Pollits' wild war of opposites, with Henny dead, becomes a tame peace. Even Louie, the resistance, leaves, and Sam-the-Bold, the Great I-Am, the Man Who Loved Children, is left to do as he pleases with the children. *For a while*: Sam has laid up for himself treasures that moth and rust can't corrupt, but that the mere passage of the years destroys. Children don't keep. In the end Sam will have to love those hard things to love, grown-ups; and, since this is impossible for Sam, Sam won't despair, won't change, but will simply get himself some more children. He has made the beings of this world, who are the ends of this world, means; when he loses some particular means what does it matter?—there are plenty of other means to that one end, Sam.

The process the book calls Louie is that of a child turning into a grown-up, a duckling turning into a swan, a being that exists in two worlds leaving the first world of the family for the world outside. The ugly duckling loves the other pretty ducklings and tries to save them from the awful war between the father duck and the mother duck—though the war is ended by Henny's act, not Louie's. Yet Louie knows that they are not really her brothers and sisters, not really her parents, and serenely leaves them for the swan world in which, a swan, she will at least be reunited to her real family, who are swans. Or do swans have families? Need families? Who knows? Louie doesn't know and, *for a while*, doesn't need to care.

The last fourth of the book makes Ernie, the child closest to Henny, a queer shadow or echo of Henny. The episodes of Ernie's lead, Ernie's money box, and Ernie's beating bring him to a defeated despair like Henny's, to a suicide-in-effigy: he makes a doll-dummy to stand for himself and hangs it. But all this is only a child's "as if" performance—after Henny's death the penniless Ernie is given some money, finds some more money, forgets Henny, and starts out all over again on the financial process which his life will be.

The attempted murder and accomplished suicide that are the conclusion of Henny and the climax of *The Man Who Loved Children* are prepared for by several hundred events, conversations, speeches, phrases, and thoughts scattered throughout the book. Henny's suicide- or murder-rhetoric; the atmosphere of violence that hangs around her, especially where Sam and Louie are concerned; the conversation in which she discusses with her mother and sister the best ways to kill oneself, the quickest poisons: these and a great many similar things have established, even before the sixty or seventy pages leading directly to Henny's death, a situation that makes plausible—requires, really—her violent end. And yet we are surprised to have it happen, this happening as thoroughly prepared for as anything I can remember in fiction.

It is no "tragic flaw" in Henny's character, but her character itself, that brings her to her end: Henny is her own fate. Christina Stead has a Chinese say, "Our old age is perhaps life's decision about us"—or, worse, the decision we have made about ourselves without ever realizing we were making it. Henny's old age may be life's decision about Henny; her suicide is the decision she has made about herself—about life—without ever knowing she was making it. She is so used to thinking and saying: *I'll kill myself! Better kill myself!* that when Louie gives her the chance she is fatally ready to take it. The defeated, despairing Henny has given up her life many times, before that drinking of the breakfast cup of tea with which she gives it up for good. What life has made of Henny, what Henny most deeply is, drinks—she is never more herself than when she destroys herself.

Many things in her life are latent or ultimate causes of Henny's death; but its immediate, overt causes—the series of extraordinarily imagined and accomplished finalities that leads to this final finality, that demands as its only possible conclusion Henny's death—all occur in the sixty or seventy pages before that death. At the beginning of the series, there is finality in the episode in which Henny feels her heart break "for good and all"; in the episode in which the aging Henny becomes, suddenly, "a dried-up, skinny, funny old woman." Miss Aiden's visit makes the reader see that this family sinking into poverty has become, without his realizing it, *poor*, abjectly, irretrievably poor. Everything valuable is gone, Henny's dearest possessions have been sold or pawned: the treasure drawers are empty.

Next day Ernie finds his money box empty, blankly sobs, and Henny, who has stolen the money, cries "Ugh-ugh" and tries to comfort him. She has stolen, from the child she loves most, the one thing that is indispensable to him. When Henny, later on, begins to beat Ernie over the head, and goes on hysterically beating him until she faints, it is as if she felt so guilty about him that it is unbearable to her to have him exist at all. The life in which what has happened can happen is more than Henny can endure—she tries to obliterate Ernie and life, and then faints, momentarily obliterating herself.

The awful end of her affair with Bert Anderson is a kind of final, public, objective degradation of Henny; she begs for a last trifle, nothing almost, and the world refuses her even that. The long nightmarish episode of the rendering of the marlin into oil is the final incarnation of all the senseless busynesses with which Sam has tormented her: "one marlin had been enough, with their kneading, manuring, trotting about, plastering, oiling, and dripping, to give Spa House a scent of its own for many years to come." But nothing else in *The Man Who Loved Children* has the empty finality of Henny's last game of solitaire. She has played it her whole life and never once won; now she wins. "The game that she had played all her life was finished; she had no more to do; she had no game." And, a little later, Henny breaks down as she has never broken down before: " 'Ai, ai,' cried Henny, beginning to cry like a little girl, and putting the dressing gown to her face, 'ai, ai!' " The world has been too much for Henny, the old woman has changed back into a child. As there has never before been anything childlike about Henny, the scene has a pitiable finality. The quarrel with Sam which follows (a quarrel monotonous with Henny's repetitions of *kill everybody, kill myself*) is the last, the worst, and the most violent of their quarrels. The next morning Henny admits to Ernie that she will never be able to pay him back, and says with a perplexed, wondering conclusiveness: "I don't know what to do." Ernie is Henny's main connection to life, her only connection to hope and to the future: when life makes her steal his money, beat him until she faints, and then tell him that she can never pay him back, what is there left to her but the "All right, I will!" that is her last word to life?

VIII

After you have read *The Man Who Loved Children* several times you feel that you know its author's main strengths and main weakness. The weakness is, I think, a kind of natural excess and lack of discrimination: she is most likely to go wrong by not seeing when to stop or what to leave out. About most things—always, about the most important things—she is not excessive and does discriminate; but a few things in *The Man Who Loved Children* ought not to be there, and a few other things ought not to be there in such quantities.

When you look at these passages that—it seems to you—ought not to be there, it is as if you were seeing an intrusion of raw reality into the imagined reality of the book: some actual facts are being rapidly, scrappily, and vivaciously described. You don't feel that these had to go into the book, nor do you feel that they have been through the process of being created all over again that the rest of the material of the book has been through. They are, so to speak, God's creation, not Christina Stead's; and Christina Stead's fairly effective reporting of this first creation is a poor substitute for her own second creation. Such accidental realities seem to have slipped into the book unquestioned—or perhaps, when a part of the author questioned them, another part answered, "But that's the way it really was." (One of the most puzzling things about a novel is that "the way it really was" half the time is, and half the time isn't, the way it ought to be in the novel.) Another sort of unrequired and consequently excessive passage seems to be there because the author's invention, running on automatically, found it easy to imagine it that way; such a passage is the equivalent, in narrative, of a mannered, habitual, easily effective piece of rhetoric.

Isn't there a little too much of the Pollits' homecoming party, of Henny's tirades, of Sam's dream sermons? Aren't these slightly excessive representations of monstrously excessive realities? Aren't there a few too many facts about Annapolis and Harpers Ferry, about Henny's more remote relatives? When Christina Stead is at her worst—in *The Man Who Loved Children* she never is—you feel that there is just too much of Christina Stead. At its worst her writing has a kind of vivacious, mechanical overabundance: her observation and invention and rhetoric, set into autonomous operation, bring into existence a queer picaresque universe of indiscriminate, slightly disreputable incidents. Reading about them is like listening to two disillusioned old automata gossiping over a cup of tea in the kitchen.

Ruskin says that anyone who expects perfection from a work of art knows nothing of works of art. This is an appealing sentence that, so far as I can see, is not true about a few pictures and statues and pieces of music, short stories and short poems. Whether or not you expect perfection from them, you get it; at least, there is nothing in them that you would want changed. But what Ruskin says is true about novels: anyone who expects perfection from even the greatest novel knows nothing of novels. Some of the faults of *The Man Who Loved Children* are the faults a large enough, live enough thing naturally has; others (those I have been discussing) are the faults a book of Christina Stead's naturally has—they are, really, the other side of her virtues. An occasional awkwardness or disparity is the result of her having created from an Australian memory an American reality; but usually you are astonished at how well acclimated, re-created, these memories are. Two or three Joyce-ish sentences—one seems consciously and humorously Joyce-ish—make you remember that the rest of the sentences in the book are pure Stead. What Louie reads and quotes and loves is more what she would have read in 1917 than in 1937; but objecting to *that* is like objecting to Tolstoy's making the characters in *War and Peace* his own contemporaries, not Napoleon's—Christina Stead understands that it is only her own realities, anachronistic or not, that can give Louie the timeless reality that Louie has.

A reader of *The Man Who Loved Children* naturally will want to know something about Christina Stead. I know only what I have found in reference books or guessed from her novels. Let me repeat some of the first: it will have for the reader the interest of showing where Sam and Louie (and, no doubt, Henny) began.

Christina Stead was born in Australia, in 1902. Her mother died soon afterwards, her father remarried, and she "became the eldest of a large family." Her father was a rationalist, a Fabian socialist, and a naturalist in the Government Fisheries Department. As a girl she was particularly interested in "fish, natural history, Spencer, Darwin, Huxley . . . the sea . . . I had plenty of work with the young children, but I was attached to them, and whenever I could, told them stories, partly from Grimm and Andersen, partly invented."

She went to Teachers' College, disliked teaching, took a business course at night, went to London in 1928 and worked there, went to Paris in 1929 and worked there for several years. She had been a public-school teacher, a teacher of abnormal children, a demonstrator in the psychology laboratory of Sydney University, and a clerk in a grain company; in Paris she was a clerk in a banking house. She lived in the United States during the late thirties and early forties, and now lives in England. Her husband is William Blake, the author of several novels and of the best and most entertaining textbook of Marxian economics that I know. In 1934 Christina Stead published *The Salzburg Tales*; in 1935, *Seven Poor Men of Sydney*; in 1936, *The Beauties and the Furies*; in 1938, *House of All Nations*; in 1940, *The Man Who Loved Children*; in 1944, *For Love Alone*; in 1946, *Letty Fox, Her Luck*; in 1948, *A Little Tea, a Little Chat*; in 1952, *The People with the Dogs*.

Her books have had varying receptions. *House of All Nations* was a critical success and a best-seller; *The Man Who Loved Children* was a failure both with critics and with the public. It has been out of print for many years, and Christina Stead herself is remembered by only a few readers. When the world rejects, and then forgets, a writer's most profound and imaginative book, he may unconsciously work in a more limited way in the books that follow it; this has happened, I believe, to Christina Stead. The world's incomprehension has robbed it, for twenty-five years, of *The Man Who Loved Children*; has robbed it, forever, of what could have come after *The Man Who Loved Children*.

IX

When we think of the masterpieces that nobody praised and nobody read, back there in the past, we feel an impatient superiority to the readers of the past. If we had been there, we can't help feeling, *we'd* have known that *Moby Dick* was a good book—why, how could anyone help knowing?

But suppose someone says to us, "Well, you're here now: what's our own *Moby Dick*? What's the book that, a hundred years from now, everybody will look down on *us* for not having liked?" What do we say then?

But if I were asked something easier—to name a good book that we don't read and that the people of the future will read—I'd be less at a loss. In 1941 I bought two copies of *The Man Who Loved Children*, one to read and the other to lend. In the long run a borrower of one died and a borrower of the other went abroad, so that I have nothing left but a copy from the library. Lending a favorite book has its risks; the borrower may not like it. I don't know a better novel than *Crime and Punishment*—still, every fourth or fifth borrower returns it unfinished: it depresses him; besides that, he didn't believe it. More borrowers than this return the first volume of *Remembrance of Things Past* unfinished: they were bored. There is no book you can lend people that all of them will like.

But *The Man Who Loved Children* has been a queer exception. I have lent it to many writers and more readers, and all of them thought it good and original, a book different from any other. They could see that there were things wrong with it—a novel is a prose narrative of some length that has something wrong with it—but they felt that, somehow, the things didn't matter.

To have this happen with a book that was a failure to begin with, and that after twenty-five years is unknown, is strange. Having it happen has helped me to believe that it is one of those books that their own age neither reads nor praises, but that the next age thinks a masterpiece.

But I suppose I'd believe this even if every borrower had told me it was bad. As Wordsworth and Proust say, a good enough book in the long run makes its own readers, people who believe in it because they can't help themselves. Where *The Man Who Loved Children* is concerned, I can't help myself; it seems to me as plainly good as *War and Peace* and *Crime and Punishment* and *Remembrance of Things Past* are plainly great. A few of its less important parts are bad and all of its more important parts are good: it is a masterpiece with some plain, and plainly negligible, faults.

I call it a good book, but it is a better book, I think, than most of the novels people call great; perhaps it would be fairer to call it great. It has one quality that, ordinarily, only a great book has: it does a single thing better than any other book has ever done it. *The Man Who Loved Children* makes you a part of one family's immediate existence as no other book quite does. When you have read it you have been, for a few hours, a Pollit; it will take you many years to get the sound of the Pollits out of your ears, the sight of the Pollits out of your eyes, the smell of the Pollits out of your nostrils.

[1965/TBC]

A Sad Heart
at the Supermarket

THE EMPEROR AUGUSTUS would sometimes say to his Senate: "Words fail me, my Lords; nothing I can say could possibly indicate the depth of my feelings in this matter." But in this matter of mass culture, the mass media, I am speaking not as an emperor but as a fool, a suffering, complaining, helplessly non-conforming poet-or-artist-of-a-sort, far off at the obsolescent rear of things; what I say will indicate the depth of my feelings and the shallowness and one-sidedness of my thoughts. If those English lyric poets who went mad during the eighteenth century had told you why the Age of Enlightenment was driving them crazy, it would have had a kind of documentary interest: what I say may have a kind of documentary interest. *The toad beneath the harrow knows / Exactly where each tooth-point goes*: if you tell me that the field is being harrowed to grow grain for bread, and to create a world in which there will be no more famines, or toads either, I will say: "I know"; but let me tell you where the tooth-points go, and what the harrow looks like from below.

Advertising men, businessmen speak continually of *media* or *the media* or *the mass media*. One of their trade journals is named, simply, *Media*. It is an impressive word: one imagines Mephistopheles offering Faust *media that no man has ever known*; one feels, while the word is in one's ear, that abstract, overmastering powers, of a scale and intensity unimagined yesterday, are being offered one by the technicians who discovered and control them—offered, and at a price. The word has the clear fatal ring of that new world whose space we occupy

Randall Jarrell

so luxuriously and precariously; the world that produces mink stoles, rockabilly records, and tactical nuclear weapons by the million; the world that Attila, Galileo, Hansel and Gretel never knew.

And yet, it's only the plural of *medium*. "*Medium*," says the dictionary, "that which lies in the middle; hence, middle condition or degree ... A substance through which a force acts or an effect is transmitted ... That through or by which anything is accomplished; as, an advertising *medium* ... *Biol.* A nutritive mixture or substance, as broth, gelatin, agar, for cultivating bacteria, fungi, etc."

Let us name *our* trade journal *The Medium*. For all these media—television, radio, movies, newspapers, magazines, and the rest—are a single medium, in whose depths we are all being cultivated. This Medium is of middle condition or degree, mediocre; it lies in the middle of everything, between a man and his neighbor, his wife, his child, his self; it, more than anything else, is the substance through which the forces of our society act upon us, and make us into what our society needs.

And what does it need? For us to need.

Oh, it needs for us to do or be many things: workers, technicians, executives, soldiers, housewives. But first of all, last of all, it needs for us to be buyers; consumers; beings who want much and will want more—who want consistently and insatiably. Find some spell to make us turn away from the stoles, the records, and the weapons, and our world will change into something to us unimaginable. Find some spell to make us see that the product or service that yesterday was an unthinkable luxury today is an inexorable necessity, and our world will go on. It is the Medium which casts this spell—which is this spell. As we look at the television set, listen to the radio, read the magazines, the frontier of necessity is always being pushed forward. The Medium shows us what our new needs are—how often, without it, we should not have known!—and it shows us how they can be satisfied: they can be satisfied by buying something. The act of buying something is at the root of our world; if anyone wishes to paint the genesis of things in our society, he will paint a picture of God holding out to Adam a checkbook or credit card or Charge-a-Plate.

But how quickly our poor naked Adam is turned into a consumer, is linked to others by the great chain of buying!

No outcast he, bewildered and depressed:
Along his infant veins are interfused
The gravitation and the filial bond
Of nature that connect him with the world.

Children of three or four can ask for a brand of cereal, sing some soap's commercial; by the time that they are twelve or thirteen they are not children but teenage consumers, interviewed, graphed, analyzed. They are well on their way to becoming that ideal figure of our culture, the knowledgeable consumer. Let me define him: the knowledgeable consumer is someone who, when he comes to Weimar, knows how to buy a Weimaraner.

Daisy's voice sounded like money; everything about the knowledgeable consumer looks like or sounds like or feels like money, and informed money at that. To live is to consume, to understand life is to know what to consume: he has learned to understand this, so that his life is a series of choices—correct ones—among the products and services of the world. He is able to choose to consume something, of course, only because sometime, somewhere, he or someone else produced something—but just when or where or what no longer seems to us of as much interest. We may still go to Methodist or Baptist or Presbyterian churches on Sunday, but the Protestant ethic of frugal industry, of production for its own sake, is gone.

Production has come to seem to our society not much more than a condition prior to consumption. "The challenge of today," an advertising agency writes, "is to make the consumer raise his level of demand." This challenge has been met: the Medium has found it easy to make its people feel the continually increasing lacks, the many specialized dissatisfactions (merging into one great dissatisfaction, temporarily assuaged by new purchases) that it needs for them to feel. When in some magazine we see the Medium at its most nearly perfect, we hardly know which half is entertaining and distracting us, which half making us buy: some advertisement may be more ingeniously entertaining than the text beside it, but it is the text which has made us long for a product more passionately. When one finishes *Holiday* or *Harper's Bazaar* or *House and Garden* or *The New Yorker* or *High Fidelity* or *Road and Track* or—but make your own list—buying something, going somewhere seems a necessary completion to the act of reading the magazine.

Reader, isn't buying or fantasy-buying an important part of your and my emotional life? (If you reply, *No*, I'll think of you with bitter envy as more than merely human; as deeply un-American.) It is a standard joke that when a woman is bored or sad she buys something, to cheer herself up; but in this respect we are all women together, and can hear complacently the reminder of how feminine this consumer-world of ours has become. One imagines as a characteristic dialogue of our time an interview in which someone is asking of a vague gracious figure, a kind of Mrs. America: "But while you waited for the intercontinental ballistic missiles what did you *do*?" She answers: "I bought things."

She reminds one of the sentinel at Pompeii—a space among ashes, now, but at his post: she too did what she was supposed to do. Our society has delivered us—most of us—from the bonds of necessity, so that we no longer struggle to find food to keep from starving, clothing and shelter to keep from freezing; yet if the ends for which we work and of which we dream are only clothes and restaurants and houses, possessions, consumption, how have we escaped?—we have exchanged man's old bondage for a new voluntary one. It is more than a figure of speech to say that the consumer is trained for his job of consuming as the factory worker is trained for his job of producing; and the first can be a longer, more complicated training, since it is easier to teach a man to handle a tool, to read a dial, than it is to teach him to ask, always, for a name-brand aspirin—to want, someday, a stand-by generator.

What is that? You don't know? I used not to know, but the readers of *House Beautiful* all know, so that now I know. It is the electrical generator that stands in the basement of the suburban house owner, shining, silent, till at last one night the lights go out, the furnace stops, the freezer's food begins to—

Ah, but it's frozen for good, the lights are on forever; the owner has switched on the stand-by generator.

But you don't see that he really needs the generator, you'd rather have seen him buy a second car? He has two. A second bathroom? He has four. When the People of the Medium doubled everything, he doubled everything; and now that he's gone twice round he will have to wait three years, or four, till both are obsolescent—but while he waits there are so many new needs that he can satisfy, so many things a man can buy. "Man wants but little here below / Nor wants that little long," said the poet; what a lie! Man wants almost unlimited quantities of almost everything, and he wants it till the day he dies.

Sometimes in *Life* or *Look* we see a double-page photograph of some family standing on the lawn among its possessions: station wagon, swimming pool, power cruiser, sports car, tape recorder, television sets, radios, cameras, power lawn mower, garden tractor, lathe, barbecue set, sporting equipment, domestic appliances—all the gleaming, grotesquely imaginative paraphernalia of its existence. It was hard to get everything on two pages, soon it will need four. It is like a dream, a child's dream before Christmas; yet if the members of the family doubt that they are awake, they have only to reach out and pinch something. The family seems pale and small, a negligible appendage, beside its possessions; only a human being would need to ask: "Which owns which?" We are fond of saying that something is not just something but "a way of life"; this too is a way of life—our way, the way.

Emerson, in his spare stony New England, a few miles from Walden, could write: "Things are in the saddle / And ride mankind." He could say more now: that they are in the theater and studio, and entertain mankind; are in the pulpit and preach to mankind. The values of business, in a business society like our own, are reflected in every sphere: values which agree with them are reinforced, values which disagree are canceled out or have lip service paid to them. In business what sells is good, and that's the end of it—that is what *good* means; if the world doesn't beat a path to your door, your mousetrap wasn't better. The values of the Medium—which is both a popular business itself and the cause of popularity in other businesses—are business values: money, success, celebrity. If we are representative members of our society, the Medium's values are ours; and even if we are unrepresentative, non-conforming, our hands are—too often—subdued to the element they work in, and our unconscious expectations are all that we consciously reject. Darwin said that he always immediately wrote down evidence against a theory because otherwise, he'd noticed, he would forget it; in the same way, we keep forgetting the existence of those poor and unknown failures whom we might rebelliously love and admire.

If you're so smart why aren't you rich? is the ground-bass of our society, a grumbling and quite unanswerable criticism, since the society's non-monetary values *are* directly convertible into money. Celebrity turns into testimonials, lectures, directorships, presidencies, the capital gains of an autobiography *Told To* some professional ghost who photographs the man's life as Bachrach photographs his body. I read in the newspapers a lyric and perhaps exaggerated instance of this direct conversion of celebrity into money: his son accompanied Adlai Stevenson on a trip to Russia, took snapshots of his father, and sold them (to accompany his father's account of the trip) to *Look* for $20,000. When Liberace said that his critics' unfavorable reviews hurt him so much that he cried all the way to the bank, one had to admire the correctness and penetration of his press agent's wit—in another age, what might not such a man have become!

Our culture is essentially periodical: we believe that all that is deserves to perish and to have something else put in its place. We speak of planned obsolescence, but it is more than planned, it is felt; is an assumption about the nature of the world. We feel that the present is better and more interesting, more real, than the past, and that the future will be better and more interesting, more real, than the present; but, consciously, we do not hold against the present its prospective obsolescence. Our standards have become to an astonishing degree the standards of what is called the world of fashion, where mere timeliness—being orange in orange's year, violet in violet's—is the value to which all other values are reducible. In our society the word *old-fashioned* is so final a condemnation that someone like Norman Vincent Peale can say about atheism or agnosticism simply that it is old-fashioned; the homely recommendation of the phrase *Give me that good old-time religion* has become, after a few decades, the conclusive rejection of the phrase *old-fashioned atheism.*

All this is, at bottom, the opposite of the world of the arts, where commercial and scientific progress do not exist; where the bone of Homer and Mozart and Donatello is there, always, under the mere blush of fashion; where the past—the remote past, even—is responsible for the way that we understand, value, and act in, the present. (When one reads an abstract expressionist's remark that Washington studios are "eighteen months behind" those of his colleagues in New York, one realizes something of the terrible power of business and fashion over those most overtly hostile to them.) An artist's work and life presuppose continuing standards, values extended over centuries or millennia, a future that is the continuation and modification of the past, not its contradiction or irrelevant replacement. He is working for the time that wants the best that he can do: the present, he hopes—but if not that, the future. If he sees that fewer and fewer people are any real audience for the serious artists of the past, he will feel that still fewer are going to be an audience for the serious artists of the present: for those who, willingly or unwillingly, sacrifice extrinsic values to intrinsic ones, immediate effectiveness to that steady attraction which, the artist hopes, true excellence will always exert.

The past's relation to the artist or man of culture is almost the opposite of its relation to the rest of our society. To him the present is no more than the last ring on the trunk, understandable and valuable only in terms of all the earlier rings. The rest of our society sees only that great last ring, the enveloping surface of the trunk; what's underneath is a disregarded, almost mythical foundation. When Northrop Frye writes that "the preoccupation of the humanities with the past is sometimes made a reproach against them by those who forget that we face the past: it may be shadowy, but it is all that is there," he is saying what for the artist or man of culture is self-evidently true. Yet for the Medium and the People of the Medium it is as self-evidently false: for them the present—or a past so recent, so quick-changing, so soon-disappearing, that it might be called the specious present—is all that is there.

In the past our culture's body of common knowledge—its frame of reference, its possibility of comprehensible allusion—changed slowly and superficially; the amount added to it or taken away from it, in any ten years, was surprisingly small. Now in any ten years a surprisingly large proportion of the whole is replaced. Most of the information people have in common is something that four or five years from now they will not even remember having known. A newspaper story remarks in astonishment that television quiz programs "have proved that ordinary citizens can be conversant with such esoterica as jazz, opera, the Bible, Shakespeare, poetry, and fisticuffs." You may exclaim: "Esoterica! If the Bible and Shakespeare are esoterica, what is there that's common knowledge?" The answer, I suppose, is that Elfrida von Nordroff and Teddy Nadler—the ordinary citizens on the quiz programs—are common knowledge; though not for long. Songs disappear in two or three months, celebrities in two or three years; most of the Medium is little felt and soon forgotten. Nothing is as dead as day-before-yesterday's newspaper, the next-to-the-last number on the roulette wheel; but most of the knowledge people have in common and lose in common is knowledge of such newspapers, such numbers. Yet the novelist or poet or dramatist, when he moves a great audience, depends upon the deep feelings, the living knowledge, that the people of that audience share; if so much has become contingent, superficial, ephemeral, it is disastrous for him.

New products and fashions replace the old, and the fact that they replace them is proof enough of their superiority. Similarly, the Medium does not need to show that the subjects which fill it are interesting or timely or important; the fact that they are its subjects makes them so. If *Time, Life,* and the television shows are full of Tom Fool this month, he's no fool. And when he has been gone from them a while, we do not think him a fool—we do not think of him at all. He no longer exists, in the fullest sense of the word *exist*: to be is to be perceived, to be a part of the Medium of our perception. Our celebrities are not kings, romantic in exile, but Representatives who, defeated, are forgotten; they had, always, only the qualities that we delegated to them.

After driving for four or five minutes along the road outside my door, I come to a row of one-room shacks about the size of kitchens, made out of used boards, metal signs, old tin roofs. To the people who live in them an electric dishwasher of one's own is as much a fantasy as an ocean liner of one's own. But since the Medium (and those whose thought is molded by it) does not perceive them, these people are themselves a fantasy. No matter how many millions of such exceptions to the general rule there are, they do not really exist, but have a kind of anomalous, statistical subsistence; our moral and imaginative view of the world is no more affected by them than by the occupants of some home for the mentally deficient a little farther along the road. If some night one of these outmoded, economically deficient ghosts should scratch at my window, I could say only: "Come back twenty or thirty years ago." And if I myself, as an old-fashioned, one-room poet, a friend of "quiet culture," a "meek lover of the good," should go out some night to scratch at another window, shouldn't I hear someone's indifferent or regretful: "Come back a century or two ago"?

When those whose existence the Medium recognizes ring the chimes of the writer's doorbell, fall through his letter slot, float out onto his television screen, what is he to say to them? A man's unsuccessful struggle to get his family food is material for a work of art—for tragedy, almost; his unsuccessful struggle to get his family a stand-by generator is material for what? Comedy? Farce? Comedy on such a scale, at such a level, that our society and its standards seem, almost, farce? And yet it is the People of the Medium—those who struggle for and get, or struggle for and don't get, the generator—whom our society finds representative: they are there, there primarily, there to be treated first of all. How shall the artist treat them? And the Medium itself—an end of life and a means of life, something essential to people's understanding and valuing of their existence, something many of their waking hours are spent listening to or looking at—how is *it* to be treated as subject matter for art? The artist cannot merely reproduce it; should he satirize or parody it? But by the time the artist's work reaches its audience, the portion of the Medium which it satirized will already have been forgotten; and parody is impossible, often, when so much of the Medium is already an unintentional parody. (Our age might be defined as the age in which real parody became impossible, since any parody had already been duplicated, or parodied, in earnest.) Yet the Medium, by now, is an essential part of its watchers. How can you explain those whom Mohammedans call the People of the Book in any terms that omit the Book? We are people of the television set, the magazine, the radio, and are inexplicable in any terms that omit them.

Oscar Wilde said that Nature imitates Art, that before Whistler painted them there were no fogs along the Thames. If his statement were not false, it would not be witty. But to say that Nature imitates Art, when the Nature is human nature and the Art that of television, radio, motion pictures, magazines, is literally true. The Medium shows its People what life is, what people are, and its People believe it: expect people to be that, try themselves to be that. Seeing is believing; and if what you see in *Life* is different from what you see in life, which of the two are you to believe? For many people it is what you see in *Life* (and in the movies, over television, on the radio) that is real life; and everyday existence, mere local or personal variation, is not real in the same sense.

The Medium mediates between us and raw reality, and the mediation more and more replaces reality for us. Many radio stations have a news broadcast every hour, and many people like and need to hear it. In many houses either the television set or the radio is turned on during most of the hours the family is awake. It is as if they longed to be established in reality, to be reminded continually of the "real," "objective" world—the created world of the Medium—rather than to be left at the mercy of actuality, of the helpless contingency of the world in which the radio receiver or television set is sitting. And surely we can sympathize: which of us hasn't found a similar refuge in the "real," created world of Cézanne or Goethe or Verdi? Yet Dostoevsky's world is too different from Wordsworth's, Piero della Francesca's from Goya's, Bach's from Wolf's, for us to be able to substitute one homogeneous mediated reality for everyday reality in the belief that it *is* everyday reality. For many watchers, listeners, readers, the world of events and celebrities and performers—the Great World—has become the world of primary reality: how many times they have sighed at the colorless unreality of their own lives and families, and sighed for the bright reality of, say, Elizabeth Taylor's. The watchers call the celebrities by their first names, approve or disapprove of "who they're dating," handle them with a mixture of love, identification, envy, and contempt. But however they handle them, they *handle* them: the Medium has given everyone so terrible a familiarity with everyone that it takes great magnanimity of spirit not to be affected by it. These celebrities are not heroes to us, their valets.

Better to have these real ones play themselves, and not sacrifice too much of their reality to art; better to have the watcher play himself, and not lose too much of himself in art. Usually the watcher is halfway between two worlds, paying full attention to neither: half distracted from, half distracted by, this distraction; and able for the moment not to be too greatly affected, have too great demands made upon him, by either world. For in the Medium, which we escape to from work, nothing is ever *work*, makes intellectual or emotional or imaginative demands which we might find it difficult to satisfy. Here in the half-world everything is homogeneous—is, as much as possible, the same as everything else: each familiar novelty, novel familiarity has the same treatment on top and the same attitude and conclusion at bottom; only the middle, the particular subject of the particular program or article, is different. If it *is* different: everyone is given the same automatic "human interest" treatment, so that it is hard for us to remember, unnecessary for us to remember, which particular celebrity we're reading about this time—often it's the same one, we've just moved on to a different magazine.

Francesco Caraccioli said that the English have a hundred religions and one sauce; so do we; and we are so accustomed to this sauce or dye or style of presentation, the aesthetic equivalent of Standard Brands, that a very simple thing can seem obscure or perverse without it. And, too, we find it hard to have to shift from one genre to another, to vary our attitudes and expectations, to use our unexercised imaginations. Poetry disappeared long ago, even for most intellectuals; each year fiction is a little less important. Our age is the age of articles: we buy articles in stores, read articles in magazines, exist among the interstices of articles: of columns, interviews, photographic essays, documentaries; of facts condensed into headlines or expanded into nonfiction best-sellers; of real facts about real people.

Art lies to us to tell us the (sometimes disquieting) truth. The Medium tells us truths, facts, in order to make us believe some reassuring or entertaining lie or half-truth. These actually existing celebrities, of universally admitted importance, about whom we are told directly authoritative facts—how can fictional characters compete with these? These *are* our fictional characters, our Lears and Clytemnestras. (This is ironically appropriate, since many of their doings and sayings are fictional, made up by public relations officers, columnists, agents, or other affable familiar ghosts.) And the Medium gives us such facts, such tape recordings, such clinical reports not only about the great but also about (representative samples of) the small. When we have been shown so much about so many—*can* be shown, we feel, anything about anybody—does fiction seem so essential as it once seemed? Shakespeare or Tolstoy can show us all about someone, but so can *Life*; and when *Life* does, it's someone real.

The Medium is half life and half art, and competes with both life and art. It spoils its audience for both; spoils both for its audience. For the People of the Medium life isn't sufficiently a matter of success and glamour and celebrity, isn't entertaining enough, distracting enough, *mediated* enough; and art is too difficult or individual or novel, too much a matter of tradition and the past, too much a matter of special attitudes and aptitudes—its mediation sometimes is queer or excessive, and sometimes is not even recognizable as mediation. The Medium's mixture of rhetoric and reality, in which people are given what they know they want to be given in the form in which they know they want to be given it, is something more efficient and irresistible than any real art. If a man has all his life been fed a combination of marzipan and ethyl alcohol—if eating, to him, is a matter of being knocked unconscious by an ice cream soda—can he, by taking thought, come to prefer a diet of bread and wine, apples and well water? Will a man who has spent his life watching gladiatorial games come to prefer listening to chamber music? And those who produce the bread and the wine and the quartets for him—won't they be tempted either to give up producing them, or else to produce a bread that's half sugar and half alcohol, a quartet that ends with the cellist at the violist's bleeding throat?

Any outsider who has worked for the Medium will have observed that the one thing which seems to its managers most unnatural is for someone to do something naturally, to speak or write as an individual speaking or writing to other individuals, and not as a subcontractor supplying a standardized product to the Medium. It is as if producers and editors and supervisors—middle men—were particles forming a screen between maker and public, one which will let through only particles of their own size and weight (or as they say, the public's). As you look into their strained puréed faces, their big horn-rimmed eyes, you despair of Creation itself, which seems for the instant made in their own owl-eyed image. There are so many extrinsic considerations involved in the presentation of his work, the maker finds, that by the time it is presented almost any intrinsic consideration has come to seem secondary. No wonder that the professional who writes the ordinary commercial success—the ordinary script, scenario, or best-seller—resembles imaginative writers less than he resembles editors, producers, executives. The supplier has come to resemble those he supplies, and what he supplies them resembles both. With an artist you never know what you will get; with him you know what you will get. He is a reliable source for a standard product. He is almost exactly the opposite of the imaginative artist: instead of stubbornly or helplessly sticking to what he sees and feels—to what is right for him, true to his reality, regardless of what the others think and want—he gives the others what they think and want, regardless of what he himself sees and feels.

The Medium represents, to the artist, all that he has learned not to do: its sure-fire stereotypes seem to him what any true art, true spirit, has had to struggle past on its way to the truth. The artist sees the values and textures of this art-substitute replacing those of his art, so far as most of society is concerned; conditioning the expectations of what audience his art has kept. Mass culture either corrupts or isolates the writer. His old feeling of oneness—of speaking naturally to an audience with essentially similar standards—is gone; and writers no longer have much of the consolatory feeling that took its place, the feeling of writing for the happy few, the kindred spirits whose standards are those of the future. (Today they feel: the future, should there be one, will be worse.) True works of art are more and more produced away from or in opposition to society. And yet the artist needs society as much as society needs him: as our cultural enclaves get smaller and drier, more hysterical or academic, one mourns for the artists inside and the public outside. An incomparable historian of mass culture, Ernest van den Haag, has expressed this with laconic force: "The artist who, by refusing to work for the mass market, becomes marginal, cannot create what he might have created had there been no mass market. One may prefer a monologue to addressing a mass meeting. But it is still not a conversation."

Even if the rebellious artist's rebellion is wholehearted, it can never be whole-stomach'd, whole-unconscious'd. Part of him wants to be like his kind, is like his kind; longs to be loved and admired and successful. Our society—and the artist, in so far as he is truly a part of it—has no place set aside for the different and poor and obscure, the fools for Christ's sake: they all go willy-nilly into Limbo. The artist is tempted, consciously, to give his society what it wants—or if he won't or can't, to give it nothing at all; is tempted, unconsciously, to give it superficially independent or contradictory works which are at heart works of the Medium. But it is hard for him to go on serving both God and Mammon when God is so really ill-, Mammon so really well-organized.

"Shakespeare wrote for the Medium of his day; if Shakespeare were alive now he'd be writing *My Fair Lady*; isn't *My Fair Lady*, then, our *Hamlet*? shouldn't you be writing *Hamlet* instead of sitting there worrying about your superego? I need my *Hamlet*!" So society speaks to the artist, reasons with the artist; and after he has written it its *Hamlet* it is satisfied, and tries to make sure that he will never do it again. There are many more urgent needs that it wants him to sat-

isfy: to lecture to it; to be interviewed; to appear on television pro-
grams; to give testimonials; to attend book luncheons; to make trips
abroad for the State Department; to judge books for Book Clubs; to
read for publishers, judge for publishers, be a publisher for publish-
ers; to edit magazines; to teach writing at colleges or conferences; to
write scenarios or scripts or articles—articles about his home town for
Holiday, about cats or clothes or Christmas for *Vogue,* about "How I
Wrote *Hamlet*" for anything; to—

But why go on? I once heard a composer, lecturing, say to a poet,
lecturing: "They'll pay us to do *anything,* so long as it isn't writing
music or writing poems." I knew the reply that as a member of my so-
ciety I should have made: "As long as they pay you, what do you care?"
But I didn't make it: it was plain that they cared . . . But how many
more learn not to care, to love what they once endured! It is a whole
so comprehensive that any alternative seems impossible, any opposi-
tion irrelevant; in the end a man says in a small voice: "I accept the
Medium." The Enemy of the People winds up as the People—but
where there is no enemy, the people perish.

The climate of our culture is changing. Under these new rains,
new suns, small things grow great, and what was great grows small;
whole species disappear and are replaced. The American present is
very different from the American past: so different that our awareness
of the extent of the changes has been repressed, and we regard as or-
dinary what is extraordinary—ominous perhaps—both for us and for
the rest of the world. The American present is many other peoples' fu-
ture: our cultural and economic example is to much of the world mes-
meric, and it is only its weakness and poverty that prevent it from hur-
rying with us into the Roman future. But at this moment of our power
and success, our thought and art are full of a troubled sadness, of the
conviction of our own decline. When the President of Yale University
writes that "the ideal of the good life has faded from the educational
process, leaving only miscellaneous prospects of jobs and joyless he-
donism," are we likely to find it unfaded among our entertainers and
executives? Is the influence of what I have called the Medium likely
to lead us to any good life? to make us love and try to attain any real
excellence, beauty, magnanimity? or to make us understand these as
obligatory but transparent rationalizations behind which the realities
of money and power are waiting?

The tourist Matthew Arnold once spoke about our green cul-
ture in terms that have an altered relevance—but are not yet irrele-
vant—to our ripe one. He said: "What really dissatisfies in American
civilization is the want of the *interesting,* a want due chiefly to the

want of those two great elements of the interesting, which are ele-
vation and beauty." This use of *interesting*—and, perhaps, this tone
of a curator pointing out what is plain and culpable—shows how far
along in the decline of the West Arnold came: it is only in the latter
days that we ask to be interested. He had found the word, he tells us,
in Carlyle. Carlyle is writing to a friend to persuade him not to emi-
grate to the United States; he asks: "Could you banish yourself from
all that is interesting to your mind, forget the history, the glorious in-
stitutions, the noble principles of old Scotland—that you might eat a
better dinner, perhaps?" We smile, and feel like reminding Carlyle of
the history, the glorious institutions, the noble principles of new
America—of that New World which is, after all, the heir of the Old.

And yet . . . Can we smile as comfortably, today, as we could have
smiled yesterday? Nor could we listen as unconcernedly, if on taking
leave of us some other tourist should conclude, with the penetration
and obtuseness of his kind:

"I remember reading somewhere: that which you inherit from
your fathers you must earn in order to possess. I have been so much
impressed with your power and your possessions that I have neglected,
perhaps, your principles. The elevation or beauty of your spirit did not
equal, always, that of your mountains and skyscrapers: it seems to me
that your society provides you with 'all that is interesting to the mind'
only exceptionally, at odd hours, in little reservations like those of
your Indians. But as for your dinners, I've never seen anything like
them: your daily bread comes *flambé*. And yet—wouldn't you say—
the more dinners a man eats, the more comforts he possesses, the
hungrier and more uncomfortable some part of him becomes: inside
every fat man there is a man who is starving. Part of you is being
starved to death, and the rest of you is being stuffed to death. But this
will change: no one goes on being stuffed to death or starved to death
forever.

"This is a gloomy, an equivocal conclusion? Oh yes, I come from
an older culture, where things are accustomed to coming to such con-
clusions; where there is no last-paragraph fairy to bring one, always,
a happy ending—or that happiest of all endings, no ending at all.
And have I no advice to give you as I go? None. You are too successful
to need advice, or to be able to take it if it were offered; but if ever you
should fail, it is there waiting for you, the advice or consolation of all
the other failures."

[*1960/SHS*]

RANDALL JARRELL (1914–1965) received the National Book Award for his book of poems *The Woman at the Washington Zoo*. His children's book *The Animal Family* was named a Newbery Honor Book, and his translation of *The Three Sisters* was produced by The Actors Studio Theatre.

For some years Jarrell was professor of English at the University of North Carolina at Greensboro. He was a member of the National Institute of Arts and Letters, a chancellor of the American Academy of Poets, and the Poetry Consultant of the Library of Congress.

BRAD LEITHAUSER is the author of a book of essays, *Penchants and Places*, as well as four books of poems and four novels. He is the recipient of many awards for his writing, including a Guggenheim Fellowship, an Ingram Merrill grant, and a MacArthur Fellowship.

He and his wife, the poet Mary Jo Salter, live with their two daughters, Emily and Hilary, in South Hadley, Massachusetts.